Variation in the Form and Use of Language

Variation in the Form and Use of Language

A Sociolinguistics Reader

Ralph W. Fasold
editor

Georgetown University Press, Washington, D.C. 20057

Printed in the United States of America

Library of Congress Cataloging in Publication Data
Main entry under title:

Variation in the form and use of language.

1. Language and languages--Variation--Addresses, essays, lectures. I. Fasold, Ralph W.
P120.V37V36 1983 401'.9 83-20620
ISBN 0-87840-214-4

CONTENTS

I.
Variation in Language Form

ON THE NATURE OF VARIABLE CONSTRAINTS

HENRIETTA J. CEDERGREN

Université du Québec à Montréal

Phonology has provided the first testing ground for theories of linguistic variability partly due to the possibility of constructing data sets large enough for simultaneous analysis along many dimensions of variation. With massive data, we are more likely to be bound to the patterning existing in the data, and less likely to resort to generating biased artificial data in order to fill vacant 'cells' in tables, to be tempted into lengthy 'a posteriori' speculations to explain away each piece of data which does not fit our models, or to dismiss systematically patterned exceptions as 'performance error'.

This paper reports some results of a sociolinguistic survey of the Spanish of Panama City involving a sample of seventy-nine speakers (Cedergren 1973). The particular variable described was measured some 22, 000 times, a number sufficient for a consideration of all the relevant dimensions of variation.

The analytical framework. Quantitative studies of language use in the speech community have demonstrated regular cooccurrence patterns between language variables and features of both linguistic and extralinguistic dimensions such as style, status, age, and regional origin. To describe this phenomenon, Labov (1969) introduced variable rules, thus replacing optional rules, in order to account for the regular patterns of covariation between the frequency of rule execution and contextual elements. For each variable rule in every environment there exists a quantity p which represents the probability of rule execution.

As a working hypothesis, it has been proposed (Cedergren and D. Sankoff 1972) that it is a universal tendency for p to be in the form of:

$$p = 1 - (1 - p_o)(1 - \alpha)(1 - \beta) \ldots (1 - \omega)$$

where p_o is an input probability independent of context and $\alpha, \beta \ldots \omega$ represent the contribution of each relevant feature in the environment. This formalization assumes that each of the environmental factors affects the probability of rule application in a consistent and independent manner, regardless of the presence or absence of other features relevant to the rule. Note, that we incorporate social and stylistic constraints into this hypothesis in the same way as linguistic factors, thereby permitting the comparison of linguistic and non-linguistic constraints and the investigation of language independence from the social system.

In empirical studies, the unmarked relation of variable constraints is indeed noninteraction or independence. This situation predominates among stable sociolinguistic variables in the speech community. Numerous examples are found in the literature. Here we will present a slightly more complicated case and discuss the methodological implication of non-negligible interaction.

Syllable final S. The variability of syllable final S is a well-known phenomenon in Spanish dialectology and has an extensive geographical distribution covering wide areas of American and European Spanish-speaking communities. Historically the alternation dates at least from the XVI century (Alonso 1962:47).

Quantitative studies of Puerto Rican Spanish by Ma and Herasimchuk (1971) and of Cuban Spanish by Vallejo-Claros (1970) indicate the different phonetic realizations of S are subject to variable linguistic and external stylistic and social constraints.

Three relevant variants of S, a strident, an aspirate, or null are considered in the analysis. The distribution of these variants in our corpus is displayed in Table 1.

TABLE 1. Distribution of variants.

Variants	%
s	11
h	41
ø	48
N	22, 167

We have postulated a variable rule of the form

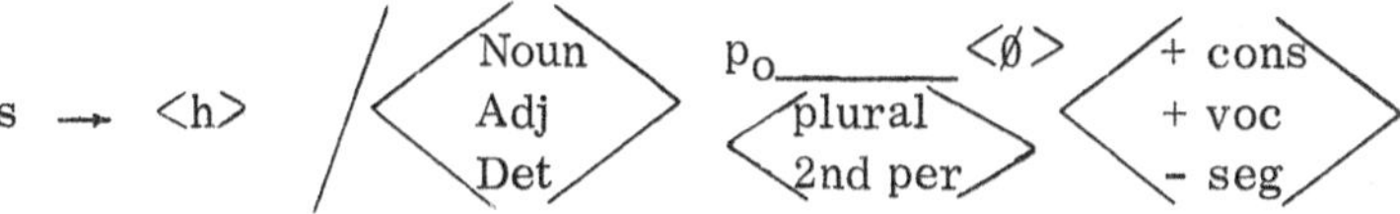

to account for the aspiration of S where the frequency of rule execution is shown to be the result of a combination of factors: the nature of the following segment, the existence of word boundary, the morphemic status of S, the type of S suffix, and the grammatical form co-occurring with the plural.

The raw data cross-classified according to all possible linguistic environment is presented in Table 2.

A maximum likelihood procedure for estimating the probabilistic contributions as in the formula for the variable rule, produces the values in Table 3. We can deduce from Table 3 that the single environmental factor most conducive to the application of the S-aspiration rule is a following consonant with a probability coefficient of 0.89. Another feature which encourages rule application is internal position in the word. Monomorphemes are quite susceptible to aspiration and among form classes in the noun phrase the plural forms of nouns favor rule execution. The degree of formality of the conversational topic is not as great as the linguistic conditioning but it is not negligible.

Table 2 also reveals the extent to which the model captures the systematicity observed in the data. Generally speaking the fit is quite reasonable for a situation where only nine parameters have been estimated to predict twenty-eight cells in a table; independence is thereby verified. However, it should be noted that determiners generally act in a nonindependent manner. Noticeable divergences appear between the distribution of determiners and the expected incidence in the model in either prevocalic or preconsonantal position.

Ma and Herasimchuk also found that the class of determiners exhibited an extraordinary proportion of standard forms in prevocalic position. In attempting to explain this phenomenon, they hypothesized that the S morpheme is retained more often because the initial position in the noun phrase would make the determiner the first element to transmit the information of plurality. Nouns need not preserve the redundant information of the plural morpheme. In an earlier partial study of the variable we obtained similar results. Both these studies, however, lacked the methodology for estimating the appropriate probabilistic parameters underlying the problem.

In terms of the formal characteristics of our model, the discrepancies that were found for determiners indicate the nonindependent

TABLE 2. Observed frequency of s per total cases of S with predicted values in parenthesis.

Style A: Informal	Cons	Voc	Pause
Internal	34/1791 (30)		
Monomorphemic	89/1701 (67)	157/976 (174)	153/500 (174)
Verb	3/30 (2)	5/13 (5)	
Determiner	22/862 (61)	89/179 (57)	
Adjective	3/142 (5)	13/59 (8)	13/68 (19)
Noun	36/754 (22)	69/498 (67)	146/544 (142)
Style B: Formal			
Internal	61/3654 (65)		
Monomorphemic	158/2617 (122)	219/1346 (284)	503/1120 (459)
Verb	21/88 (8)	21/72 (30)	
Determiner	51/1238 (103)	167/359 (135)	
Adjective	12/466 (17)	23/96 (16)	34/101 (33)
Noun	60/1247 (44)	98/617 (97)	233/849 (261)

TABLE 3. Contribution of each factor influencing S aspiration.

p_o = 0.21					
[Det] 0	[Adj] 0.66	[Noun] 0.58			
[monomorphemic] 0.49	[plural] 0.08	[verb] 0			
[final] 0	[internal] 0.62				
[cons] 0.89	[voc] 0.49	[pause] 0			
[informal] 0.15	[formal] 0				

interaction between the environmental factors of the rule. A closer look at the set of determiners in the corpus was warranted to explicate the type of interaction between the phonological constraints and the determiners. The hypothesis which emerged was that the distribution of variants is conditioned not by a single phonological factor, but by the conjoined presence of stress and a following vowel.

To verify this hypothesis, data from eleven informants was searched. Each occurrence of determiner was cross-classified for the nature of the phonological environment and the presence of stress in the following syllable. The results displayed in Table 4 unmistakeably show that stress is a variable constraint affecting the distribution of determiners. We therefore assume that this feature should be incorporated into the structural environment of our rule.

An exhaustive search of all S tokens, not just determiners was also effected to delimit the range of the stress effect. The result confirmed that the effect of stress was limited only to determiners and led us to conclude that the configuration of determiner-vowel-stress was governed by a separate rule in the grammar.

TABLE 4. Distribution of s for determiners by following segment and stress (N = 11).

Consonant				Vowel			
stressed		unstressed		stressed		unstressed	
3/134	2%	3/170	2%	28/40	70%	7/42	17%

This illustration reveals the use of variable rules as an adjunct to discovery procedures for the detection of hidden linguistic constraints.

S is a well developed sociolinguistic variable in covariation with both stylistic and social features. The exact contribution of each nonlinguistic factor was also estimated following the established procedure. The effect of sex, age group, socioeconomic status, and local origin of speaker were separately correlated with the linguistic constraints. In each and every case, the analysis revealed that the linguistic constraints do not interact with the social constraints; for the probability coefficients assigned to the linguistic features do not noticeably change in the different analyses. This independence is an important characteristic of the relation between language structure and social structure. Also it serves as evidence against the hypothesis that linguistic variation along sociolinguistic dimensions always proceeds by successive reweighting of the features or constraints in rules. Here the configuration of constraints with respect to one another remains relatively fixed, while the input probability varies from one socioeconomic group to another or from one person to another.

CH lenition. The acceleration of rule application rates can occur in selected linguistic environments across certain social and age groups in the context of a rapid sound change. An example of an ongoing sound change in the history of the community is the lenition of CH. This variable presents three variants which are the standard form [č], reduced occlusion [š̊] and a sibilant [š]. We have postulated (Cedergren 1973) two rules to account for the distribution of the newer variants, which represent the step-wise phonetic implementation of the sound change.

Table 5 displays the distribution of the variants when aggregated by the relevant linguistic environments and age groups of the sample. The estimated coefficient values assigned to the social variable clearly indicate that the frequency of CH lenition is not evenly distributed among the speakers of the sample, as seen in Table 6.

The younger speakers under 35, groups I and II, favor the execution of both rules and are the vehicles of the change. The 20-35 age group reveals slightly atypical values for the variable constraints. This group, as seen in Table 5, is more sensitive to the effect of word boundary than the youngest group of speakers, indicating a reweighting of linguistic constraints as the rule is being generalized in the community.

In such cases of relatively rapid rule spread, the variable rule calculation enables us to estimate the rate of increase of rule application in different time periods. From Table 6 we can calculate that the first rule, reduced occlusion, applies, in least favorable environments, 13 per cent of the time for the oldest group, average age 60, 15 per cent for the group of average age 42, 51 per cent for the group of average age 28, and 56 per cent for the group of average age 18. Under the assumption that these represent variable constraints

TABLE 5. Distribution of CH variants by age groups and the preceding linguistic environment. I, age 14-20; II, age 21-35; III, age 36-50; IV, age 51+.

Age group	Variant	Initial CH V	Initial CH K	Initial CH P	Internal CH V	Internal CH K
	CH-1	40	40	17	36	76
I	CH-2	7	10	14	3	0
	CH-3	53	50	69	60	23
	N	(30)	(29)	(10)	(339)	(13)
	CH-1	65	52	58	29	50
II	CH-2	8	17	12	6	13
	CH-3	27	31	30	63	35
	N	(62)	(29)	(43)	(357)	(30)
	CH-1	65	75	63	66	90
III	CH-2	17	13	26	7	6
	CH-3	28	12	11	25	3
	N	(46)	(16)	(43)	(322)	(33)
	CH-1	77	70	71	69	78
IV	CH-2	7	20	29	11	10
	CH-3	16	10	0	19	10
	N	(30)	(10)	(17)	(198)	(19)

acquired during childhood, we estimate that from about 1938 to 1952, this rule probability increased at an average rate of .025 or 2 1/2 per cent per year, and has more or less ceased to increase since then. The second rule on the other hand increased even more, 3 per cent per year during the 1940s and has continued to increase at half that rate since then until it now applies to about every eligible input string.

We would contend that insofar as rule diffusion rates can be estimated from synchronic data, this is the methodology of choice. Methods not based on age-related variability, on the other hand, run the risk of imputing or exaggerating dynamic qualities in situations

TABLE 6. Linguistic and age factors influencing CH lenition.

Rule 1: Reduced occlusion							
$p_o = 0.13$							
[k-]	0	[v]	0.18	[p-]	0.21		
[internal]	0.06	[initial]	0				
[I]	0.47	[II]	0.44	[III]	0.02	[IV]	0
Rule 2: Lenition							
$p_o = 0$							
[k-]	0.16	[v-]	0.49	[p-]	0		
[internal]	0.35	[initial]	0				
[I]	0.84	[II]	0.69	[III]	0.27	[IV]	0

which may well have exhibited stable variability over many centuries, e.g. S variation in Spanish.

Recurrent linguistic patterns. Our work on variability in Panamanian Spanish and Montreal French provides an opportunity to independently corroborate or refine certain sociolinguistic principles which have been proposed by Labov (1971) and Wolfram (1971). The factors contributing to the deletion of L in Montreal French (Sankoff and Cedergren 1971), word final D and N deletion, and S aspiration in Spanish (Cedergren 1973) all indicate that the following phonological environment of consonant reduction or deletion rules does not affect rule executability idiosyncratically. If the following segment is not a vowel, the probability of rule application increases.

The presence of a grammatical feature is another condition which receives cross-linguistic validation of interaction patterns. The S suffixes in Spanish tend to constrain the aspiration and deletion of the variable. This conservative effect on rule application converges with the results of the study of consonant cluster deletion in Black English (Labov et al. 1968, Wolfram 1969). However, the deletion of intervocalic D and final R in Spanish appears to provide counter examples to this principle. In both instances, the presence of a grammatical form favors rule execution rather than constraining it. Intervocalic D of the past participle formative as in pasado and cantado, and the formative R, as in the infinitive cantar and chupar tend to delete more than monomorphemic forms. These grammatical forms, however, are both introduced by obligatory transformational rules, and thus it is likely that predictable grammatical surface markers should be susceptible to variability. As a result, statements about the typical behavior of grammatical forms should be refined in terms of the surface predictability of the form.

Conclusions. We have provided empirical evidence about certain characteristics of variable constraints. These constraints tend not to interact. Cases of non-negligible interaction indicate the possible presence of hidden constraints or discontinuity in the grammar of the speech community due to rapid on-going sound changes. The variable rule calculation permits us to estimate the rate of increase of rule application across time. The probability coefficients contributed by factors influencing certain types of variable rules in Spanish and French confirm sociolinguistic principles that have been proposed from the study of English.

ACKNOWLEDGMENTS

I would like to particularly thank David Sankoff who developed the procedure for estimating rule probabilities. I am also grateful to Gillian and David Sankoff for their helpful suggestions and comments on work which led to this paper.

REFERENCES

Alonso, Dámaso. 1962. Sobre la -s final de sílaba en el mundo hispánico. In: Enciclopedia de Lingüística Hispánica. Suplemento.

Cedergren, Henrietta J. 1971. Una descripción sociolingüística del español de Panamá. Manuscript.

_____. 1973. The interplay of social and linguistic factors in Panama. Unpublished Ph.D. dissertation, Cornell University.

_____ and David Sankoff. 1972. Variable rules: Performance as a statistical reflection of competence. Manuscript.

Labov, William. 1969. Contraction, deletion and inherent variability of the English copula. Language. 45.715-62.

_____. 1971. Methodology. In: A survey of linguistic science. Ed. by W. O. Dingwall.

_____, Paul Cohen, Clarence Robins, and John Lewis. 1968. A study of the non-standard English of Negro and Puerto Rican speakers in New York City. Cooperative Research Report 3288.

Ma, Roxana and Eleanor Herasimchuk. 1971. The linguistic dimensions of a bilingual neighborhood. In: Bilingualism in the barrio. Ed. by Fishman, Cooper, and Ma. The Hague, Mouton.

Sankoff, Gillian and Henrietta J. Cedergren. 1971. Some results of a sociolinguistic study of Montreal French. In: Linguistic diversity in Canada. Ed. by R. Darnell.

Vallejo-Claros, Bernardo. 1970. La distribución y estratificación de /r/ /r̄/ y /s/ en el Español Cubano. Unpublished Ph. D. dissertation, University of Texas at Austin.

Wolfram, Walter. 1969. A sociolinguistic description of Detroit Negro Speech. Urban Language Series 5. Washington, D. C., Center for Applied Linguistics.

_____. 1971. Overlapping influence in the English of second generation Puerto Rican teenagers in East Harlem. Final Report, U. S. Office of Education Grant No. 3-70-0033(508). Washington, D. C., Center for Applied Linguistics.

ABOVE AND BEYOND PHONOLOGY IN VARIABLE RULES

GILLIAN SANKOFF

Université de Montréal

The principal goal of this paper is to extend the scope of an analytical framework which treats variation in linguistic behavior as being entirely natural, rather than anomalous, error-laden, or otherwise unmanageably messy. Perhaps the very success of such a framework in dealing with phonological data and with morphophonemic reduction rules has led many to believe that concepts of variation are applicable only in these domains, and that strict application of all-or-nothing principles are still defensible at other levels of grammar. I will argue that this is a misconception based in large part on an overly mechanistic view of language, which in turn stems from the traditional deterministic postulates underlying most of modern linguistics, including both structuralist and generative schools of various persuasions. Thus I think that work on systematic variability has often been misperceived by those who react to numbers and tables as being boring, trivial, or alarming, as being simply a detailed 'description' of 'performance'. My view is quite the opposite: I think from the beginning, and I refer principally to the continuing ground-breaking research of Labov and associates, the attempt has been to find more adequate ways of dealing with the great subtleties of competence in some of its most complex and interesting, i.e. noncategorical, aspects.

This is not to argue for chaos; quite the reverse. Perception of a set of observations as chaotic or otherwise disorderly may well stem from the inadequacy of the analyst's model to account for the kinds of diversity represented in the observations. It is to be hoped that the reason for a renewed interest of linguists in the study of language in context is not only to widen the field in which it is permissible to search for categorical constraints on linguistic behavior, e.g. to disambiguate referentially synonymous expressions 'categorically' by reference to social context. There is, in my view, mounting evidence that such semantic, discourse, or cultural constraints will be no more (or less) categorical than the type of linguistic constraints now agreed to be allowable. Both Hymes (1964, 1972) and Labov (1966, 1969, 1972a), from somewhat different traditions of enquiry, have for some years supported this point of view. Sherzer (n. d.) has recently provided some very cogent arguments as to why it is inadequate to deal with cultural and interactional context only in an ad hoc way and only when strictly 'necessary' (i. e. when all else appears to fail), why a systematic study of the latter is indicated, and careful work by Gumperz (e.g. Gumperz and Wilson 1971, Blom and Gumperz 1972) and others has shown the complexity of the two-way interactions between language behavior and its context. In brief, the study of the context of language use as an integral part of linguistic description is necessary on a number of grounds, but there is no reason to suppose that it will in any way simplify the linguist's task or provide easy, categorical solutions to current linguistic problems. The futility of the search for complete determinacy in language was not found at the level of the so-called idiolect, and it is difficult to imagine why it might be found to any greater degree at the level of speech act context.

Briefly, I posit that linguistic behavior, like other behavior, is subject to statistical variation which can best be accounted for by an underlying model which is probabilistic rather than deterministic in nature. This position has been argued recently by a number of researchers, and I will not go into any details here except to state one salient point: such a model contains no implication that any or all rules will be variable, i. e. it can deal with the kinds of structures involved in both variable and categorical rules.

In order to demonstrate that variability occurs and can be dealt with at levels of grammar above (or beyond) the phonological, I have chosen some examples from syntax and semantics, drawn from the current work of myself and coworkers on two linguistic communities: native, French-speaking Montrealers, and urban New Guineans who speak Tok Pisin, formerly a pidgin language with about 70 per cent English-derived vocabulary and which now boasts a first generation of native speakers.

1. The first example has to do with the placement of the future marker in New Guinea Tok Pisin (cf. Sankoff and Laberge 1972). This was a study in which we did an extensive series of recordings of members of about a dozen families in the town of Lae, as well as

a considerable number of other recordings of individuals, groups, public gatherings, and the like. There was no formal sample: families were chosen for intensive study on the basis of their having children of at least seven or eight years old who spoke Tok Pisin as a first language. The families were members of a close-knit multilinguistic neighborhood. Few of the adults had a native language in common, and this included most spouses: all were fluent second-language speakers of Tok Pisin.

One of the results of an investigation of the syntactic marking of futures in the speech of eight adults and eight children in seven of the families was that bai, the marker, is variably placed before or after the subject NP. This has historical implications, as it seems that 50 or 60 years ago the standard order was to place baimbai or bai (now reduced to [ba] or [bə] by fluent speakers in informal conversation) before the subject NP. Though generational differences between our speakers appear in reduction of stress on bai, there appears to be no generational difference, nor a difference between individual speakers, with respect to order. Rather, there are a series of syntactic constraints, some of them categorical and others variable. Table 1 indicates the influence of the various pronominal subjects as well as nonpronominal noun phrases.

TABLE 1. Bai placement in terms of subject NP.

Subject NP Definition	Form	Position of bai: __NP	Position of bai: __VP
1st sing.	mi	78	7
2nd sing.	yu	52	1
3rd pl.	ol	31	1
1st pl. incl.; {1st pl. excl. / 2nd pl.}	yumi; {mi / yu} pela	22	6
3rd sing.	em	11	47
other NP		22	36
∅ subject			53

We see that all pronouns except the 3rd person singular characteristically follow bai, whereas em and nonpronominal NP's generally precede, though with considerable variation. Further examination of the structure of nonpronominal subject NP's shows (Table 2) that there is a categorical rule which inserts bai after the NP when the latter contains an embedding whether the embedding contains a surface verb or not. The transformation for bai-movement is given as Rule 1.

Rule 1. bai + ⟨NP / N-S⟩ + VP
1 2 3 ⟹ < 2 + 1 + 3 >

2:	NP	N-S
p	0.5	1.0

TABLE 2. Bai placement in terms of structure of nonpronominal subject NP.

Structure of NP	Position of bai __NP	NP__	__NP__
NP containing bilong (possessive)	--	8	2
NP containing embedding (with surface verb)	--	6	1
Other NP	17	17	2
Total	17	31	5

Thus a sentence like (1) applies the same bai-movement rule as a sentence like (2).

(1) Na meri bilong en bai igo bek.
And his wife will go back. (Speaker #7)

(2) Igat planti man bai igo.
There are lots of people who'll go. (Speaker #7)

In the case where the subject NP is nonpronominal and contains no embedding, the bai-movement rule operates with a probability of approximately .5, no further grammatical, social, or contextual constraints being evident. Thus the same speaker will use sentences like (3) and (4).

(3) Dispela kot ating bai i pinis nau.
That court case will probably soon be finished. (Speaker #8)

(4) Bai wara igo insait.
The water will get into it. (Speaker #8)

There is one further point of interest, and that is the existence of sentences containing a bai both preceding and following the subject NP. Thus there seems to be a 'copying' alternative to the bai-movement rule based on the length of the subject NP, as this pattern seldom appears with NP's of less than three phonological words.

A rather long example is the following:

(5) Bai man i wok gaden o mikim wonem istap long bus, bai tingting.
The people working in the fields or whatever they may be doing in the forest, will be thinking. (Speaker #14)

In summary, we can say that though we have not completed our investigation of the bai-movement rule, it is found to be quite stable in some syntactic environments, operating always (in the case of subject NP's containing embeddings) or almost never (in the case of most NP's consisting of a single pronoun other than em). Interestingly, most of the exceptions to the latter applied the bai-movement rule to indicate particular emphasis on the pronoun subject to the exclusion of other people, as in (6):

(6) Mi bai kisim!
I [not you guys] will get it. (Speaker #3)

In the case of the pronoun em, however, bai-movement applies with a probability of approximately .85, and in the case of an NP consisting of more than a single pronoun, it applies with a probability of .5.

2. More on Montréal que. A preliminary analysis of the deletion of complementizer que in the speech of sixteen Montrealers (Sankoff, Sarrasin, and Cedergren 1971) indicated a structure of variable phonological deletion constraints. Further work on other constructions containing que has shown that not only is que absent in a great many places where there is every indication that it is present earlier in the derivation, but also that it is present on the surface at places where one would not postulate its introduction by standard French transformations (Cedergren and Laberge 1972). Examples (7) and (8) show the alternation of que after quand for speaker #109; and examples (9) and (10) show the same kind of alternation with comment.

(7) Quand qu'on sort, bien on va pas loin.
When you leave, you don't go far. (Speaker #109)

(8) Quand tu as tout en main puis ça va bien, bien là tu te décourages moins.
When you have everything in hand and things are going well, you don't get so discouraged. (Speaker #109)

(9) Tu sais comment qu'ça se passe.
You know how it happens. (Speaker #6)

(10) Je sais pas comment ça se fait.
I don't know how it works. (Speaker #6)

Insertion of que results in a grammatically different structure, as the subordinator quand or comment appears to lose its subordinating function and act like an adverb, the subordinating function being taken over by an attached que. Examples (11) through (13) indicate, moreover, that more complexity is possible, with various representations of est-ce appearing between the WH-form and que.

(11) Je trouvais ça formidable comment c'que c'est.
I thought it was great, how it is. (Speaker #89)

(12) Je sais pas comment c'est qu'ils la faisaient dans ce temps-là.
I don't know how they did it in those days. (Speaker #24)

(13) Ils ont déterminé au juste qu'est-c'est que c'est j'avais.
They found out just what it was . . . that I had. (Speaker #52)

Sentence (13) contains the maximum number of que-attachments we have found, and Table 3 gives an idea of the complexity of the data.

We see that for some forms, most speakers categorically produce a que-less or a que-containing pattern, but that for most, the majority of speakers exhibit variation. We also see that there is the now familiar 'scaly' look to the pattern, and a reasonably good implicational relationship such that having comme que implies having quand que, and so on. Table 4 adds further information, showing that speakers tend to incorporate some sort of que-attachment consistently in the various possible environments. I have sketched a variable rule (Rule 2) involving que-attachment which takes into account only the syntactic constraints, and shows that parce is a very favorable (i.e. categorical) environment for que, whereas comme is a distinctly unfavorable environment.

TABLE 3. Ordering of speakers according to presence or absence of forms in their speech. [ETC[1] = other est-ce embeddings beginning with ce; ETC[2] = other embeddings beginning with que; que[3] = qu'est-ce que]

Speakers	comme	que	quand	que	comment combien pourquoi où	ETC[1]	que	ce	ETC[1]	ETC[2]	que[3]
30	+		+		+			+			
25	+		+		+			+			
20	+		+		+			+		+	
68	+		+		+			+	+		
87	+		+		+			+	+		+
75	+		+		+	+		+			
89	+		+		+	+	+	+	+		
98	+		+		+		+				+
13	+		+		+	+		+		+	+
97	+		+	+	+	+		+	+	+	+
83	+		+	+	+	+	+	+	+		+
24	+		+	+	+	+	+	+		+	+
2	+		+		+	+	+	+	+	+	+
36	+		+	+	+	+	+	+		+	+
14	+		+	+	+		+	+	+		+
6	+	+	+	+	+	+	+	+		+	+
40	+	+	+	+	+	+		+			+
52	+	+	+	+	+	+	+	+		+	+
23	+	+	+	+	+	+	+	+		+	+
105	+	+	+	+	+		+			+	+
94		+	+	+		+					+
17		nil		+		+	+				+
22		+		+		nil					+

TABLE 4. Ordering of speakers according to percentage of subordinators without que or other est-ce embeddings.

Speakers	comme	quand	comment combien pourquoi où	ce
30	1.00	1.00	1.00	1.00
25	1.00	1.00	1.00	1.00
20	1.00	1.00	1.00	.91
68	1.00	1.00	1.00	.96
87	1.00	1.00	1.00	.78
75	1.00	1.00	.71	1.00
89	1.00	1.00	.71	.79
98	1.00	1.00	.50	0
13	1.00	1.00	.57	.55
97	1.00	.89	.56	.43
83	1.00	.83	.50	.61
24	1.00	.98	.12	.64
2	1.00	1.00	.33	.12
36	1.00	.89	.33	.77
14	1.00	.75	.33	.66
6	.57	.57	.14	.56
40	.33	.33	.66	.40
52	.25	.68	.36	.15
23	.50	.50	.08	.13
105	.50	.36	.70	0
94	0	.23	0	0
17	-	.38	0	0
22	0	0	0	0

Rule 2: WH - raising rule

VP + [NP + V + Adv. Pron. $]_S$

1 2 3 4 ⟹ 1 + 4 + <que> + 2 + 3

Approximate probability values for variable que:

term 4	comme	quand	où comment combien pourquoi	__ce	parce
p	.1	.3	.4	.4	1.0

At this point, however, we encounter a major problem. Presence of que added as an adjunct with WH-raising appears in Table 5 to be highly unlikely in anything but a succeeding vocalic environment, in which its surface representation is generally the consonant [k]. The thought that this [k] may simply be a liaison-like phenomenon can rapidly be dismissed on the grounds of numerous full-form que's before consonants and pauses, as well as on the grounds that est-ce embeddings also occur almost entirely before vowels. How can we explain this? As a result, I think, of the same low level phonological rule that deletes que in constructions such as complements

TABLE 5. [k] (= que) and [sk] (= est-ce-que) deletion according to succeeding phonological environments for speakers who use que and ETC (= other est-ce embeddings).

	Succeeding phonological environments								
	[+sib]			[+cons, -sib]			[-cons]		
Forms	que	ETC-que	∅	que	ETC-que	∅	que	ETC-que	∅
comme; quand	2	--	113	1	--	56	96	--	50
où; pourquoi; combien; comment	2	1	41	3	--	16	26	53	54
Total	4	1	154	4	--	72	122	53	54

where it appears earlier in the derivation (Cedergren and Laberge 1972). This rule appears as Rule 3. *Est-ce* would be added as an optional complication of Rule 2, but would then be virtually always removed as a further consequence of Rule 3 in the favored environments. But if, as we have shown, presence of *que* is a result of both an optional attachment rule followed by an optional deletion rule, it becomes difficult to state the conditions under which attachment applies, since absence of *que* may result from it never having been attached in the first place, or from it having been attached and later deleted. It would seem at best inappropriate to postulate both attachment and deletion for those individuals and those forms where *que* never appears on the surface.

Rule 3: *que*-deletion rule

$$\textit{que} \rightarrow \emptyset \;/\!/ \left\langle \begin{array}{c} [+\text{sib}] \\ \begin{bmatrix} +\text{cons} \\ -\text{sib} \end{bmatrix} \\ [-\text{cons}] \end{array} \right\rangle \;\_\_\; \left\langle \begin{array}{c} [+\text{sib}] \\ \begin{bmatrix} +\text{cons} \\ -\text{sib} \end{bmatrix} \\ [-\text{cons}] \end{array} \right\rangle$$

Effects:	[+sib]	[+cons -sib]	[-cons]
pre. seg.	.13	.02	0
fol. seg.	.36	.09	0

(1 - deletion prob.) = [1 - effect (pre. seg)] x [1 - effect (fol. seg.)]

Perhaps here we can look at some of the probabilities attached to various constraints in clear deletion cases (e.g. *parce que*, complements, relatives) and, comparing them to the observed data on possible attached, then deleted cases, infer what such frequencies might represent in terms of cases originally attached. For even if, turning back to the figures in Table 4, the phonological rule sweeps across surface *que*'s of every grammatical stripe, it is clear that some of the forms are simply less amenable to *que* attachment. It seems, for example, that *que* is what some might call 'less good' with *comme* 'like' than it is with *quand* 'when'. Again, compare *quand*, which we see only occurring by itself and with *que*, but not taking any est-ce in between. Informants questioned about the acceptability of a construction like quand est-ce que, or quand c'est que all said this would be fine, but not with comme, thus *comme ce que, *comme est-ce que, etc. In fact the student who tabulated the forms in Tables 3 and 4 left columns for est-ce insertion for the quand form, but not for comme. Referring back to the table under Rule 2, which shows very approximate probabilities of que attachment for the various forms in the tables as well as for parce, we might also note that in comparing que deletion in complements versus relatives, we have found the latter to be a much more conservative environment--though the phonological constraints pattern in the same way. All speakers would be less likely to say a sentence like (14) than a sentence like (15).

(14) C'est la fille ∅ j'ai vue.
'That's the girl I saw' instead of 'That's the girl that I saw'

(15) Je pense ∅ ça a été plutôt un snobisme.
'I think it was more a kind of snobbery' instead of 'I think that it was more a kind of snobbery'

We have not yet investigated distinctions in the way a grammatical difference like restrictive versus nonrestrictive relatives would affect presence or absence of que, or, to turn the thing on its head, what que attachment can tell us about the nature of the NP which follows it, in terms of being more or less like other NP's. But we can already see that presence or absence of que is differentially allowable for different grammatical constructions in a way that is clearly important to an understanding of the grammar of French. This would seem to be the kind of area one might also investigate from the perspective of universals proposed by Wolfram at this conference. I might add that the difference between est-ce allowability with quand and comme might stem partially from the fact that comme can never be used in a surface direct question, whereas quand can.

Before passing to the last example, which is taken from the area of semantics, I would like to say a little more about the relationship between variability studies and the work of linguists who do not explicitly base their formulations on systematic studies of speech production. It is clear that Chomsky was correct in pointing out that there is no necessary connection between frequency of occurrence and grammaticality. Yet it is also clear that the questions of degrees of grammaticality or acceptability discussed so elegantly at this conference by Ross and by Sag fit very naturally into the overall framework of variability that we base our work on. The problem comes back to a question of the interpretation one would be able to give to a table like Table 4. What does it mean to note that speaker 97, say, was never observed to use comme que, though he did use quand que a little, and made considerable use of constructions like comment que? Is comme que disallowed by his grammar? Would he react to its use by others as being 'funny'? Could we say that comme que would be more likely to be grammatical for him in some sense, even though he does not use it, than it would be for speaker 20, who also does not use it, but does not use any of the others either? Here we get into the problems of production versus reception, the fact that we can receive correctly and without thought that they are 'peculiar', messages in forms that we would never ourselves use, and so on, as Peter Trudgill pointed out during this conference. Further, questioning people about whether they find such forms 'grammatical' runs into a great deal of interference due to their recognition as nonstandard both by those who use them and those who do not (cf. Labov 1970 on this general point).

3. My last example deals with pronoun semantics in Montreal French, and is drawn from Laberge (1972). I am presenting only one small part of the system: the variation Laberge found in the surface representation of the pronoun she defined as 'indefinite marked'. This is the indefinite par excellence, traditionally represented as on on the surface in French grammar, and which contains no features indicating inclusion or exclusion of the speaker (ego) or hearer, nor the singular/plural distinction. Some examples taken from our recordings are listed here:

(16) Tu as beau parler de l'éléphant, du serpent, mais si on peut pas le décrire, hein?
It's all very well to talk about elephants, about snakes, but if you can't describe them, eh? (Speaker #99)

(17) Quand une personne élevait une famille à ce temps-là, vous étiez pas capable d'avoir de luxe.
When a person was bringing up a family at that time, you couldn't afford luxuries. (Speaker #37)

(18) J'aime mieux boire une bonne brosse, c'est mieux que fumer de la drogue, je trouve. Le lendemain matin tu as un gros mal de tête mais ça fait rien, tu es tout là. Tandis qu'avec la drogue, tu sais pas si tu vas être là le lendemain. Tu peux te prendre pour Batman ou Superman puis tu te pitch dans les poubelles.

I'd rather have a good drink, it's better than smoking drugs, I find. The next morning you have a terrible headache but it doesn't matter, you're all there. But with drugs, you don't know if you're going to be there the next day. You might think you were Batman or Superman and throw yourself into the garbage pail. (Speaker #62)

Often what the speaker appears to be doing is talking about an experience of his own, but which he is generalizing to apply as a general rule. In sentence (17) the speaker does not imply that the 22-year-old addressee has herself raised a family during the depression; this is the indefinite vous which is distinguished clearly from personal vous in its underlying representation. Further evidence for this distinction (tu and vous personal versus tu and vous indefinite) comes from a comparison of speakers' address terms with their indefinite usage. Several older speakers consistently used the vous politeness form in addressing young interviewers, yet used tu (alternating with on) as an indefinite. This was the case for speakers 82 and 109 in the bar graph of Figure 1, and an example is given as sentence (19).

(19) Aussi, vous savez, quand tu as tout à la main puis ça va bien, bien là le courage vient.
So, you know, when you have everything and things are going well, it's then that you get courage. (Speaker #109)

The graph shows that speaker 37 uses tu very occasionally to express the marked indefinite, that he uses vous for the marked indefinite about 60 per cent of the time, and on for the rest. Thus speakers over fifty are shown to use on frequently, alternating on with either tu (in the case of three speakers), or vous in the case of the other eleven. Speakers under twenty-five, however, use on very seldom indeed in the indefinite sense. More than half of them use over 80 per cent tu. For most younger speakers, as Laberge shows in a chapter not reported on here, on is used almost categorically to represent nous or 'we' as a verb subject. A typical example would be a sentence like (20).

(20) Dans notre famille, on a toujours fait ça.
In our family, we always did that.

In over a thousand examples of underlying nous, Laberge found only one case of surface nous for one speaker under twenty-five.

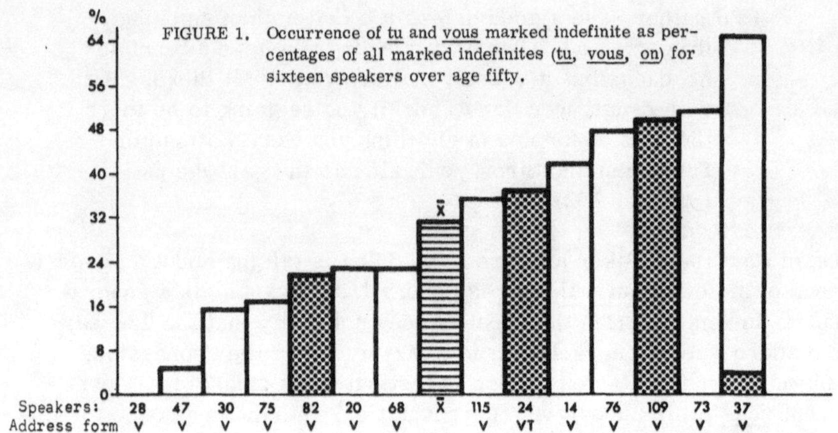

FIGURE 1. Occurrence of tu and vous marked indefinite as percentages of all marked indefinites (tu, vous, on) for sixteen speakers over age fifty.

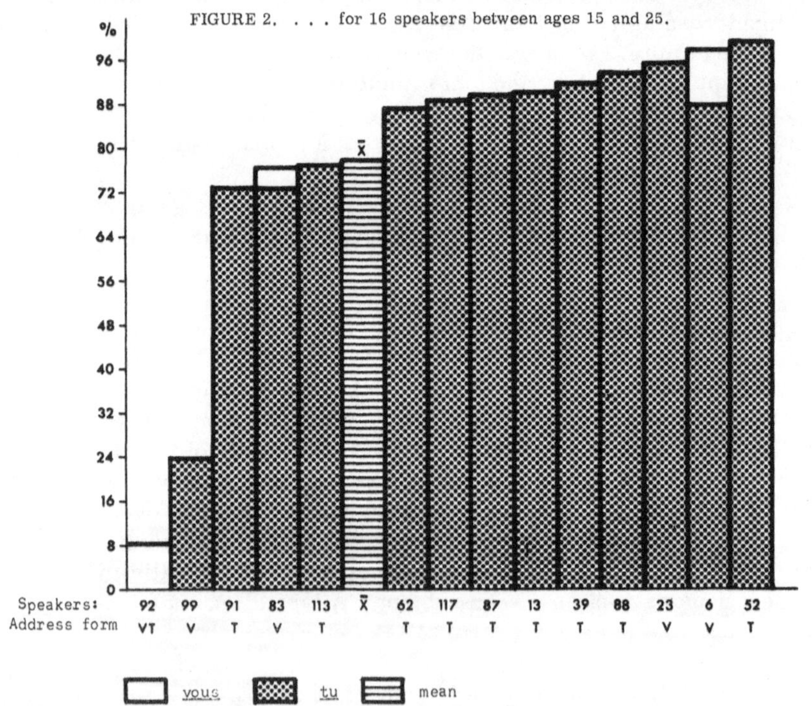

FIGURE 2. . . . for 16 speakers between ages 15 and 25.

Contrary to the que example, this example shows a dramatic and rapid usage change, which Laberge has described in terms of the articulation of the pronoun system as a whole. She has analyzed the alternation between on and either tu or vous as a variable rule with increasing input probabilities for younger speakers. This is not to suggest that younger speakers do not understand older speakers when they use on as in (16); and this again fits into some notion of passive competence. It is simply that such usage has become archaic, and gives every sign of disappearing. I might add that Laberge used only male speakers for the present analysis, as she felt the change tendencies would be clearer in the speech of men, given the greater conservative hypercorrection of women speakers in North American society, noted in our own previous work on Montreal French (Sankoff and Cedergren 1971) as well as in American English by Labov (1966), Shuy (1969), and Lakoff (n. d.).

4. The extension of probabilistic considerations from phonology to syntax is not a conceptually difficult jump. Whenever there are options open to a speaker, we can infer from his or her behavior an underlying set of probabilities. It seems clear to us that in the increasing number of situations which have been studied in depth, this inference is more than an exercise in data organization, since the underlying probabilities are consistently and systematically patterned according to internal (linguistic) and external (social and stylistic) constraints. There is no reason not to expect similar patterning elsewhere in grammar, aside from the phonological rules and syntactic transformations we have been discussing. Indeed, though there has been relatively little of the type of systematic data collection associated with variable rule studies, a certain amount of linguistic and probabilistic theorizing has been taking place à propos of other components of grammar.

On the level of phrase structure grammar, for example, considerable work has been done. The choice of one of a number of possible rules to rewrite a nonterminal node in a phrase marker is not strictly comparable to the application or nonapplication choice of a meaning-preserving transformation; nonetheless it frequently involves a certain freedom in the way a speaker organizes what he is saying. Furthermore, in the base component of many grammars, rewrite choices in phrase structure rules involve a strong stylistic component. The extension of phrase structure grammar to include probabilistic considerations has been suggested, largely independently and in ways which are mathematically almost identical, by Klein (1965), and by the mathematicians Grenander (1967), Horning (1970), Suppes (1970) working with Roger Brown's acquisition data, and D. Sankoff (1971, 1972). See also Peizer and Olmsted (1969).

Without going too far into problems of lexical choice and lexical insertion, it is not difficult to see how phenomena such as synonymy, overlapping meanings, specificity versus generality, and referents which are marginal or on the border between two semantic domains could all lead to probabilistic considerations of the lexicon. In this connection we can point particularly to the work of Lehrer (1970) on probabilistic weights of features in the semantic domain of 'containers'. The mathematical and probabilistic implications of this approach were investigated by D. Sankoff (1971b). Finally we may cite Labov's paper at this conference (1972b) as showing the role of probabilistic choice near the boundaries between semantic domains.

Much of the work done thus far, including our own, is fragmentary. Nevertheless, it seems readily discernible that there is a natural and behaviorally motivated trend to extend grammatical theory, which is primarily discrete and algebraic in character, by the introduction of well-defined probabilistic notions.

REFERENCES

Blom, J.-P. and J. J. Gumperz. 1972. Social meaning in linguistic structures: Code-switching in Norway. In: Directions in sociolinguistics. Ed. by J. J. Gumperz and D. Hymes. New York, Holt, Rinehart and Winston. 407-34.

Cedergren, H. J. and S. Laberge. 1972. Les règles variables du que explétif dans le français parlé à Montréal. Paper read at the Annual Meeting of the Canadian Linguistic Association.

Grenander, U. 1967. Syntax-controlled probabilities. Technical report, Brown University, Division of Applied Mathematics.

Gumperz, J. J. and R. Wilson. 1971. Convergence and creolization: A case from the Indo-Aryan/Dravidian border. In: Pidginization and creolization of languages. Ed. by D. Hymes. Cambridge, Cambridge University Press. 151-67.

Horning, J. J. 1969. A study of grammatical inference. Technical report No. CS-139, Stanford Artificial Intelligence Project, Memo A1-98. Stanford University, Computer Science Department.

Hymes, D. 1962. The ethnography of speaking. In: Anthropology and human behavior. Ed. by T. Gladwin and W. C. Sturtevant. Anthropological Society of Washington. 13-53.

_____. 1972. Models of the interaction of language and social life. In: Directions in sociolinguistics. Ed. by J. J. Gumperz and D. Hymes. New York, Holt, Rinehart and Winston. 35-71.

Klein, S. 1965. Control of style with a generative grammar. Language. 41.619-31.

Laberge, S. 1972. Observation d'un changement linguistique: Les pronoms indéfinis dans le français Montréalais. Unpublished M.A. Thesis, Département d'Anthropologie, Université de Montréal.

Labov, W. 1966. The social stratification of English in New York City. Washington, D.C., Center for Applied Linguistics.

_____. 1969. Contraction, deletion, and inherent variability of the English copula. Language. 45.715-62.

_____. 1972a. Where do grammars stop? In: Georgetown University Monograph Series on Languages and Linguistics, Monograph 25. Washington, D.C., Georgetown University Press.

_____. 1972b. The measurement of vagueness in semantic structures. Paper read at NWAVE Colloquium, Georgetown University.

Lakoff, R. n.d. Language and woman's place. Unpublished manuscript.

Lehrer, A. 1970. Indeterminacy in semantic description. Glossa. 4.87-110.

Peizer, D. B. and D. L. Olmsted. 1969. Modules of grammar acquisition. Language. 45.60-96.

Ross, J. R. 1972. The fake NP squish. Paper read at NWAVE Colloquium, Georgetown University.

Sag, I. 1972. On the state of progress on progressives and statives. Paper read at NWAVE Colloquium, Georgetown University.

Sankoff, D. 1971a. Branching processes with terminal types: Application to context-free grammars. Journal of Applied Probability. 8.233-40.

_____. 1971b. Dictionary structure and probability measures. Information and Control. 19.104-13.

_____. 1972. Context-free grammars and nonnegative matrices. Linear Algebra and its Applications. 5.277-81.

Sankoff, G. and H. J. Cedergren. 1971. Some results of a sociolinguistic study of Montreal French. In: Linguistic diversity in Canadian society. Ed. by R. Darnell. Linguistic Research, Inc. 61-87.

Sankoff, G. and S. Laberge. 1972. On the acquisition of native speakers by a language. To appear in: Kivung (Journal of the Linguistic Society of Papua New Guinea), vol. 5.

Sankoff, G., R. Sarrasin, and H. J. Cedergren. 1971. Quelques considérations sur la distribution de la variable <u>que</u> dans le français de Montréal. Paper read at the Congrès de l'Association Canadienne-française pour l'Avancement des Sciences.

Sherzer, J. n.d. Some current issues in linguistic theory: A sociolinguistic perspective. Unpublished manuscript.

Shuy, R. 1969. Sociolinguistic research at the Center for Applied Linguistics: The correlation of language and sex. International Days of Sociolinguistics. Rome, Istituto Luigi Sturzo. 849-58.

Trudgill, P. 1972. Diasystemic rules and variation in Norwich English. Paper read at NWAVE Colloquium, Georgetown University.

Wolfram, W. 1972. On what basis variable rules? Paper read at NWAVE Colloquium, Georgetown University.

THE BOUNDARIES OF WORDS AND THEIR MEANINGS

WILLIAM LABOV

University of Pennsylvania

If we take seriously the traditional notion that linguistic signs represent the union of a form and a meaning, there can be no limit to our interest in the meanings of words. But for a number of reasons, linguists have concentrated their attention on the forms of words and their combinations, and the meanings of only a small number of grammatical particles. The description of the meanings of words has been left to the lexicographers, for better or for worse; and linguists have long contented themselves with glosses which are labels but not descriptions. Recent activity in combinatorial semantics has not extended as yet to the meanings of words.

The reason for this neglect is certainly not a lack of interest, since linguists like any other speakers of a language cannot help focusing their attention on the word, which is the most central element in the social system of communication.[1] It is the difficulty of the problem, and its inaccessibility to the most popular methods of inquiry, which is responsible for this neglect.

We encounter many ordinary objects that are clearly and easily named, but many more where it is difficult to say exactly what they are if we confront them directly. In any kitchen, there are many containers that are obviously bowls, cups, mugs, and dishes. But there are others that might be called cups, or might not; or might be a kind of a cup, according to some, but a kind of a dish according to others. This is a problem of formal description more than a problem of the language; for the puzzled expressions that we get when we hold up such an object for naming rarely appear in the everyday use of the language. The most casual observation suggests that the language has many adroit ways of dealing with the problem, but that has not helped lexicographers when they attempted formal definitions of words.

Words have often been called slippery customers, and many scholars have been distressed by their tendency to shift their meanings and slide out from under any simple definition. A goal of some clear thinkers has been to use words in more precise ways. But though this is an excellent and necessary step for a technical jargon, it is a self-defeating program when applied to ordinary words. It is not only that words are shifters; the objects to which they must be applied shift with even greater rapidity. Words that are bound to simple conjunctive definitions will have little value for application in a world which presents us with an unlimited range of new and variable objects for description. Words as well as the world itself display the 'orderly heterogeneity' which characterizes language as a whole (Weinreich, Labov, and Herzog 1968). Again we would argue that this orderly heterogeneity is functional. Rather than complain about the variable character of the meanings of words, we should recognize the existence of an extraordinary ability of human beings to apply words to the world in a creative way. The problem is no less central than the one which Chomsky has identified in relation to syntax. Just as we employ a finite set of rules to produce an unlimited number of sentences, so we employ a finite set of words to describe an unlimited number of objects in the real world around us.

The ordinary methods of investigation which have been used to define words represent only a part of the methods which might be used to attack this problem. Language can be studied through introspection, formal elicitation, the study of texts, experiment, and/or observation (Labov 1971). But only the first three approaches have been taken to the study of words and their meanings. This paper will report for the first time a series of experimental studies of the use of words which have been carried out over the past ten years.[2] The main focus has been on the denotation of cups and cuplike containers, and the use of words such as _cup_, _bowl_, _dish_, _mug_, _glass_, _pitcher_, etc., and their corresponding terms in other languages. New techniques have been developed for the study of the variable conditions which govern denotation. But there are also invariant components among these conditions, and the entire study must be firmly located as an aspect of the basic categorizing activity of human beings. Before we consider the experiments themselves, it will be necessary to outline the traditional categorical view which attempts to capture this aspect of linguistic behavior and the problem of defining boundary conditions within that view.

1. The categorical view and its limitations

If linguistics can be said to be any one thing it is the study of categories: that is, the study of how language translates meaning into sound through the categorization of reality into discrete units and sets of units. This categorization is such a fundamental and obvious part of linguistic activity that the properties of categories are normally assumed rather than studied. Behind all of the theories of linguistic structure that have been presented in the twentieth century there is a common set of assumptions about the nature of structural units. This set of assumptions can be called the 'categorical view'. It includes the implicit assertions that all linguistic units are categories which are:

(1) discrete
(2) invariant
(3) qualitatively distinct
(4) conjunctively defined
(5) composed of atomic primes

By 'discrete', it is meant that the categories are separated from each other by clear-cut discontinuities of form or function; by 'invariant', that the category as a type recurs as precisely the same in each occurrence, despite the fact that tokens may vary; by 'qualitatively different', that the units are completely different from each other, and not distinguished as homogeneous elements in a linear or ordered sequence; by 'conjunctively defined', that there is a set of properties associated with the unit which are in some way criterial or necessary, essential as opposed to other properties which are unnecessary, accidental, or redundant, and that all of these essential properties must be present for the category to be recognized.

The fifth property may be considered an extension of discreteness: although some categories are compounded of others, there is a limit to any such subdivision, and all categories are ultimately composed of a set of integral categories which cannot be subdivided.

Membership in these categories, and relations of inclusion and exclusion among categories, are established by rules which are obligatory or optional, but optionality cannot be further characterized. No statements can be made as to whether one such rule applies more often than another.[3]

These properties of linguistic categories are far from arbitrary. They appear to correspond well to the basic structure of language as we deal with it everyday. It is sometimes said that man is a categorizing animal; it is equally appropriate to say that language is a categorizing activity. The total abandonment of any one of these properties might be shown to have unfortunate consequences for linguistic analysis. But some modification appears to be necessary, as the present report and other recent work demonstrates.

Scholars have assumed the properties of the categorical view for a wide range of categories: features, phonemes, morphemes, intonation contours, verbs, modals, nouns, nodes, cycles, derivations, styles, languages, manner adverbs, dialects, etc. Because this characterization of language seems to be firmly based on the nature of linguistic activity, it has provided a useful base for a first approximation to grammars and the principles of writing grammars.

But this view of man as a categorizing animal fails if it takes categorizing activity for granted, since it cannot deal with the facts of linguistic change which have been studied over several centuries, nor with the orderly variation within linguistic structure which we have charted in some detail in recent years (Weinreich, Labov, and Herzog 1968).

In the categorical view, the properties of categories are assumed. Scholars then typically argue how many categories exist, and what items are assigned to what categories.[4] This is an important and essential activity: many fields which study human behavior deal with categories which are not firmly enough established to allow the question, one category or two?[5] But in many areas of linguistics, we have extracted as much profit as we can from these debates, and we can turn to the resolution of long-standing questions by examining the correspondence of the categorizing process to linguistic activity. Instead of taking as problematical the existence of categories, we can turn to the nature of the boundaries between them. As linguistics then becomes a form of boundary theory rather than a category theory, we discover that not all linguistic material fits the categorical view: there is greater or lesser success in imposing categories upon the continuous substratum of reality.

There are cases where the categorical nature of a boundary is immediate and obvious, as suggested in a property-item matrix such as Figure 1. Here there are a series of eight items (a-h) which may be thought of variously as languages, dialects, villages, parts of speech, words, phonemes, etc., and seven properties (1-7) detectable in them. The presence of these properties is associated with category X, their absence with category Y. In Figure 1 it is plain that items a-d are X's, and e-h are Y's. Though it is possible to select a single property as the distinctive, or criterial, or essential one, we feel much more confident about categories which are defined by the co-occurrence of a large number of items. Thus it is clear that French and English are different systems, and we use these terms without misgivings. But we are not so happy with such categories as dialects established by the evidence that two speakers disagree with each other on the acceptability of a single sentence type[6] and we are particularly critical of sub-categorizations of parts of speech which are justified by only one property.[7]

FIGURE 1. Property-item matrix for a clearly categorical boundary.

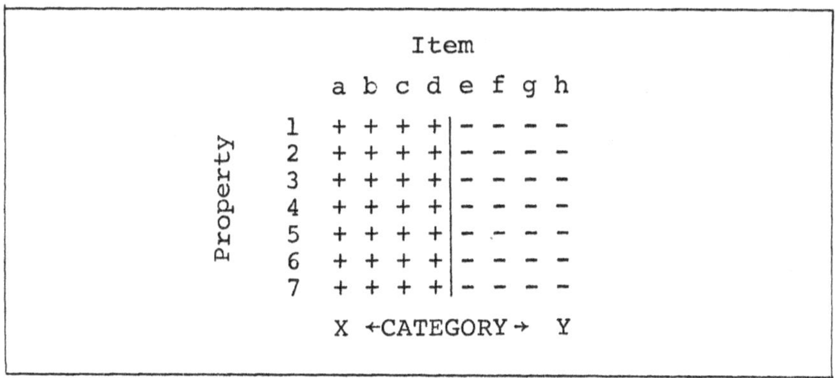

Property	Item a	b	c	d	e	f	g	h
1	+	+	+	+	-	-	-	-
2	+	+	+	+	-	-	-	-
3	+	+	+	+	-	-	-	-
4	+	+	+	+	-	-	-	-
5	+	+	+	+	-	-	-	-
6	+	+	+	+	-	-	-	-
7	+	+	+	+	-	-	-	-

X ←CATEGORY→ Y

However, a certain degree of vagueness is often characteristic of boundaries. In the most extreme case, categories can be justified even when no boundaries can be set up between them.

Thus, in Figure 2, any decision to locate the boundary between categories X and Y would obviously be an arbitrary one. Yet the fact that the data on properties (1-7) can be organized in the implicational series shows that there is a structure here, which effectively constrains the data to eliminate at least half of the possible permutations

FIGURE 2. Property-item matrix for the absence of a boundary between two categories.

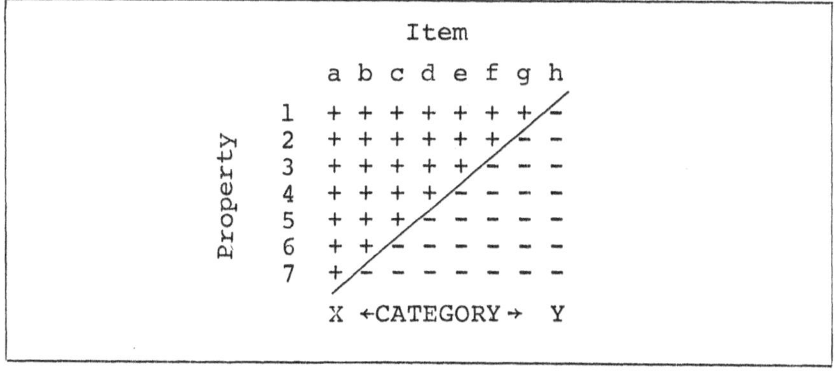

Property	Item a	b	c	d	e	f	g	h
1	+	+	+	+	+	+	+	-
2	+	+	+	+	+	+	-	-
3	+	+	+	+	+	-	-	-
4	+	+	+	+	-	-	-	-
5	+	+	+	-	-	-	-	-
6	+	+	-	-	-	-	-	-
7	+	-	-	-	-	-	-	-

X ←CATEGORY→ Y

of items and properties. Given empirical data which resembled Figure 2, we could not say with any certainty whether any given item b-g was to be classed as a sonorant or an obstruent, a verb or a modal, a speaker of the white vernacular or of the black vernacular, a Romance or a Germanic language, a pidgin or a creole, as the categories X and Y may variously assign membership. The transition between X and Y occupies the entire property-item space. Such matrices have been discussed as theoretical possibilities by a number of recent writers, beginning with Quirk (1965) in regard to grammatical categories, and DeCamp (1971) in regard to sociolinguistic systems and the Creole continuum. But in regard to geographical dialects, it has long been argued that such gradient models are characteristic of the diffusion of linguistic features across a territory and the challenge has been to establish that boundaries between dialects are anything but arbitrary (Weinreich 1954, Stankiewicz 1957).

The most vigorous development of the modal of Figure 2, on both the theoretical and empirical side, is to be found in the work of Bickerton, who proposes that linguistic structures contain no homogeneous categories at all, but only continuous transitions bound by implicational series, with no properties showing co-occurrence restrictions at all (1971, 1972). Nevertheless, even in dialect geography, most investigators agree that properties do bundle, and that it is possible to show boundaries of varying degrees of clarity even when all variable features are superimposed upon a single map. This type of bundling or co-occurrence of properties in a variable matrix is illustrated in Figure 3, where the division between categories X and

FIGURE 3. Discontinuity reflecting co-occurrence restrictions on properties in a variable matrix.

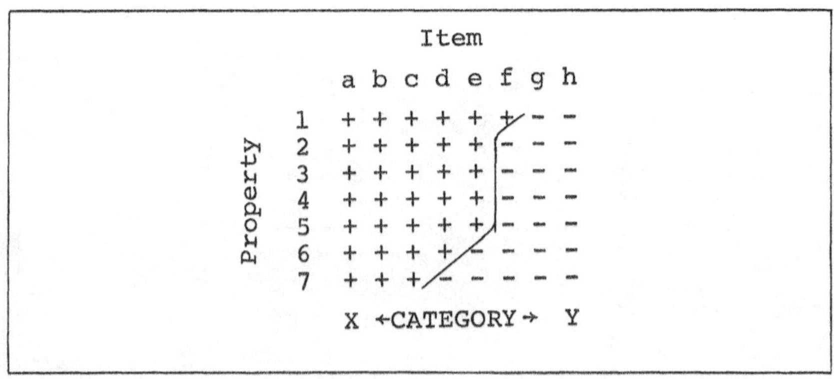

Y appears to be less arbitrary than in Figure 2. Items a, b, c are clearly X, and d and e appear to be X's as well, though a bit defective in relation to properties 6 and 7. Items g and h are clearly Y, and f is again a Y, though imperfect. The important feature of Figure 3 which makes this division possible is the simultaneous shift or co-occurrence restrictions exhibited by properties 2-5. These provide us with evidence of systematicity within the rules which govern property 2 and tie them to those which govern properties 3, 4, and 5. In dialect geography, the discontinuity of Figure 3 would represent a bundle of isoglosses; in an urban speech community, it would represent a subsystem characteristic of a class or ethnic dialect. If Figure 3 represents the distinction between modals and other verbs, the bundling properties might be subject to inversion, reproduction in tag questions, and not contraction. In phonology, we find that initial stops show co-occurrence of initial aspiration, voicing lag, and stronger release of air pressure. Whether or not we choose one of these properties as distinctive, the co-occurrence reinforces our confidence in the existence of the categories.

Another sort of discontinuity in a variable matrix appears in Figure 4. Here there is no co-occurrence of any two properties, but there are items that clump together. Items e-h are all characterized by properties 1-3 but not properties 4-7. This situation

FIGURE 4. Discontinuity reflecting a concentration of homogeneous items in a variable matrix.

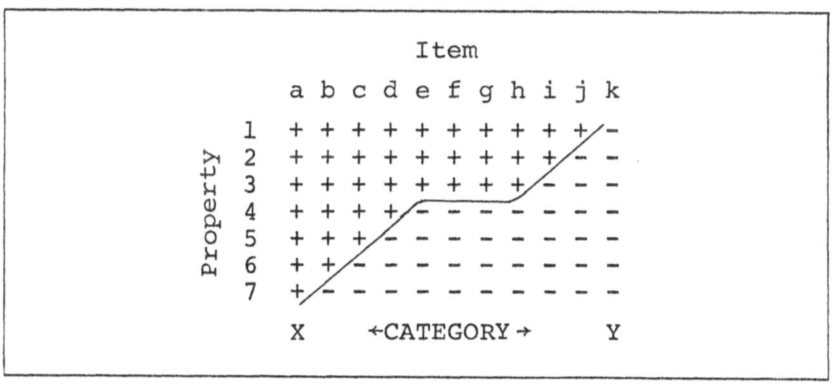

tempts us to redefine our category system, possibly setting up a third category X' which is defined by properties 1-3 only. In dialect geography, this would mean that relatively homogeneous speech communities exist; in phonology, it would mean that some combinations of features were more heavily exploited than others for some functional reason. It is clear that this second type of discontinuity appears in Bickerton's data, and is one of the main focuses of Bailey's approach in building rate into models of phonological linguistic description (1971).

In large-scale studies which are accountable to a given population or body of data, we may find no examples of perfect co-occurrence or perfectly homogeneous groups. But given an empirical approach to the problems of linguistic analysis we can report the actual discontinuities in transition which exist. Thus if we are to take seriously the categorical property of language, we must pass beyond the categorical view which takes it as given, and study the process of categorization itself by focusing on such discontinuities directly. By avoiding the categorical view, or some equally rigid principle of distribution, we are free to study the real properties of such boundaries, and deduce the higher level properties which govern the use of language.

This paper will introduce the study of variability in denotation, systematically displacing the categorical view which has dominated previous studies in order to discover the regularities which relate the properties of shape, function, material, etc. as they govern the conditions for the act of denotation. To do so, we will have to reject in particular property (d)--the notion that categories are to be defined conjunctively through their distinctive features. These distinctive features or essential attributes are the working apparatus of the scholastic tradition which has dominated almost every school of linguistic thought until recently, and our pursuit of a secular mode of inquiry will inevitably bring us into conflict with that tradition.

2. Conditions for denotation

In this study, we will be dealing with the conditions which govern denotation, that is, the act of naming or reference which associates a linguistic sign with an element of the extra-linguistic world. Denotation or reference has been especially excluded from some recent studies of combinatorial semantics, as if this topic were outside of the proper domain of linguistics (Katz and Fodor 1963). Yet the fundamental relation of form to meaning in designation is to be seen only in the conditions which govern the act of reference: that is, the significatum of the sign.

Though this investigation deals with the application of signs to concrete objects, it is not a study of the act of reference, and should not be confused with the point of view that identifies meaning with use. We are dealing rather with the knowledge of ability to apply a term to a range of objects in a way that reflects the communicative system utilized by others. Following Weinreich (1962), we define the significatum or meaning of a sign, as the conditions which govern denotation. Given a situation in which such conditions are actually fulfilled, so that the sign can be used in reference to the situation, the token of the sign is said to denote. Thus

(1) L(x) if C_1 and C_2 and C_3.

That is, the sign L denotes the object x if all of the conditions C_1, C_2 . . . are fulfilled. These conditions C_1, C_2 . . . are sometimes called criteria, or conditions of criteriality. The relationship here is one of intersection: each of them must be fulfilled, or the sign does not denote. In other words, these are essential conditions, or distinctive features of the designatum. They are quite parallel in this respect to the distinctive features of the Jakobson-Halle framework (1952): essential properties that are always present (except when they are replaced), and the only properties which need to be included in a specification of the phoneme or the sign. All other--redundant--properties can be discarded from the specification of meaning.

In the present state of semantic investigations, most articles draw upon the intuitions of the theorist in order to isolate these distinctive features and their internal structure. A great deal can be learned through such introspection, especially if intuitions are sharpened, by the use of the right linguistic frames. Let us see how much can be achieved within the categorical view by the use of our linguistic intuitions, beginning with a definition of a cup cast in the model of (1):

(2) The term cup is used for an object which is (a) concrete and (b) inanimate and (c) upwardly concave and (d) a container (e) with a handle (f) made of earthenware or other vitreous material and (g) set on a saucer and (h) used for the consumption of food (i) which is liquid [(j) and hot] . . .

In order to find out which of these ten conditions are criterial, we can apply the test frame proposed by Weinreich, <u>It's an L but C</u>. If the property is essential and expected to be present, the result is absurd since <u>but</u> implies something contrary to expectation. Thus the absurdity of <u>It's a chair but you can sit in it</u> establishes that there is something about the property of seating someone that is essential to chairs. In the test sentences given below, we insert first the property listed as an essential condition in definition (2); on the right, a contrary or opposing property. If the original property cited is essential, criterial, or distinctive, we should have unacceptable or absurd sentences on the left, and acceptable or sensible sentences on the right.

(3)

It's a cup but . . .	
a. *it's concrete.	it's abstract.
b. *it's inanimate.	it's alive.
c. *it's concave.	it's convex.
d. *it holds things.	it doesn't hold anything.
e. *it has a handle.	it doesn't have a handle.
f. *it's pottery.	it's made of wax.
g. *it's on a saucer.	it has no saucer.
h. *it's used at meal times.	they use it to store things.
i. *you can drink out of it.	you can eat out of it.
j. ?you can drink hot milk out of it.	?you can drink cold milk out of it.
k. ?it has a stripe on it.	?it doesn't have a stripe on it.

My own reactions to these sentences are indicated by asterisks or question marks; they suggest that properties (a–i) satisfy this approach to essentiality or criteriality. For item (j) we get two sentences that are equally irrelevant or questionable. There is no reason to think it surprising that we can drink hot milk out of a cup; but equally so, it is not surprising that we can drink cold milk out of it. Similarly, if we add a feature which is obviously accidental and not essential, like a stripe (k), we get questionable results on both sides.[8] It is of course the lack of symmetry between the two opposing sentences rather than the absolute judgment which makes the test reasonably precise.

If the study of linguistic intuitions were a satisfactory approach to the defining of terms, it would seem that linguists have a great deal to contribute to the writing of dictionaries. But lexicography as it has been practised is an art of a different kind, where the intuitions of the lexicographer combine with traditional lore (the definitions found in other dictionaries) and a large body of citations from published sources. The dictionary maker does not rely upon his intuitions to cover the full range of applications and meanings which the term cup might have, but tries instead to frame a definition that circumscribes as narrowly as possible the whole range of uses that he can collect. The result is a kind of definition which linguists usually find quite unsatisfactory.

(4) cup, n. 1. A small open bowl-shaped vessel used chiefly to drink from, with or without a handle or handles, a stem and foot, or a lid; as a wine cup, a Communion cup; specif., a handled vessel of china, earthenware, or the like commonly

set on a saucer and used for hot liquid foods such as tea, coffee, or soup. --Webster's New International Dictionary, Second edition.

There are quite a few features of this definition which linguists might find peculiar, but the most objectionable is the use of qualifying words like chiefly, commonly, or the like, etc. These are the kinds of indefinite quantifiers that linguistics has been trying to escape from since the early days of comparative method. In the current linguistic framework, a property can be optional or obligatory. If it is optional, then it is in 'free variation'. and nothing more can be said about its frequency.[9] Even more objectionable is with or without a handle, or handles. Such a phrase is hardly specific to cups; it can be applied to any object in the universe. I myself, for example, come with or without a handle or handles.

Let us ask how a reader is expected to use this definition. Suppose an object is not used to drink from. How does the reader utilize the expression used chiefly to drink from? Is the object he is examining less of a cup? Should he then call it cuppish, or a thing like a cup, or can he go ahead and call it a cup just the same? The definition does not help to make the kind of decision which was discussed in section 1, where the categorizing spirit of language is invoked to decide if in fact, an object is, or is not, a cup.

Webster's definition goes far beyond this categorizing activity; it has an encyclopedic quality, which could seemingly expand indefinitely to tell us anything or everything ever known about cups. There are of course many other entries besides the principal one that I have quoted. The sixth is the principle generalizing entry which covers the extended and metaphorical uses of cup most freely:

(5) 6. A thing resembling a cup (sense 1) in shape or use, or likened to such a utensil; as (a) a socket or recess in which something turns, as the hip bone, the recess which a capstan spindle turns, etc. (b) any small cavity in the surface of the ground. (c) an annular trough, filled with water, at the face of each section of a telescopic gas holder, into which fits the grip of the section next outside. (d) in turpentine orcharding, a receptable shaped like a flowerpot, metal or earthenware, attached to the tree to collect resin.

We wonder whether the first part of this definition could not be added to every noun in the dictionary. Is there any term which cannot be applied to a thing resembling its main referent in shape or use, or likened to it? Beyond this, we have four uses of dazzling specificity, which are obviously inserted only to cover some particular three-by-five slips which the dictionary staff happened to have collected. If the reader is not capable of understanding uses (a-d) without help from the dictionary, it seems unlikely that he will be able to survive in everyday life where terms are freely extended in such a way to even more specific objects.

Thus the Webster definition seems to be overly specific in some areas, but terribly vague in others. No current linguistic text would hold it up as a proper model or guide for semantic description. It is true that it will be contradicted far less often by experience than definition (2). But definition (2) can be defended by saying that it covers only the essential or distinctive properties of a cup; the Webster definition seems to be governed only by the need to cover all of the uses of cup that have been accumulated in its files.

The balance of this paper will report experimental studies of the use of the term cup. Surprisingly enough, these studies will show that the Webster definition is superior to the criterial definition (2) in every respect. A first indication of this situation appears when we consider some properties of such criterial statements which raise great difficulties for empirical investigations.

The conditions specified in formula (1) are usually taken to indicate the presence or absence of a given feature: that is, they govern the denotation of L by binary decisions. Thus a cup may or may not be concave, may or may not be used as a container. Similarly, in componential analysis we define a relative as either male or female, either colineal or ablineal. But the generation condition is a linear scale; we must establish some criterial value along that scale, such as first ascending generation, to locate father (Wallace and Atkins 1960). We do find many such cases of simply yes-no conditions, such as whether a tree has cones or not. But we more commonly encounter dimensions which require us to establish criterial values to complete our definition. For L to denote, C_1 must achieve a critical value. Thus we need a formulation such as

(6) $L(x)$ if C_p and D_r and E_t . . .

where C, D, and E each vary along separate dimensions, and L does not denote if the value of C is less than p, etc. Thus a tree is not a white pine unless it has five needles in each fascicle. But again, it is unusual to find such discrete criterial values in empirical work: normally, the criterial condition is a range of values within which L will denote. Thus we must formulate

(7) $L(x)$ if C_p^q and D_r^s and E_t^u . . .

where L does not denote if the value of C is less than p or greater than q, etc. Thus a tree is not a yellow pine if its needles are in bundles of less than two or more than three.

We may note here one further limitation of the traditional, categorical approach to denotative conditions which may cause difficulties: the various conditions C, D, E are normally considered to be independent of each other. It is possible that one condition is dependent on the other in the sense that it is a precondition for the other. Thus the leaves of a pine tree must be needles, implying some maximum of cross-section relative to length. And the needles must be in bundles of a certain number, entailing the existence of needles as a feature superordinate in the taxonomy. But the criterial values for a needle, and the criterial values for numbers of needles in a fascicle, are independent of each other. The number of needles in a bundle required if white pine is to denote are usually independent of the specification of maximum cross-section of the leaves. We do not, for example, say that a white pine is a tree with bundles of five needles if they are thick or three to four when they are thin.[10]

This property of independence of criterial conditions is firmly entrenched in the componential analysis of kinship terms, plant taxonomy, etc., which is the area where the most progress has been made in descriptive semantics. Nevertheless, our empirical investigations will show us that the independence of criterial values is not a fundamental property which governs native competence in the use of words. The formal modifications of (7) necessary to cope with this situation will be developed at the conclusion of our report.

The remaining limitation of the modified categorical formula (7) which we must amend is its discreteness. The criterial conditions C_p^q imply discrete cutting points p and q. Yet in the world of experience all boundaries show some degree of vagueness, and any formal system which is useful for semantic description must allow us to record, or even measure, this property.

3. The measurement of vagueness

When we approach the empirical problems of naming things, we find that vagueness is almost a universal property of the criterial ranges C_p to C^q. In kinship terminology, we have ready-made discreteness: there is no intermediate step in the nuclear family between first and second generation, and no vague borderland or fringe area between them. But the borderline between a tree and a shrub is not discrete. Leaves may be deeply lobed or shallowly lobed, but there is a vague area in-between where we are in doubt. This vagueness is not a property of our perception or the weakness of our instruments, nor the abstractness of our objects. Some of the most concrete data are by nature vague, and some concrete objects are in themselves vague, as for example, fog.

Can we measure vagueness? At first glance, this may seem to be a self-defeating idea. Yet if we follow the reasoning of Max Black (1949), it seems quite feasible to measure the vagueness of terms within a given context. A term's vagueness, following Black, consists of the existence of objects concerning which it is impossible to say either that the term does or does not denote. He constructs a consistency profile upon three fundamental notions: (1) users of a language; (2) a situation in which a user of a language is trying to apply a term L to an object x; and (3) the consistency of application of L to x. The subjective aspect of vagueness may be thought of as the lack of certainty as to whether the term does or does not denote; and this may be transformed into the consistency with which a given sample of speakers does in fact apply the term. The problem of vagueness is seen most clearly when we have a large number of objects which differ by only small degrees from each other, as in Black's example of a series of chairs which gradually become indistinguishable from a series of blocks of wood. At one end of the series, a single term L clearly denotes; at the other end, it does not; and in the middle we are left in doubt. If the consistency of application of L to x for each of these objects is measured, we obtain a consistency profile. Measurements are not of course comparable except in a given situation, but we can distinguish various types of gradients and opposing relations within that situation and regular transformations of it. A precise symbol will show a sharp gradient, while a vague term will show a very slight one. But more importantly, we will be able to use this mechanism to demonstrate the effect of changes in various properties upon the application of the term, and their mutual interaction.

The present series of studies is based upon the series of cup-like objects shown in Figure 5. The first four cups across the top show increasing ratios of width to depth. If the proportional width of the cup at upper left is taken as 1, then the widths of the cups 1, 2, 3, 4 increase in the ratios of 1.2, 1.5, and 1.9 to 1, all with constant depth.[11] A fifth decrease in width (No. 20, not shown here) gives us a ratio of 2.5 to 1. Proceeding downward along the left margin, we have five increments of depth with constant width; the depth is increased in the ratios of 1.2, 1.5, 1.9, 2.4, and 3.0 to 1. In the center of the diagram are cups which depart from the concave shape of 1-4 and 5-9. Cups 10, 11, 12 are cylindrical, with increasing depth; and cups 13, 14, 15 show the same increments for the tapering pattern of a truncated cone. In the lower right we have forms that depart maximally from the modal cup at upper left. The short- and long-stemmed cups show variation in the form of the base, and

FIGURE 5. Series of cup-like objects.

the square and triangular objects show variation in the contour of the perimeter. The drawings of cups are presented to subjects one at a time, in two different randomized orders; the subjects are simply asked to name them. They are then shown the same series of drawings again, and this time asked to imagine in each case that they saw someone with the object in his hand, stirring in sugar with a spoon, and drinking coffee from it (or in some languages, tea), and to name them in this context. In a third series, they are asked to imagine that they came to dinner at someone's house and saw this object sitting on the dinner table, filled with mashed potatoes (rice for some languages). In a fourth series, they are asked to conceive of each of these objects standing on a shelf, each with cut flowers in it. We will refer to these four contexts as the 'Neutral', 'Coffee', 'Food', and 'Flower' contexts.

There is another set of diagrams with no handles, and a third with two handles, which are used in a more limited series of namings. In other series, we specify the material of these cups as china, glass, paper, and metal.

The responses to these tests are in the form of noun phrases, often with a wide range of modifiers. In our present analyses, we consider only the head noun. That is, we do not care whether the object is called a long cup, a funny cup with a stem, or a kind of a cup; as long as the head noun is cup, it will be classed here as 'cup'. We have carried out these tests in a fair range of languages, and recently extended this study to contrast bilingual and monolingual speakers of Spanish and English, in various degrees of proficiency. But the material reported here will be drawn from a series of eight investigations of speakers of English, with sample sizes ranging from eleven to twenty-four subjects. The fundamental relations to be discussed here are confirmed with great consistency in each of these tests. The first series was drawn from exploratory interviews in the speech community, but most of the others from classes or series of individual students at Columbia University and at the University of Pennsylvania.[12]

Figures 6 and 7 show a series of consistency profiles for the application of cup to a series of objects of increasing width. Figure 6 is for Group A of eleven subjects from the first series in 1964 (without cup No. 20), and Figure 7 is an immediately following series with Group B, also with eleven subjects. The solid lines show the consistency profiles for cup and bowl in the first, Neutral context. For Group A, the applicability of cup is 100 per cent for the first two cups, drops slightly for a ratio of 1.5 to 1, and then plunges sharply to less that 25 per cent for the wider objects. The line crossing from lower left shows the percentage of applications of bowl to the same objects. At about the width of 2.2 to 1, the

FIGURE 6. Consistency profiles for cup and bowl in Neutral and Food contexts, Group A, N = 11.

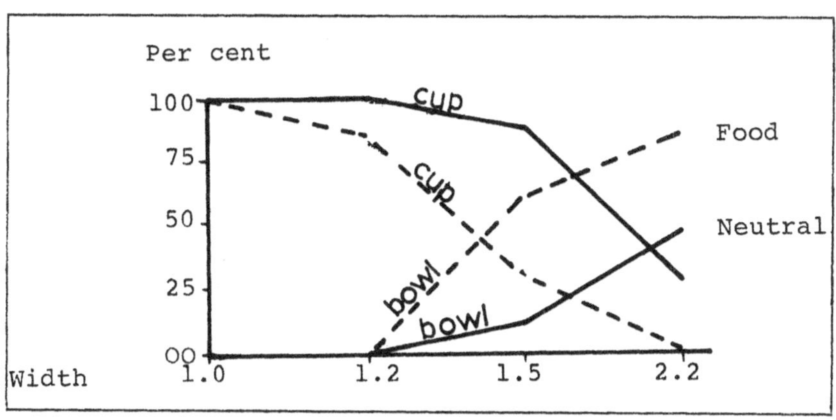

FIGURE 7. Consistency profiles denoted as cup and bowl in Neutral and Food contexts, Group B, N = 11.

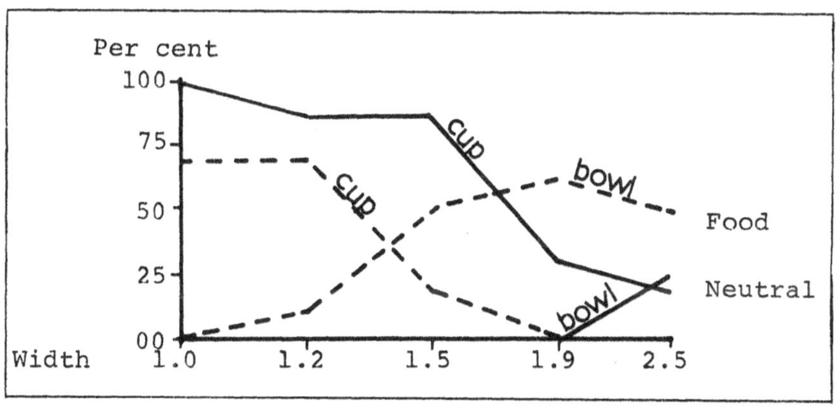

likelihood of the object being called a bowl is roughly equal to the likelihood of its being called a cup. This is the fringe area, in which it is possible to assert with equal truth that the object is a cup and that it is not a cup.

The same relations for the Neutral context appear again in Figure 7, this time with five degrees of width. Again the fringe area cross-over point is at a width ratio of 2.2 to 1.

The dotted lines show the effect of switching the context of denotation to Food--that is, containing mashed potatoes. The pattern is the same as for Neutral, but it is shifted to the left. Now the abrupt drop in the cup pattern is after cup No. 2, and the cross-over point is between 2 and 3, that is between the width ratios of 1.2 and 1.5. The same phenomenon appears in both Figures 6 and 7. The term bowl is applied more frequently in the transitional area than cup, although the modal values are immune from the shift.

Figure 8 shows consistency profiles for objects of increasing depth. Only Group A is shown here; Group B gives similar results. The term mug is shown superimposed on instances of cup, since as all informants agree that cup is a superordinate term for mug: that is, mug is a kind of cup.[13] On the other hand, vases are not kinds of cups. The number of items named as vase in the Neutral context is shown by the solid line at the lower right of Figure 8. In Figure 9,

FIGURE 8. Consistency profiles for cup, mug, and vase in Neutral context, by depth for Group A, N = 11.

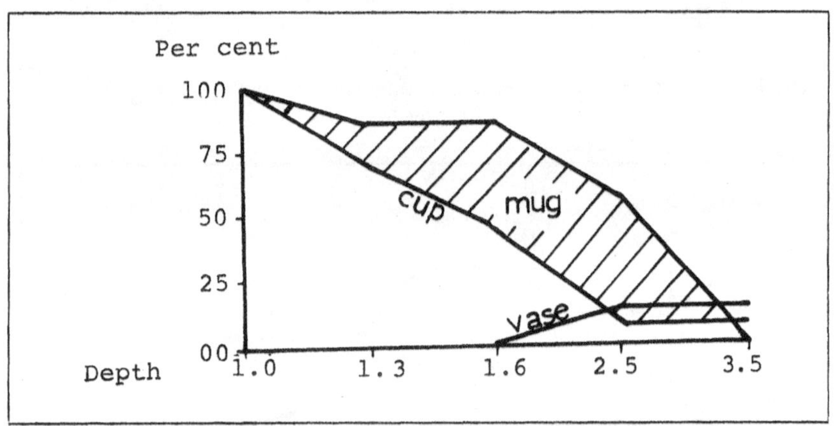

the same series of objects are shown in the Flower context; more favorable to vase, and less favorable to cup and mug. In fact, mug does not appear in the Flower context at all. Here again we see a regular shift of consistency profiles, so that now the crossover area lies between depths of 1.3 and 1.6, rather than at 3.5.

4. The interdependence of conditions for denotation

Many different dimensions and sub-tests within these series confirm the general pattern of Figures 5 and 6: the consistency profiles for any given term are radically shifted as the subjects conceive of the objects in different functional settings.[14] The consistency profiles are regularly elevated for cup by the Coffee context, depressed by Food, and even further depressed by the Flower context. The

FIGURE 9. Consistency profiles for cup and vase in Flower context, by depth, for Group A, N = 11.

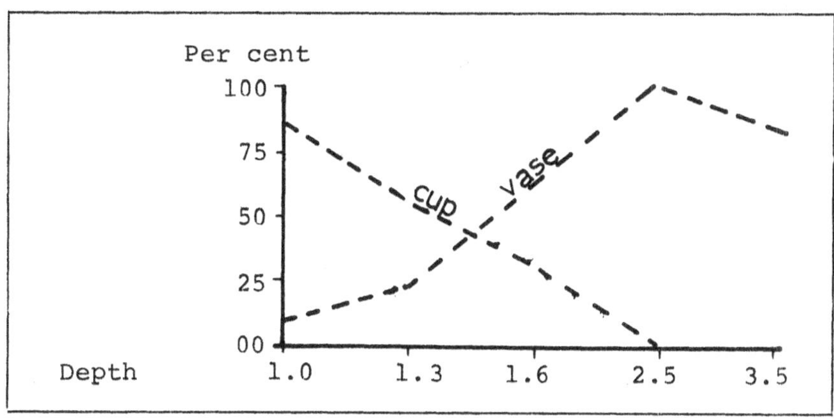

clarity and strength of the effect is illustrated by the fact that it emerges consistently with groups of less than ten subjects. Figure 10 shows the effect of all four contexts on the application of cup to

FIGURE 10. Consistency profiles for cup by width in four contexts, Group C, N = 24.

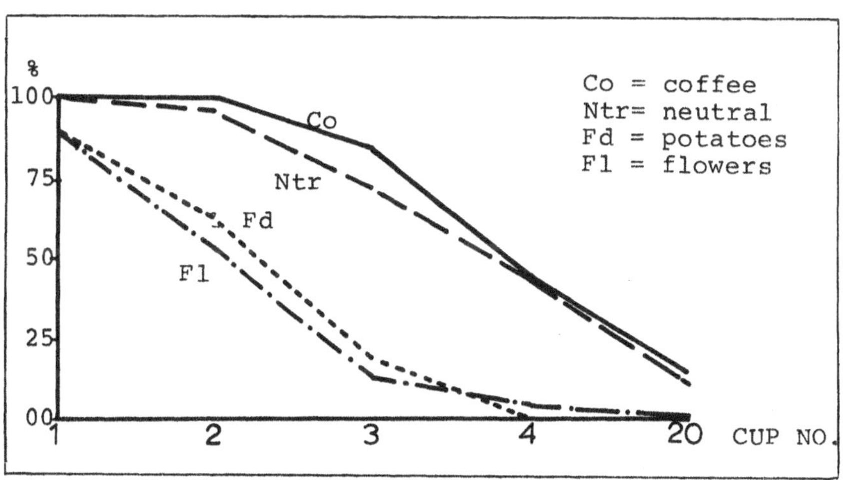

containers of increasing width, and Figure 11 the effect on containers of increasing depth. This was a series carried out in 1968 on Group C, with twenty-four subjects. The increment of Coffee over the Neutral context is a slight one in Figure 10, and for these shallow containers the Flower context decreases the use of the term only a

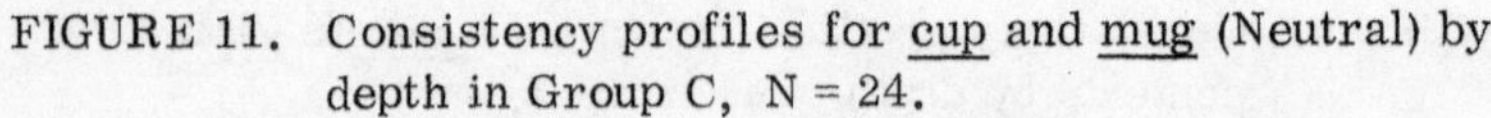
FIGURE 11. Consistency profiles for cup and mug (Neutral) by depth in Group C, N = 24.

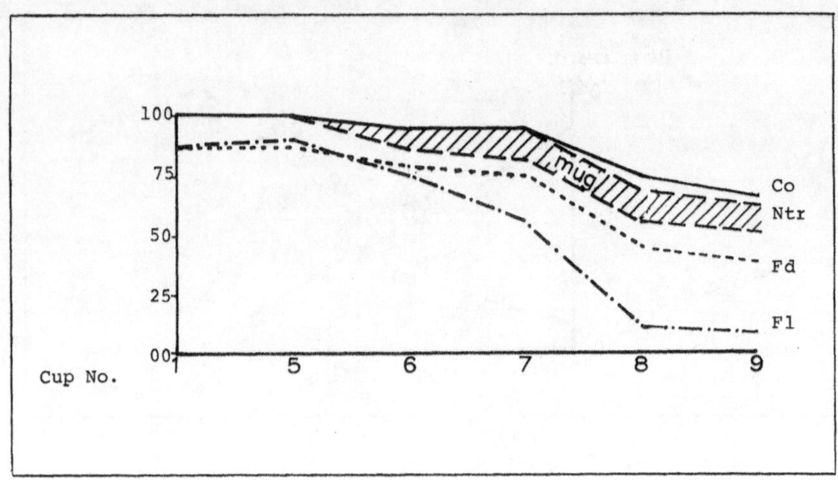

little more than Food. In Figure 11 this effect is much greater, as bowl competes with cup less in the Food context and vase competes more with cup. The effect contributed by mug to cup is shown here for the Neutral context only; in the others, mug is added to cup, but not shown separately.

Formal representations. It is normally assumed, as we noted above, that the criteria for denotation are established and selected independently of each other. The relations of form and function would therefore appear on a two-dimensional graph as a rectangular block bounded by the straight lines C = p and C = q, as in Figure 12. This is the pattern which we normally find in the schematic representations of componential analysis (Wallace and Atkins 1960, Figure 1). If we take condition C as referring to form (e.g. ratio of width to depth), and condition D as referring to use (e.g. function as a container), then the term always denotes if C lies between p and q, and D lies between r and s. This is the categorical view of denotation, corresponding to formula (1).

The data we derive from our studies of cup, bowl, vase, etc., corresponds to a very different model. Figure 13 shows a linear model which approximates the data. Instead of locating the outer and inner limits of the conditions C and D, we locate at the origin the modal values of C and D, p_o and r_o. The values of p and r which depart in various ways from this modal value will be located along the ordinate and abscissa respectively. The diagonal line shown in Figure 13 is merely one of many that connect points of

FIGURE 12. Orthogonal model for independent conditions for denotation.

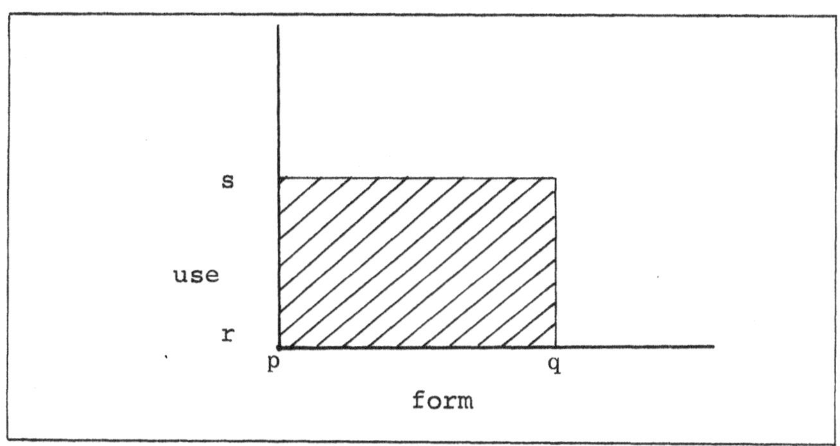

FIGURE 13. Linear model for relations between conditions for denotation.

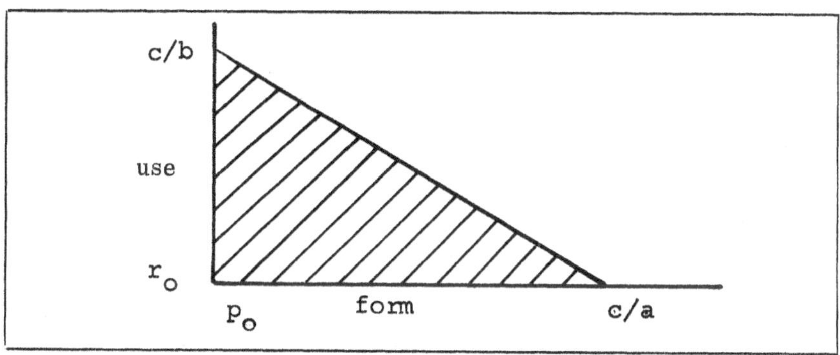

equal probability of the term L denoting. To express a quantitative relationship between the values of form and function presupposes that function has been quantified, and in our present state of knowledge this does not seem likely. If that could be done, however, the relationship between form and function might appear as

$$(8)\quad a \cdot (p - p_0) + b \cdot (r - r_0) = c$$

If the diagonal line of Figure 13 is taken to represent the outer limits of all cases where the probability of L denoting is more than zero, then it will show two specific limits of form and function for cup.

When p is equal to the modal value for form p_o, then $(r_o - r) = c/b$, and similarly, when r is equal to the modal value for form r_o, then the outer limits of $(p_o - p)$ will be equal to a quantity c/a. This means that under no circumstances will any object with a form beyond c/a be called a cup.

If this is not the case, and if there is no outer limit of shape or function which limits the use of cup, then we would have a hyperbolic model such as Figure 14. Here there are no outer limits. When

FIGURE 14. Hyperbolic model for relations between two conditions for denotation.

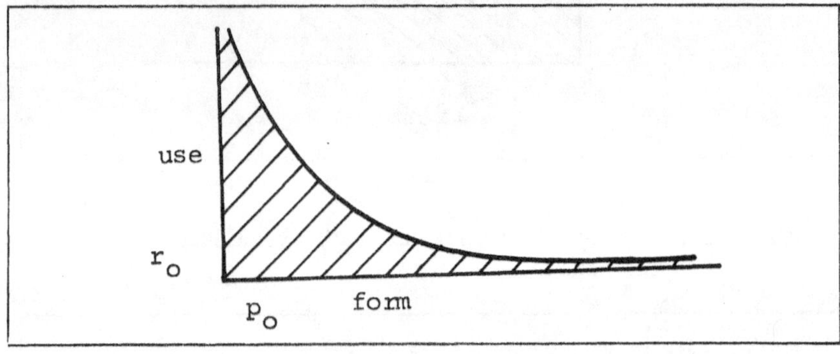

$p = p_o$, then almost any value of r will permit the application of the term cup, and when $r = r_o$, then any value of the shape p will permit the term to denote. In this case, the relations of use and form would appear as

(9) $(p - p_o) \cdot (r - r_o) = c$

Thus as $(p - p_o)$ approaches zero, $(r - r_o)$ becomes indefinitely large.

We do not yet have a wide enough range of data to test these models, although the evidence of Figures 6, 8, 9, 10, and 11 argues for an approximation to the linear model of Figure 13. The linearity is most evident in the slopes for cup, especially in Neutral and Coffee contexts. In some arrays, we note sudden discontinuities when vase, for example, begins to compete actively with cup and mug in the deepest containers. There are further interrelationships between the invariant core or modal values of one term and the variable skirt of another which must be explored if the model is to be refined.

The location of a subordinate term. Figure 10 showed combined figures for cup and mug, based on the notion that mug is included within the superordinate cup. This claim can be supported by examining responses to the cylindrical series of cups 10, 11, and 12, where mug is most strongly favored. Figure 15 shows that in the Coffee and Neutral contexts, mug expands to its maximum extent with No. 11; in the Coffee context it denotes in over three-quarters of the total responses. Note that the most sensitive index of the

FIGURE 15. Consistency profiles for cup, mug, and vase for cylindrical cups of increasing depth in three contexts, Group C, N = 24.

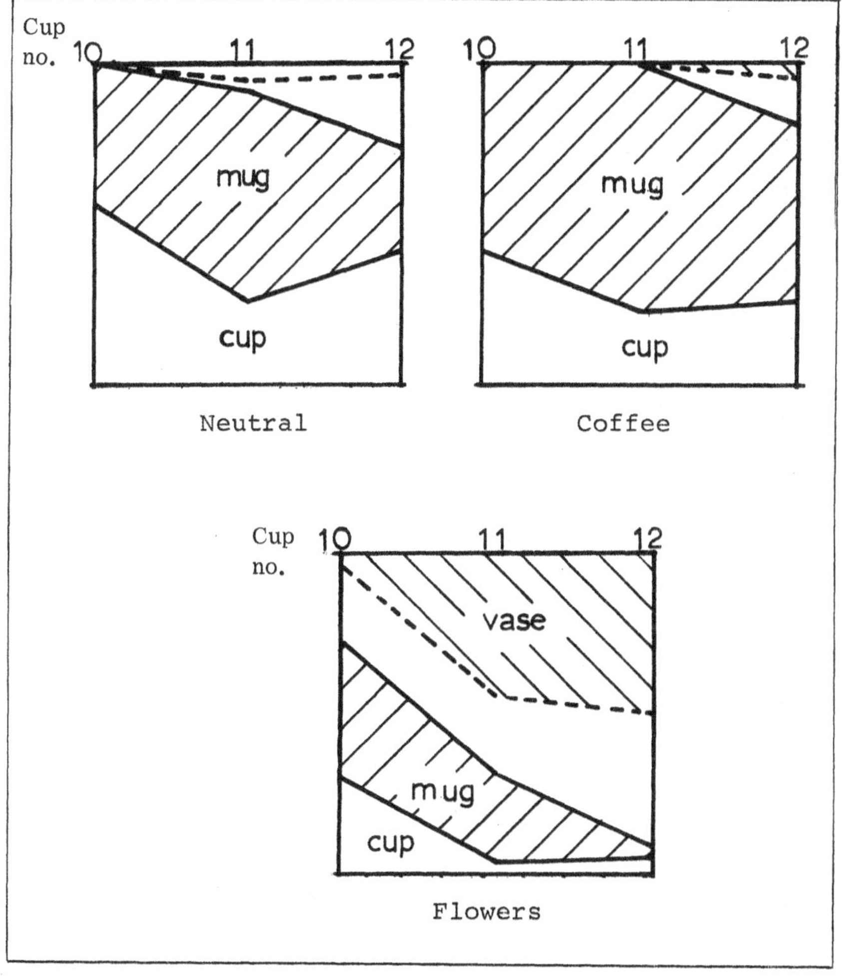

predominance of mug is its relation to cup, for No. 11, the ratio of mug to cup is quite high, but in No. 10, it represents only about half of the combined category, and in the longer cylinder of No. 12, the proportion of mug to cup again recedes. The fact that mug reaches a maximum at a certain depth, and then recedes, flanked by greater proportions of cup on both sides, indicates that cup is the residual or unmarked category out of which mug is specified. Thus in the most favored Coffee and Neutral contexts, we observe the following pattern in the ratios of mug to cup:

	Mug/Cup No. 10	No. 11	No. 12
Coffee context	1.4	2.4	1.5
Neutral context	.8	1.8	.8

It appears that the empirical study of denotation can offer us further insight into the superordinate/subordinate relationship through the study of such regular patterns.

Further articulation of function and form. In recent tests we have explored the possibility of further subdividing the functional scale, in order to show more delicate shifting, and looking forward to ordering the functional contests by more exact criteria. Figure 16 shows the consistency profile for cup in a recent test with the

FIGURE 16. Consistency profiles for cup in four contexts, Group D, N = 15.

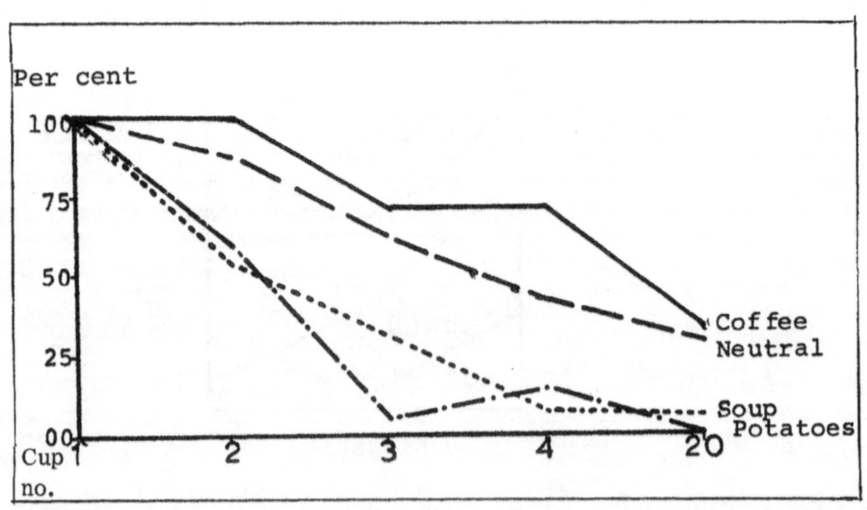

fifteen subjects of Group D, where the Food context was subdivided into Soup and Potatoes. Soup is normally a hot liquid, like coffee, but it is eaten rather than drunk, and is often served in a bowl. Potatoes, as a solid food, is regularly served in a bowl and never in a cup, and we would thus expect that Potatoes favors *cup* even less than Soup. Figure 16 does not bear out this expectation, however. Again, the largest break is between Coffee and Neutral contexts, on the one hand, and the food contexts on the other. But Soup and Potatoes are evidently not distinguished. This may be due to the fact that both of these contexts favor *bowl* strongly at the expense of *cup*, except in the modal values of *cup*.

Figure 17 shows the same contexts in a range of cups of increasing depth, with some additional details. Here the role of Soup is

FIGURE 17. Consistency profiles for *cup* in five contexts by depth, and *bowl* and *glass* in one context (Neutral, no handle). Group D, N = 15.

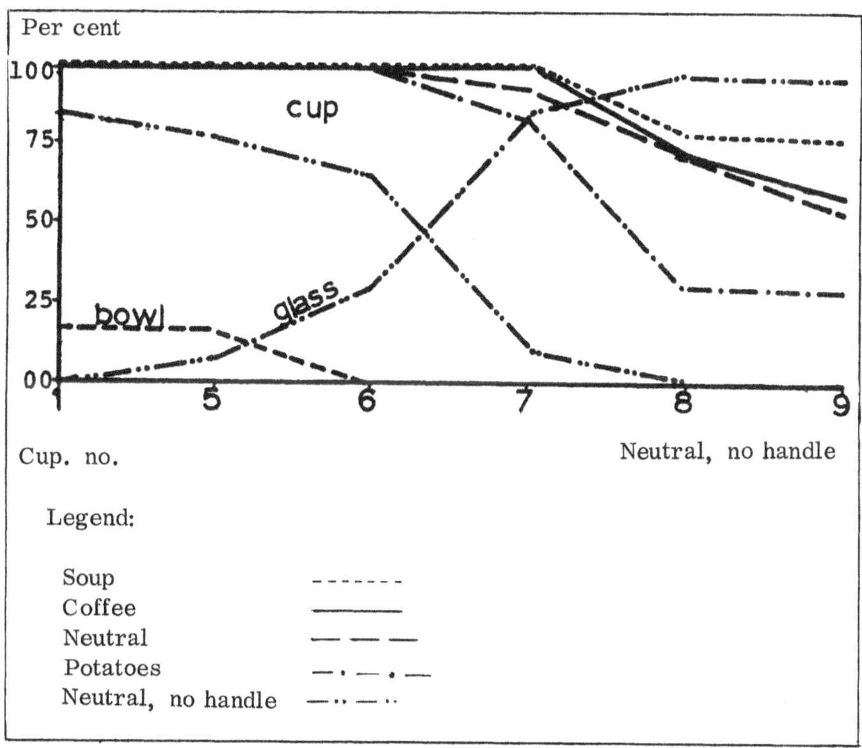

suddenly reversed. Instead of being confounded with the Potato context, it now appears to be the context which favors cup more strongly than any other, even coffee. This must be because cup is not now competing with bowl in the Soup context, since the deeper containers are less like bowls than the modal cup container No. 1. Again, we note that the largest difference between contexts is that which separates Food (potatoes) from the others.

Below the Potatoes profile, there is one in which cup is even more disfavored. This is the series of diagrams of cup without handles (see Figure 17). Even in the neutral context, the effect of removing the handle appears to be greater than the shifting context with the handle. Here we can see how strongly glass competes with cup in this handle-less condition, with a cross-over point between Nos. 6 and 7. The effect of removing the handle from the containers is seen even more clearly in Figure 18, which shows the application of cup to objects of increasing width, with and without a handle.

FIGURE 18. Consistency profiles for cup with and without a handle in Neutral context, for Group D, N = 15.

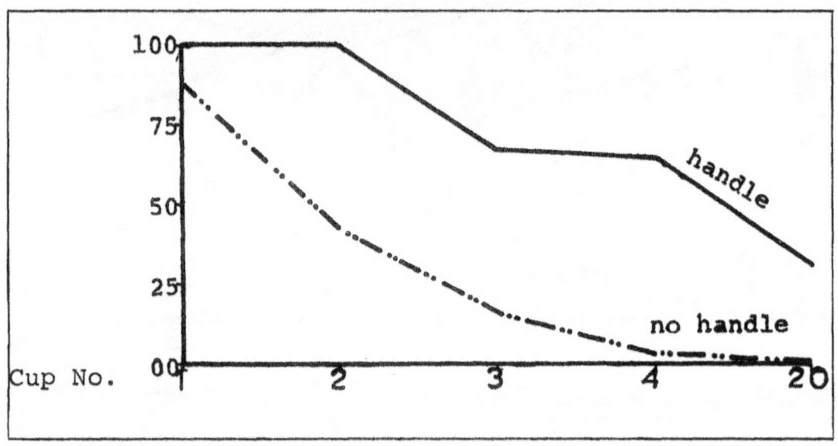

5. Redefining cup

We may now attempt to utilize our new information about the conditions for denotation of cup in reconstructing the definition of this term. Returning to the two definitions presented in section 2, we find that (2) is even less attractive than ever, but Webster's second edition definition (4) does not look quite as bad as it did at first. The expression with or without a handle can now be read as usually with a handle, sometimes without, in line with the findings presented in Figure 18. Expressions such as used chiefly to drink from, commonly set on a saucer, used for hot liquid foods, etc., express the regularities which were brought out in Figures 6-11. The writers of the definition seemed to anticipate by one means or another many of the findings of our more objective procedures, and they have resolutely adhered to terms which may appear uselessly vague to less experienced lexicographers. This should not be surprising, as we have found similar tendencies in the treatment of variability by practicing phonologists, who have undertaken the task of describing new languages (Labov 1971). Though the theory they are operating under strongly forbids them to characterize the frequency of free variants, they regularly insist on inserting such informal qualifiers after they have stated the principal allophonic distributions. Thus we find Bucca and Lesser writing about Kitsai voiceless I:

> It is in free variation with i. The free variation is less frequent in final position where i is more used; and in medial position before the consonantal groups ts, st, sk, sn, tjk, where I is predominant (1969:11).

Such statements about relations or more or less express informally the variable constraints which are formalized in recent direct studies of variability (Labov 1969, Cedergren and Sankoff to appear). In the same way, good lexicographers make an informal attempt to capture the variable properties which reflect the deep and subtle competence of the native speaker, a competence he must have to name the wide variety of new and intermediate objects in the world.

But the Webster definition still fails to capture the most systematic and intricate aspect of variability in the use of cup. On the one hand, there seems to be a wide range of objects that we call cup without hesitation. But the size of that invariant range fluctuates systematically according to function, material, and other properties. As we examine the figures given above, there appears beyond the invariant range a systematic decline, almost linear, in the probability of an object being called a cup. Though a hyperbolic, asymptotic model like Figure 14 may be possible, most of our data is linear, and whenever we actually observe a terminal point, it is quite sharp. We can therefore construct a definition which reflects this double variability: the invariant core is itself variable in extent, controlled by the interrelation of a number of factors, while the variable skirt follows a relatively simple downward slope.[15]

> The term cup is regularly used to denote round containers with a ratio of width to depth of $1 \pm r$ where $r \leq r_b$, and

$r_b = \alpha_1 + \alpha_2 + \ldots \alpha_\nu$ and α_i is a positive quantity when the feature i is present and O otherwise.

feature 1 = with one handle
2 = made of opaque vitreous material
3 = used for consumption of food
4 = used for consumption of liquid food
5 = used for consumption of hot liquid food
6 = with a saucer
7 = tapering
8 = circular in cross-section

Cup is used variably to denote such containers with ratios of width to depth of $1 \pm r$ where $r_b \leq r \leq r_t$ with a probability of $r_t - r/r_t - r_b$. The quantity $1 \pm r_b$ expresses the distance from the modal value of width to height.[16]

The various factors controlling the invariant core are ordered in accordance with the data presented here, rather than the dictionary definition itself, but there is no contradiction between them. The expression regularly used is intended to capture the fact that there are objects which in the range of contexts indicated will be called cups by practically all speakers.

The second half of the definition reflects the general fact that the vagueness profile of cup is approximately linear, so that the probability of applying cup to an object is proportional to the distance one has moved from the outer limit of the invariant core and the cut-off point r_t. The quantity $(r_t - r_b)$ may vary considerably, and so alter the slope of the variable skirt or fringe of cup-like objects.

This definition is thus designed to register the categorical character of our lexicon along with its flexibility and adaptability for application to a wide range of objects. We can schematize this relation by Figure 19, which shows the two aspects of variability superimposed upon an item-speaker matrix similar to the item-property matrices of section 1.

The model of Figure 19 is an elaboration of Figure 3: it reflects the categorical nature of the phenomenon by delineating an invariant core; but it also specifies the variable location of the boundary which marks the limits of categories and the limitations of the categorizing process.

The study of variability is the obverse of the study of invariance; one without the other has little significance, and a linguistic study devoted to only one or the other misses the richness of the phenomenon. It is not true that everything varies, anymore than it is true that everything remains distinct and discrete. We must locate the boundary between the invariant and variable areas of language with

FIGURE 19. Invariant core and variable range for denotation of items by speakers.

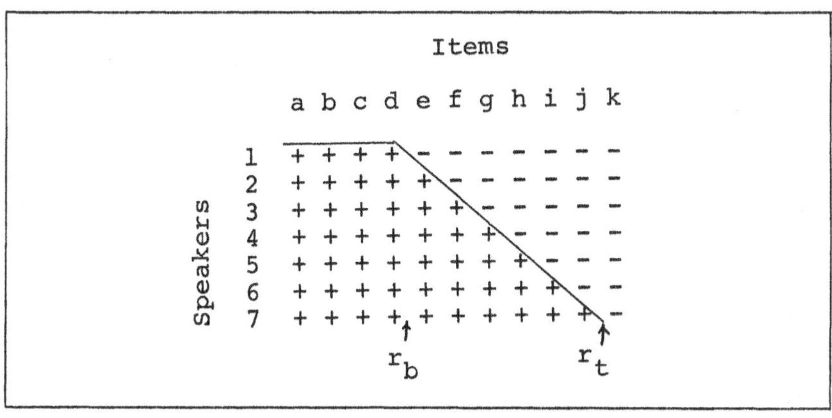

the same precision that we have learned to use in studying the variable elements themselves (Labov 1972b). We cannot escape the overall implications of section 1: that language is essentially a categorical device. If we want to understand it, we have to do more than count the categories; we have to measure them, weigh them, and eventually record them at work.

5. How an object is not known *per se*

A review of the linguistic literature on distinctive features reinforces our conviction that there is no significant difference between the distinctive/redundant opposition and the Aristotelian notion of essence and accident. A search for distinctive features is fundamentally a search for the Aristotelian essence, through which the thing itself is to be known.

> The essence (τὸ τί ἦν) of each thing is that which it is said to be *per se* (καθ αὑτό).
>
> *Metaphysics* VII. IV. 4

Essence is opposed to accident, and reflects the way things really are, intrinsically, and cannot help being. One's essence is identical with one's own nature, as Aristotle points out, continuing the above passage:

> 'To be you' is not 'to be cultured', because you are not of your own nature cultured. Your essence, then, is that which you are said to be of your own nature.

Furthermore, it is clear that for Aristotle, the essence of a substance is identical with and inseparable from the thing itself. But essence is somehow the verbalizable aspect of substance:

> It is obvious, then, that the definition is the formula (λόγος) of the essence. VII. V. 7

The definition we have presented in section 4 is obviously not the essence of a cup, nor limited to essential attributes. There is no question of a handle or a saucer being an essential attribute of a cup, anymore than 'white' is an essential part of the essence of 'man' (to use Aristotle's favorite example). One cannot separate an essential attribute from the object, and cups without handles are common enough. In our definition, properties such as these play an important role in circumscribing the outer range of regular usage, which varies with their presence or absence. Our ability to recognize a cup depends upon our ability to recognize such accidents, contrary to the opinion of Aristotle:

> That each individual thing is one and the same thing with its essence, and not merely accidentally so, is apparent, not only from the foregoing considerations, but because to have knowledge of the individual is to have knowledge of its essence. VII. VI. 9.

These quotations from the philosopher should make it quite evident that scholastic linguistic theory is quite in harmony with Aristotle's categorical viewpoint, which is in almost every detail the categorical view sketched in section 1. It is not uncommon for linguists to insist that one or the other aspect of property of an object is the essential property for the naming of it; as for example, the claim that function is the essential thing in naming objects while form is accidental.[18] The empirical evidence presented here will serve to underline the interrelation of form and function, and their symmetry in the process of denotation. A secular approach to further research in semantic description will necessarily carry us outside of the schools, beyond the limitations of scholastic intuitions, and beyond the categorical view which survives intact in the doctrines of the schoolmen.

The experimental studies reported here represent only one step outward from this scholastic setting. Further research will carry us towards experimentation in a more natural setting (Labov 1971). But the results so far are encouraging enough to suggest that semantic theory, like phonological theory, can find firm ground if we take even one step away from the intuition of the theorist and towards the observation of language in use.

NOTES

[1]One of the classic problems of defining the boundaries of a category is that of defining the word in English (Hockett 1958:166). The difficulties of providing a categorical definition are so great that many linguists have abandoned word as a technical term and substituted lexeme, formative, etc. But the word seems to be the linguistic unit of greatest social significance in our own and many other cultures. The problem of defining the category word can be taken as one of the important issues to be attacked as linguistics shifts from being a theory of category to a theory of limits and boundaries (see section 1).

[2]The first report of this work was to the Linguistic Society of America at the Annual Meeting in New York City on December 28, 1964, entitled 'Interdependent conditions for denotation'. The present report incorporates results from a number of further studies carried out at Columbia University, and recent work at the University of Pennsylvania in 1972 with the help of Franklin Jones.

[3]The analysis of the categorical view presented here is based upon Labov (1965); for the additional consideration of the prohibition on constraining free variation, see Labov (1971).

[4]See for example Martinet 'Un ou deux phonèmes' (1939) and countless other discussions of category assignment in the literature.

[5]Several other fields concerned with human behavior have not yet been able to formulate questions precisely enough to answer such questions. For example, it is very difficult to argue in role theory whether certain small differences in rights, duties, and obligations represent one role or two; there seems to be no principled way of deciding whether being the father of a five-year-old child is a different role from being the father of an eight-year-old child.

[6]On the questionable status of such idiosyncratic dialects, see Labov (1972a).

[7]Such ad hoc categories are regularly criticized in syntax as having no explanatory adequacy. But when a category can be shown to have two relatively independent properties, one property at least is said to be 'explained'; that is, the overall rule statements can then be simplified by the use of the category in question. The distinction of count-nouns vs. mass nouns, for example, is associated with differences in co-occurrence with the plural, with the indefinite article, and partitive quantifiers like some.

[8]Of course one can construct contexts in which it is reasonable to say either form of (k). For example, 'All of the cups in this

store have stripes on them. This is a cup but it doesn't have a stripe on it.' But such contexts can be constructed with equal facility for both the positive and negative forms.

[9]This is a property associated with the categorical view, as discussed in section 1 above; for further discussion, see Labov 1971.

[10]There are a few disjunctive statements of this sort in plant taxonomy, but they are rare. As a plant grows, its leaves may become thicker, develop more lobes, and its bark may develop an entirely different form. The difficulties of recognizing immature specimens may require such interdependence of the criterial properties. The fact that the formal taxonomy usually does not reflect such interdependence does not mean that people do not utilize more sophisticated models when they actually recognize trees.

[11]The actual ratio of width to depth in the drawings is not immediately obvious, since they are slightly foreshortened in depth. The figures used throughout this discussion are the relation of the width or depth of a given cup to the width and depth of cup No. 1. I am indebted to Felix Cooper, the well-known illustrator of scientific texts, for the precise execution of this series of drawings.

[12]I am indebted to Franklin Jones of the University of Pennsylvania, who carried out an extensive series of studies of the denotation of cups and other objects in connection with a study of differences in Spanish and English bilingualism, and to Beatriz Lavandera who completed a comparable series in Buenos Aires.

[13]For more objective evidence on this point, see below.

[14]The subjects show an extraordinary ability to register the effect of different contexts through verbal instructions. Some preliminary tests with more concrete instances of contextual shifting did not show any clearer results, although this is an area to be explored further.

[15]The basic form of the rule presented here is due to David Sankoff of the Centre des Recherches Mathématiques in Montreal.

[16]The slope of the variable area is itself quite variable, but it cannot be specified as long as function is not a quantified linear scale.

[17]In actual fact, the ratio of width to height which is most typical of coffee cups in American households is considerably less than 1, reflected in the way we have located cup No. 1. Cup No. 5 exhibits in perspective this 1:1 ratio, and a glance at the various representations of increasing depth shows that it is in fact favored as strongly as No. 1.

[18]From an oral presentation of Noam Chomsky in Los Angeles, 1966, developing a point of view based upon thought experiments performed by Philippa Foot.

REFERENCES

Aristotle. 1933. The metaphysics. With translation by H. Tredennick. Cambridge, Harvard University Press.

Bailey, Charles-James N. 1971. Building rate into a dynamic theory of linguistic description. Working Papers in Linguistics. Honolulu, University of Hawaii.

Bickerton, Derek. 1971. Inherent variability and variable rules. Foundations of Language. 7.457-92.

_____. 1972. The structure of polylectal grammars. In: Georgetown University Monograph Series on Languages and Linguistics, Monograph 25, Report of the 23rd Annual Round Table. Washington, D.C., Georgetown University Press.

Black, Max. 1949. Language and philosophy. Ithaca, Cornell University Press.

Bucca, Salvador and Alexander Lesser. 1969. Kitsai phonology and morphophonemics. IJAL. 35.7-19.

Cedergren, Henrietta and David Sankoff. Variable rules: Performance as a statistical reflection of competence. To appear in Language.

DeCamp, David. 1971. Toward a generative analysis of a post-creole speech continuum. In: Pidginization and creolization of languages. Ed. by Dell Hymes. Cambridge, Cambridge University Press. 349-70.

Hockett, Charles F. 1958. A course in modern linguistics. New York, Macmillan.

Jakobson, R., G. Fant, and M. Halle. 1952. Preliminaries to speech analysis. Cambridge, MIT Press.

Katz, Jerrold J. and Jerry A. Fodor. 1963. The structure of a semantic theory. Language. 39.170-210.

Labov, William. 1966. The linguistic variable as a structural unit. Washington Linguistics Review. 3.4-22. Available through the ERIC System, ED 010 871.

_____. 1969. Contraction, deletion, and inherent variability of the English copula. Language. 45.715-62.

_____. 1971. Methodology. In: A survey of linguistic science. Ed. by William Dingwall. College Park, Md., Linguistics Program, University of Maryland. 412-97.

_____. 1972a. For an end to the uncontrolled use of linguistic intuitions. Paper presented to the Linguistic Society of America, Atlanta, December.

_____. 1972b. Negative attraction and negative concord in English grammar. Language. 48.773-818.

Martinet, A. 1939. Un ou deux phonèmes? Acta Linguistica. 1.94-103.

Quirk, Randolph. 1965. Descriptive statement and serial relationship. Language. 41.205-17.

Stankiewicz, Edward. 1957. On discreteness and continuity in structural dialectology. Word. 13.44-59.

Wallace, Anthony F. and John Atkins. 1960. The meaning of kinship terms. American Anthropologist. 62.58-80.

Weinreich, Uriel. 1954. Is a structural dialectology possible? Word. 10.388-400.

_____. 1962. Lexicographic definition in descriptive semantics. Problems in Lexicography. 28(4)April.

_____, William Labov, and Marvin Herzog. 1968. Empirical foundations for a theory of language change. In: Directions for historical linguistics. Ed. by W. Lehmann and Y. Malkiel. Austin, University of Texas Press. 97-195.

THE NECESSITY OF VARIABLE RULES

ROBERT BERDAN

SWRL Educational Research and Development

Since Labov (Labov et al. 1968) first introduced the notion of variable rules there have been several examples of the way in which they account for the data of sociolinguistics (e.g. Fasold 1972). There have also been significant advances in understanding the way variable rules operate, most notably the papers by Cedergren and the Sankoffs (e.g. Cedergren & Sankoff 1974). Wolfram (1973) presented arguments for the adequacy of variable rules. This paper expands on Wolfram's presentation to argue that variable rules are an essential component of any notion of linguistic competence that attempts to explain linguistic knowledge in a real-world context.

There is no argument that variation exists in speech. Variation has always been noted by careful observers of real speech. The argument is: does variation exist in language, given the traditional distinctions drawn between speech and language? More recently, variation has been assumed to be part of performance. The question becomes: can there be a meaningful notion of competence that excludes variation?

Wolfram (1973) observed that if one assumes that inherent variation does not exist, its existence can never be proven by linguistic data. Any putative instance of observed inherent variation can always be discounted as failure to observe some categorical conditioning environment. This has the form of the classical argument from ignorance: one does not know that all inherent variation will not ultimately be proven to be categorically determined. Such arguments are never very strong.

There is another equally unsatisfying argument. If one assumes that inherent variation does exist, it can never be proven by linguistic data that it does not. Demonstrating that some putative instance of inherent variation is in fact categorically conditioned by some exotic environment can disprove only that particular instance as inherent variation. It can never disprove the notion of inherent variation itself. These arguments do little to advance an understanding of variation. To pursue them is to be reduced to a shouting match of 'I like my assumptions better than yours.'

Code switching

The existence of inherent variation has been challenged from another direction. Rather than arguing that variation results from unidentified influences, this is an argument which suggests that it results from alternation among grammars, i.e. code switching. That there is code switching among bi-linguals is well-established. But recently, publications such as Dillard's (1972) work on Black English seem to argue that what has in the past been identified as inherent variation is better described as code switching. The notion of code switching implies that there is some set of rules underlying the code that may be observed to covary.

Figure 1 is a display of runs of realizations against word count. The word count is from the conversation of a black kindergarten girl from Los Angeles.[1] A run is a sequence of instances of one realization of a variable, with no intervening instances of another realization of that variable. Symbols above the zero line represent instances of a standard realization, symbols below the line represent a nonstandard realization. Vertical distance from the center line at any point in the text represents the length of a run of realizations without variation for that feature. Slope of the line reflects the density of the variable in the text. A switch from standard to nonstandard realizations, or nonstandard to standard, is shown by a line crossing the horizontal axis.

At about word 430 the girl begins to tell a rather intense story in which she claims initially that her dog and cat were shot. Later she reveals that the shot was medicine from the veterinarian as treatment for the dog, who had been run over by a car. The story continues through word 620. At that point she begins a recitation of 'Eenie, meanie, minee, moe.' This extends about to word 782.

Throughout the story and the recitation of the familiar jingle, the five variables in Figure 1 have almost exclusively nonstandard realizations. By word 800 she begins to count and to spell, or at least recite letters of the alphabet. These are school tasks and the distribution of the realizations changes markedly.

This is the type of phenomenon that is usually referred to as code switching. In this instance it is a style shift. But if this nearly simultaneous switching of linguistically distinct processes from

FIGURE 1. Runs by word count

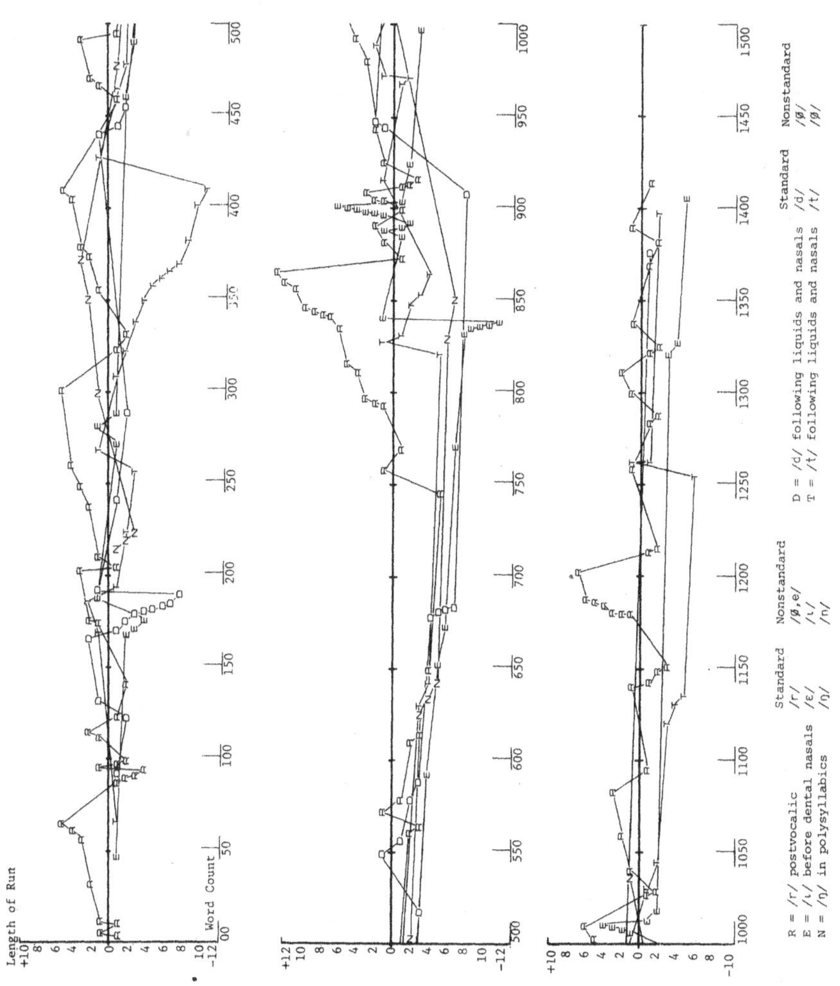

nonstandard to standard is code switching, then the situation in the first 400 words of the conversation is markedly different. There different features are observed to switch simultaneously, but in different directions. In that part of the text the five features do not covary. There are no instances of simultaneous switching of all features. Nor is there any hierarchical arrangement among features, as posited by DeCamp (1971) for sets of related codes. What there appears to be is the independent cooccurrence of randomly distributed realizations.

If this were code switching it would constitute counter-evidence to the DeCamp notion of hierarchies of codes. However, to call this code switching is to make the term synonymous with what has been called inherent variation: independent alternations among surface forms with none of the external cues associated with code switching. The fact that this is so very different from what is usually meant by code switching, that there are no predictable relationships among the 'codes', argues rather that this is not code switching at all.

Randomness

Another type of argument accepts the notion of inherent variation, but contends that the variation is random and therefore not properly described by rules in a grammar (Gobel and Kypriotaki 1973). However, this position represents a misapprehension of the notion of randomness.

It is possible to subject the data in Figure 1 to a runs analysis (Siegel 1956). One way to determine whether the realizations of some variable are randomly distributed is to count the number of runs and calculate the probability of that number occurring by chance. There are established statistical procedures for determining the number of runs to be expected in a random distribution. If the observed number of runs is greater or less than the expected, one can reject the hypothesis that the variants are randomly distributed throughout the text. Table 1 gives the probabilities associated with the number of runs observed for each of the five variables in Figure 1. None of the distributions of the variables is significantly different from chance.[2]

There is a certain imprecise but useful sense in which 'random' and 'probabilistically determined' mean essentially the same thing. To describe variation as random does not preclude describing it as 'probabilistically determined'. It is in fact the randomness of the distribution of realizations summarized in Table 1 that allows formulation of statements for the probability of any particular realization.

Variation does exist in speech. It is not just a reflex of some code switch, nor have there yet been discovered categorical explanations

TABLE 1. Runs analysis for five phonological variables

Variable	No. std.	No. nst.	Runs	Probability
/r/	67	43	43	.037
/ɛ/	14	29	13	.015
/ŋ/	4	10	4	>.05
/d/	7	24	11	.652
/t/	9	34	15	.912

within a single code. The variation is, however, random and amenable to description in probabilistic terms. From this it does not automatically follow that the facts of variation merit incorporation into the grammar.

It is true that the variation in Table 1 can be described as a set of percentages. But no motivation has been presented here for including those percentages in the grammar. They are the simple consequence of the application of an arithmetic operation to this particular corpus spoken by this particular speaker within some particular time-frame. To the extent that the variable rule claims nothing more, its detractors are quite right in excluding the variable rule from the provenience of the competence grammar. However, there are sociolinguistic data that do argue strongly for the necessity of incorporating variable rules into the grammar.

Patterns across time

Successive samples of speech from a single individual show that patterns of variation are constant across time. To minimize the enormous amount of work involved in transcription and analysis of casual conversation, Legum and Coots (1971) explored the possibility of analyzing some sample of the available corpus. Transcripts of the Los Angeles Child Language Survey data (Legum et al. 1971) were divided into ten equal segments on the basis of word count. Analysis of variance for 23 high-frequency variables on 11 transcripts failed to show interaction between segment and realization.[3] From this it was concluded that a sample from any segment would produce essentially the same results as analysis of the entire text.

This means that although alternation between realizations for any variable was random, there were no significant differences in relative frequency as one moved through time from segment to segment of the transcript.

In a study of plurals used by first and sixth grade black children in Los Angeles, responses were compared across two interviews separated by several months of time. When the samples were matched for phonological characteristics of the final consonants of the nouns, two observations could be made. First, there were no changes between studies in the relationships among the relative frequencies for the different allomorphs of the plural morpheme. Secondly, there were virtually no significant changes in the absolute relative frequencies for any allomorph for any child.

The 'transcript segment study' and the repeated plural study show that although variation is random, for the individual the rate of variation does not vary significantly across time; in one instance it is throughout the duration of extended discourse and in the other instance it is constant between two interviews separated by several months.

This constancy argues that relative frequencies and the resulting variable rules are not simply descriptive of some corpus; they have predictive value as well. Frequency statements derived from one sample predict the rate of occurrence of realizations in other samples. In moving from describing a sample to making predictions about the population from which the sample is drawn, the notion of probability is introduced. In associating variable rules with statements of probability rather than relative frequencies, Cedergren and Sankoff (1974) have made explicit an important property of the variable rule. The variable rule, with its integral statement of probability of application, becomes the ideal device for making linguistic generalizations about the random or probabilistic distribution of realizations of linguistic variables.

Variable rules with statements of probability have predictive value for the individual. That does not preclude their being totally idiosyncratic on the one hand, or a product of some universal constraint on human behavior on the other.

Language acquisition

However, there have been other observations of regularities in variation. Consider the case of language acquisition. Language is a discontinuous phenomenon; it is learned anew by each generation. We posit for the child a Language Acquisition Device that enables him to sort through the linguistic data of his environment, make appropriate generalizations, and establish a grammar.

G. Sankoff (1973), in an interesting paper discussing syntactic variation, studied the use of a future marker by New Guinean speakers of Tok Pisin. She found that placement of the marker was best described by a variable rule, with rate of application conditioned by syntactic environment. Although both parents and their children applied the rule variably, Sankoff found no differences across generations. This suggests that when the child acquired the rule for placing the future marker, he also acquired a knowledge of the probabilistic influence of syntactic environments on its application.

If one admits variable rules in the competence grammar, this is readily accounted for by the existing mechanisms posited for language acquisition. The alternative which dismisses variation as 'vagaries of performance' puts one in the uncomfortable position of explaining how the child who acquires not only significant generalizations about his language, but also 'random' performance errors, ever makes any significant generalizations in the first place.

Cross-generation studies have, in general, not been looking for constancy in variation, and the evidence is limited. That, however, is a reflection on the paradigm of sociolinguistic research, not necessarily a reflection of the facts of language. Should future studies find more cases of cross-generational uniformity in variation, the acquisition argument will become much more important.

Socialization

Language acquisition is not the only place to look for nonidiosyncratic variation. There are many studies indicating that persons who undergo a similar socialization process are similar with respect to certain kinds of linguistic variation. Studies that only report mean rates of variation for groups provide no evidence for this argument. Irrespective of how the group is constituted or how linguistically divergent the individuals in it are, they will be described by some mean rate of variation. Rather, the evidence comes from statements like those in Labov (1970:53) concerning consonant cluster reduction:

(a) There are no speakers who never have these clusters; nor are there any who always preserve them; it is a case of inherent variation in NNE.
(b) For every speaker and every group, the second consonant is absent more often when the following word begins with a consonant than when it begins with a vowel.

The similarity among groups mentioned by Labov is of course a consequence of the similarity among individuals, all exhibiting variation, but each having the same pattern of variation. Wolfram (1973) and Fasold (1972), reporting independent studies in different cities, found the same pattern to hold.

Unlike Sankoff's acquisition data where children evidenced the same patterns of variation as their parents, the individuals in these studies have in all likelihood never heard or heard of the individuals in the other studies. Nonetheless, they are in possession of a single cultural artifact: a pattern of language variation. The phenomenon is readily explained if indeed one is willing to posit the pattern of variation as a fact of the language. Then the distribution of the pattern is simply a result of the socialization mechanism by which we can say that they all speak the same language. If patterns of variation exist as part of that cultural institution language, then they are difficult to exclude from what linguists describe as competence.

Universals

There is a counter argument, one suggested by Kiparsky (1971) and elaborated on by Fraser (1972). It could be that the regularities in patterns of variation have nothing to do with particular linguistic rules, or even language particular grammars. Rather, they may result from universal properties of language: tendencies toward CVCV syllable patterns, and tendencies to avoid sequences of stressed or sequences of unstressed syllables, for example.

A possible candidate for these universal principles would be that a phonetic sequence is deleted less often if it is a morphological marker than if it is not. The three studies mentioned above of consonant cluster simplification found that, in addition to the influence of following environment, dental consonants were deleted less often when they marked past tense than when they were part of a single lexical item. Cedergren (1973) reported similar effect of morphemic status on the deletion of word final D and N in Spanish. However, she found medial D in past participles and final R in infinitives to be deleted more often than in similar monomorphemic contexts. In other words, morphological content cannot be considered a language-universal inhibiting influence on consonant deletion.

Besides such possible universals that do not hold, there are also observed instances of variation that cannot result from any universal principles. If a principle were truly universal it must apply to all speakers alike. However, there are cases where patterns of variation are different for different groups of people.

For many black children, deletion of the third person agreement marker is conditioned by whether the verb takes the regular morpheme or irregular form, as with do/does and have/has. Among children in a low income Los Angeles school, the non-use of inflection was more probable with irregular verbs, less probable with regular verbs. Exactly the opposite relationship held for children in a middle income black neighborhood. For these children the probability that agreement did not occur was greater for regular verbs than for irregular verbs (Berdan 1973a).

Although variation is not idiosyncratic, it is not necessarily universal. There are some conditioning factors that are not universal across different language situations. There are also some patterns of variation that are not universal across different social groups.

These facts suggest that variation cannot be described only as universal. It must be language, and grammar, specific.

The general principles Fraser proposes do not necessarily preclude the influence of specific environments on the probability of rule application. The effect of this is not to argue against the incorporation of probabilistic statements into the grammar, only to suggest that the situation is more complex than had been reported.

Style and dialect

A theory of language that disallows probabilistic statements cannot account for the uniformity of patterns of variation across generations and across social groups. It also cannot account for differences in patterns that individuals produce and perceive.

Much of style shift is not shift from categorical use of a rule to categorical non-use of a rule; rather, it is shift in the rate of application of the rule. Labov (1966) found a consistent pattern across individuals and across phonological features: the more formal the context, the greater the probability of standard realizations of phonological variables. If probability statements are part of the grammar, then style shifts may be viewed as a regular, grammatical process. On the other hand, a theory that does not recognize relative frequencies as meaningful data cannot even observe that these style shifts are taking place.

Failure to accept probability statements as meaningful data has also compounded the problem of dialect definition and the recognition of dialect differences. The 'check-list' approach to dialect definition (e.g. McDavid 1967) historically has been quite distinct from the tradition of generative grammar. Nonetheless, they share the inability to recognize gradient differences. Williamson (1971) catalogs surface structures that have been reported as typical of Black English, and cites parallel structures used by southern Anglos. She concludes that the features are neither 'black nor white, but American'.

Anshen (1972) points out that those who argue that there are no ethnic dialect differences must still account for the accuracy with which ethnic differences in dialect are perceived. He cites a study by Bryden (1968) in which Anglo and black listeners from Charlottesville, Virginia, perceived the race of other Anglo and black speakers with 84 percent accuracy. The speakers, from a range of social and educational backgrounds, read a passage of only sixteen-second duration. Other studies have also shown high degrees of accuracy in ethnic identification. Stroud (1956) found that listeners were 93 percent accurate in distinguishing the recorded voices of Anglo speakers from those of black speakers.

Bryden found no categorical differences between the Anglo and black speakers in his study. But he did find significant differences in what he called 'number of phonetic errors' and 'number of misarticulated phonemes'. The study also showed high correlation between perceived race and number of 'errors'. In other words, there was a high correlation between perceived race and rate of nonstandard usage. Correlation does not imply causation, but the observed correlates were perception and variable use of nonstandard realizations, not categorical use of realizations.

Anshen examined the distribution of realizations of two phonetic variables, /r/ and /ŋ/, among Anglo and black informants. Both Anglos and blacks used standard and nonstandard forms of each. However, the rates of nonstandard realizations were differentially distributed through the populations. The differences, always in the same direction, were significant among men, and among women, at each educational level, and in each age group. This consistent pattern of differences would be readily explained as dialect difference, if probability were part of the grammar.

The distinction between competence and performance has been supported by showing that some characteristics of speech, such as memory limitations on center embeddings or long sentences, are not properly part of the grammar. They are better treated as some general limitation on cognitive processing. If probability functions are likewise explicable outside the grammar, one must speculate on what that explanation could be. Racial differences in the physical characteristics of the vocal apparatus have been suggested in the past (Wiggam 1949) to explain dialect differences. Hopefully, advances in application of the scientific method have put that notion to rest. The alternatives are cognitive differences or cultural differences (excluding language, of course). There is absolutely no evidence whatsoever to suggest that the propensity to pronounce /n/ rather than /ŋ/ is associated with any racially differentiated cognitive mechanism, if such did exist. Cultural differences do exist. But the a priori exclusion of language as an explanation of differences in speech, in deference to unrelated areas of culture, is indefensible. If the probabilistic nature of a rule is a fact of competence, then the differences noted by Anshen follow from differences in the distribution of grammars among Anglo and Black populations.

Language change

There are systematic, nonidiosyncratic differences in language among social groups. There are also differences among age groups. The New Guinean situation reported by Sankoff (1973), with no difference between generations, is the exception, not the rule, in cross-generation studies of language variation. And, although Sankoff found no difference across generations in the syntax of the future marker, she did find differences in stress.

Languages do change. Linguists have debated for decades whether those changes are gradual or instantaneous. Since Labov's (1963) pioneering work on Martha's Vineyard there have been a number of studies looking at language across apparent time, that is, across age groups. What has been found has rarely been categorical innovation or extinction of some form. Rather there have been changes in the relative proportions of variant realizations.

In New York, Labov (1966) found that the probability a person used retroflection of preconsonantal /r/ varied inversely with the age of the informant: younger informants were more likely to use retroflection than older informants. Cedergren (1973) observed language change in a different framework. Rather than the spread of a rule throughout a population, she observed that younger informants applied a rule for lenition of CH in Panamanian Spanish at a higher rate than did older speakers.

A grammar that disallows statements of probability can recognize three synchronic states: a grammar prior to the innovation, a grammar with the innovating form and the preexisting form in 'free variation', and a later grammar with only the innovating form. The observed dynamic process is describable only as static grammars. The problem has been stated lucidly by Weinreich, Labov, and Herzog (1968). If the grammar allows probability, then what is observed to be change in language can in fact be described as change in grammars. That change is gradual ceases to be a problem for the historical linguist; it is rather the type of change the grammar predicts.

Bailey (1971, 1972), responding largely to the problems of describing language change, created what he calls the 'dynamic' model of grammar, distinct from former 'static' models. However, incorporation of probability into the competence grammar is not without consequences, consequences that have been largely overlooked by those who discuss variable rules.

Problems

A grammar, as traditionally conceived, is a device capable of generating all and only the sentences of a language. It makes no claims whatsoever about the relative frequencies with which any rules are applied. 'Sentences' of the language are implicitly assumed to be 'sentence types', not 'sentence tokens' or utterance tokens. That is, two languages are not different simply because one contains two tokens of some sentence and another language contains three tokens of the same sentence. A grammar is not defined by some corpus, but by what the hypothetical idealized speaker-hearer would accept as sentences of his language.

The probabilities of rule application, on the other hand, are computed by observing the relative frequencies of variant realizations in some corpus, or speech sample. If the corpus contains repeated tokens of a single sentence type, and the tokens contain a realization being studied, then the relative frequency of the realization is based on data undefined in the generative grammar. The resulting probability statements must also be undefined in the generative grammar. If variable rules and probability statements are to become part of the competence grammar, there needs to be serious rethinking of the way in which language is defined and of the definition of the grammar that accounts for language.

Evaluation of grammars

The incorporation of variable rules into the grammar makes the grammar more powerful. That is not necessarily desirable. But the increased power is justifiable in terms of the increased range of language phenomena for which the grammar can account.

It also makes different claims about language behavior. The orthodox grammar claims that language behavior is either categorical or outside the scope of grammatical description. The probabilistic grammar recognizes that much of language behavior is probabilistically determined and must be explained in probabilistic terms.

Variable rules not only make the grammar more powerful, they make the grammar more strong; they increase the ability of the theory to evaluate competing grammars. For example, there are several proposals in literature for accounting for the facts of English inflectional morphology. One proposal, by Luelsdorff (1969) suggests that the underlying form of the plural morpheme is syllabic [əz]. The rules that provide for contraction of the singular copula *is* also provide for the reduction of this plural morpheme before nonstrident consonants and vowels. An alternative proposal by Hoard and Sloat (1971) has an underlying consonant with a rule of epenthesis to give the inflectional morpheme the proper phonetic shape.

The facts of variation provide evidence for choosing between these analyses for Black English. For many children the plurals of *ghost* and *desk* alternate between *ghos* and *ghoses*, and *des* and *desses*, respectively. In the Luelsdorff grammar we hypothesize that *ghoses* and *desses* result from deleting the final consonant by the consonant cluster simplification rule, thus bleeding the contraction rule.

Luelsdorff grammar

Underlying	ghost#əz
Cluster simplification	ghos #əz
Nonconsonant deletion	N. A.

For the Hoard and Sloat grammar we hypothesize that consonant cluster simplification occurs and feeds the epenthesis rule. Either grammar will account for the facts.

Hoard and Sloat grammar

Underlying	ghost#z
Cluster simplification	ghos #z
Epenthesis	ghos #əz

But these children are no exception to the pattern found in eastern cities for consonant cluster reduction: consonants delete less often when followed by a vowel than when followed by a consonant. Many of the same children who have dusses as the third person singular of dust have dusting in the progressive. If we chose the Luelsdorff grammar, the underlying schwa inhibits consonant deletion. The rate of consonant cluster simplification followed by vowels is insufficient to account for the rate at which dusses and ghoses occur. Thus, we have to posit a special case of consonant cluster simplification for consonants followed by inflectional morphemes. Any supposed generalizations that the Luelsdorff grammar would provide, are lost.

On the other hand, the Hoard and Sloat grammar posits an underlying form that makes consonant cluster simplification most probable: cluster followed by a consonant. The variable rule that simplifies clusters in this environment is sufficient to account for these facts of inflectional morphology. In this way, the use of probabilities provides evidence for choosing among alternate grammars.

Another case in which the facts of probability offer evidence is the deletion of the copula in Black English. Labov (1969) has proposed that the deletion is essentially a phonological process. Others claim it is grammatical. The phonological explanation exploits rules that are needed elsewhere in the grammar to delete final consonants; the siblant of contracted is and the /r/ of contracted are. The question to be asked is: are the patterns of deletion of phonologically distinct is and are more similar than either of those patterns to the respective noncopula consonant deletion rules? If so, there is good reason to believe the deletion is syntactic. If not, the phonological deletion argument is much stronger.

Conclusions

Variation with respect to the individual is truly random. Variation with respect to different features of the grammar is independent, it is not code switching. Because variation is random, its rate can be observed in a speech sample and predicted for the language. Patterns of variation are not idiosyncratic; they can be observed across generations. Children do not only acquire the form of a rule, they acquire the probability of its use. Patterns of variation are observed to co-occur with other linguistic entities; they are language and dialect specific, not universal. Changes in probabilities provide the mechanism for gradual language change. Incorporating probability into the grammar not only provides a framework for explaining language variation; it facilitates the description of language acquisition, language change, and the delineation of languages and dialects. The facts of variation and variable rules provide the grammar a strong mechanism for determining among alternate solutions to grammatical problems.

The grammar is a theoretical construct that attempts to provide an explanation for the phenomenon of human language. Sociolinguists in the past decade have amassed a large body of facts that argues that language is in part probabilistic. The grammar must attempt to explain those facts. The variable, or probabilistic, rule provides the grammar the necessary mechanism to account for the facts of variation.

NOTES

1. These data are from a transcript summarized and tabulated in Legum et al. (1971).

2. The [I, ɛ] variation before nasals, which would be significant at 0.05, reflects a lexical bias.

3. One interaction was significant. That was for post-consonantal /r/. However, there were virtually no realizations of [ə] or [Ø]. This means that the interaction was not between segment of the transcript and realizations of the variable, but between segment and density of the variable.

REFERENCES

Anshen, Frank. 1972. Some statistical bases for the existence of Black English. Florida FL Reporter 10.19-20.

Bailey, C.-J.N. 1971. Trying to talk in the new paradigm. Papers in Linguistics 4.312-338.

Bailey, C.-J.N. 1972. The integration of linguistic theory: Internal reconstruction and the comparative method in descriptive analysis. In: Linguistic change and generative theory. Edited by R. Stockwell and R. Macaulay. Bloomington, Indiana University Press. 22-31.

_____ and Shuy, R. W., eds. 1973. New ways of analyzing variation in English. Washington, D.C., Georgetown University Press.

Berdan, R. 1973a. The use of linguistically determined groups in socio-linguistic research. Professional Paper 26, Southwest Regional Laboratory.

_____. 1973b. Probability and variable rules: A formal interpretation. Paper read at the Summer LSA Meeting, Ann Arbor.

Bryden, James D. 1968. An acoustic and social dialect analysis of perceptual variables in listener identification and rating of Negro speakers. Charlottesville, University of Virginia. ERIC No. ED 022 186.

Cedergren, Henrietta. 1973. On the nature of variable constraints. In: Bailey and Shuy (1973). 13-22.

_____ and Sankoff, David. 1974. Variable rules: Performance as a statistical reflection of competence. Language 50.333-355.

DeCamp, David. 1971. Toward a generative analysis of a post-creole speech continuum. In: Pidginization and creolization of languages. Edited by Dell Hymes. Cambridge, University Press. 349-370.

Dillard, J. L. 1972. Black English: Its history and usage in the United States. New York, Random House.

Fasold, Ralph W. 1972. Tense marking in Black English. Washington, D.C., Center for Applied Linguistics.

Fraser, Bruce. 1972. Optional rules in grammar. In: Georgetown University Round Table on Languages and Linguistics (GURT) 1972. Edited by R. W. Shuy. Washington, D.C., Georgetown University Press. 1-16.

Gobel, E. C., and Kypriotaki, L. 1973. Mouses and mices: A study in grammatical variation. Paper presented at the Summer LSA Meeting, Ann Arbor.

Hoard, J. and Sloat, C. 1971. The inflectional morphology of English. Glossa 5:1.47-56.

Kiparsky, Paul. 1971. Historical linguistics. In: A survey of linguistic science. Edited by William O. Dingwell. College Park, University of Maryland. 576-649.

Labov, W. 1963. The social motivation of a sound change. Word 19.273-309.

_____. 1966. The social stratification of English in New York City. Washington, D.C., Center for Applied Linguistics.

Labov, W. 1969. Contraction, deletion, and inherent variability of the English copula. Language 45:4.715-762.

_____. 1970. The study of language in its social context. Studium Generale 23.30-87.

_____, P. Cohen, C. Robins, and J. Lewis. 1968. A study of the non-standard English of Negro and Puerto Rican speakers in New York City. Final Report, Cooperative Research Project 3288, 2 vols. Washington, D.C., Office of Education.

Legum, S. E. and Coots, J. 1971. Transcript homogeneity study. Technical Note No. TN2-71-40, November 23, 1971. Southwest Regional Laboratory.

Legum, S. E., C. Pfaff, G. Tinnie, M. Nicholas, and W. Riley. 1971. The speech of young Black children in Los Angeles. TR 33. Southwest Regional Laboratory.

Luelsdorff, P. A. 1969. On the phonology of English inflection. Glossa 3:1.39-48.

McDavid, Raven I. 1967. A checklist of significant features for discriminating social dialects. In: Dimensions of dialect. Edited by E. Evertts. Champaign, Illinois, N.C.T.E. 7-10.

Sankoff, Gillian. 1973. Above and beyond phonology in variable rules. In: Bailey and Shuy (1973). 44-61.

Siegel, Sidney. 1956. Nonparametric statistics for the behavioral sciences. New York, McGraw-Hill.

Stroud, R. 1956. A study of the relation between social differences of White and Negro high school students of Dayton, Ohio. Unpublished Master's Thesis, Bowling Green State University.

Weinreich, U., W. Labov, and M. Herzog. 1968. Empirical foundations for a theory of language change. In: Directions for historical linguistics. Edited by W. P. Lehmann and Y. Malkiel. Austin, University of Texas Press. 97-195.

Wiggam, Albert E. 1949. Let's explore your mind. Cleveland Plain Dealer, July 3, 1949. Cited by R. I. McDavid and V. G. McDavid. 1951. The relationship of the speech of American Negroes to the speech of American Whites. American Speech 26.3-17.

Williamson, Juanita. 1971. A look at Black English. Crisis 169-185.

Wolfram, Walt. 1973. On what basis variable rules? In: Bailey and Shuy (1973). 1-12.

VARIABLE CONSTRAINTS AND RULE RELATIONS

WALT WOLFRAM

Federal City College and Center for Applied Linguistics

The formulation of new theoretical paradigms must be seen in terms of several stages. Initially, there is the claim that the theoretical model can handle data not dealt with in earlier models or account for it in some systematic way not afforded by a previous model. At this point, there appears to be a giant step in the formulation of the paradigm. Once this giant step is taken, however, a number of small steps (not all forward) follow. These are the so-called 'mopping-up' operations. Quite rightly, Kuhn (1962:24) has observed that lots of what we call mopping-up operations are directed to force nature into a preformed and inflexible box that the paradigm supplies. But there are also, as a part of authentic mopping-up operations, the necessary considerations of sorts of phenomena which the giant step may have leaped over in its initial formulation. Mopping-up operations, then, become important in order to see the full implications of the paradigmatic leap. Without either maximizing the contribution of so-called 'variable-rule theory' or minimizing my own janitorial role, I would like to consider this paper as a type of mop-up operation.[1] One must be fully aware that in mopping-up, we may find that we discover more dirt under the rug than we thought existed in our clean paradigm. But at least if we know where the dirt is, we can always try cleaning it up with a different solution.

In this paper, we shall be looking at how variable constraints may affect rule relationships. In order to look at this matter, it is of course necessary to accept fundamental notions concerning structured variability (cf. Wolfram 1973a). We can then start out with the acceptance of the notion that there are independent linguistic constraints on variability which must be included in the formal account of non-categorical rules. At the very least, I am claiming that as part of a speaker's competence in his language, he has knowledge of variable rules, the linguistic factors favoring rule operation, and the hierarchical order in which these factors are ranked. (The acceptance of stronger claims, as put forth by Cedergren and Sankoff (1974), does not appear to affect the following discussion in any significant way.) I am further claiming that at least some of the hierarchical ordering of the constraints on variable rules are language particular in that they do not necessarily derive from some universal principle of constraint hierarchies (cf. Wolfram 1973a:8-10).

Since we shall also be discussing rule ordering to some extent, it is necessary to accept here the notion that the rules of, at least, phonology are ordered with respect to each other. It is further necessary to accept the notion of some extrinsic rule ordering (cf. Koutsoudas 1972, Campbell 1973, Bailey 1973) although most of the discussion pertaining to rule ordering may apply equally to a position which only allows ordering which derives from universal principles.

In the discussion that follows, we will look at two aspects of rule relationships and how they may or may not be affected by considerations of variable constraints. The general question I am interested in is the extent to which variable constraints may provide formal motivation (i.e. a 'discovery procedure', if you will) in the consideration of rule separation and collapsing, and rule ordering. Do considerations of variability serve as a principled basis in the consideration of rule relations, and if so, under what sorts of conditions? I am concerned here with elucidating and illustrating how variable rules reveals that, in some cases, a principle has been followed, either explicitly or implicitly, to arrive at the 'correct' solution. In other cases, the failure to apply a principle has resulted in a faulty analysis. The intent of this paper then, is to elucidate general principles of rule relationships affected by variable constraints and to illustrate them.

Rule separation and collapsing

The first claim that I would like to make is that considerations of variable constraints may provide a principled basis for combining or separating linguistic processes. Now where there are other types of 'conventional' motivations which can operate to provide a principled basis for separating or collapsing processes, the variability of variable constraints is, at best, simply confirmation. But I would like to go one step further and maintain that in the absence of other types of conventional motivations, variable constraints may be independently powerful enough to provide a principled basis for considering processes as distinct or identical. An examination of certain types of variable constraints, in fact, turns out to be the deciding factor in the resolution of different analyses of the same phenomenon. Several cases can be cited to demonstrate this capability of variable constraints.

The case of post-consonantal and post-vocalic *t*, *d* deletion.

To illustrate how variable constraints can provide formal motivation for treating linguistic processes as unitary or disparate, we can first look at the case of word-final alveolar stop deletion which takes place in at least Vernacular Black English and Puerto Rican English in East Harlem, among other English lects. In these lects, there is a process(es) in which final post-vocalic and post-consonantal alveolar stops may be deleted. That is, we have items such as *tes'*, *buzz'*, *rabbi'*, and *rapi'* for *test*, *buzzed*, *rabbit*, and *rapid* respectively.[2] Although Labov, et al. (1968), and I have both described the same type of phenomenon, we have arrived at conclusions which are somewhat different. (For a complete discussion of our differences, see Fasold 1972:58-60, 76-82.) In Labov's et al. analysis, both post-vocalic and post-consonantal alveolar stop deletion are considered to be part of the same rule. That is, there is only one rule which affects final *t* and *d* whether they are the final member of a consonant cluster or following a vowel. Labov (1972:111) has formulated the rule as follows:

$$[-\text{cont}] \rightarrow \langle \emptyset \rangle \;/\; \langle +\text{cons} \rangle \; \langle \emptyset \rangle \; \underline{\qquad} \#\# \; \langle -\text{syl} \rangle$$ [3]

As formulated by Labov, there are three ordered constraints on the operation of this rule: (1) deletable *t*, *d* preceded by a consonant, (2) deletable *t*, *d* followed by a non-vowel, and (3) deletable *t*, *d* preceded by a non-morpheme boundary. Unmistakenly, Labov's rule is written to include post-vocalic and post-consonantal *t*, *d*. A version of this rule, with a more extended hierarchy of constraints, is followed by Fasold (1972:98). Both of these treatments, then, differ from my earlier account in which post-vocalic *t*, *d* deletion and post-consonantal *t*, *d* deletion were considered to be a part of different processes. Although we then argued for the analysis on other grounds in that description, a reopening of this issue in our more recent study of Puerto Rican English in New York City has demonstrated how the examination of the constraint hierarchy can be utilized to resolve this matter. In the account that follows, we will illustrate with data from Puerto Rican English, but a comparison of these speakers with Vernacular Black English speakers who were a part of the study indicates that the same arguments are operative in the resolution of this question in Black English as well.

If post-consonantal and post-vocalic t, d deletion were to be considered as a part of the same process, we would expect that independent tabulations of t, d deletion would show that the constraint hierarchies are isomorphic. With the exception of the post-consonantal/vocalic environments, which may be a variable constraint in itself incorporated into the hierarchy, the constraint hierarchy should match whether post-consonantal or post-vocalic t, d is the input for the deletion process. If it does not, then the generalization of the rule is inadequate and the environments for the rule must be considered at least disjunctive if not part of a separate rule. If an independent tabulation of these two potentially separate processes indicates isomorphic hierarchies, this may provide, in the absence of other types of formal motivation to separate them, a principled basis for considering them as part of the same general process. If, on the other hand, our independent tabulation turns up a genuinely different hierarchy of constraints, then the generalization of the rule must be considered as inaccurate. (By genuinely different, we here mean to exclude differences which are artifacts of unreliable tabulation such as different categorization of linguistic categories, inadequate numbers of tokens, etc.) With this in mind, let us compare what happens when the constraints for post-vocalic and post-consonantal t, d are tabulated separately. This is done in the versions of the rule given by Shiels (1972) and Wolfram (1973). Shiels has tabulated the totals for post-consonantal t, d deletion and Wolfram has tabulated the results for post-vocalic t, d. Shiels' rule for post-consonantal stop deletion is as follows:

$$\begin{bmatrix}\text{-voc}\\ \text{+cons}\\ \text{-cont}\\ \alpha\text{voice}\end{bmatrix} \longrightarrow (\emptyset) \;/\; \begin{bmatrix}\text{+cons}\\ \alpha\text{voice}\\ \Delta\,(\text{+cont})\end{bmatrix} \;\Gamma\;(\text{-}\#)\underline{\quad}\begin{matrix}\text{A}([\text{+cons}])\\ \text{B}([\text{-seg}])\end{matrix}$$

(Shiels 1972:237)

In Wolfram's analysis of variable constraints for post-vocalic t, d deletion, using the same sample as Shiels, the rule is written as:

$$\begin{bmatrix}\text{-cont}\\ \text{+ant}\\ \text{+cor}\\ \text{-nas}\end{bmatrix} \longrightarrow (\emptyset) \;/\; \begin{bmatrix}\text{V}\\ \Gamma\text{-stress}\end{bmatrix} \;\Delta\text{-}\#\; \begin{bmatrix}\underline{\qquad\quad}\\ \text{B + vd}\\ \text{E - PAST}\end{bmatrix}\#\#\text{A-V}$$

(Wolfram 1973:146)

The ordered constraints for post-consonantal t, d deletion are then:

1. deletable consonant followed by consonant.
2. deletable consonant followed by pause.
3. deletable consonant preceded by non-morpheme boundary.
4. deletable consonant preceded by continuant consonant.

The constraints for post-vocalic t, d deletion are ordered as follows:

1. deletable consonant followed by non-vowel.
2. deletable consonant is voiced.
3. deletable consonant in an unstressed syllable.
4. deletable consonant preceded by non-morpheme boundary.
5. deletable consonant part of derived adjective.

As we stated previously, we would expect the two hierarchies not to differ in any significant ways, if both aspects of this process were handled by one general rule. Obviously, there are some parallels, such as the first order effect of the following non-vowel. But the hierarchies also appear to differ in non-trivial ways. Perhaps the most important difference is the constraint of voicing which operates on the post-vocalic deletable consonant but not on post-consonantal consonants. Independent of considering post-vocalic t, d deletion, studies of final consonant deletion (e.g. Labov et al 1968, Wolfram 1969, Fasold 1972, Shiels 1972) have not shown voicing of the deletable stop to be a significant constraint on variability.[4] But quite clearly, it is shown to be a high order constraint for post-vocalic t, d deletion. It should also be noted that the constraint of grammatical inflection (i.e. following a morpheme boundary) is ordered lower in the hierarchy of constraints for post-vocalic t, d deletion than it is for post-consonantal t, d deletion. The effect of stress, which is ordered before a grammatical inflection, is not even mentioned by Shiels, and other studies (e.g. Fasold 1972) tend to find stress for post-consonantal t, d deletion ordered below the constraint of grammatical inflection.

The solution, then, seems to be quite clear. The rules should be kept as distinct in some sense, since the more general version of the rule obscures crucial differences in the constraint hierarchies of post-consonantal t, d deletion. Stated as a general process which includes both aspects of the t, d deletion, the rule does not account in an adequate way for what actually takes place (i.e. it is observationally inadequate). It should, however, be noted here that the evidence taken from considering post-consonantal and post-vocalic t, d deletion separately is based on an assumption that constraint effects will operate independent of each other. If we found that the effects worked synergistically or antagonistically, our evidence might be questioned, but at this point, there is little counter-evidence to the assumption of constraint independence (cf. Cedergren and Sankoff 1974).[5] Apart from the motivational principle which variable constraints can be shown to provide for separating or combining processes, there is an obvious tabulational principle which emerges from this simple case. If there is some question as to whether processes should be generalized or separated in a descriptive account of non-categorical rules, tabulations of variable frequency treating them separately should be undertaken. If the hierarchies differ based on this separate tabulation, then they should be considered disjunctive in some sense. If, however, the processes are not tabulated as potentially different, the disjunction may not be revealed. In my dispute with Labov and Fasold's version of the rule, the apparent failure to carry out this simple procedure seems to be the reason why they did not arrive at the correct solution.

One might point out that it is not necessarily procedurally expedient to consider the tabulations of the potential disjunctive set completely independently, since a simple tabulation of all the logical possibilities of the combination of constraints for the potential generalized process might reveal the disjunction. Although this is certainly true in some cases, this procedure may leave the analyst in a difficult position of having to distinguish between non-significant hypothesized constraints for a general process and a significant disjunction. In distinguishing this important difference, the more statistically sophisticated program of Cedergren and Sankoff (1973) is obviously heuristically superior to the traditional impressionistic basis for deciding this difference (cf. Cedergren 1973:17 for an illustration of detecting 'hidden linguistic constraints' which suggest this sort of rule disparity).

The case of ARE copula absence and post-vocalic r desulcalization

The second example of how variable constraints may provide motivation concerning rule relations comes from a recent examination of present tense copula absence in Southern white speech. It is generally recognized that in white Southern speech, as well as in Vernacular Black English, there is a process by which copula forms involving the contracted forms of ARE can be deleted (i.e. You're ugly → You ugly). Although there is general acceptance of this observation, there is some question as to the process(es) by which this deletion comes about. This has become particularly important in comparing copula deletion in Southern white speech with copula deletion in Vernacular Black English (cf. Wolfram forthcoming). The basic question seems to be whether copula absence is to be derived from a general 'auxiliary deletion' rule which operates on the r remaining after contraction or whether absence is derived through a process related to general Southern r-lessness. Labov (1969) has presented an attractive alternative in which 're deletion is derived through a process related to *r* desulcalization (in his terminology, 'vocalization') and subsequent post-vocalic schwa loss. As Labov has shown, these two rules are needed for reasons quite independent of copula deletion (cf. Labov (1969:754) where items like *po'* [po] and *do'* [do] are derived by first desulcalizing the *r*, giving [poə] and [doə], and then removing the *ə* by post-vocalic schwa deletion. The summary of the operations which derive *ARE* deletion are given by Labov in the following paradigm. In this paradigm, the number of Labov's original rules is specified in the parentheses following each rule title.

(a) ## ăr ## weak word rule (2)
(b) ## ər ## vowel reduction (4)
(c) ## əə ## vocalization of *r* (5)
(d) ## ə ## loss of post-vocalic *ə* (6)
(e) ## ## contraction (9)
(f) ## ## auxiliary deletion

In the above paradigm of rules, the weak word rule (a) prepares unstressed copula to undergo vowel reduction (b). At that point, the desulcalization rule (c) operates on post-vocalic *r* generally. The final *r* of *ARE* is desulcalized by this general rule. Operating on the output of desulcalization is a rule to delete the post-vocalic *ə* which results from desulcalization (d). As has been pointed out by the above, this is a rule which is required in Southern white speech and Vernacular Black English for reasons independent of copula absence. The *ə* remaining after the application of the post-vocalic schwa loss rule is the original nucleus of *ARE*, and this is then removed by contraction (e). In effect, then contraction is equivalent to deletion for *ARE*, and there is nothing left for the deletion rule (f) to operate on with reference to *ARE*.

Although this analysis has been accepted by a number of scholars, there are several problems that arise in choosing to account for deletion in this way. One of the most persuasive of these is based on constraint effects. If copula deletion were derived from a process of desulcalization and subsequent post-vocalic schwa loss, we would expect that the constraints affecting *r*-lessness derived from copula *ARE* to match those which effect *r*-lessness from other sources, with, of course, the exception of copula itself which may be a constraint. That is, if *r* is affected by a following consonant, then we would expect this constraint to obtain for both copula-derived and non-copula derived *r*'s. With respect to *r* desulcalization involving non-copula *r*'s, we find that a following consonant heavily favors desulcalization. The following rule, which may delete the remaining post-vocalic schwa shows no constraints to neutralize this effect. If copula-derived *r* were related to this process, we would expect this process to also operate for these forms. But compare the figures given in Table 1, which compares r desulcalization for non-copula r's with deletion for copula ARE. These figures are taken from my recent study of copula deletion in white Southern speech (Wolfram 1974). For r derived from copula ARE, the figures are broken down according to the following syntactic environment, so that they can be compared independent of any skewing effect that the following syntactic environment may have on the figures. The tabulation only includes a following consonant across word boundary for the sake of comparability.

TABLE 1. Influence of following vowel and consonant (a) on ARE deletion and (b) on non-copula r desulcalization; Franklin County, Mississippi, whites.

(a) Deletion

Following phonological environment	Following syntactical environment									
	___NP		___PA/Loc		___Vb-ing		___gonna		Total	
	No. D/T	%D	No. D/T	%D	No. D/T	%D	No. D/T	%D	No. D/T	%D
___ ##V	2/5	20.0	47/88	53.4	8/12	66.7	NA		57/105	54.3
___ ##C	9/30	30.0	59/130	45.4	84/128	65.6	59/69	85.5	211/357	59.1

(b) Desulcalization

Following phonological environment	No. Des/T	% Des
___ ##V	30/100	30.0
___ ##C	54/100	54.0

Table 1 indicates that a following consonant does not favor deletion to any significant extent for ARE deletion. In fact, when the figures for gonna are excluded because of the possible skewing effect (since there are no possible examples of gonna, the most favorable syntactic environment for deletion, beginning with a vowel) there is actually more deletion when followed by a vowel. With or without gonna, however, the difference is not significant. The pattern for copula ARE clearly contrasts with the pattern found for non-copula r, where a following consonant significantly favors desulcalization. Based on this lack of isomorphy in a variable constraint, we conclude that the two processes are disparate in some way. The evidence from constraint effects, then provides a principled basis for supporting the disjunction of the processes.[6]

In many respects, the argument for separating post-vocalic and post-consonantal t, d deletion and copula ARE and non-copula r processes are quite similar. Our arguments in both cases are based on differences in constraint effects and hierarchies. There is, however, a sense in which the argument for separating copula ARE deletion and other types of r-lessness is less direct in that it argues from a 'carry-over' effect of variable rules in a feeding relationship.[7] It will be recalled here that my argument for different constraint effects for non-copula r-lessness and copula ARE deletion was based on a comparison of the constraints for r desulcalization and copula ARE absence. But desulcalization is only Step 1 on the process which has been claimed to account for ARE copula absence, since it still leaves the vestige of a schwa which must be deleted by post-vocalic schwa deletion (e.g. [wɪ ə] 'we're, [yvə] 'you're', etc.). Since the input of the second rule (i.e. post-vocalic schwa loss variable rule feeds on the variable output of the first rule (i.e. desulcalization), the argument is based on the observation that the second rule will reveal the constraint effects of the first rule unless there is a constraint in the second rule which neutralizes this effect. If we have more r' desulcalized when followed by a consonant in the first rule, there will be more tokens in this environment which become the input for the post-vocalic schwa deletion variable rule.

Suppose, for example, that we have 200 tokens available for desulcalization, 100 followed by a consonant and 100 followed by a vowel. Of the 100 followed by a consonant, 80 are desulcalized; of the 100 followed by a non-consonant, 40 are desulcalized. This rule then feeds into the post-vocalic schwa loss rule. The schwa loss rule can only operate on the 80 desulcalized r's followed by a consonant and the 40 desulcalized r's followed by a non-consonant. If there is no neutralizing constraint found in this rule (and following Labov's (1969) analysis, there is not), then we may expect that this variable rule will operate on more items when followed by a consonant. The constraint effect of the previous rule will then be realized in a variable rule which feeds off of it. This description is illustrated by the following rules, which incorporate the choice of tokens into the approximate rule:

1. r → (ə) / [+V] ___## 80/100 + C
   40/100 - C

2. 40/80__ + C
   20/40__ - C ə → (∅) / [+V] ___##

The argument for separating non-copula r desulcalization and copula deletion then, must be considered by looking at the cumulative constraining effect of two rules in a feeding relationship. This observation extends the use of variable constraints as a principled basis for separating or generalizing rules slightly beyond that of the t, d deletion case.

Extended rules and variable constraints

The use of variable constraints as a basis for separating or combining rules is not, of course, unique to the cases we have illustrated in the previous description. What we have tried to demonstrate here, however, is that such evidence can, of itself, serve as a principled basis for separating or combining processes; it is not simply an ad hoc procedure that allows for a convenient fit between quantitative data and formal rules. As mentioned earlier, a search of the literature on variable rules reveals that arguments quite similar to the ones presented here have been put forth to justify a rule generalization or separation into different rules. One of the prominent cases that has come up in the literature concerns the use of variable constraints to motivate the distinction between 'extended processes' and separate rules. A process of the type X → Y → Z is considered to be extended and therefore to be distinguished from separate rules of the type X → Y and Y → Z.[8] Labov's discussion of contraction and deletion examines both alternatives (Labov's Case 4, where Z → Z → ∅; Case 1, where Z → Z and Z → ∅) and resolves the issue largely on the basis of variable constraints. There are two aspects of variable constraints which provide the basis for Labov's conclusion that deletion is an independent process operating on the output of contraction. One is the fact that some of the constraints in the preceding environments are different for the two processes. Thus, we find that a preceding vowel favors contraction and a preceding consonant favors deletion. This sort of motivation is similar to the type of principled basis for separating rules as discussed previously. The second motivation is based on the fact that the constraints for the following syntactic environment (NP, PA, Verb-ing, and gonna) although ordered identically for contraction and deletion, apply to both contraction and deletion. That is, the constraints apply twice, making the constraints for deletion more exaggerated than they are for contraction. If the constraints applied only once, deletion would presumably be a fixed proportion of contraction in each following syntactic environment. (Compare Figure 8b and 8c in Labov 1969:734 for a graphic representation of this difference in application.)

Without questioning the ultimate relationship of contraction and deletion (since there may be other types of very sound reasons for viewing them as separate), I would like to address myself to the matter of reapplication of variable constraints as a principled basis for distinguishing between extended processes and separate rules. In an extended rule with two variable inputs, it would not appear to be particularly unnatural to have the variable constraints apply twice. In the light of other types of identical features of such processes (e.g. conflated identical environment specifications), it is questionable whether this reapplication can provide the formal basis for separation. Is this reapplication attributed too much motivational power?

Although there are few cases of variable constraints applying to extended rules of this sort, there is one case from Labov et al., where a variable rule is applied to an extended rule of this type. This is found in the discussion of the rule which changes morpheme-initial underlying interdental fricatives first to affricates, and then to stops. Labov et al. have formalized this rule as follows:

$$\begin{bmatrix} \text{+cons} \\ \text{-voc} \\ \text{+diff} \\ \text{-grave} \\ \text{-strid} \end{bmatrix} \longrightarrow (\text{[-cont] ([+abr off])}) / \; \# \underset{\alpha \text{ voiced}}{\underline{\qquad}}$$

Labov et al. observed that there is one main constraint on the rule, namely voicing. This means that more voiced segments will become affricates and subsequently more will become stops than their voiceless counterparts. Assuming that the variable constraint only applies once to the two variable inputs, we will have a frequency distribution something like the following:

TABLE 2. Comparison of interdental fricatives → affricates → stops with one application of variable constraints.

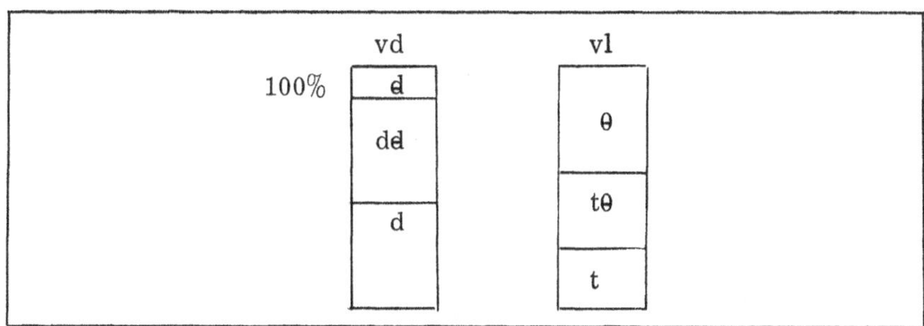

With one application of the variable constraints to the two variable inputs, we should find that there are more voiced segments that become affricates than voiceless ones. Then taking a fixed proportion of both voiced and voiceless affricates to become stops, the end result will be both more voiced affricates and more voiced stops than the corresponding voiceless affricates and stops. But this is apparently not what actually happens since according to Labov et al. (1968: 96) there are 'a great many affricates for (th), (th-2) but that the prevailing form for the (dh) is the stop, (dh-3).' Since there are more voiceless affricates than voiced ones, I understand this to mean that the actual configuration is like Table 3 rather than Table 2.

TABLE 3. Comparison of interdental fricatives → affricates → stops with two applications of constraint effects.

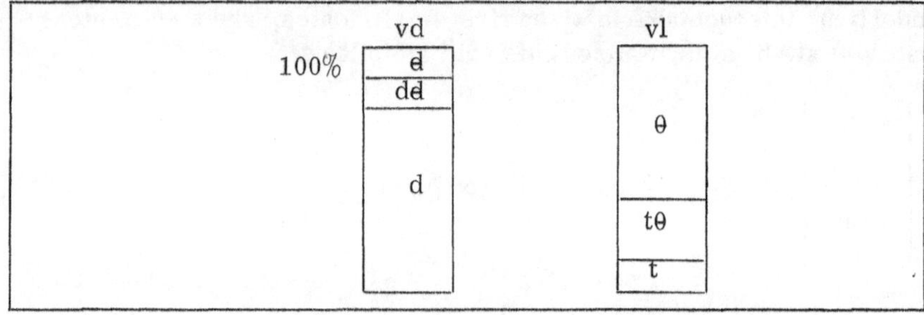

This figure, which represents the actual quantitative dimensions, can apparently be derived only from allowing the constraint effect of voicing to apply to both variable inputs of the rule. But it is noted that the rule is written as an extension type rule rather than two separate rules. How, then, do we deal with the lack of motivation provided by reapplying constraints in the one case (viz. the interdental fricatives) and the appeal to this same sort of reasoning in another case (viz. copula contraction and deletion) as a principled basis for rule separation? If we followed Labov's reasoning in the description of contraction and deletion, then the process for changing interdental fricatives to affricates and then stops must be considered as separate rules, with the effect of voicing as a constraint on each rule. But if we allow for the reapplication of constraints in an extended process, then there is no basis for arguing the separation of rules on these grounds in either case. The allowance of reapplication appears to be consonant with other identical aspects of extended processes (e.g. the conflated specified environment for application, identical constraint hierarchies) so that at this point we opt for latter solution. Further studies of variable constraints as they apply to processes considered extended on the basis of other types of 'conventional' evidence may reveal that we have underestimated the motivational powers of constraints, but it appears that counterevidence must be provided if the use of variable constraints in such cases is not to be considered ad hoc.

Variable constraints and rule ordering

In the previous discussion, we have only described the implications of variable constraints in terms of separating or combining processes. No mention has been made of the possible effect that constraints may have on rule ordering. The questions we want to ask with regard to rule ordering is what possible motivation variable constraints may provide for sequencing rules? Can variable constraints provide a type of principled basis for ordering which might be somewhat analogous to the type of motivation constraints may provide for rule separation?

We must first of all point out that from a purely quantitative standpoint, variable constraints do not appear to provide independent evidence for ordering related rules in only one particular sequence. The cumulative quantitative effect of two rules appears to be the same regardless of the order. For example, consider the case of the two rules needed to account for underlying //d// and //t// in Puerto Rican English. First of all, there is a rule which may delete word-final d or t. This is the post-vocalic alveolar stop deletion rule which was discussed earlier in connection with the description of the effect of constraint hierarchies on rule separation and combining. Then there is another rule which changes underlying //d// to surface t. This means that both t and ∅ may be the surface realizations of underlying //d//. For reasons elaborated elsewhere (Wolfram 1973), these rules must be kept separate. Both of the rules are variable, showing several different constraints favoring their operation. Without going into all the various constraints on their operation, let us look at some approximate overall variable relations. For every 100 tokens of underlying //d//, approximately 70 get realized ultimately as ∅ and 10 become t in their surface realizations. Of the 100 tokens of underlying //t//, 20 get realized as ∅ and the remainder are unchanged. The graphic distribution of the ultimate surface realizations is shown in Table 4. Now let us suppose that the rule ordering for the two processes involved in the realization of these forms is first d, t → ∅ and then d → t. Placing the number of items affected into the rule input, we have the following:

$$1.\quad \begin{Bmatrix} 70/100\ \text{d} \\ 20/100\ \text{t} \end{Bmatrix} \rightarrow (\emptyset)/\ \ldots$$

$$2.\quad 10/30\ \text{d} \rightarrow (\text{t})/\ \ldots$$

TABLE 4. Graphic representation of surface forms for underlying //d// and //t// in Puerto Rican English.

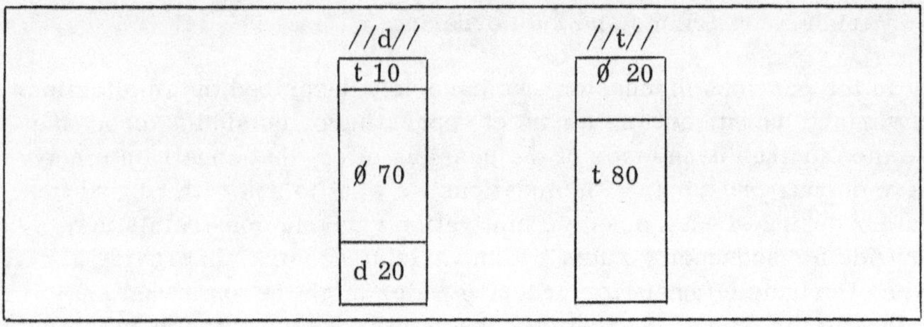

//d//	//t//
t 10	Ø 20
Ø 70	t 80
d 20	

The output of the first rule allows only 30 d's out of the original tokens to become the output for the second process, and this process operates to change 10 of the remaining d's to t.

Now let us suppose that the order is the opposite; that is, the proper ordering of these two variable rules is first d → t and then d, t → Ø. Placing our tokens again into the variable output of the rule, we have:

1. 10/100 d → (t)/ . . .

2. $\left\{ \begin{array}{l} \text{70/90 d} \\ \text{20/100 t} \end{array} \right\} \rightarrow$ (Ø)/. . .

Although the variable input may be different for the two rules based on how they are ordered, the end quantitative result of the application of the two rules is the same. From a quantitative standpoint, it really does not make any difference whether the totals of t are added to Ø and d, or Ø to d and t. The individual rules may turn out to have different application frequency values (e.g. 10 or 100 t's for //d// is very different from 10 out of 30), but the quantitative dimensions are essentially neutral to the order, and can equally accommodate either order.

Although the ultimate quantitative dimensions of two related variable rules will ultimately add up to the same cumulative output regardless of the way in which they are ordered, this is not to say that the ordering of the rules cannot have a significant impact on the constraint effects. The significance of different ordering has been rather dramatically illustrated by Labov (1969) in his discussion of the relations of contraction and deletion of the English copula. If we, for the sake of discussion, assumed that contraction operated on the output of deletion, we would find that the constraints of the following syntactic environment contraction would be illustrated by Figure 4a

FIGURE 4.

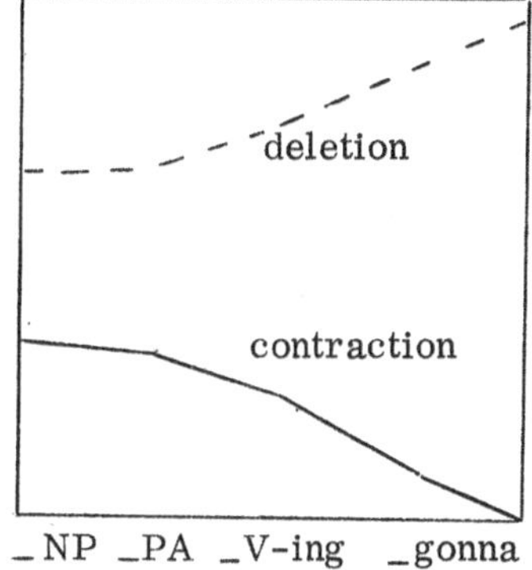

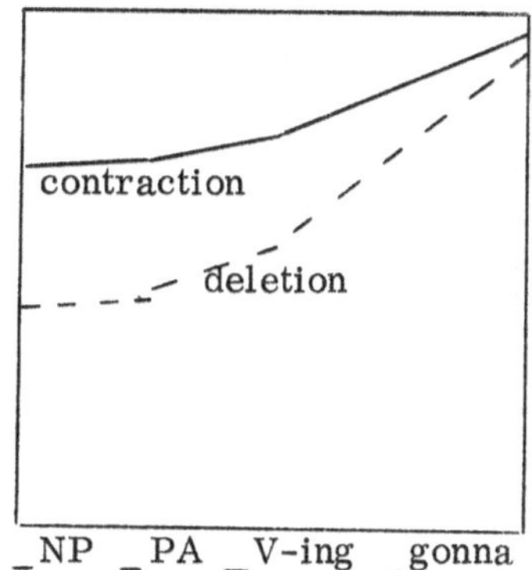

instead of the relationships of Figure 4b, which is the actual relationship of these rules. If the rules were sequenced so that deletion operated first and then contraction, the constraint hierarchies of contraction and deletion would be mirror images of each other. That is, deletion would be favored by gonna, V-ing, PA, and NP in that order, while for contraction the order would be NP, PA, V-ing, and gonna. But if we ordered contraction before deletion as Labov has done (quite correctly), the order would be gonna, V-ing, PA, and NP for both contraction and deletion. The cumulative quantitative effect of the two rules, however, might be the same regardless of the order (since the variable inputs of the individual rules would simply have different frequency values) but the constraint hierarchy would be quite different. I am not here disputing Labov's ordering of contraction before deletion, but simply pointing out that the motivation for this order cannot be justified from the quantitative dimensions of the rules, since either order can be accommodated by them.

At this point, it may be difficult to conceive of actual instances in which constraint effects may allow only one ordering of rules, but it seems reasonable to expect that further exploration of universal aspects of constraint effects and orders may provide a principled basis for only one particular sequence of rules. In terms of the above case, for example, we may find that there is universal prohibition of mirror images in constraint hierarchies of related rules. If there were an apparent option to order two rules with respect to each other and one of the orderings allowed a mirror-image of hierarchical constraints, then the constraint hierarchy might provide a basis for allowing only one order.

One could conceive of other instances where a particular ordering changed the effect of the constraints. Let us assume (and there appears to be some basis for this assumption, cf. Wolfram 1973a) that constraint effects are universal (i.e. particular environments will always have a particular effect on variability). Suppose we have a universal effect in which a following consonant always favored deletion of a consonant. In a particular language, we find that there is no type of 'conventional' motivation to order two rules with respect to each other. But ordering them in one sequence results in a non-consonant favoring deletion while ordering them in the other order reveals the consonant to favor deletion. If this were the case, the universal constraint effect would then provide evidence for ordering them only in one particular order. In this way, then, variable constraints could provide an independent basis for motivating a given order.

At this point, my comments on the effect that variable constraints may have on rule ordering consist of considerable speculation. A search of the literature turns up short in its attempt to substantiate claims about the formal evidence provided by variable constraints for particular orders. Several instances of supposed implication for rule ordering turn out to be inadequate.[9] This, of course, does not mean that there can be no such evidence, and we have speculated several possible types of evidence which might be relevant. But at this point, there are no cases in the variable rule literature which, to my knowledge, demonstrate convincingly that variable constraints can independently provide formal motivation for a particular rule ordering. Maybe this statement will provide an impetus for someone to provide counterevidence. That would be nice since I once read in an introductory textbook that that was what the advance of science was all about.[10]

NOTES

1. In defense of the dignity of mop-up operations, I simply quote here Kuhn's comment: 'Few people who are not actually practitioners realize how much mop-up work this sort of paradigm leaves to be done or quite how fascinating such work can prove in the execution' (1962:24). In several instances in the history of linguistic theory, I think the failure to undertake 'mop-up' operations has led to the ultimate dismissal of the theory, irrespective of its potential as a theoretical construct.

2. In my earlier study of alveolar stop deletion for Vernacular Black English (Wolfram 1969), I considered the relatively infrequent examples of post-vocalic t deletion, at least in some environments, to be due to performance factors rather than an integral part of the lect. This matter is still not quite resolved to my satisfaction, but in our discussion here we will consider t to be variably deleted as an authentic part of the lect.

3. The more recent version of this rule, while revised in conventions for its representation, does not essentially differ from the earlier version by Labov (1969:748). There is, however, correction of what apparently was a typographical error in the earlier version; namely, the omission of an 'in the absence of' sign to indicate that it is the non-grammatical boundary which favors the operation of the rule. In the earlier version, the preceding environment should read $\not{\mathcal{C}}$ (~ #) instead of $\not{\mathcal{C}}$ (#). However, in this version of the rule, the title t, d deletion is given but the designation of [-cont] as an input allows considerably more than t and d.

4. In an earlier version of the t, d deletion rule, Labov et al. (1968:136) did actually include voicing as a low order (fifth) constraint on deletion. Since the tabulational procedure is only given for the high order constraints, however, it is difficult to determine if this was due to the inclusion of post-vocalic t, d deletion along with post-consonantal deletion or an authentic low-order constraint for post-consonantal t, d deletion. At any rate, it is quite clear that if the two potentially different processes had been tabulated separately, the results would not have been isomorphic. Fasold's t, d deletion rule, which goes into considerably more detail for the constraints on post-consonantal stop deletion but does not actually include any tabulations of post-vocalic t, d deletion, does not include voicing even as a low-order constraint (cf. Fasold 1972:75-76).

5. Even if we were to find that some constraints did operate synergistically or antagonistically, it would not necessarily rule out such evidence, since there may be some principles of non-independent constraint operation (e.g. a constraint does not operate synergistically with all other constraints in the hierarchy of a given rule) by which we would differentiate them from apparent synergism.

6. In presenting my case for the separation of copula ARE deletion and non-copula r desulcalization and post-vocalic ə loss, there are two other arguments which would be sufficient to motivate this analysis independent of constraint effect (cf. Wolfram forthcoming). Interestingly, however, this was the first motivation which I became aware of, and the two other reasons became obvious after this argument was developed. In the absence of the other motivations, I would still maintain that the argument presented here is sufficient in itself.

7. Feeding relationship is here to be defined following Kiparsky (1968). That is, two rules, A and B, are functionally related so that the application of A creates representations to which B can apply. The application of A converts forms to which B cannot apply into forms to which B can then apply.

8. There are two basic differences between the extended process of the type X → Y → Z as opposed to the separate processes X → Y,

and Y → Z. In the former case, the environmental specification must be identical for the entire process while in the latter case, it may be different. Also, the former case only allows forms to change to Z which have been derived ultimately from X whereas in the latter case, a form not derived from X may become the input for Y → Z (e.g. A → Y, X → Y, Y → Z).

9. There are at least two cases in the literature on variable rules where constraints are suggested as providing formal motivation for rule ordering. One is my discussion on post-vocalic t, d deletion and its relation to the devoicing of d (Wolfram 1973:146). In this case, I simply failed to understand the frequency relations between related rules in terms of the second rule operating on the frequency output of the first rule. The second case is Labov's arguments for ordering deletion to operate on the output of the contraction rule. In this case, the argument is tautological. He first implies an ordered relationship in setting up his quantitative dimensions and then notes that 'deletion first and contraction second would not fit any of the quantitative results shown above for there is no reason for contraction of undeleted [əz] to be dependent upon the deletion of some other [əz]' (1969:733). In reality the quantitative dimensions are neutral to the ordering, and either order could theoretically result in the same cumulative effect. In both cases cited here, the order suggested is apparently the correct one, but for reasons unrelated to the variable constraints.

10. Extended discussions with Peg Griffin have been particularly helpful in the preparation of this paper. I am also grateful to Ralph W. Fasold and Tim Shopen for comments on an earlier draft. As always, I alone am responsible for remaining inadequacies.

REFERENCES

Bailey, Charles-James N. 1973. Variation resulting from different rule orderings in English phonology. In: New ways of analyzing variation in English. Edited by Charles-James N. Bailey and Roger W. Shuy. Washington, D.C., Georgetown University Press. 211-252.

Cedergren, Henrietta J. and David Sankoff. 1974. Variable rules: Performance as a statistical reflection of competence. Language 50:333-355.

Cedergren, Henrietta J. 1973. On the nature of variable constraints. In: Bailey and Shuy (1973). 13-22.

Campbell, Lyle. 1973. Extrinsic ordering lives. Indiana Linguistics Club Publications.

Fasold, Ralph W. 1972. Tense marking in Black English: A linguistic and social analysis. Arlington, Virginia, Center for Applied Linguistics.

Labov, William, Paul Cohen, Clarence Robins, and John Lewis. 1968. A study of the non-standard English of Negro and Puerto Rican speakers in New York City. USOE Final Report, Research Project Number 3288.

Labov, William. 1969. Contraction, deletion, and inherent variability of the English copula. Language 45:715-762.

_____. 1972. Language in the inner city: Studies in the Black English vernacular. Philadelphia, University of Pennsylvania Press.

Kiparsky, Paul. 1968. Linguistic universals and language change. In: Universals in linguistic theory. Edited by Emmon Bach and Robert T. Harms. New York, Holt, Rinehart and Winston. 171-204.

Koutsoudas, Andreas. 1972. The strict order fallacy. Language 48:88-96.

Kuhn, Thomas. 1962. The structure of scientific resolutions. Chicago, University of Chicago Press.

Sankoff, Gillian. MS. A quantitative paradigm for the study of communicative competence.

Shiels, Marie Eileen. 1972. Dialects in contact: A sociolinguistic analysis of four phonological variables of Puerto Rican English and Black English in Harlem. Unpublished Ph. D. dissertation, Georgetown University.

Wolfram, Walt. 1969. A sociolinguistic description of Detroit Negro speech. Washington, D. C., Center for Applied Linguistics.

_____. 1973. Sociolinguistic aspects of assimilation: Puerto Rican English in East Harlem. Arlington, Virginia, Center for Applied Linguistics.

_____. 1973a. On what basis variable rules? In: Bailey and Shuy (1973).

_____. 1974. The relationship of white Southern speech to vernacular Black English: Copula deletion and invariant be. Language 498-577.

CARRYING THE NEW WAVE INTO SYNTAX: THE CASE OF BLACK ENGLISH BÍN[1]

JOHN R. RICKFORD

University of Pennsylvania

1. Introduction. Ever since the first conference on New Ways of Analyzing Variation in English was held in 1972, the abbreviated title--NWAVE--has become something of a rallying cry ('The New Wave') to those interested in the study of linguistic variation. The enthusiasm is doubtless justified. Uneasiness with categorical frameworks has been growing for some time, and the remarks made by C.-J. N. Bailey in the introduction to the papers from NWAVE I (Bailey and Shuy 1973) would probably be endorsed by a great many (though by no means all) linguists today:

> I am happy to be rid of static homogeneous models and to be rid of the fudges represented by 'my dialect', 'performance component', 'optional', and the rest . . . (xiv)

However, as we move beyond initial revolutionary fervour, and begin a more sober stock-taking, certain weaknesses in our line of attack become increasingly clear. One salient limitation is the extent to which we have become preoccupied with morphophonemic and phonological variation to the exclusion of everything else. Syntax and semantics, for instance, have come to represent lone islands far out at sea, increasingly untouched by any waves--old or new.

The problem is particularly acute for those 'variationists' whose data consists of large samples of tape-recorded speech, covering as wide a range of stylistic contexts as possible (cf. Labov 1966, Bickerton 1972). While the advantages of this method in terms of 'accountability' etc. should be clear to most of us by now, it has a built-in limitation in providing large masses of data only on those phenomena which show up with high frequency in natural speech. In most cases, these are phonological variables; hence the disproportionate number of variation studies in phonology.

It was precisely in response to this problem that Gillian Sankoff (1973) entitled her paper presented at the first NWAVE meeting 'Above and beyond phonology in variable rules'. There can be little doubt about the soundness of her primary thesis--that 'variability occurs, and can be dealt with, at levels of grammar above (or beyond) the phonological'. However, we can hardly fail to note that the pool of data examined in some of the studies she cited (for example, bai in Tok Pisin) is far smaller in the more customary studies of phonological phenomena. And that in others (Montreal que; cf. also the English copula as examined by Labov 1969) phonological features in the environment act as significant variable constraints. What of the other syntactic variables which show no or very little phonological conditioning? (We certainly know such cases exist.)

Finally, what of the other syntactic phenomena which tend to occur even less frequently than these--things about which not even the most basic linguistic facts are known, much less the kind of variation they display? Bickerton, in a recent issue of the Lectological Newsletter (March 1973) complained about the 'reams that have been written about the different things Black speakers do with their D's and Z's', but the 'next to nothing that has been written about the different ways Black speakers organize their tense systems'. But this is again because of the low frequency with which many of the most interesting Black English tense and aspect markers (e.g. Invariant Be, Remote BÍN) tend to show up in tape-recorded speech. This in turn is so not only because speakers have some awareness of the stigmatized nature of such forms, but also because the semantic conditions which they are normally introduced to express may occur rarely, if at all, in the course of a sociolinguistic interview.

Overcoming these limitations of tape-recorded data should certainly rank as one of the major challenges to riders of the 'New Wave'. But the problem has so far not received the attention it deserves. Innovations made in this area (cf. Labov 1972a) have not sparked off a chain of repeat performances (as many of Labov's innovations in sociolinguistic interview technique did in the 1960's). And issues of validity and reliability involved in such innovations still remain to be raised.

The purpose of this paper is to draw attention to some of the innovations in methodology which have already been achieved, and to demonstrate the application of two such methods to a syntactic case about which very little has been written so far--BÍN in Black English. Let us first review some of the methods available for overcoming the limitations of tape-recorded data with respect to syntactic and other low-frequency phenomena.

One possibility is the method of 'surreptitious' or 'candid' recording. As it has been demonstrated publicly and dramatically for us most recently, this method involves tape-recording what people say without their knowledge or permission. The hope of the strongest advocates of this method is that speakers, unhampered by the constraints of the typical interview situation, will produce more of those syntactic and other variables which are normally stigmatized. While this is certainly true to the extent that other aspects of the speech-situation (for example, nature of the participants) do not have a more powerful over-riding effect, it is simply the case that we cannot have our 'hidden tape-recorder' with us at all times. We will always be exposed to more speech than we shall ever have the opportunity to record. The other disadvantages of this method--poor quality of recordings, discovery and its consequences, quite apart from the ethics involved, are also well known. Together, they suggest that despite its devilish appeal, this possibility will be of limited utility.

Another method involves 'enriching the data of tape-recorded conversation' by including questions and topics which stimulate more frequent use of rare forms or environments than might occur naturally (Labov 1972b). The method works excellently in some cases. If you will pardon the use of a phonological example for effect, let me cite one case from recent studies at the University of Pennsylvania, of the tensing and raising of (æ). The problem was to elicit a natural production of the word 'sad'. One student discovered that a highly successful way of doing this was to ask interviewees if they had ever seen the movie 'Love Story'. Almost inevitably the word would crop up--repeatedly--in the ensuing discussion.

The method demands careful attention to the nature of everyday conversational interaction. But it demands more. Most of the crucial syntactic/semantic variables (like B. E. BÍN) are extremely difficult to elicit, paradoxically, unless we already know a great deal about their meaning and use.

The final two methods are more immediately feasible to the researcher. Both move beyond the use of tape-recorded data, though in very different ways. The first has been used extensively by students of variation in 'abstract syntax', for example, those interested in syntactic features which have no clear regional or social roots. In its more sophisticated form, this method involves eliciting the intuitions of other people and analyzing the results for patterns of variation, increasingly, with the help of implicational scales (Elliot, Legum, and Thompson 1969; C. J. Bailey 1970; Baltin 1973; Carden 1971; Sag 1973). The method has been extended, with important innovations, to the study of syntactic variation which is governed by regional and social factors (Labov 1972a), and is being hailed by others (Butters 1973) as the most promising methodology for overcoming the limitations of tape-recorded data. However, as mentioned before, issues of validity and reliability are most acute with this method, and as it is usually employed, no independent check on the results is available.

The final method is one which has been used very rarely in studies to date. It involves careful and intense participant observation. Whether our interest is in Black English, Puerto-Rican English, British English, or more abstract varieties, we exploit our contacts with native speakers to record on 3-by-5 cards every possible use of the variable in which we are interested. At the suggestion of Bill Labov, several students at the University of Pennsylvania have been using this method for some time now. We never cease to be amazed at the frequency with which even the rarest variables begin to show up once we are constantly attending to them in this way. The advances of this method over the others are also clear. Not only are we able to gather the most reliable data--from natural conversation--but we can gather it anywhere, anytime, without the need of any technical equipment. (Note too that permission to scribble away in the midst of ongoing conversations is more easily extended than permission to run a tape-recorder, partly because it is less potentially damaging to participants.)

My own studies of B. E. BÍN have depended largely on a combination of the last two methods. The 'intuitive data' consists of the responses of a sample of twenty-five Black and twenty-five White subjects to a questionnaire designed to explore their ability to interpret, predict, and evaluate the use of BÍN. This questionnaire, entitled Q-SCOM-IV, was an extension of similar ones (Q-SCOM-I to III) which had been developed and used by Bill Labov and other members of a research group in which I participated two years ago (cf. Labov 1972a). In Q-SCOM-IV, several more aspects of BÍN usage were attacked, and the questions about other variables served principally as 'distractors'. The subjects were drawn from very diverse geographical backgrounds (including Pennsylvania, New York, California, North Carolina, and Massachusetts), and were interviewed individually. [I should like to thank here Angela Rickford and Karl Reisman for their help with this time-consuming process.]

Participant observation was carried out in two widely separate Black communities--one in West Philadelphia, the other in the Sea Islands off the coast of South Carolina. Living in these communities, I was able to draw on a wide range of conversational encounters in which BÍN, supposedly rare, was frequently used. Although I heard many more than I was able to note down, I was able to gather about sixty-six sentences with stressed BÍN. Most of my sentences, it should be noted, come from adults over the age of twenty-four--providing strong contradictory evidence to the frequently voiced claim that the central syntactic structures of Black English are regularly used only by young Black children or adolescents.

It is clearly impossible to present all the findings of this research in the time available to me today. I shall consider only three central aspects about BÍN on which there seems to be disagreement or limited information in the published literature: (A) The significance of stress (i.e. BÍN = bĭn?); (B) Meaning and Use; (C) Productivity--Cooccurrence Relations. I shall try to maintain a balance between substantive findings about BÍN itself and theoretical questions about the two methods employed. In particular I shall be interested in the internal consistency of the intuitive responses, and the extent to which they are supported by data from participant observation.

2. Three issues in the study of Black English BÍN

A. The significance of stress (i.e. BÍN = bĭn?). The <u>been</u> which we are interested in is the form which has been mentioned in the literature as signalling some 'remote' past tense or perfective aspect.[2] We shall explore the precise meaning of the form in the next section. Here we simply want to know how significant stress is to the remote function with which the form has typically been associated.

Previous researchers have been quite divided on this point.[3] Stewart (1965), the first to draw attention to the form, indicated that stress was obligatory. Fasold and Wolfram (1970) feel that stress on <u>been</u> is an optional element only, its function being to 'doubly emphasize the total completion of an action'. Fickett (1970) shares their view on the optionality of stress, but for her its function is to distinguish <u>been</u> as a Phase Auxiliary (with remote function) from <u>been</u> as the auxiliary of a passive. The latter, in her analysis, never receive stress.

Dillard (1972) suggests that there may have existed two systems all along: one in which stressed BÍN is a remote, and unstressed <u>bĭn</u> a recent perfective; and another in which <u>been</u> (regardless of stress) is remote, and <u>done</u> a recent perfective. He adds that the latter system 'has had most widespread influence in the U.S.' but that the former 'still survives in some forms of Black English'.

When we turn to the intuitive responses of Black subjects on this point, we find similar divisions and ambiguities. (1) below indicates the questions relevant to this is Q-SCOM-IV:

(1) 17b. Could you say 'I <u>bĭn</u> know it' (unstressed) and mean the same thing as 'I BÍN know it' (stressed)? Yes___ No___

9a. He BÍN had one. 9b. He bĭn had one. Same___ Different___
15a. He BÍN sick. 15b. He bĭn sick. Same___ Different___

Question 17b for instance, was asked after subjects had responded to the meaning of stressed BÍN, usually with tremendous agreement on the remote function of this form. The question was whether one could say the unstressed form bĭn and mean the same thing. Nine said yes, ten said no. Similarly, twelve felt that 9a and 9b were the same, and ten that they were not.

As Table 1 indicates, the number of informants who were consistent in their responses on this issue is even smaller:

TABLE 1. Consistency response of Black subjects to 17b, 9 and 15 in Q-SCOM-IV

N	Positive responses			Negative responses		
	Yes to 17b	Yes 17b Same 9	Yes 17b Same 9 Same 15	No to 17b	No 17b Diff 9	No 17b Diff 9 Diff 15
19	9	8	6	10	7	7

Positive responses are those which suggest that BÍN and bĭn are equivalent. Negative responses, that they are different. While there are only six informants who consistently see the two forms as equivalent, and seven who consistently see them as different, note again what an even split this is. This is the pattern that is repeated regularly, no matter how the question of BÍN = bĭn is put, nor how the answers are analyzed. This might be taken to suggest that Dillard (1972) is right--that there are two systems for signalling 'remote' tense. In one the stress on been is significant, in the other it is not.

As variationists, there should be nothing uncomfortable about this conclusion. But before we accept it, let us turn to the data gathered in participant observation. From a total of sixty-six BÍN sentences, and over two hundred with unstressed bĭn, the data is quite clear and conclusive on this point. Only stressed BÍN can signal remote function by itself, as is clear from the contexts in which it is used.

Unstressed bin occurs frequently with temporal adverbs or 'specifiers', as in

(2) I bĭn playing cards since I was four. (BF 38, Pa)[4]

Since this is often the case, it is possible to see how one might arrive at the mistaken impression that unstressed bĭn signals remote aspect. However, it is the time adverbial that signals the function in these cases, not the unstressed bĭn form. Not only are such time-adverbials unnecessary with stressed BÍN, they are restricted from co-occurring with it. This syntactic consequence of the semantic difference between the two forms is illustrated most strikingly when the two follow close upon each other in the discourse:

(3) I BÍN know you, you know. I bĭn knowing you for years. BM 59, Pa)

The only case in which time adverbials appear to co-occur with BÍN is in utterances like (4):

(4) He BÍN home--since last week. (BM 41, Pa)

However the time adverbial here does not, as in (2) or (3) occur as part of a single 'sentence intonation pattern'. It is separated from the main clause both by pause and by falling intonation on home. And in fact an analysis of (4) as derived from (4') seems quite sound:

(4') He BÍN home. He bĭn home since last week.

There is other evidence that BÍN and bĭn are different. Note the following sentence:

(5) He bĭn doing it ever since we was teenagers, and he still doing it. (BM 41, Pa)

The conjoined qualification 'and he still doing it' would be redundant if BÍN+V-ing were used. As we shall see in a moment, the meaning 'Remote Phase Continuative' would be implicit in the form itself.

Although most of the examples with unstressed bĭn are not preceded by forms of have, there are a few which are, and seem nevertheless to carry the same semantic force. For instance:

(6) Cause I've bĭn through it. I've bĭn through them changes. (BM 26, Pa)

On the basis of this, it may be possible to describe most instances of B. E. bĭn for Philadelphia, at least, as 'Present Perfects'. This is not the case with stressed BÍN.

There are also several cases of unstressed bĭn with done as first auxiliary, as in:

(7) Get to work, start talking to them girls, they done bĭn locked up fifteen times! (BF 38, Pa)

There is a rare occurrence of BÍN + done, as in the Sea-Island sentence:

(8) Boy, if we had shrimp, we'd a BÍN done got us some fish! (BM 11, SI)

but none whatsoever of done + BÍN.

In the Sea-Island data, stressed BÍN and unstressed bĭn must also be separated on syntactic and semantic grounds. One difference between the two forms, here as in Philadelphia, is the possibility of treating many instances of bĭn as 'Present Perfects'. But there are other differences here. Unstressed bĭn is sometimes used as a straight equivalent of was, indicating simple past tense. Note the close alternation between the two forms in (9):

(9) I don't know if that snake bĭn coil, or either was stretch out or what. (BM 52, SI)

Used before a verb-stem, unstressed bĭn has the additional ambiguity of signalling either 'Past' or 'past before the Past':

(10) But the real medicine what I bĭn want fuh get fuh Joo-Joo . . . (BF 78, SI)
'But the real medicine which I had wanted to get for Joo-Joo . . .'

Finally, bĭn but not BÍN occurs before continuative a:

(11) How bout that thing wuh B bĭn a tell you? (BM 67, SI)
'How about that thing which B was telling you?'

These uses of unstressed bĭn are of course well known in other creole areas (cf. for Jamaican Creole, B. Bailey 1966; for Sierra Leone Krio, Jones 1968; for Guyana Creole, Bickerton 1974). The point here is not to pursue the use of bĭn in any detail, but simply to indicate the ways in which it differs from BÍN in semantic function and syntactic co-occurrence restrictions.

Enough has been said so far to demonstrate the point with which I started out, that on the basis of the participant observation data, BÍN and bĭn must be distinguished. In the light of this, what are we to make of the intuitive judgments of Black respondents, who, as indicated above, were evenly divided on this issue? It may be that those who claimed the forms were equivalent were speakers of some 'other' dialect which has simply not been tapped in my own participant observation. This is possible, but I think, unlikely. First of all, the respondents were, as we shall see, in unanimous agreement on the meaning and interpretation of stressed BÍN. Secondly, I know that at least one of the respondents who suggested that the two forms were equivalent, consistently distinguishes them in his everyday speech. I am more inclined to think that what we are dealing with here is a weakness of the 'intuitive method' itself.

Let me mention two possible sources of error which have already come to light. One is the real difficulty which some subjects had in hearing 'unstressed' forms of b̆in. They would repeat question 9b, for instance, with lighter stress on bin than the stress on BÍN in 9a, but it would still be primary in that sentence.

This difficulty may have been the result of a second factor. For some informants, unstressed b̆in + V-ed (non-passive) is not a real possibility at all. These informants accept and say 'I BÍN had that' but not 'I b̆in had that'. Faced with the latter, they cannot see it as contrastive, may not even hear the difference in this environment. Note that when BÍN and b̆in are contrasted in another environment in which both are possible for all informants, as in question 15: He BÍN sick vs. He b̆in sick, five of the twelve informants who had seen them as equivalent in 9 now saw them as different. It is clear that in any repeated version of this questionnaire serious attempts to overcome these difficulties will have to be made. What is demonstrated here, in this very first issue about BÍN, is the value of data from participant observation in challenging and qualifying the data from intuitive responses.

B. BÍN--meaning and use. Previous researchers have applied a variety of labels to the Black English form BÍN (I ignore henceforth the issue of stress): 'Completive Perfect' (Stewart op. cit.) 'Remote Past' (Fasold and Wolfram 1970), 'Remote Perfective' (Dillard 1972) 'Perfect Phase' (Fickett 1970). What they are all trying to express via these different labels is essentially the same. That BÍN places the action in the distant past (relative to the present axis) and/or that it expresses 'total completion of the event'. One Standard English paraphrase that has been used frequently to register this fact is the time adverbial 'a long time ago'. This is perfectly appropriate for some of the BÍN sentences which I collected in Philadelphia and the Sea Islands, for instance (12):

(12) She ain't tell me that today, you know. She BÍN tell me that. (BF 32, SI)
'She told me that a long time ago'

However, this gloss, and the semantic notion of a totally completed action in the distant past, is appropriate only for a subset of the Participant-observation data--those in which BÍN is followed by non-stative verbs. With stative verbs, or with either kind in the progressive, the function of BÍN is different. Instead of expressing completion of the associated process (a cover term for action or state) it asserts only that it began in the distant past and is still very much in force at the moment of speaking. In both of these cases, a better S. E. paraphrase would be 'for a long time', e.g.:

(13) I BÍN had this. (BM 6, Pa)
'I've had this for a long time'
(14) I BÍN treating them like that. (BF 25, Pa)
'I've been treating them like that for a long time'

The similarities and differences between BÍN as used with non-statives on the one hand, and statives and progressives on the other, is more graphically illustrated in (15)

(15)

	Remote Anterior	Anterior	Point of Orientation
Statives	X-------------	---------	------
Non-statives	XY		
Progressives	X-------------	---------	------

In (15), X indicates the initiation of the 'process' and Y the end-point.

If we wish to formulate a conjunctive definition for BÍN we would have to say that it places the initiation of a process at some point in the distant past. 'Remote Phase' is perhaps the most appropriate label for this function.[5] It could then be extended (Remote Phase Continuative, Remote Phase Completive) to describe the particular effect of using the form with statives and progressives as against non-statives. It should be mentioned here that almost all the examples given by previous researchers involve non-stative verbs. This may be one element in their failure to perceive the more comprehensive nature of BÍN. This failure in turn is reflected in the labels they chose for the form--all of which suggest a Remote Phase Completive function only. Let us now turn to the intuitive responses on the meaning and use of BÍN to discover the extent to which they support or qualify the above analysis. In (16), the main questions in Q-SCOM-IV relevant to this issue are presented. Note that they go beyond simply asking what the form means, and try to get subjects to look through the grammar into the real world (cf. Labov 1972a).

(16) Q-SCOM-IV questions on the meaning of BÍN:

1. Someone asked, 'Is she married?' and someone else answered, 'She BÍN married'. Do you get the idea that she is married now? Yes___ No___
3. Bill was about to be introduced to this guy at a party, but when he saw him, he said, 'Hey, I BÍN know his name!' Which of these three things do you think he's most likely to say next:
   a. Give me a minute and I might remember it.
   b. He's John Jones. I saw his picture in the papers yesterday.
   c. He's John Jones. I've been hearing about him for years.

   So, what do you think Bill meant when he said, 'I BÍN know his name?' Choose the one that is closest to what you think:
   d. Used to know.
   e. Already knew.
   f. Know, but can't quite remember.
   g. Know right now.
   h. Have known for a long time, and still do.
   i. Other______________________________.
16. Frank asked his friend if he had paid off the bill on his new stereo, and got the answer, 'I BÍN paid for it'. Does he mean:
   a. I've already paid for it.
   b. I was paying for a long time, but I'm finished now.
   c. I paid for it long ago.
   d. I've been paying for it for a long time, and haven't finished yet.
   e. Other______________________________.

The responses appropriate to a 'Remote Phase' interpretation of BÍN were: Yes to 1, (c) and (h) to 3, (c) to 16. If we multiply the number of responses by the number of individuals in each group, we derive a total of one hundred possible responses. From the start, the difference between Black and White respondents on this issue is clear. For the Blacks, 87 percent of the responses were appropriate to a 'Remote Phase' interpretation. Only 37 percent of the White subjects' responses were.

The overwhelming agreement among Black respondents and their difference from White subjects on this issue is demonstrated even more clearly in Table 2, which displays the number of consistent Remote Phase interpretations:

TABLE 2. Consistent 'Remote Phase' interpretations to Q's 1, 16, 3

Group	N	Yes to 1	Yes to 1 (c) to 16	Yes to 1 (c) to 16 (c) to 3	Yes to 1 (c) to 16 (c) to 3 (h) to 3
Blacks	25	23	21	19	15
Whites	25	8	4	1	1

Note that while fifteen of the Black respondents end up giving completely consistent 'Remote Phase' interpretations, only one of the White respondents manages to do so. As it turns out, he is a native of Greensboro, North Carolina, who claims to have extensive contact with Blacks throughout his life.

The responses can be just as dramatically reviewed the other way around. In Table 3, the consistent Non-'Remote Phase' interpretations of Blacks and Whites are tabulated:

TABLE 3. Consistent Non-'Remote Phase' interpretations to Q's 1, 16, 3

Group	N	No to 1	No to 1 ~ (c) to 16	No to 1 ~ (c) to 16 ~ (c) to 3	No to 1 ~ (c) to 16 ~ (c) to 3 ~ (h) to 3
Blacks	25	2	1	0	0
Whites	25	17	14	12	10

Note that there are only two Black respondents who give Non-'Remote-Phase' interpretations to 1 to begin with, and by the time non-remote interpretations to 1, 16, and 3 are combined, none of the Black respondents are involved. By contrast, seventeen of the White respondents gave non-remote interpretations to 1, and ten maintained the same interpretation throughout.

Considering that a certain amount of chance error may always be present in investigations of this type, the tremendous regularity that is revealed here is highly significant. Both the 'participant observation' and the 'intuitive' data converge strongly to endorse a 'Remote Phase' interpretation for Black English BÍN. In addition, both data sources suggest that Black and White speakers are sharply divided in their abilities to use and interpret the form. The only other feature which has ever been shown to differentiate the two groups so sharply and reliably is their ability to understand the African-derived forms

'Cut-eye' and 'Suck-Teeth' and enact the non-verbal behavior to which these refer (cf. Rickford and Rickford 1974).

Finally, we may consider the overt responses of Black and White subjects to questions designed to explore their familiarity with and use of BÍN. The results are tabulated in Table 4.

TABLE 4. Positive responses to familiarity and use questions

Group	Have you ever heard BÍN?	Do you say BÍN yourself?
Blacks	24/25 = 96%	17/25 = 68%
Whites	16/24 = 67%	3/22 = 13%

Insofar as these results indicate what we would have suspected from participant-observation anyway, that more Blacks have heard and use BÍN than Whites, they seem generally valid. But the details are questionable. Sixteen Whites claim to have heard BÍN, and three to use it themselves. But in view of their responses on the 'meaning' questions reported on above, these claims are at least suspect. Interestingly enough, of the three Whites who claimed to 'say BÍN' themselves, two gave consistent Non-'Remote-Phase' interpretations to all four meaning-questions, and the other one gave a similar interpretation to two out of four. It is probable that these particular subjects were trying to claim familiarity with what they perceived as a 'Black' idiom because it was in some sense fashionable to do so.

The reverse process undoubtedly operated in the case of some Black subjects. Some of those who claimed not to say the form themselves modified it in subsequent discussion to 'at least not anymore'. For them, BÍN as a non-standard feature had a stigma which they would just as soon avoid.[6] In any case, the almost unanimous claim of Black subjects that they had at least heard the form is more credible, in the light of the high percentage of 'Remote Phase' interpretations on the meaning questions.

I might only add that BÍN is understood by a range of Black subjects considerably wider than is normally associated with the Black English vernacular. I once informally asked a few of the 'meaning' questions at a dinner party. The lone Black informant in this group, a Philadelphia judge, was rather surprised to discover that he was immediately distinguished from the other 'subjects' by his ability to give the 'correct' Remote-Phase interpretations. From his normal level of speech, one would hardly have classed him as a speaker of 'Black English'. But his ability to interpret BÍN in the same way that other B. E. speakers do, indicates the deep-seated sensitivity and exposure to this form that exists among Black Americans, of all levels, and suggests a possible creole history. It also raises the crucial issue of whether linguistic grammars should be written on the basis of 'productive' or 'receptive' competence. To explore this issue at any further length is clearly beyond the scope of this paper.

C. The productivity of BÍN--co-occurrence relations. The final issue which I shall take up is the productivity of BÍN in the grammar of Black English. The only environment in which earlier investigators found BÍN to occur was before V+ed. Dillard (1972) also found it before V-ing. But the picture that emerges from the participant-observation data is that BÍN is far more productive in Black English than this. In addition to V+ed and V-ing, it can be followed by:

(a) Locatives:
(17) Oh, it BÍN in this house. (BM 6, Pa)

(b) Adverbs:
(18) Them crab BÍN off. (BM 46, SI)

(c) Verb-Stem alone
(19) She BÍN quit school. (BM 15, SI)

(d) Passive Participles (contrary to Fickett 1970's claim), both with and without got:
(20) My hair BÍN cut. (BM 29, SI)
(21) He shoulda BÍN got shot. (BM 25, Pa)

(e) Modal or Done + Verb-(ed):
(22) I BÍN could walk on them stilts. (BF 16, SI)
(23) Boy, if we had shrimp, we'd a BÍN done got us some fish. (BM 11, SI)

Finally, as some of the examples here have already indicated, BÍN is frequently preceded by the modals coulda, shoulda, and woulda.

In order to discover the reliability of co-occurrence patterns which showed up in the participant-observation data and to discover the status of patterns which had not been attested at all, we included a series of sentences (a-n) in Q-SCOM-IV, and asked subjects to indicate whether they found them acceptable ('Given that you could say "I BÍN know that", could you also say . . . ?'). The sentences themselves are reprinted in Table 6 which displays the results in the form of an implicational array. First, however, we want to consider the extent to which Black and White groups differed in their acceptability ratings in general. This data is tabulated in Table 5.

TABLE 5. Positive acceptability ratings for sentences in Q. 18, Q-SCOM-IV

Group	N	a	b	c	d	e	f	g	h	i	j	k	l	m	n
Blacks	25	23	23	18	18	19	8	15	15	15	18	19	23	22	5
Whites	23	17	14	17	18	13	8	12	17	10	15	14	11	14	7

There are one or two striking differences in the acceptability ratings given to particular sentences by members of the two groups: twenty-three Blacks but only eleven Whites endorsed (18l): 'They BÍN ended that war'; twenty-two Blacks but only fourteen Whites endorsed (18m): 'I BÍN knowing that guy'. But these are sentences which were already well-documented from the participant observation data. On the acceptability ratings of lesser attested or unattested sentences, the difference between the two groups are virtually identical (cf. ratings for (18d) and (18f). This is surprising, in view of the overwhelming difference between the two groups which was registered in their interpretations of the meaning of BÍN. This equivalence in the ratings of the two groups is the first piece of evidence to suggest that there is more random variation here; that somehow, in this section of the questionnaire, we have failed to elicit the richer knowledge of the syntactic relations of BÍN which Black speakers must certainly possess in order to understand and use it as consistently as we know they do. Many different interpretations for our failure here suggest themselves. Part of the difficulty may lie in the technique of asking subjects to rate a string of sentences all at once. But Labov's (1971) remarks on idiosyncratic judgments made by informants to extremely rare alternants undoubtedly also apply here. Labov suggested that these might not be part of langue, but rather some kind of intuitive parole, and 'if so, we need techniques that will enable us to stop short of (such) intuitive judgments' (1971:447-448). Finally, it may be that both groups predict the extension of BÍN to other points in the grammar on the basis of their knowledge of the syntactic possibilities with Standard English unstressed bĕen. If this is so, we have again failed to get at the true set of possible co-occurrence patterns with Black English BÍN, for as indicated in section A above, these can be quite different from bĭn.

I have not yet identified the real source of the problem here, nor have I attempted as yet any workable solutions. However, the data remains useful--if only for demonstrating the kinds of difficulties which we might encounter in asking for acceptability ratings for sentences. There are more. Disregarding the questions Table 5 has already led us to raise concerning the reliability of the data we are getting here, let us go on to squeeze it, as is usually done, for all that it is worth.

Table 6 represents the results of the acceptability ratings of Black subjects in the form of an implicational array. As usual, what this 'implicational scale' implies is: (a) sentences to the left are more generally acceptable than sentences to the right; (b) if a subject finds a certain sentence acceptable, he will also find all sentences to the left of this (in the implicational array) acceptable.

In general, the hierarchical ranking of these sentences in terms of acceptability can be supported somewhat by the participant observation data. As already indicated, the two sentences most acceptable (furthest to the left) are well represented in the data from actual speech. And the three least acceptable (or furthest to the right): (h) He done BÍN locked up, (f) He BÍN bin gone, and (n) I have BÍN had that, have never been attested. The two next least acceptable sentences, including BÍN-could and BÍN-done have been attested only rarely, and only in the Sea-Islands. Since none of the respondents were from this area, their low acceptability rating is understandable. However, there are a few striking surprises. For instance, 'He BÍN got messed up', a pattern represented in the Philadelphia data, is ranked much further down the line than we would expect. And the BÍN-NP pattern represented in (a) He BÍN the leader, is ranked as third most acceptable, but has never been attested. Thus the ranking of the sentences cannot be simply taken at face-value either.

To continue the discussion at this level would be to miss the whole point of the methodology of 'implicational scaling' as it is usually applied to linguistic behavior or intuitions (cf. Bailey 1970, Bickerton 1973). Implicational scales are less valuable for the ranking of particular sentences (we could achieve more or less the same results just by noting percentages of positive responses) than for isolating the 'lects' (and their membership) which they may be taken to define. If we follow the solid line as it cuts upward and to the right across the table, separating mainly 'positive' ratings from mainly 'negative' ones, we find that no less than eleven different 'lects' are found to exist among these twenty-five different subjects. (For instance, B15 and B5 share lect 1, the most 'liberal' lect; and B1 is the only representative of lect 11, the most 'conservative' one). This by itself seems highly questionable. If we could find so many 'lects' among only twenty-five speakers, what would happen if we increase both the number of sentences, and the pool of subjects, to any significant extent? Would we truly be prepared to accept the proliferating number of 'lects' as having any solid basis in reality?

Furthermore, there is absolutely no evidence in the participant-observation data for these eleven different lects. Obviously, the method here is telling us far more than we can reasonably assume to be true. Its results are not supported by any of the independent evidence presently available. All this is the more striking because of the

TABLE 6. Implicational array for Black subjects' acceptability ratings to BÍN sentences in question 18, Q-SCOM-IV (Deviations circled, Scalability = 88.9%)

Subjects	__Ved	__Ving	__NP	've __had	__Pass.	__knew	got __Pass.	__have	__Adj.	__Modal	__done	done__	__bin	have __had
	They BÍN ended that war.	I BÍN knowing him.	He BÍN the leader.	I've BÍN had that car.	The chicken BÍN ate.	I BÍN knew your name.	He BÍN got messed up.	I BÍN have that.	She BÍN nice.	I BÍN could do that.	He BÍN done gone.	He done BÍN locked up.	He BÍN bin gone.	I have BÍN had that.
	l	b	a	m	d	k	e	j	c	i	g	h	f	n
B 15	+	+	+	+	+	+	+	+	+	+	⊖	+	+	+
B 5	+	+	+	+	+	+	+	+	⊖	+	+	+	+	+
B 19	+	+	+	+	+	+	+	+	+	+	+	+	+	−
B 8	⊖	+	+	+	+	+	+	+	+	+	+	+	+	−
B 21	+	+	+	+	⊖	+	+	⊖	+	⊖	+	+	+	−
B 12	+	+	+	+	+	+	+	+	+	+	+	+	−	−
B 3	+	+	+	+	+	+	+	+	+	⊖	+	+	−	−
B 24	+	+	+	+	⊖	+	+	+	+	+	+	+	−	−
B 4	+	+	+	+	⊖	⊖	+	+	+	+	+	+	−	−
B 22	+	⊖	+	⊖	+	+	+	+	+	+	+	+	−	−
B 25	+	+	+	+	+	+	+	+	+	+	+	−	−	−
B 6	⊖	+	+	⊖	+	⊖	+	+	+	+	+	−	⊕	−
B 11	+	+	+	+	+	+	+	+	+	+	−	−	−	−
B 16	+	+	+	+	+	+	+	+	+	+	−	−	−	−
B 23	+	+	+	+	+	+	+	+	+	+	−	−	−	−
B 13	+	+	+	+	+	+	+	+	+	+	−	−	−	⊕
B 14	+	+	+	+	+	+	⊖	+	+	+	−	⊕	⊕	−
B 7	+	+	⊖	+	+	+	+	+	−	−	−	⊕	−	−
B 17	+	+	+	+	+	+	−	−	−	−	⊕	−	−	−
B 18	+	+	+	+	+	+	−	−	−	−	⊕	−	−	−
B 2	+	+	+	+	+	−	⊕	−	−	−	⊕	−	−	−
B 20	+	+	+	+	−	−	−	−	⊕	−	⊕	⊕	−	−
B 9	+	+	+	+	−	−	−	−	⊕	−	−	⊕	−	⊕
B 10	+	+	−	−	⊕	⊕	−	⊕	−	−	⊕	−	−	−
B 1	+	−	⊕	⊕	−	−	−	−	−	−	−	−	⊕	−

high scalability (88.9%) which this table manages to achieve.[7] Scalability figures like these are often included in the literature, supposedly to represent the 'statistical reliability' of the implicational array. But the evidence suggests that in this case, and perhaps others, such figures may mean very little. Far more work remains to be done in developing reliable statistical and linguistic measures of the reliability and validity of implicational arrays.[8]

3. Conclusion

The weaknesses in the intuitive data revealed at various points in the preceding discussion of BÍN merit serious attention. For it is precisely the same method, eliciting judgments of the equivalence or acceptability of various sentences, and arranging the results in implicational arrays, which, as mentioned before, is most frequently used in the study of abstract syntactic 'squishes', and is winning devotees among those interested in social and regional variation. The results revealed in this paper, along with other limitations previously noted (Labov, Hindle, and Baltin [to appear]) should give us pause. They should also force us to consult, perhaps for the first time, a handful of research which has already explored in some detail various issues involved in the elicitation of linguistic judgments (Bolinger 1968, Gleitman 1967, Quirk and Svartvik 1966). I discovered these too late to affect the course of my own elicitations. But most work involving the study of linguistic intuitions seems equally uninformed by the insights and suggestions represented in this tiny literature.

We might indicate in closing one way in which the work on BÍN discussed in this paper seems to relate to some of this work on 'intuitive judgment methodology'. Bolinger (1968:39) had suggested:

> Perhaps we are not asking the right question when we inquire whether a given sentence or sentence-type is grammatical--we should ask instead whether it has a meaning, (and) determine what the meaning is . . .

The highly successful results of our 'intuitive data' on the meaning of BÍN, contrasted with the far more ambiguous and questionable results on the acceptability of BÍN sentences, suggests that Bolinger may well be right on this point. (Cf. also the successful investigations of the meaning of 'Cut-Eye' and 'Suck-Teeth'--Rickford and Rickford 1974). But this again is exactly the opposite of what is being done in the growing number of variation studies employing 'intuitive' data.

It is clear that we shall have to be far more critical about the use of elicited intuitive data than we are presently. Intuitions can be invaluable resources. But, contrary to past and present expectations, they are not necessarily or universally so. What questions we can ask, what answers we can accept, and what we can do with such answers, are things that remain very much to be worked out, both in general, and for specific cases. There is much work to be done here, and much work to be done also in developing other methods, like participant observation,[9] which can serve as independent 'checks and balances'.

The prospects for overcoming the limitations of tape-recorded data and carrying the 'New Wave' into syntax, seem promising but not easy. However, there is no reason to limit our goals and methods to those that require the least effort and/or imagination. This is no way to run a revolution.

NOTES

1. This paper is full of references to the work and influence of William Labov. It is not inordinately or accidentally so, however, for he has been in the forefront of innovations in (socio-) linguistic methodology for the past ten years. I welcome this opportunity to thank him for provoking me to a critical awareness of the importance of 'methodology' and for stimulating my own work both by example and suggestion.

2. As used in this paper, <u>been</u> is an abstract form in which stress is not distinguished. It is introduced primarily to facilitate discussion of the work of previous researchers. BÍN and <u>bĭn</u> are more concrete--the former referring to the stressed form, the latter to the unstressed.

3. The work of Loflin (1969) is omitted in the body of this paper. This might be surprising to some, since Loflin does discuss BÍN, and his paper is often cited as a high point in the formal analysis of Black English. But we must not be 'snowed' by apparent applications of the transformational-generative framework to the field of 'sociolinguistic variation'. Loflin 'accounts' for BÍN by 'postulating a formative E of emphatic stress which could be given in the rule rewriting VP and which could be converted into appropriate realizations, e.g. E+V+ed ⇒ BÍN+V+ed'. In recognizing the obligatory nature of stress, Loflin is justified. But his rule for generating the form is totally ad hoc and unmotivated, most seriously because the meaning of the form is not discussed at any point. Loflin's methodology, drawing on the intuitive reactions of an isolated fourteen-year-old informant, has also received widespread criticism.

4. The notation in parentheses following each sentence records in this order the following information: race, sex, age, and geographical community of the speaker.

5. We cannot explore here in any depth the fascinating issue of how 'remote' the initiation of a process must be to justify the use of BÍN. One thing is certain--no absolute distance in objective time from the point of orientation can be set. What BÍN expresses is the speaker's subjective feelings about the event and the 'time' involved. Thus an old woman stepping out of a dentist's office she had entered only a few minutes before said, 'He finish so quick. I ask him was he finished, and he say "I BÍN finished"'.

There are, however, 'consensus definitions' of how 'remote' the initiation of a process must be, relative to certain cases. And there is a rich arena for research in the use of BÍN contrary to such 'consensus' definitions for dramatization and self-aggrandizement, or 'styling'. Thus a young woman who was complimented on the fine dress she had bought only the day before replied nonchantly, 'Oh, I BÍN had this!' This 'styling' use of BÍN is open to challenge, however.

These considerations are not totally irrelevant to the methodological issues with which we are concerned in this paper. For instance, Gary M. of New York hesitated before giving the 'Remote Phase' interpretation to question 3 in Q-SCOM-4 (see (15) below), because, in his words 'I don't know if he bin know that guy. A lot of dudes go around running off at the mouth bout how they BÍN know this and they BÍN know that. Ain't nothing but a bunch of jive!'

6. This section may be taken to illustrate the general principle that questioning people on their own use of linguistic forms or varieties which have high social effect (either positive or negative) is likely to produce unreliable results unless checked against other evidence.

7. The scalability figure is arrived at by the formula:

$$100 - \left(\frac{\text{No. of deviations}}{\text{No. of cells}} \cdot \frac{100}{1}\right)$$

In this case: 100 - (39/350 · 100).

8. The whole question of what is to be retained, what modified in borrowing techniques like 'sociometric scaling' from social-survey methodology is quite problematic. For instance, 'factors' which are marked by a high number of 'deviations' are often omitted in psychological and sociological work. But so far no one has suggested in linguistic circles that sentences like 18g should be thrown out of consideration altogether. (I am thankful to Wolfgang Wölck for raising this issue.) The closest anyone has come to this is Labov (1971), see page 176 above.

9. At the risk of being accused of descending to the trivial or ephemeral, let me suggest here one or two methods for extending

the method of participant-observation to include information on the frequency of pre-coded variables which occur more often than BÍN. The art is to develop idiosyncracies like doodling or breaking matches in half. With each occurrence of a variant (for example que vs. ∅) one makes the appropriate 'doodle' on a handy napkin or whatever, or puts the broken half of a matchstick in the appropriate pile. So long as one remembers to collect the napkins, or put the matchstick pieces into different pockets, these 'extensions' can prove extremely informative and reliable. Needless to say, however, they put a tremendous strain on the 'participant-observer' of natural conversation, and require some practice.

REFERENCES

Bailey, B. L. 1966. Jamaican Creole syntax. London, Cambridge University Press.

Bailey, C.-J. N. 1970. Using data variation to confirm, rather than undermine, the existence of abstract syntactic structures. Working Papers in Linguistics 2.8:77-86. Honolulu, University of Hawaii.

_____ and R. W. Shuy, eds. 1973. New ways of analyzing variation in English. Washington, D.C., Georgetown University Press.

Baltin, Mark. 1973. A reanalysis of quantifier-negative dialects. Mimeo. University of Pennsylvania.

Bickerton, Derek. 1972. The structure of polylectal grammars. In: GURT 1972. 17-42.

_____. 1973. On the nature of a creole continuum. Lg. 49:640-669.

_____. 1974. Bin in the Atlantic Creoles. In: Journal of African Languages, Special Issue devoted to the English Pidgins and Creoles. Edited by I. Hancock.

Bolinger, D. 1968. Judgments of grammaticality. Lingua 21:34-40.

Butters, R. 1973. Acceptability judgments for double modals in Southern English. In: Bailey and Shuy (1973). 276-286.

Carden, G. 1971. A note on conflicting idiolects. Linguistic Inquiry 1.3.

Dillard, J. L. 1972. Black English--Its history and usage in the United States. New York, Random House.

Elliot D., S. Legum, and S. Thompson. 1969. Syntactic variation as linguistic data. In: Papers from the Fifth Regional Meeting, Chicago Linguistic Society. Edited by Binnick, et al. Chicago, University of Chicago. 52-59.

Fasold, R. W. and W. Wolfram. 1970. Some linguistic features of Negro dialect. In: Teaching Standard English in the inner city. Edited by R. W. Fasold and R. W. Shuy. Washington, D.C., Center for Applied Linguistics. 41-86.

Fickett, Joan G. 1970. Aspects of morphemics, syntax, and semology of an inner-city dialect. West Rush, New York, Meadowbrook Publications.

Gleitman, Lila R. 1967. An experiment concerning the use and perception of compound nominals by English speakers. Unpublished Ph. D. dissertation, University of Pennsylvania.

Jones, E. D. 1968. Some tense, mode, and aspect markers in Krio. African Language Review 7:86-89.

Labov, William. 1966. The social stratification of English in New York City. Washington, D. C., Center for Applied Linguistics.

_____. 1969. Contraction, deletion, and inherent variability of the English copula. Lg. 45.4:715-762.

_____. 1970. The study of language in its social context. Studium Generale 23:30-87.

_____. 1971. Linguistic methodology. In: A survey of linguistic science. Edited by W. O. Dingwall. College Park, University of Maryland. 412-497.

_____. 1972a. Where do grammars stop? In: GURT 1972. 43-88.

_____. 1972b. Some principles of linguistic methodology. Language and Society 1:97-120.

_____, D. Hindle, and M. Baltin. [To appear] For an end to the uncontrolled use of intuition in linguistic analysis.

Loflin, M. 1969. On the structure of the verb in a dialect of American Negro English. Linguistics 14-28.

Quirk, R. and J. Svartvik. 1966. Investigating linguistic acceptability. The Hague, Mouton and Co.

Rickford, John and Angela Rickford. 1974. Cut-eye and suck-teeth. In: Journal of African Languages. Special issue devoted to the English pidgins and creoles. Edited by I. Hancock.

Sag, Ivan. 1973. On the state of progress on progressives and statives. In: Bailey and Shuy (1973). 83-95.

Sankoff, Gillian. 1973. Above and beyond phonology in variable rules. In: Bailey and Shuy (1973). 44-61.

Stewart, William A. 1965. Urban Negro speech: Sociolinguistic factors affecting English teaching. In: Social dialects and language learning. Edited by Roger W. Shuy. Champaign, Illinois, The National Council of Teachers of English. 10-18.

POLYLECTAL COMPREHENSION AND THE POLYLECTAL GRAMMAR

ROBERT BERDAN

SWRL Educational Research and Development

In theory, generative grammar makes no claims to being either a grammar of production or a grammar of comprehension. It is conceived of as neutral with respect to speaker or hearer. In practice, argumentation tends to be analogized to the speaker and to production. Data on comprehension have played a minimal role in our understanding of grammar. Thus it is not surprising to find, even among linguists, inferences based on comprehension that are highly problematic.

In this paper two claims from comprehension are discussed. The first is a claim made by certain educationalists and psychologists, notably Hall and Turner (1974). They reason that because children from ethnic minorities can hear a Standard English sentence, translate it, and repeat back the appropriate dialectal equivalent, educational problems of the children cannot be accounted for by language differences. Obviously, if the children can repeat the semantic equivalent, they comprehend the language of instruction. The second claim is most explicitly articulated by Bailey (1973:17, 23-24). He argues that speakers exposed to more than one lect have polylectal comprehension, and therefore necessarily polylectal grammars.

It will be convenient for the present to define comprehension rather casually as the hearer's act of associating a semantic structure with a phonetic string. A communication is successful if the semantic structure of the hearer is equivalent to that of the speaker. If it is not, it can be said that they have miscommunicated, or that the hearer has miscomprehended the speaker.

In the real world, comprehension is a complex event. In comprehending statements, persons draw not just on their linguistic knowledge but on all of their knowledge of the real world. Further, as linguists know, but seem at times to forget, linguistic knowledge is highly complex, including semantic relations, syntactic rules, phonological rules, and a knowledge of possible lexical items. The combination of linguistic knowledge and real world knowledge frequently introduces redundancy into the message of any particular sentence. Comprehending a sentence does not necessarily imply comprehending all of the intricacies of its syntax. To comprehend a particular sentence it may be sufficient, in real world contexts, to understand the meaning of the lexical items without comprehending any of the implicit rules of syntax. In some limited contexts, a message is so culturally constrained that it is not necessary to have any linguistic understanding of the utterance to make an appropriate response.

Communication between persons necessarily involves a discontinuity. The formal attributes of the grammar of the speaker are not accessible to the hearer. The hearer knows only what can be inferred from the sentences he hears. The speaker and the hearer may or may not share identical grammars and they have no direct way of determining this. At best they can attempt to assess whether or not they have comprehended each other.

Consider for the moment the minimal case of one speaker, one hearer, and the utterance of one sentence. The speaker may or may not share the grammar of the hearer. The hearer may or may not comprehend the speaker. There are thus four logically possible communication situations, as shown in the 2 x 2 table in Figure 1. While all the combinations are logically possible, it remains to be shown that they are linguistically plausible.

FIGURE 1. Possible relations between comprehension and grammars.

		Grammars of speaker and hearer	
		Same	Different
Comprehension	Yes	Situation 1	Situation 2
	No	Situation 4	Situation 3

The first situation is perhaps what would be considered the unmarked case; the grammars of the speaker and the hearer, or at least the relevant portions, are identical, and comprehension takes place. The second situation may be somewhat less obvious, but would be predicted if there exist weakly equivalent grammars, i.e. grammars generating the same set of strings but assigning them different derivational histories. Such grammars could differ without impeding comprehension.

One example is *got* as a verb of possession. For many speakers *got* is understood as possessive only with auxiliary *have*, as in (1a, b):

(1a) My friend ~~ha~~s got a new car.
(1b) My friends ~~ha~~ve got a new car.

Many of the speakers who produce the sentences of (1) allow for deletion of contracted *have* (2b), but not of contracted *has* (2a) (McDavid 1967:10):

(2a) *My friend ~~has~~ got a new car.
(2b) My friends ~~have~~ got a new car.

The use of possessive *got* for many other speakers, particularly black Americans, is quite different. For these speakers, it is a regular main verb (Berdan 1973) which negates with *do* (3) and questions with *do* (4).

(3) My friends *don't got* a new car.
(4) *Do* my friends *got* a new car?

For some of these speakers who use agreement markers in the present tense, *got* can be inflected:

(5) My friend *gots* a new car.

The speaker who utters (2b), using a grammar where *have*-deletion operates, will be comprehended perfectly by a hearer whose grammar only has *got* as a regular main verb, giving (6):[1]

(6) My friends ~~do~~ got a new car.

This would then be a case where the grammars are different, but comprehension exists.

The situation in cross-dialect communication is not always as fortuitous as the one just described. Differences in grammars may also result in differences in comprehension, Situation 3. Sentence (6) is phonetically indistinguishable from (2b). It is also indistinguishable from (7):

(7) My friend ~~ha~~s got a new car. (=1a)

In this environment, as in most, contracted has is not perceptibly different from the plural morpheme (Palmer 1968:32). The sentence is ambiguous across dialects. Thus (7) uttered by a have-got speaker may be understood by a main-verb got hearer to be an utterance of (6). In this case miscomprehension occurs. The nature of the miscomprehension is made apparent by the tag questions in (8), which provide disambiguation.

(8a) My friend ~~ha~~s got a new car, {hasn't / doesn't} he?

(8b) My friends ~~do~~ got a new car, don't they?

The nature of the miscommunication would be, in most cases, trivial, and the parties may never become aware of its existence. At some subsequent point, however, it may become apparent that a miscommunication has occurred. For example, the hearer, comprehending plural (6) rather than the speaker's singular (7), might ask a question like (9a). The response from the speaker of (7) is likely to be a very confused (9b):

(9a) Which one gets it on Saturday nights?

(9b) Which one what?

As far as the speaker is concerned, no plural exists in the conversation, and (9a) has no possible referent. By this point the source of the miscommunication could be totally obscured.

The fourth possible situation in Figure 1 seems to be not at all infrequent in actual communication: speaker and hearer share the same grammar, but they fail to comprehend each other. There is another sentence that is phonetically indistinguishable from (2b), (6), and (7). This is sentence (10) where got is the regular past tense of get, meaning obtained.

(10) My friends got a new car (didn't they)

The grammar of the speaker of (7) also generates (10); thus both readings are possible within a single lect. Potential for this type of situation occurs whenever a single string has more than one possible derivational history associated with it within a single grammar.

Given the linguistic possibility of all four situations, it is apparent that from many cases of comprehension, or lack of it, there can be no direct arguments for similarity or difference of grammars.

In all the examples discussed thus far, it has been assumed that comprehension is necessarily consistent with the syntactic cues of a surface string. There may be several different ways of comprehending a sentence, but the possible semantic structures are those predicted by the syntactic and lexical form of the sentence. However, in the actual process of comprehending, the hearer must integrate many cues besides those provided by the syntax. In particular, the semantic cues of one portion of a sentence may override syntactic cues in another portion, thus influencing comprehension. This point can be illustrated with experimental data.

It is possible to determine how a hearer comprehends a particular sentence by observing the tag question he constructs for it. At least it is possible to determine what the hearer comprehends to be the number, person, and gender of the subject, and what he comprehends to be the tense and aspect of the verb. The readings of the potentially ambiguous got sentences are uniquely disambiguated by their tag questions, as (8a, b) and (10). The pronominalized equivalent of the sentential subject is explicitly marked for number; if third singular, it is also marked for gender. Further, the carrier of tense and aspect marking is much more immune from phonological deletions in the tag than it is in the full sentence. [2]

The following data derive from a study in which four classes of undergraduates at California State University, Long Beach, listened to 60 potentially ambiguous sentences and constructed tag questions for them. [3] Two classes were of students enrolled in the Educational Opportunities Program. All of these students identified themselves as black. Two other English composition classes were largely Anglo and only students who identified themselves as Anglo are included here. The sentences were sequenced in two random orders and read by the author. Each order was heard by one class of blacks and one class of Anglos. Students made their responses by checking one of twelve possible verb alternatives and one of six possible pronouns for each item.

Like contracted has, contracted is is often phonetically indistinguishable from the plural morpheme. Thus the sequence [frɛnz] in (11a) with contracted is is indistinguishable from the plural [frɛnz] in (11b).

(11a) Her best friend ~~i~~s playing jump rope.
(11b) Her best friends are playing jump rope.

There is, of course, no sentential ambiguity because of the plural copula are in (11b). But not everybody says (11b). There are many speakers who use instead the semantically equivalent (12), with deleted copula.

(12) Her best friends ~~are~~ playing jump rope.

Sentence (12) with plural subject is phonetically identical to (11a). Tag questions again function to disambiguate in (13a, b):

(13a) Her best friend ~~i~~s playing jump rope, isn't she.
(13b) Her best friends ~~are~~ playing jump rope, aren't they.

On hearing sentence (11a) or (12), speakers of a dialect that does not allow copula deletion could understand them both only as (13a). Speakers of a dialect that optionally deletes the copula would find the sentence ambiguous, with either (13a) or (13b) as possible interpretations.

For the sentence, *Her best [frɛnz] playing jump rope,* all 25 of the Anglo students provided *isn't she* or *isn't he* as a tag, showing that they understood the sentence as (11a). So did all but two of the 26 black students. Such a difference is not significant. This suggests either that the copula-deleting dialect is not well represented in the sample, or that this item is simply skewed toward a singular reading. It appears to be possible to change semantic and contextual cues in an ambiguous sentence to make one reading more plausible than another without making either reading ungrammatical. For example, superlatives like *best* seem to facilitate a singular reading, but still allow plurals, as in (14).

(14) They are my best friends.

Also, the singular possessive pronoun *her* would seem to facilitate a singular reading, while a plural pronoun like *their* would increase the possibility of a plural reading.

In order to explore the effects of contextual cues, the four sentences of (15) were included among the test items.

(15a) Her best friend's playing jump rope.
(15b) Her friend's playing jump rope.
(15c) Their best friend's playing jump rope.
(15d) Their friend's playing jump rope.

It was predicted that order of magnitude of influencing a singular reading would be in the sequence of (15a) to (15d). The possessive pronoun with overt number would exert a stronger influence than the superlative adjective, with its weak implication of singularity.

Table 1 gives the percent of singular responses for each sentence in each classroom. The prediction of order of effect was confirmed in all four classrooms. In each class the singular possessive pronoun facilitated a singular understanding of the sentence. So to a lesser extent did the superlative adjective.

TABLE 1. Percent of singular interpretations of four auxiliary be sentences.

	Anglo 1 N=12	Anglo 2 N=13	Black 1 N=12	Black 2 N=14
(a) Her best friend[z]	100	100	100	85
(b) Her friend[z]	100	92	83	64
(c) Their best friend[z]	58	77	36	21
(d) Their friend[z]	33	54	25	7

It had been predicted that this would be found in the black classes, but not in the Anglo classes. The people who were expected to be susceptible to this kind of contextual conditioning were only those people for whom the sentences would be ambiguous: persons who could delete auxiliary is and are. What was not expected was the large number of plural readings, particularly for sentence (d), from a population not known to allow this deletion.

It appears that the relationship between comprehension and grammar is less direct than might have been anticipated. For some informants, contextual cues, such as the plurality of a possessive pronoun, are sufficient to override syntactic cues such as the absence of a plural copula. Compounding of contextual cues increases the effect. The magnitude of the conditioning effect is smaller in the Anglo classrooms than in the black classrooms. It appears that the influence of contextual cues is stronger when they do not conflict with syntactic cues than when they do conflict.

The pattern found for groups obtains for individuals as well. The hierarchy of contextual weighting predicts that individuals will use one of the five patterns shown in the columns of Figure 2. Some individuals will understand all of the sentences as singular, some will understand all as plural, and the rest will use one of the three other patterns out of the remaining fourteen logically possible patterns.

FIGURE 2. Patterns of interpretations of four auxiliary be sentences.

Sentence	Pattern 1	2	3	4	5
(a) Her best friend[z]	Sing.	Sing.	Sing.	Sing.	Plural
(b) Her friend[z]	Sing.	Sing.	Sing.	Plural	Plural
(c) Their best friend[z]	Sing.	Sing.	Plural	Plural	Plural
(d) Their friend[z]	Sing.	Plural	Plural	Plural	Plural

Most of the individuals do conform to these predictions; 83 percent of the blacks and 92 percent of the Anglos evidenced one of the five patterns in Figure 2. The percentage of the population in each ethnic group using each of the five patterns is shown in Figure 3. Other individuals are randomly distributed across the nonpredicted patterns.

FIGURE 3. Percent of individuals of each ethnicity showing each pattern.

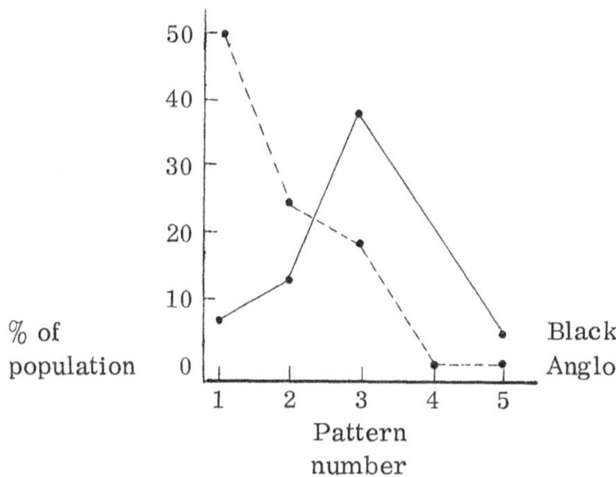

This patterning of contextual influence is not an isolated phenomenon in these data. The test included four more sentences.

(16a) His favorite horse[ɨz] got long legs.
(16b) His horse[ɨz] got long legs.
(16c) Their favorite horse[ɨz] got long legs.
(16d) Their horse[ɨz] got long legs.

Here the ambiguity rests on the possibility of using got as a possessive verb without auxiliary has or have. For some speakers got is a regular main verb that requires no have auxiliary. Other speakers who use have got can delete have, apparently by phonological processes. Speakers who, for one reason or another, can use got without auxiliary can interpret the [Z] morpheme as a syllabic plural marker on horse; other speakers who require an auxiliary with possessive got will interpret the [z] morpheme as the contracted form of has. The two interpretations result in the tags (17a) and (17b), respectively.

(17a) His favorite horse[ɨz] got long legs, don't they?
(17b) His favorite horse[ɨz] got long legs, hasn't/doesn't he?

As with the deleted copula case, the perception of singularity for the four sentences conformed to the predicted hierarchy in all four classrooms: in each group, more individuals understood (16a) as singular, than did (16b), than did (16c), than (16d). The effect of the singular or plural possessive pronoun is the same as was previously observed; the adjective favorite, though not morphologically a superlative, appears to have an effect comparable to that of best.

Again, most individuals used one of the patterns comparable to those in Figure 1: 91 percent of the black group and 88 percent of the Anglo group did so. Distribution of these individuals across the predicted patterns is shown for each ethnic group in Figure 4. Again, the remaining individuals are randomly distributed across the nonpredicted patterns.

FIGURE 4. Percent of individuals of each ethnicity showing each pattern.

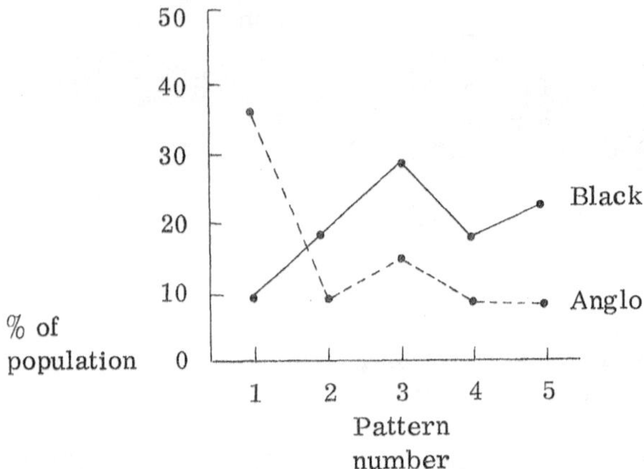

The populations are clearly distinct in one respect. Most of the Anglos show no sensitivity to these conditioning factors, but most of the blacks do. Almost half of the Anglos understood all of the sentences to be singular, but only about 8% of the black listeners did. For the be sentences that difference was greater than for the have sentences. Given that many Anglos delete have in production, but few delete are and is (cf. Wolfram 1974), this is not surprising.

There are many other sources of potential ambiguities and miscomprehensions across dialects. For example, there is a set of verbs in English that has the same form in the present tense and in the past tense, e.g. cut, hit, put. However, a sentence like (18a) is unambiguously past tense for many speakers; if it were present tense they would use an agreement morpheme as in (18b).

(18a) Everyday the teacher put up new pictures.
(18b) Everyday the teacher puts up new pictures.

Many speakers in the black community, however, do not require the use of that agreement morpheme in the present tense. For them (18a) is ambiguous, and can be disambiguated as either (19a) or (19b).

(19a) Everyday the teacher put up a new picture, didn't she.
(19b) Everyday the teacher put up a new picture, {doesn't / don't} she.

The tag question task included five sentences of this type. Each of the sentences was weighted toward present tense with devices such as adverbial every day. Figure 5 shows the distribution of past tense comprehensions in each of the ethnic groups. About half of the black students understood none of the five sentences as past tense. On the other hand, almost half of the Anglo students understood all five sentences to be past tense. Among the individual sentences there were no notable differences in the proportions of past tense tags.

FIGURE 5. Percent of individuals of each ethnicity by number of past tense responses for unmarked verbs.

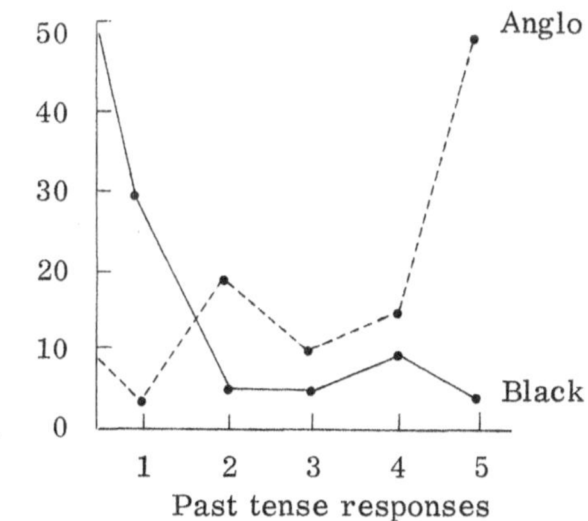

A similar situation can be created when the past tense marker is masked by assimilation with a following dental. Speakers who do not require the agreement morpheme could thus use either (20a) or (20b); speakers who do require the agreement morpheme would only use (20a).

(20a) My sister always walked to school, didn't she.
(20b) My sister always walk to school, {don't / doesn't} she.

The percent of each ethnic group giving 0 to 5 past tense responses for the five masked past tense items is shown in Figure 6. The differentiation across ethnic groups is comparable to that shown in Figure 5.

FIGURE 6. Percent of individuals of each ethnicity by number of past tense responses in masking environments.

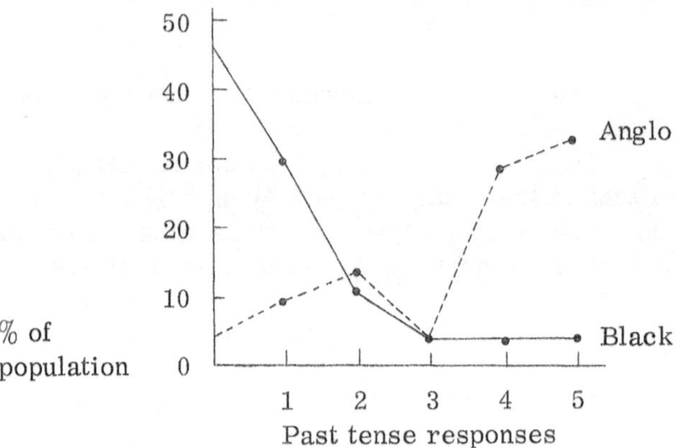

This could be expected, given that the grammatical elements of the ambiguity are the same: lack of overt past tense markers and present agreement markers. More surprising is the stability of individual scores. If a person understood all of the unmarked verbs as past, he tended to understand all or most of the masked past tense constructions as past tense. However, if he understood some of the unmarked pasts as present, he understood about the same number of masked pasts as present. For over half of the individuals, the number of past tense responses was exactly the same on the two sets of sentences. For all but four of the rest, there was a difference of only one in the number of past tense responses on the two sets.

The inferences being made here from tag question indications of how sentences are comprehended are not hard to support. Extraneous responses to these sentences were minimal, despite the large number of possible tags available to students. In other words, virtually all responses are amenable to linguistic explanation. Where the ambiguity involved singular and plural differences, there are attested grammars with and without copula deletion. Where the ambiguity involved tense, it could be predicted from the known existence of grammars that do and do not employ an agreement morpheme.

More interesting, however, is the support of inferences between the comprehension of ambiguous sentences and the grammars for the individuals involved. As has been shown, there is no absolute relationship in all cases between comprehension and grammars. However, in the past tense sentences there is very strong evidence of a direct relationship. Formation of the tag question is itself an act of language production. Of particular interest here is the possibility that present tense singular tags may or may not be marked for agreement. Thus in (19b) and (20b) there is the possibility of either don't she or doesn't she as a tag. Summing across all 60 test items, three-fourths of the black students and one-fourth of the Anglo students gave at least one present tense singular tag without agreement. Each of these students who constructed tags without agreement also gave tags that indicate a comprehension of present tense without agreement. They are not randomly distributed with respect to present tense comprehensions; they are exclusively in the half of the population that perceived most of the sentences as present tense: the left-most columns of Figures 5 and 6. There seems to be a direct relationship in this instance between production and comprehension.

I return now to the two claims mentioned initially. The pedagogical claim is summarized by Hall and Turner (1974). They introduce their review of research by asking rhetorically, 'Does the black child have a difficult time comprehending the SE speaking teacher or vice versa?' (1974:70). They conclude that there is no language difference sufficient to cause comprehension problems:

> In general, no acceptable, replicated research has found that the dialect spoken by black children presents them with unique problems in comprehending SE. If there are problems, they occur in relatively rare cases (e.g., possessive sentences). What really seems to occur is that speakers of NNE automatically translate the SE into their dialect. It is this translation which is given in imitation studies (1974:79).

Linguists, in general, do not endorse this conclusion by psychologists and educationalists that language differences are insufficient to cause educational problems. Linguists do, however, seem tacitly to endorse a fundamental premise of the argument: imitation of this type implies comprehension. Butters, for example, in discussing material from the Natalicio and Williams (1971) study of sentence repetition, mentions the situation in which a child hears (21a) and responds with (21b):

(21a) Mother helps Gloria.
(21b) Mother help Gloria.

Butters concludes that 'obviously the respondent understands the utterance, even though he can repeat it exactly only with difficulty (if at all)' (1972:31).

Given the possible relationships between utterances and comprehension, nothing is obvious in this instance. A child who could respond to (21a) with (21b) could use the latter equally well as a repetition of (22).

(22) Mother helped Gloria.

One could argue equally well that there has been a compounding of miscomprehension: the child misunderstood the tense of the original sentence, and the linguist misunderstood the intent of the child. Such sentence repetition tasks simply have very little to say about comprehension.

Hall and Turner do, in fact, recognize this. In another study (Hall, Turner, and Russell 1973) they devised a modification of the Osser, Wang, and Zaid (1969) task to test imitation and comprehension independently. The child is given a sentence to imitate and then chooses from among a set of pictures the one which best exemplifies the sentence. The sentences are constructed to have potential ambiguities, with three pictures matching possible readings of each sentence. They used four sentences to test imitation and comprehension of past tense (23a-d).

(23a) The man chopped the oak logs.
(23b) The boy jumped over the puddle.
(23c) The woman washed the dirty clothes.
(23d) The boy kicked the big ball.

Consider first the imitation task. All four of the verbs end in nondental consonants and the past tense morpheme is thus represented by a single consonant. In three of the four test sentences, the past tense morpheme is followed by the definite article. There is a phonological process of assimilation operating across this word boundary, making perception of the past tense marker phonetically impossible in most cases. This is true particularly for speakers of a dialect in which the initial phoneme of the article may be a stop, affricate, or fricative ([dIs, dðIs, ðIs] respectively). In three of the sentences, the child would not be able to hear the past tense marker; the experimenter could not hear its repetition.

As would be expected, the mean number of sentence imitations containing past tense markers is about 1.0 (range 1.0–1.8) for the lower-class black and lower-class white children. It is somewhat more surprising that for the suburban, middle-class white fourth graders, the average number of past tense responses was 2.7, in spite of the fact that each child has only one sentence in which the presence of the past tense morpheme can be ascertained reliably. It would seem that there is, in fact, an act of comprehension involved in sentence repetition tasks. That act is the experimenter's comprehension of the child's response. In this instance comprehension appears to be based on sociological cues as much as or more than it is based on linguistic cues.

What is being comprehended by the child in the three sentences is not presence of the past tense marker, but the absence of any present tense agreement marker. The published pictures are somewhat obscure. Not surprisingly, mean rates of comprehension for the groups of children on the four sentences ranged from 0.8 to 1.4, suggesting that many of the children may be performing randomly.

The task includes another set of sentences which are supposed to measure comprehension of the agreement morpheme (24a–d).

(24a) The sheep eats all the hay.
(24b) The girl slides down the hill.
(24c) The deer runs across the road.
(24d) The boy climbs up the ladder.

Two of the sentences (24b, d) are described as double cue sentences, being marked both by the absence of a plural marker and by the presence of the agreement morpheme on the verb. The other sentences with *sheep* and *deer* are marked only on the verb. But that is a strictly ethnocentric view of language. For many children, particularly black children, the plural of *sheep* is *sheeps,* and the plural of *deer* is *deers.* For such children there should be no difference among the four sentences.

That is exactly what the study found. Means for the Anglo children are about twice as high on the *boy* and *girl* sentences as on the *sheep* and *deer* sentences; for the black children the difference is negligible. Apparently, the children are responding to perceived plural cues, or their absence, on the nouns, rather than to verb markers. Not surprisingly, no significant differences were found among the groups of children in their comprehension of these sentences. There is no reason to believe that deletion of plural markers plays a major factor in distinguishing among ethnic dialects.

A third set of sentences in Hall et al. (1973) tests the imitation and comprehension of the possessive marker (25a-d):

(25a) The girl wears the clown's hat.
(25b) The boy carries the cowboy's boots.
(25c) The girl paints the dog's house.
(25d) The boy takes the baby's doll.

The results are exactly what can be predicted from knowledge of the dialects involved. In imitation, black children repeat the possessive marker less often than do the white children, but in comprehension no significant differences are observed among groups. It appears that the possessive marker is understood, but is deleted in production, black children giving responses like (26):

(26) The girl wears the clown~~'s~~ hat.

Unfortunately, the task tests the wrong question. The interesting question is, what does the Anglo experimenter comprehend when he hears the black child utter (26)? Does he comprehend the child's intended possessive construction, or does he comprehend only the noun phrase construction that his own grammar allows? The potential for ambiguity is only in the sentences with no overt possessive marker, not in the sentences with the marker.

The fourth set of sentences used in this task contain what are termed 'critical phrase markers'. These contain subordinating conjunctions in constructions that have never been shown to be dialectally differentiated (27a-d):

(27a) Mother puts the cake where he can reach.
(27b) Father throws it so they can catch.
(27c) The boy sees that the girl runs.
(27d) The girl swings before the boy slides.

Again, not surprisingly, no significant differences are noted either in imitation or comprehension among ethnic groups.

From another study, beset with comparable linguistic problems, Hall and Turner (1971:1749) conclude that

> if the superior comprehension performance of the [white lower class] sample reflected a true difference in that group's ability to comprehend the sentences, it was probably due to

a difference between the two groups in reasoning ability rather than in linguistic competence.

Comprehension is very difficult to test, and testing comprehension of particular linguistic structures is even more difficult. Testing comprehension across dialects requires extraordinary caution to ensure that all relevant aspects of the grammars involved are being considered. Demonstration of comprehension problems across dialects is not a socially negative finding. Rather it is a demonstration of the linguistic basis for a situation that is known tacitly to exist. The fact that black students responded differently than Anglo students did on the tag question task does not demonstrate a failure to comprehend. The black students did comprehend these ambiguous sentences, but not in the same way that Anglo students did. The cross-dialect communication problem is in many cases not failure of comprehension, as seen by the parties to the communication. The problem is rather that the expectations based on those asymmetrical comprehensions are not shared by both parties to the communication.

The second claim mentioned initially relates to the concept of the polylectal grammar. Under the heading 'Justification of polylectal grammars', Bailey makes the following statement:

> Since it is known that women are about a generation ahead of men in some changes, the language of one's mother will be different from that of one's father, even if their age and class traits are similar. Each of the interlocutors encountered by a child has a multitude of styles which he or she must competently deal with (1973:24).

The form of the argument is that the child comprehends different lects. Therefore, receptively at least, he must have a polylectal grammar. Setting aside any objections to the rather dubious universal generalization that women lead men by a generation in language change, is there any evidence for the argument, and what characteristics would the evidence have to possess?

Suppose, for whatever reason, mother and father employ different lects, different grammars. From that fact, and the observation that the child makes the socially appropriate responses, what can be inferred about the child's receptive grammar is very little indeed. It may be Situation 1 (Figure 1) with identical grammars; it may be Situation 2, with unlike grammars but comprehension. In most instances it will be difficult to determine if the child's comprehension results from particular syntactic cues, or from constraints placed on the possible meanings by real world contexts. Even if the child does comprehend both sets of syntactic cues, it does not follow that this must represent polylectal comprehension. The production may involve different grammars for mother and father, but the child's comprehension may well be a variable process integrated into one grammar. In order to demonstrate the need for a polylectal grammar from comprehension data it is necessary not only to show that the different sets of linguistic cues are in fact part of comprehension, but also that they are comprehended to be parts of different linguistic systems. In many cases that will be difficult to do.

For example, Politzer and Hoover (1972) had children listen to sentences in what they termed 'standard Black English' and 'nonstandard Black English'. The children were asked to identify the sentences as 'school talk' or 'dialect'. From their results it can be determined that most second grade children and many fourth grade children reliably make distinctions. Even then it is not clear what cues the children use to make distinctions, or that they comprehend the semantic import of those cues.

The polylectal grammar undoubtedly exists. It can be observed that there are persons who switch in their production. That the polylectal grammar exists in comprehension for persons who do not also have it in production, however, is based on unsubstantiated inferences, not on experimental data. The complexity of comprehension is such that those inferences are not well supported by available data. Grammars of polylectal comprehension may well exist. However, documented cases of comprehension across lects fail to provide sufficient evidence for the polylectal grammar.

Responses to the tag question task show that comprehension is conditioned, though not absolutely determined, by grammar. It is also conditioned by contextual cues that may or may not produce comprehension consistent with the syntactic cues of the sentence. Showing that a black child comprehends a certain Standard English sentence does not show that he comprehends all of Standard English. To the contrary, there appear to be systematic differences in grammars that lead to major differences in comprehension for certain kinds of sentences.

NOTES

1. For the present argument it is irrelevant whether <u>do</u> is present in underlying structures and deleted or is inserted by a <u>do</u>-Support Rule.

2. Depending on how one wishes to analyze tags (see, for example, Stockwell et al. 1973:620ff.), this may be related to the nonreduction of stress before deletion sites (Baker 1971).

3. Arrangements for the testing were made with the kind assistance of Professors Steven Ross and Edward Twum-Akwaboah.

REFERENCES

Bailey, C.-J. N. 1973. Variation and linguistic theory. Washington, D.C., Center for Applied Linguistics.

Baker, C. L. 1971. Stress level and auxiliary behavior in English. Linguistic Inquiry, 2(2).167-181.

Berdan, R. 1973. Have/got in the speech of Anglo and Black children. Professional Paper No. 22. Los Alamitos, Calif. SWRL Educational Research and Development.

Butters, R. R. 1972. Competence, performance, and variable rules. Language Sciences, No. 20, 29-32.

Hall, V. C. and R. R. Turner. 1971. Comparison of imitation and comprehension scores between two lower-class groups and the effects of two warm-up conditions on imitations of the same groups. Child Development, Vol. 42, 1735-1750.

Hall, V. C. and R. R. Turner. 1974. The validity of the 'different language explanation' for poor scholastic performance by black students. Review of Educational Research, 4.69-81.

Hall, V. C., R. R. Turner, and W. Russell. 1973. Ability of children from four subcultures and two grade levels to imitate and comprehend crucial aspects of Standard English: A test of the different language explanation. Journal of Educational Psychology, 64.147-158.

McDavid, R. I. 1967. A checklist of significant features for discriminating social dialects. In: Dimensions of dialect. Edited by E. Evertts. Champaign, Ill., NCTE. 7-10.

Natalicio, D. and F. Williams. 1971. Repetition as an oral language assessment technique. Austin, Center for Communications Research, School of Communications, University of Texas.

Osser, H., M. D. Wang, and F. Zaid. 1969. The young child's ability to imitate and comprehend speech: A comparison of two subcultural groups. Child Development, Vol. 4, 1063-1075.

Palmer, F. R. 1968. A linguistic study of the English verb. Coral Gables, Fla., University of Miami Press.

Politzer, R. L. and M. R. Hoover. 1972. The development of awareness of the black standard/nonstandard dialect contrast among primary school children: A pilot study. R&D Memorandum No. 83. Stanford Center for Research and Development in Teaching.

Stockwell, R. P., P. Schachter, and B. H. Partee. 1973. The major syntactic structures of English. New York, Holt, Rinehart and Winston.

Wolfram, W. 1974. The relationship of white Southern speech to Vernacular Black English. Lg. 50.498-527.

VARIATIONS ON RELATIVE CLAUSES IN ITALIAN

DONNA JO NAPOLI

Georgetown University

1.0. Introduction. All speakers of Italian produce at least two types of relative clauses, those introduced by a relative pronoun and those introduced by che 'that' with no pronoun coreferential with the head NP (call it Pro_{rel}) present. Many speakers also produce relatives introduced by che with Pro_{rel} present. For these speakers there is a deletion rule (call it DEL) which deletes Pro_{rel} in certain syntactic configurations.[1] DEL cannot apply, optionally applies, or must apply, depending on two factors which are shown to form a squish on the application of DEL.

I propose that for those speakers who never have Pro_{rel} present in the surface, DEL is an obligatory rule. Thus all relatives introduced by che are produced in the same way by all speakers. The fact that some speakers allow che relatives with Pro_{rel} and others do not is due to the sensitivity to syntactic structure of DEL for the first set of speakers but the obligatoriness of DEL (regardless of the structural configuration) for the second set of speakers.

2.0. The data. In the examples in this section we find relatives introduced by che with and without Pro_{rel}. We find that the two factors affecting the appearance of Pro_{rel} in the surface are the structure in which the relative clause appears[2] and the role Pro_{rel} plays in the relative clause. The data presented here are not new. Keenan (1972) has found similar data for many languages.

Four distinctive roles for Pro_{rel} are examined: subject, accusative object, nonaccusative cliticizable object,[3] and noncliticizable object.[4] We see these roles exemplified here in five different structures.[5]

2.1. S_1. The lowest S dominating Pro_{rel} is S_1:

(1)

NP

NP_{head} S_1

Pro_{rel}

(2a) Subject:
Ecco il ragazzo che (*lui) studia legge.
'Here's the boy that (*he) studies law.'

(2b) Accusative object:
Ecco il ragazzo che Maria (*lo) conosce.
'Here's the boy that Mary knows (*him).'

(2c) Nonaccusative cliticizable object:
Ecco il ragazzo che gli parlavo.
'Here's the boy that I was talking to him.'

(2d) Noncliticizable object:
*Ecco il ragazzo che litigavo con (lui).
'Here's the boy that I was arguing with (him).'

In (2c) gli is optional for some speakers.

2.2. S_2. Pro_{rel} appears in an S embedded in S_1:

(3)

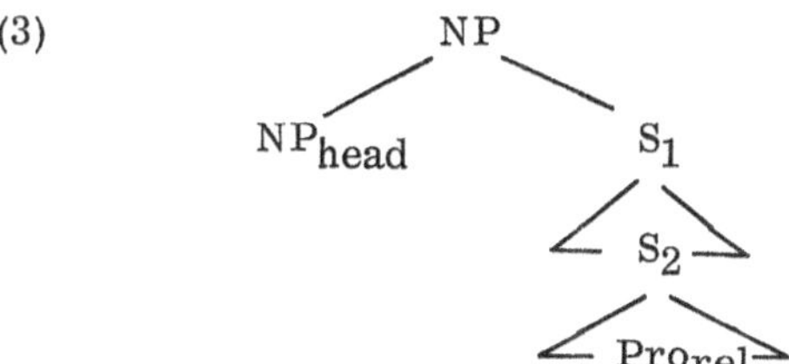

Now more roles exhibit a Pro_{rel} in the surface.

(4a) Subject:
Ecco il ragazzo che so bene che (??lui) studia legge.
'Here's the boy that I know well that (??he) studies law.'

(4b) Accusative object:
Ecco il ragazzo che so bene che Maria (lo) conosce.
'Here's the boy that I know well that Mary knows him.'

(4c) Nonaccusative cliticizable object:
Ecco il ragazzo che so bene che ne parlavi.
'Here's the boy that I know well that you were talking about him.'

(4d) Noncliticizable object:
Ecco il ragazzo che so bene che litigavi con lui.
'Here's the boy that I know well that you were arguing with him.'

Example (4d) is ungrammatical for some speakers.

2.3. Embedded Q. Pro_{rel} is in an embedded question:

(5)

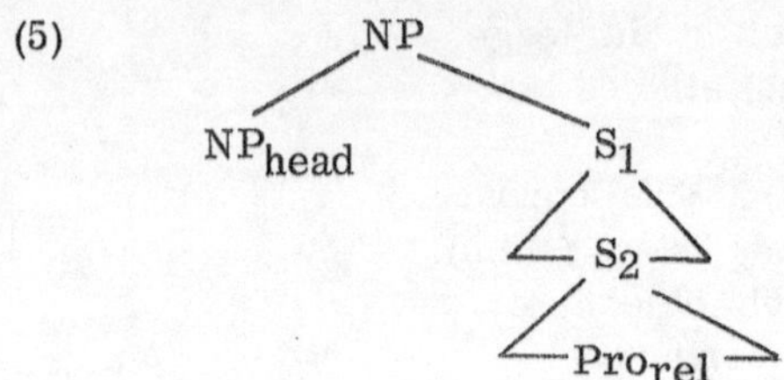

where S_2 is a question. Now Pro_{rel} must appear in all roles except subject, where it is optional:

(6) Ecco il ragazzo che non capisco perchè (lui) studia legge.
'Here's the boy that I don't understand why (he) studies law.'

Another structure which behaves exactly as embedded questions do is an adverbial of the type demonstrated in (7).

(7) Ecco il biscotto che tu gridavi a me mentre lo facevo.
'Here's the cookie that you were yelling at me while I made it.'

2.4. CNP. Pro_{rel} is in a Complex Noun Phrase.

(8)

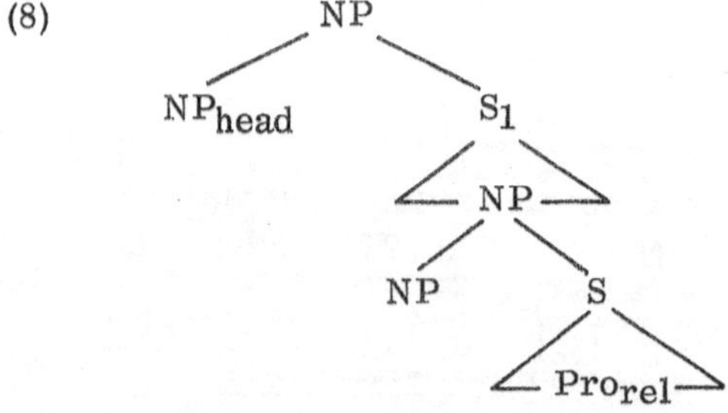

Pro_{rel} must appear in this structure in the surface regardless of its role.

(9a) Ecco il ragazzo che conosco la maestra che lui odia.
'Here's the boy that I know the teacher that he hates.'

(9b) Ecco il ragazzo che il fatto che lui odia la maestra è ovvio.
'Here's the boy that the fact that he hates the teacher is obvious.'

2.5. CS. When the relative clause is formed in a Coordinate Structure, Pro_{rel} must appear in the surface regardless of its role.[6]

(10a) NP and NP

(10b) Ecco il ragazzo che mia sorella e lui vanno al cinema domani.
'Here's the boy that my sister and he are going to the movies tomorrow.'

(11a) NP and NP [dominating Pro_{rel}]

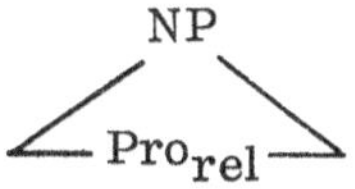

(11b) Ecco il ragazzo che ho raccomandato Maria e la signora che lui ha sposato per il posto.
'Here's the boy that I recommended Mary and the woman that he married for the job.'

Note that in (11b) Pro_{rel} is not only in a CS, it is also in a CNP.

3.0. The Relative Squish. If we arrange the two factors, role and structure, in a matrix with structure heading each column and role heading each row, and if we then fill in each square with information about whether or not Pro_{rel} appears in the surface, we find the squish shown in Table 1.[7] In this table x signifies that Pro_{rel} cannot appear in the surface; 0, that Pro_{rel} optionally appears; +, that Pro_{rel} must appear; and -, that no relative can be formed with <u>che</u> in this context. A square with two symbols signifies dialectal variation, with the first symbol representing the most frequently found data for my informants.

The roles in Table 1 have been arranged according to the Keenan and Comrie (1972) Accessibility Hierarchy. The structures have been arranged according to their degree of 'islandness', with those observing Ross's (1967) constraints being rightmost. Assuming that the positions get progressively more difficult as we go from NW to SE on the matrix, we see that Pro_{rel} does not appear in easy contexts, optionally appears in more difficult contexts, and must appear in the most difficult contexts.[8]

TABLE 1. Squish on the appearance of Pro_{rel}.

	S_1	S_2	em Q	CNP	CS
subject	x	x	0	+	+
acc. object	x	0	+	+	+
nonacc. clit. object	+, 0	+	+	+	+
nonclit. object	-	+, -	+	+	+

4.0. The Deletion Rule DEL. The squish in Table 1 is written as a squish on the appearance of Pro_{rel} in the surface. I argue here that there is a rule DEL which deletes Pro_{rel} and that DEL cannot apply, optionally applies, or obligatorily applies, depending upon the difficulty of the context. If it were possible to motivate such a rule, Table 1 would offer support for Lakoff's (1972) claim that 'rules of grammar do not simply apply or fail to apply; rather they apply to a degree'.[9]

One kind of evidence which would support the proposal of DEL would be something which would make us posit an underlying level for (2b), for example, in which Pro_{rel} was present.

(2b) Ecco il ragazzo che Maria (*lo) conosce.

Such evidence exists. Consider (12). Pensare a NP 'think about NP' is unusual in Italian, in that if a NP is replaced by a clitic we get an accusative clitic (having the same gender and number as the NP) but never a dative clitic. A NP in other predicates, however, is replaced by a dative clitic if the NP is animate.[10]

(12a) Penso a mia madre.
'I'm thinking about my mother.'

(12b) *Penso mia madre.
'I'm thinking my mother.'

(12c) *Le (dative) penso.
'I'm thinking about her.'

(12d) La penso.
'I'm thinking about her.'

In a relative clause with pensare a NP we find that Pro_{rel} cannot appear. All speakers of Italian, as far as I know, accept (13a):

(13a) La signora che pensavi entra adesso.
'The woman that you were thinking about is entering now.'

(13b) *La signora che la (accusative) pensavi entra adesso.
'The woman that you were thinking about her is entering now.'

(13c) *La signora che le (dative) pensavi entra adesso.
'The woman that you were thinking about her is entering now.'

Had the relative clause in (13a) been formed directly on an underlying full dative NP as in (14),

(14) [la signora [(tu) pensavi alla signora] entra adesso]

we would expect a dative clitic to appear in the surface obligatorily for most speakers and at least optionally for many others, since dative objects are nonaccusative cliticizable objects (see row 3 of Table 1). Yet no such clitic may appear, as (13c) shows. If, instead, the dative object in (13a) went through a pronominal stage first, it would become an accusative clitic, as (12d) shows. Then this clitic would be deleted by DEL, since accusative $\mathrm{Pro}_{\mathrm{rel}}$ does not show up in a structure like that in (13) (see the first column of Table 1). And, in fact, no clitic appears.

Thus the positing of a pronominal stage in the history of (13a) explains the absence of a clitic in the <u>che</u> relative there. Note that if we formed a relative clause with a relative pronoun in the same environment, the relative pronoun would appear after the dative marker <u>a</u> and not as an accusative object.[11]

(15a) La signora alla quale/a cui pensavi entra adesso.
'The woman to whom you were talking is entering now.'

(15b) *La signora la quale pensavi entra adesso.
'The woman who you were thinking is entering now.'

Example (15) shows that (13a) must be derived from a stage in which an accusative clitic was present and not from a stage in which a relative pronoun was present.[12]

Another argument in favor of proposing DEL depends on dialectal variation. The relative clauses given in Sections 2.1 through 2.5 are grammatical for a large number of speakers. Many other speakers reject many of the examples in Sections 2.1-2.5. All speakers, however, accept relative clauses introduced by <u>che</u> of the following types.

(16a) La ragazza che canta bene è Maria.
'The girl that sings well is Mary.'

(16b) La ragazza che so che canta bene è Maria.
'The girl that I know sings well is Mary.'

(16c) La ragazza che mi domando perchè piange è Maria.
'The girl that I wonder why she's crying is Mary.'

(16d) La ragazza che conosco bene è Maria.
'The girl that I know well is Mary.'

(16e) La ragazza che so che tu conosci bene è Maria.
'The girl that I know that you know well is Mary.'

These examples are of the type given in row 1 of columns 1, 2, and 3, and row 2 of columns 1 and 2 of the squish seen in Table 1.

Assuming DEL exists, the fact that (16) is accepted by all speakers of Italian, while the other types of relative clauses given in Sections 2.1-2.5 are accepted only by some, can be explained if we propose that DEL is an obligatory rule for the speakers who accept relatives with che only of the types seen in (16). To see this, look back at the squish in Table 1. Italian observes Ross's (1967) constraints on deletion and movement out of CNP and CS. If DEL is obligatory for a given speaker, then the speaker must delete Pro_{rel} in the environments in columns 4 and 5. But the CNP Constraint and the CS Constraint block this deletion. Since an obligatory rule is blocked from applying, such a speaker cannot produce the types of relative clauses found in columns 4 and 5.

Likewise for these same speakers, DEL must delete Pro_{rel} in row 4, yielding sentences such as:

(17a) *La ragazza che parlavi con è Maria.
'The girl that you were talking with is Mary.'

(17b) *La ragazza che so che parlavi con è Maria.
'The girl that I know you were talking with is Mary.'

(17c) *La ragazza che mi domando perchè parlavi con è Maria.
'The girl that I wonder why you were talking with is Mary.'

However, there is a constraint against stranding prepositions in Italian.[13] Since the application of DEL to sentences like those in (17) would result in a stranded preposition (con 'with'), such sentences are ungrammatical.

For the speakers with obligatory DEL the impossible grids left to be accounted for in Table 1 then, are those shown in (18).

(18)

	S_1	S_2	embed Q
accusative object			✓
nonaccusative clit. object	✓	✓	✓

Note that all the speakers who produce the che relatives of columns 2 and 3 of (18) keep Pro_{rel} in the surface. That is, for these speakers the contexts represented in columns 2 and 3 of (18) are of a level of difficulty that requires the presence of Pro_{rel}. Thus there is some kind of constraint that blocks DEL from applying in these contexts. If this same constraint operates in the grammars of those speakers who have obligatory DEL, an obligatory rule is blocked from applying in these contexts and the relatives of columns 2 and 3 of (18) cannot be produced.

The only grid left to be accounted for is the nonaccusative cliticizable object in S_1. Most speakers who produce che relatives in this context keep Pro_{rel} in the surface. Thus there is a constraint blocking DEL here for them. However, there are also speakers for whom DEL optionally applies in this context. Thus we expect that for most speakers who produce (16) but not the other types of relatives exemplified in Sections 2.1-2.5, (19) should be out.[14]

(19) Il gesto che sono capace è sputare in faccia al maestro.
'The act that I am capable (of) is spitting in the face of the teacher.'

Example (19) is out for these speakers because DEL is obligatory but at the same time it is blocked by a 'difficulty' constraint. However, there should be speakers who produce (16) and (19) but not the rest of the sentence types in Sections 2.1-2.5. That is, there should be speakers with obligatory DEL who do not consider the context in (19) difficult enough to block deletion, just as there are speakers with structure-sensitive DEL who do not consider the context in (19) difficult enough to block DEL. I have found no such speakers, and if they, in fact, do not exist, my explanations are greatly weakened. However, my sampling of speakers is small, so the possibility that such speakers exist remains.

Without a rule such as DEL, there must be a third relative clause strategy in Italian. This strategy would introduce relative clauses by che and leave no Pro_{rel}. Compare the two resulting che relative clause strategies. One has che plus Pro_{rel}. The other has che with no Pro_{rel}. If both strategies exist and are independent of one another, we would expect to find speakers with only the first of the two strategies as well as speakers with only the second of the two strategies. But, in fact, there are no speakers who produce che relatives with Pro_{rel} who cannot also produce che relatives without Pro_{rel} (of the type seen in (16)). Also, if the two strategies are independent, the fact that they are in complementary distribution (with only three exceptions) is unexplained.

4.1. Actual usage. While many speakers accept relative pronouns in relatives of the types seen in columns 1 through 3 of the squish in Table 1,[15] in actual usage relative pronouns are found in such structures usually only in the roles seen in rows 3 and 4. That is, il quale, the relative pronoun, rarely occurs as the subject or accusative object of its clause. In fact, many speakers do not even accept il quale as an accusative object.[16] For rows 3 and 4, the roles in which the NP coreferential with the head is in a prepositional phrase at some point in the derivation, the relative pronoun relative is more common than the che relative, but the preferred choice of relative pronoun is not il quale, but rather cui. Thus (20a) is more frequently used than (20b):

(20a) La ragazza con cui parlavi è Maria.
(20b) La ragazza con la quale parlavi è Maria.
'The girl with whom you were speaking is Mary.'

The preference for che and cui relatives, as opposed to il quale relatives, may be related to the fact that che and cui are invariant forms whereas il quale has different forms, depending on the number and gender of the referent. I think there is a general tendency in colloquial Italian to use invariant forms whenever one has a choice, witness the preference of (21a) to (21b):

(21a) Noi donne siamo meglio (unmarked) degli uomini.
(21b) Noi donne siamo migliori (feminine plural) degli uomini.
'We women are better than men.'

5.0. Conclusion. All relative clauses introduced by che in Italian are produced by the same relative clause strategy by all speakers. The fact that some speakers exhibit relatives with Pro_{rel} in the surface while others do not is directly due to the fact that DEL is structure-sensitive for the first group of speakers but obligatory, regardless of structure, for the second group.

NOTES

I would like to thank Judith Aissen, Nick Clements, Susumu Kuno, and Bob Rodman for suggestions and criticisms of various stages of this work; Dwight Bolinger, for some tantalizing questions and suggestions; my informants, especially Claudio Moser, Marina Nespor, and Bartolo Vattuone, for many hours and comments; and, above all, Pasquale Tatò, for his generous giving of time and incisive comments, the effects of which are apparent throughout this paper. A preliminary version of this paper was presented at the summer, 1974, LSA meeting.

1. Emonds (1970:169ff.) assumes for English that all relative clauses are introduced by _that_ and go through a stage in which the NP coreferential with the head is pronominalized or deleted. In the case of pronominalization, _wh_-fronting applies, optionally pulling along a preceding preposition and replacing _that_ in the COMP with the relative pronoun. In the case of deletion, _that_ introduces the surface relative. (_That_ may be deleted in certain instances.)

Chomsky (1973), alternatively, proposes that relative pronouns may delete and that then _that_ may be inserted in COMP.

Both linguists see relative clauses introduced by _wh_ forms and _that_ as being produced by one basic strategy, with deletion (either of a pronoun within the relative clause or of a fronted _wh_ pronoun) resulting in _that_ appearing in the surface. If _che_ relatives and _wh_ relatives in Italian were the result of one basic strategy, then _wh_-fronting would apply to Pro_{rel} before Clitic Placement or else be inapplicable to clitics (because of sentences such as (14a) in the text) and _wh_-fronting would be obligatory for some speakers in certain contexts but optional for others in the same contexts. Of course, there are some contexts (such as Complex NP's or Coordinate Structures) in which _wh_-fronting could not apply. If _wh_-fronting did not apply, Clitic Placement would apply where applicable and then DEL would apply. Determining whether or not this is the proper characterization of relativization in general in Italian is beyond the scope of this paper. In particular, the interaction of _wh_-fronting and Clitic Placement must be explored.

2. Many linguists have noted that the structure in which the relative clause appears may affect whether or not a Pro_{rel} appears. See Ross (1967), Neubauer (1970), and Givon (1973), among others.

3. Possessive NP's behave the same as nonaccusative cliticizable objects.

4. In Italian, unemphatic pronominal forms appear as clitics on the verb unless they are the object of a preposition that cannot be stranded or they are a possessive NP or they cannot be moved because of some other constraint (for example, a pronoun that was a conjunct of a Coordinate Structure could not be cliticized).

5. I have not included relativization in Sentential Subjects because the resulting sentences may well be ruled out for independent reasons. Thus, in (i)

(i) ?*Ecco il ragazzo che che (lui) ama Maria è ovvio.
'Here's the boy that that (he) loves Mary is obvious.'

the sequence che che is what most speakers say they object to. As in English, relativization into extraposed SS's is possible:

(ii) Ecco il ragazzo che non mi piace che lui sposi mia figlia.
'Here's the boy that it doesn't please me that he should marry my daughter.'

Regardless of role, Pro_{rel} must appear in relatives formed in extraposed SS's.

6. For some Italians (11) is better than (10). Grosu (1973), because of similar data in English, has proposed that the CS Constraint is not unitary but rather consists of two separate constraints, the Conjunct Constraint (which is relevant to (10)) and the Element Constraint (which is relevant to (11)). Neeld (1973) points out further distinctions between the two constraints. Neubauer (1972) has noted that SuperEqui distinguishes between the two constraints.

7. For discussions of squishes, see Ross (1972) and Lakoff (1972), among others.

8. Keenan (1972) argues that 'the more a syntactic process, such as relative clause formation, preserves logical structure, the greater the variety of contexts in which it applies and the more "difficult" the positions it applies to.' Assuming that a relative clause with a Pro_{rel} in the surface is closer to the 'logical' structure than a relative clause with a relative pronoun in clause initial position, the squish in Table 1 bears out Keenan's claim. Relative clauses introduced by relative pronouns cannot even be formed for columns 4 and 5, since Italian observes Ross's (1967) constraints on movement out of CNP and CS.

Relatives with relative pronouns also cannot be formed for the bottom square in column 3. I do not know why.

9. For another approach to the same kind of problem, see Neeld (1973), among others.

10. A NP of pensare a NP may also be replaced by the locative clitic ci, as in:

(i) Ci penso.
'I'm thinking about it.'

The major point in this example in the text is the contrast between a predicate like parlare a NP 'speak to NP' and pensare a NP. In the first, a NP is replaced by a dative clitic,

(ii) Gli parlo. (dative)
'I'm speaking to him.'

whereas in the second it is replaced by an accusative.

Also, I found a speaker from Padova who accepted (12b). For such speakers the following argument in the text is vitiated, since the NP coreferential with the head could have been an underlying accusative object, regardless of any pronominal stage.

11. Many speakers do not allow the relative pronoun to be used as the accusative object of its clause. (For a discussion of similar facts in French, see Kayne 1976.) However, even those speakers who do use the relative pronoun for accusative objects reject (15b).

12. There are some relative clauses introduced by che for which the positing of an underlying stage with Pro_{rel} present amounts to positing an underlying ungrammatical stage. For example, in (i)

(i) La ragazza che dicevo ieri è Carla.
'The girl I was talking about yesterday is Carla.'

since no Pro_{rel} can appear in the surface, we would posit an underlying accusative clitic. Thus the relative clause in (i) would derive from the ungrammatical (ii),

(ii) *La dicevo ieri.
'I was talking about her yesterday.'

The problem is that dire with the sense of 'refer to' or 'talk about' (rather than its usual meaning of 'assert') does not appear other than in relative clauses of the type seen in (i). Thus one cannot say:

(iii) *Dicevo Carlo quando tu sei entrato.
'I was talking of Carlo when you entered.'
(iv) *Dicevo di Carlo quando tu sei entrato.
(v) *Il ragazzo il quale dicevo è Carlo.
'The boy who I was talking about is Carlo.'
(vi) *Il ragazzo di cui dicevo è Carlo.
'The boy of whom I was talking is Carlo.'

Examples such as (i) are not evidence against the existence of DEL, however. Rather, since (iii)-(vi) are also bad, they are problems for any analysis of these relative clauses, regardless of the positing of a pronominal stage.

13. So-called prepositions like dietro 'behind', attorno 'around', davanti 'before', etc., which can be stranded, are really adverbs. See Napoli (1974) for evidence.

14. The version of (19) with Pro_{rel} present has ne.

(i) Il gesto che ne sono capace è sputare in faccia al maestro.

15. Relative pronouns cannot be used in columns 4 and 5 because of Ross's constraints.

16. See note 11.

REFERENCES

Chomsky, Noam. 1973. Conditions on transformations. Festschrift for Morris Halle. New York, Holt, Rinehart and Winston, Inc.

Emonds, Joseph. 1970. Root and structure-preserving transformations. Unpublished doctoral dissertation, MIT.

Givon, Talmy. 1973. Complex NP's, word order and resumptive pronouns in Hebrew. You take the high node and I'll take the low node. Comparative Syntax Festival. Chicago, Chicago Linguistic Society.

Grosu, Alexander. 1973. On the non-unitary nature of the Coordinate Structure Constraint. Linguistic Inquiry 4.188-192.

Kayne, Richard. 1976. French relative <u>que</u>. In: Current studies in Romance linguistics. Edited by Marta Luján and Fritz Hensey. Washington, D.C., Georgetown University Press. 255-299.

Keenan, Edward. 1972. The logical status of deep structures. To be published in the proceedings of the 11th International Congress of Linguists at Bologna, Italy.

Keenan, Edward and Bernard Comrie. 1972. Noun phrase accessibility and universal grammar. Unpublished mimeo of the King's College Research Centre in Cambridge, England.

Lakoff, George. 1972. Hedges: A study in meaning criteria and the logic of fuzzy concepts. Papers from the Eighth Regional Meeting. Chicago, Chicago Linguistic Society.

Napoli, Donna Jo. 1974. Reflexivization across S boundaries in Italian. Paper presented at the winter meeting of the Linguistic Society of America.

Neeld, Ronald. 1973. On the variable strength of island constraints. Papers from the Ninth Regional Meeting. Chicago, Chicago Linguistic Society.

Neubauer, Paul. 1970. On the notion 'chopping rule'. Papers from the Sixth Regional Meeting. Chicago, Chicago Linguistic Society.

Neubauer, Paul. 1972. SuperEqui revisited. Papers from the Eighth Regional Meeting. Chicago, Chicago Linguistic Society.

Ross, John. 1967. Constraints on variables in syntax. Unpublished doctoral dissertation, MIT.

Ross, John. 1972. The category squish: Endstation hauptwort. Papers from the Ninth Regional Meeting. Chicago, Chicago Linguistic Society.

A NOT IMPARTIAL REVIEW OF A NOT UNIMPEACHABLE THEORY: SOME NEW ADVENTURES OF UNGRAMMATICALITY[1]

Dwight Bolinger

The Standard Theory has been taking its lumps of late, and Terence Langendoen and Thomas Bever have made a chivalrous attempt to rescue it. Their 'Can a not unhappy person be called a not sad one?' (Langendoen and Bever 1973, hereafter L and B) has the twofold aim of analyzing a bit of English syntax in a novel way, and trying to show, by the analysis, that generative orthodoxy still has life in it. Their attempt is not a frivolous one, but it makes the not uncommon mistake of taking the theory as the lodestar and moving in directions that a fuller look at the data will not permit. I approach it as a classic example of theory getting in the way of explanation, and hope to make clear how necessary it is, in describing any part of language, to take it on its own terms. I need not add that if my proposals turn out to be better than theirs, I owe the promptings to them.

L and B are looking for a way to avoid the embarrassments which their understanding of the *not unhappy* construction causes for the Standard Theory of TGG. The problem is how to preserve the transformations that derive *sad person* from *person who is not sad* while at the same time blocking **not sad person* from *person who is not sad*, in spite of the apparently smooth operation of deriving *not unhappy person* from *person who is not unhappy*. The solution adopted is to block both operations. *A not unhappy person* is declared to be ungrammatical in spite of being perfectly acceptable; this relieves the grammar of having to explain it. (And recruits a new member for the Mere Club, the founding patriarch of which was Mere Style, with new members Mere Performance and Mere Rhetoric, and now Mere Ungrammaticality. Not that L and B's brief for admission is a crude one. They feel they have identified a principle for their use of ungrammaticality. I will touch on that later, after I have shown, I hope, that *a not unhappy person* is either grammatical or we had better close out our business.)

L and B's title gives a foretaste of the complications. The two words *unhappy* and *sad* conceal a trap that might have been more visible if the language were Spanish instead of English--they are not synonymous in the relevant sense. I will not elaborate at this point, but only illustrate with an acceptable instance of *not* + *sad* + noun. Imagine that you are a radical anti-intellectual who has just heard that the Library of Congress has burned to the ground. You report the happening, and then you add, with a diabolically wry smile, *A not, shall we say, sa:d turn of events*. Substituting *person* for that abstract noun does not get by very well: ??*A not, shall we say, sa:d person*. There are two reasons why **a not sad person* is unacceptable. I took care of one of them by inserting an illocutionary phrase, but I let the other one stand.

L and B start by assuming the validity of two transformations, that of relative clause reduction whereby *a person who is not unhappy* yields *a person not unhappy*, and that of adjective phrase preposing whereby *a person not unhappy* yields *a not unhappy person*. They decide that the difficulty for the *not sad* construction resides in the first transformation, not in the second, because they consider the sentence *Someone not happy entered the room* to be ungrammatical. This is a mistake, though not a material one. The sentence is screwy for other reasons; I will not attempt to explain, because it suffices to cite a few more examples to show that the construction itself is normal:

> Someone not happy is usually someone not healthy.
> What we need is something not commonplace, not run-of-the-mill.
> Someone not accredited is sure not to be acceptable to our Board of Directors. (*a not accredited person)

(A context for the last example might be that it serves as an answer to the question *Why have you turned down this candidate?*) It is enough to concede that the trouble lies somewhere in these two transformations.

The next step on L and B's program is to decide that the adjective, call it Adj_1, must be analyzable into Neg + Adj_2--that is, *unhappy* = *un-* + *happy*. Three examples are cited, including **His uncle left him a not dismantled clock*. This fails supposedly because there is no such thing as **mantled*. But the real reason is not the unanalyzability of the adjective. Expressions of this kind are commonplace as an extension of remarks, either added to what the speaker himself has just said or to what someone else has just said:

I was amazed at her acceptance of his proposal.--Her not ecstatic acceptance, shouldn't we say?
A not egregious error--I can understand its happening.
A not reprehensible desire. (*not blameworthy)
A not intermittent event, by any means. (not infrequent)
A not surprising outcome, I must say.
A not pretentious ambition.
A not engrossing book, God knows.
A not excruciating failure.
A not prepossessing face and a not particularly prepossessing manner.
A not preposterous assumption.
A not presumptuous request.
A not superlative achievement.
A not revolutionary idea, I must say.
A not erroneous assessment. (not incorrect)
A not prototypical event.

The next step is to provide for excluding the type **Sheila wants to meet a not unmarried man.* L and B write it off on the score that the two adjectives, *married* and *unmarried*, denote mutually exclusive states rather than the extremes of a continuous scale. I think this is correct, and explains why **Her not indescribable picture* sounds so much worse than *Her not indescribable suffering*. The intonation betrays the gradability of the adjective. Said matter-of-factly, ??*A not illiterate letter* suggests *illiterate* in an absolute sense. But if the speaker is trying to mitigate someone else's scathing criticism of a letter's style by saying

```
         lit
            e
A            r          ter,         ly?
              a
   not         t
                e
         il         let         sure
```

then *illiterate* refers to an extreme of illiteracy. But it would be wrong to mark all instances of absolute adjectives with an asterisk. Consider the parallel antonyms *complete* and *incomplete*:

Your squib is incomplete.--I deny that.--I'm afraid you'll have to accept my judgment. A not incomplete one would at least have the punctuation corrected.

The difference here is that the contrast has to be set up explicitly. One does not say **He handed me a not incomplete report* as one may say, with less explicit presuppositions, *He handed me a not uninteresting report*.

L and B's next move is to rule out cases where the two adjectives do not match as antonyms, as in

*He emitted a not unearthly scream.
*Don't take any not unhealthy risks.

Since we have already seen many examples in which there is no negative prefix at all, but the acceptability hinges on the meaning of the adjective as a whole, it is clear that this new restriction will not hold. The following are normal, in spite of the fact that there is no longer any semantic connection between *inordinate* and *ordinate*, and very little between *inadvertent* and *advertent*:

A not inordinate demand, you will surely agree. (not excessive)
A not inadvertent mistake, I assure you. (not unintentional, not unintended)

Next, L and B look for a way to rule out cases like **The bishop favored the not impious regent.* They feel they have it in the phonological change that occurs in the word *pious*. There is nothing wrong with the meaning--*pious* and *impious* are perfect antonyms; so the difficulty must be the fact that as a result of the shift of stress, *pIous* becomes *-pEous*: 'The relevant factor, clearly, is that the two forms differ phonetically as a consequence of the laxing rule in *impious*' (398). But there are plenty of cases where such changes occur without any harmful effect:

A not inimical attitude. (amicable)
A not inept performance. (apt)
Her remarks have hurt me deeply.--Her not innocuous remarks, I can well see. (noxious)
A not insipid dish. (sapid)

The problem is not with the laxing, but with the factor that causes the laxing, namely the shift of stress. There is a rhythm rule that applies directly. The word *not* is a stressed form, and like a few other similarly stressed monosyllables it is not normally used with an attributive adjective that begins with a stressed syllable. A similar case is that of *too*:

?A too unusual sight.
*A too strange sight.

Here we have the choice of reversing the position of *too* and the article, but in the second example it is required:

Too unusual a sight.
Too strange a sight.

Similarly with *not*:

A not unusual sight.
*A not strange sight.
Not an unusual sight.
Not a strange sight.

The cases are not identical, because *a not* and *not a* raise a question about what the constituents are which is less clearly true of *too*. Also the buffer syllable is introduced at a different point. But the same principle is involved, and that is why in some earlier examples I inserted an illocution at the strategic point. Similarly:

A not, I grant you, obvious error.
A not, I can assure you, minimal difference.
A not, I must say, stringent requirement.
A not, you'll agree, stellar performance.
A not, to be sure, plentiful amount.
A not, you might say, eminent success. (a not pre-eminent success, *a not eminent success)
A not, as must be obvious, fatal error.
A not, quite obviously, dazzling (brilliant) outcome.
A not, I can safely say, mind-boggling (world-beating) discovery.
A not, in all candor, open and frank discussion.
A not, shall we say, healthy situation.
A not, I respectfully remind you, impotent kind of act.

(The rule applies weakly to an initial secondary stress:

?A not universal opinion.
A not, I regret to say, universal opinion.)

Illocutions in medial positions tend to evolve into intensifiers, and we find that the more they resemble intensifiers, the better they are as rhythmic buffers in this construction:

A not, I should say, radical position.
A not, I must say, dismal prospect.
A not, God help us, glorious day for our side.
A not, exactly, thrilling experience.
A not exactly thrilling experience.
A not, truly, elegant way of doing things.
A not truly elegant way of doing things.

With the commas stripped away we have outright intensifiers. Adding to the intensification is the suspense created by the interruption--the adjective comes in with greater force after the comma. Enhancement of intensification is important in this construction, as we shall see. Illocutions that contribute nothing to intensification are a bit doubtful:

?A not, I infer (suppose, gather), delirious success.

Illocutionary insertions are not the only way of avoiding the rhythmic restriction, if we are allowed other manifestations of Neg than just the word *not*. I assume that the disjunctive conjunctions *neither ... nor* are derivable from *not* + *and* + *not*:

A remark that is not snide and that is not mean.
A remark not snide and not mean.
A remark neither snide nor mean.
A neither snide nor mean remark.
*A not snide and not mean remark.

What saves the day, of course, is that *neither* has an unstressed second syllable and *nor* normally has no stress at all. *Never* is similarly free.

Though comparatively infrequent by comparison with its negative counterpart *not*, the affirmative *indeed* is similarly restricted:

His behavior is indeed insufferable (rude).
His indeed insufferable (*rude) behavior.

With its terminal stress, *indeed* causes the same rhythmic problem as *not*.

Though simpler than the laxing rule proposed by L and B, the rhythm rule is merely an earlier stage of the same phenomenon and creates the same difficulty for the Standard Theory. L and B want to avoid it by setting up a universal constraint which they word like this: 'no syntactic transformational rule is permitted to make use of the internal morphological structure of lexical items' (402). This is intended to take care of the laxing problem, now seen as a rhythm problem, but it also has the effect of making it impossible to use the analysis of *unhappy* into *un-* + *happy*. For us, that is not the problem, because we have found that analyzability is irrelevant: *a not erroneous assessment* and *a not incorrect assessment* are both acceptable. But for L and B it is serious because their only evidence is from analyzable adjectives. So, to save the theory, they must find an explanation for the construction that will not involve formal analysis into Neg + Adj_2. This leads them to look for a beachhead in pragmatics, to explain acceptability without grammaticality. Specifically, there are perceptual strategies that assign a structure to a string not on the basis of its actual components but on the basis of what is expected. Something of this sort, L and B believe, occurs with *not unhappy*. English has a sequence of adv + adv + adj + noun that is so commonplace that it creates an expectation. The model here is such cases as

somewhat badly expressed idea
altogether neatly conceived plan
less unmistakably hostile attitude
not thoroughly agreeable stance
not very happy boy
not too clever idea

and given the model, we 'misanalyze' (their term) a combination such as *not unhappy* or *not underdeveloped* or *not supersaturated* as if the prefix were a separable adverb, 'provided that what remains after the prefix has been removed is an adjective that plausibly modifies the noun that follows it' (405).

This is an ingenious explanation and it is easy to see how one can be tempted into it by our time-honored habits of formal segmentation. But if *a not surprising* event is as good as *a not unexpected event*, the semantic plausibility of *expected* is beside the point. What is the real requirement where meaning is concerned?

L and B correctly state the chief defining feature of the construction as in some way denoting 'two ends of a continuous scale with respect to the noun being modified' (396).[2] Their only error is in being too selective with their examples and consequently defining the scale too narrowly (see Bolinger 1972:115-125): *not* + neg comes out for them meaning 'slightly to moderately' (401); that is, *not unhappy* means 'slightly to moderately happy'. As readers of Zimmer (1964) will know, there is a difference between negative formations, depending on whether the base word is favorable or unfavorable. *Ungenerous* is *un-* plus a favorable base; *unselfish* is *un-* plus an unfavorable one. The tendency, though I think it is no more than that, is for the *ungenerous* type to take on the mild meaning when negated, but for the *unselfish* type to lean more toward the extreme--whereas *not ungenerous* is 'slightly to moderately generous', *not unselfish* is 'pretty damn selfish'. The reason lies in the general conditions of use: *not unselfish* is apt to be ironically euphemistic. If a philanthropist donates a million dollars to a charitable cause, and you know, and you know your interlocutor knows, that the gift is mainly to avoid paying income tax, you may say *A not unselfish act, you'll have to admit*--implying that the interests of Number One are well up front. Other examples are *not impartial*, *not inexpensive*, *not undemanding*. But this does not depend directly on the meaning of the base. As we have seen, too often there is no base; the relevant meaning is that of the adjective itself, unanalyzed. The adjective *ingratiating* has a favorable meaning as a whole; there is no negative prefix. And *a not ingratiating manner* will probably be taken as 'a pretty disagreeable manner'.

There are other factors. One is the degree of extremeness of the adjective. The less extreme, the more the meaning when negated tends to be not extreme, that is, 'slightly to moderately'; *not unhappy* is of this kind. A more extreme adjective polarizes the scale, with a corresponding 'pretty damn'. For example, *a not infinite (infinitesimal) amount* is apt to mean 'a pretty damn small (large) amount'; the weaker synonyms in *a not excessive (insignificant) amount* bring things more toward the middle.

A further factor, affecting all those that have gone before, is intonation. It can mitigate or intensify. If I say

A amount.
insignificant
not

I probably intend 'a moderately large amount'; but if I say

not insignificant
A amount.

I probably mean 'a fairly sizable amount'; and if I say

not ni:f mou
A insig icant a nt.

I probably mean 'a whale of a lot'.

Sometimes the adjective is so neutral that only with intonational intensification do we get a suitable result. Thus ?*A not seductive prospect* is a bit doubtful, but

not
d:uc
pros
A
se
tive
pect.

with all the prosodic stops pulled out and with an added chuckle, is much improved. A still weaker adjective is *acceptable*, and with an utterance such as **A not acceptable excuse* I find that I have to pile on a vigorous gestural intensification (head-shaking) to make things right:

not
ćé:p
cu
A
ac
table ex
s
e.

Intonational intensification of a very extreme sort even makes it possible to override the rhythm rule (which was probably in the first place as an aid to intonational contrast). In oratorical style, with the syllables embodying *not* + adj + noun duly stretched, one may hear such things as *And there he lies, awaiting that not distant time when we shall all be called before the eternal judgment.*

The point is that the whole range, and not merely the 'slightly to moderately' end of it, is wide open, and there are more ways than one of achieving the necessary semantic continuum. The essential thing is that the adjective be far enough away from the middle of the range for the reversal of its position to move it significantly. Take the hackneyed word *excellent* by comparison with its stronger synonym *surpassing:*

A not, I must say, surpassing (*excellent) grade.

The weak status of *excellent* is betrayed by its use with *very, very excellent,* a fate that has not yet overtaken *surpassing.*

If the scaled continuum were the whole story on the semantic side, neither L and B's explanation nor mine, thus far, would suffice to account for the low acceptability of **A not, shall we say, sa:d person* and the higher acceptability of *A not, shall we say, sa:d turn of events,* where I hinted that Spanish might offer a clue. Similar pairs, with my judgment of acceptability:

A not, shall we say, joyous occasion.
??A not, shall we say, joyous person.
A not, I would say, intelligible answer. (with the adjective intensified intonationally)
??A not, I would say, intelligible person.
A not, I would say, loose woman. (with *loose* intensified intonationally and *woman* at low pitch with terminal rise --'whatever else she may be, she is not loose')
*A not, I would say, loose chain.
A not, I would say, laudatory remark.
*A not, I would say, laudatory person.

For reasons that I will get around to in a moment, I add a few examples with *very*, which display the same restriction though more weakly, and which allow a wider choice of adjectives and also avoid the problem of rhythm:

A not very clean joke.
?A not very clean floor.
A not very sad occasion.
?A not very sad person.
A not very dry wine.
?A not very dry handkerchief.
A not very loud cry.
?A not very loud infant.

?A not very close point--it measures a full yard from the other one.
*A not very close man--he must be at least a mile away.

Similarly with *exactly:*

A not exactly faint cry.
*A not exactly faint girl.

The doubtful examples are the ones that would call for the verb *estar* as predicator in Spanish, and the acceptable ones, with one exception, would use *ser*. The second strike against **a not sad person* is that *sad*, applied to a person, is a temporary adjective. The semantic reason for our not saying **a not sad person* is the same as the reason why we can readily say *She died of unhappiness* but not *?She died of sadness*. The Spanish equivalents are standard examples in the classroom: *happy* and *unhappy* are *feliz* and *infeliz*, and normally take *ser*; *joyous* and *sad* are *alegre* and *triste*, and take *estar* when they refer to people. Temporary *faint* contrasts with nontemporary *weak* (*a not exactly weak girl*). Temporary *sorry* contrasts with nontemporary *regretful*:

A not, I would say, regretful person. (with intonational intensification)
*A not, I would say, sorry person.

But with an abstract noun, *sorry* is all right, with a bit of intonational help:

A
not, I would say, sorry state of affairs!

The abstract noun names something that remains, timelessly, what it was at the moment of its inception. Hence the acceptability of *A not, shall we say, sad turn of events*.

So we add minus temporary to the semantic specification, which can be summed up as: 'A minus temporary degree adjective that is well off center on the scale of intensification'.

The justification for entering examples with *very* is that I believe that the construction implies a kind of underlying *very*.[3] Or perhaps a feature resembling both *very* and *too*, since the restrictions with *too* are similar:

A not too spotless reputation.
?A not too spotless windowpane.
A not too nearby point.
*A not too nearby onlooker.

With or without *very* or *too*, the temporary-nontemporary restriction lines up the same way. This is not true of all intensifiers. For example, practically all of the expressions that were doubtful with *very* and *too* turn out to be normal with *particularly: a not particularly joyous person, a not particularly loose chain, a not particularly spotless windowpane.*

With the prosodic and semantic parameters of the construction more or less framed up, we can look at the consequences, first for the effects of theory on description, and second for the empirical principle of grammaticality.

It is clear that the guidelines for L and B's investigation of *not unhappy* have been laid down by the preexistence of certain definite procedures in TGG. If the theory had not prescribed the derivational sequence of clause reduction and adjective preposing, the analysis would not have been misled into concluding that the ungrammatical expressions had their origin in the process of dropping the copula. If *The sound pattern of English* had never been written, the idea that vowel laxing was responsible for some of the difficulties would probably never have occurred to anyone. This is theory getting in the way of description. But it harms description in a more fundamental way, by shifting attention away from semantically interesting questions to semantically uninteresting ones. It is of no great moment at this stage that there is some kind of relationship between *a person who is not unhappy* and *a not unhappy person.* The interesting question, and one that has to be addressed if the construction is really to be understood as a functioning reality in English, is how this particular kind of litotes relates to other kinds. What is the basis for our choice among the three varieties represented by *This is a not insignificant amount, This is no insignificant amount,* and *This is not an insignificant amount*? How do the negatives *not* and *no* contrast with other expressions that are used in litotes, in phrases like *a hardly insignificant amount, a scarcely reasonable request, a far from easy task, his anything but careful appraisal,* where *hardly, scarcely, far from,* and *anything but* are brought inside the noun phrase? How are these now and then combined, in expressions like *a not insignificant amount, far from it,* or *a not insignificant amount, anything but*? These are the choices that a speaker faces when he sets out to code a message, not the choice between *a not unhappy person* and *a person who is not unhappy.*

As for the consequences of my reexamination for the theoretical assumption of ungrammaticality-cum-acceptability, it could be that by eliminating any need to refer to the internal morphology of the adjective--at least on the semantic side--I may have done no more than show that the construction is grammatical after all, so that no conflict between grammaticality and acceptability comes up. (There would need to be a phonological filter, of course, to take care of the rhythm rule, but that is so obviously needed for other things as well that the grammar could scarcely do without it.)

If this is the outcome, fine. All we can render then--for the case of whether acceptability can exist without grammaticality--is the Scottish verdict of not proven. But there remain one or two things to say about this construction that may get us a little closer to a verdict of disproven.

First, how does one fix a line so that everything to the left of it is available for syntactic transformations, and everything to the right is not? That is, when is structure morphological rather than syntactic? The utterances

A not overestimated figure, by a long shot.
A not too highly estimated figure, by a long shot.

are virtual equivalents, yet the first would be ungrammatical because *over-* is a prefix. Such a dichotomy is impossible in practice. There is an unbroken gradient between adverbs and prefixes. If we try to define prefixes as elements that cannot be freely used to generate new forms, then the form *ill* when it precedes an adjective has to be a prefix, while its antonym *well* remains an adverb: we can say either *a well conceived plan* or *a well thought-out plan*, and we can say *an ill-conceived plan* but are not apt to say **an ill-thought-out plan;* similarly *well designed, well worked out*, and *ill-designed*, but not **ill-worked-out*. As the antonym of *well nourished* we would be more apt to say *undernourished* than *?ill-nourished*, though both *well fed* and *ill-fed* are normal. Our uncertainty here is shown by our hesitation over using or not using the hyphen. On the other hand, if we define prefixes as forms that are always prefixed, though there is no restriction on particular members of the class to which they are attached, then the intensifier *too* is a prefix (unlike *overly* and *excessively*). To make grammaticality hinge on variably productive mechanisms is to force it to make an impossible distinction.

A more serious objection to such notions of ungrammaticality is that they stem from a one-sided view of communication. Everything is seen from the standpoint of the decoder. This is not objectionable when we are dealing with lapses; the burden is on the hearer to interpret what the speaker had in mind. When a radio announcer says *Take mercy on me*,[4] I can match it up with the two things that he is probably confusing, *Have mercy on me* and *Take pity on me*. This is the kind of matching operation that L and B assume is taking place when we are able to make sense out of *a not unhappy person*. But when I as a speaker start out with a plan to say *a not unhappy person*, then I am coding by rule. There is no 'perceptual misanalysis', as L and B call it, because no perception is involved.

In a broader sense, the source of the trouble is the refusal to assign independent status to independently signifying patterns. Predicate adjective constructions without the copula are not the same as constructions with it. Neither of these is the same as an attributive adjective construction. *Not* + adj + noun has its own special niche with its own special function. A paraphrase grammar is useful to discover what constructions have in common; its usefulness is ended when it tries to deny differences or to consign inconvenient structures to any kind of limbo, whatever the name. It should never become necessary for a grammatical theory to sacrifice the best empirical principle we have, which is that all fully acceptable utterances are grammatical utterances. To do so is to take the dictum of Chomsky's *Syntactic structures* (1957:13) which as written was 'The grammar of L will thus be a device that generates all of the grammatical sequences of L and none of the ungrammatical ones' and revise it to read 'The grammar of L is a device that generates all of the sequences of L that it generates and none that it does not generate'.[5]

NOTES

1. An earlier version of this paper was given at the Fifth Annual Colloquium on New Ways of Analyzing Variation in English, Georgetown University, October 29, 1976.

2. Their example of an unscaled adjective, *unmarried*, does not quite do justice to the possibilities. It can happen that an adjective that is actually not a degree adjective can be used in a way that implies a scale. For example, something is either *intentional* or not--we do not say **very intentional*. Yet the sentence *It was a mistake--and a not unintentional* (*unintended, inadvertent*) *one, I may add* is normal, because the implication is that it was rather conspicuously intentional, it was really intended; and those adverbs are degree adverbs. Similarly *a not unfounded rumor*.

3. The similarity with *very* is supported by what I think is the constituency of those phrases. The *not* does not modify *very* directly (as L and B assume, 405), but *very* plus its adjective. If the scope of *very* were just the following adjective, it should be possible to give it a contrastive accent, but doing so produces an unacceptable result: **She's a not VERY attractive person, only mildly* so (compare **She's a not UNattractive person, just low on the scale*). In fact, *very* is normally de-accented: *a NOT very atTRACtive PERson*. *Not* can readily be split off from *very: A not, you see, very remarkable thing after all*, vs. **A not very, you see, remarkable thing after all*.

4. Radio Station KGO, San Francisco, January 26, 1975.

5. I relegate to this note some comments on minor points.

(i) Many of L and B's starrings are due to some contextual inappropriateness. In my examples I have tried to use the *not* constructions in situations where the degree of presupposition is high enough to justify such a negation. It has been pretty well established that a negative presupposes some corresponding affirmative. So L and B's example (11b), **Did he make a not untoward remark about me?*, is bad because there is no basis for the negation (**Did a not unhappy person enter the room?* is just as bad). The comment *A not untoward remark, surely, under the circumstances?* makes due allowances for the need to presuppose.

(ii) Genericness is not a requirement for indefinite pronouns with reduced relative clauses. L and B's (12), **Someone not unhappy entered the room*, is bad again because there is no basis for the negation. If you have been speaking of candidates for a job and already know that George is unhappy, I may say *Someone not unhappy is bound to see things differently--that's why I have Melvin in mind for this.* (But in any case these expressions are not relevant, because the adjective is absolute, not graded. L and B's (13a), *Anyone not interested may leave*, does not mean 'slightly to moderately interested', but rather the contradictory of 'interested'.)

(iii) L and B commit a curious oversight when they cite their examples (14), e.g. (14a) **Any not interested person may leave*, as proof that generic nouns, unlike generic indefinite pronouns, cannot take reduced clauses. The trouble is due not to the reduction but to the preposing: *Any person not interested may leave.*

(iv) To say that 'the difference in interpretation between full and reduced relative clauses is rhetorical rather than semantic' (note 20, instancing *I see an elephant that is small* and *I see a small elephant*) is at one stroke to claim that *an eater who is big* and *a big eater* differ rhetorically but not semantically, and to measure off yet another dumping ground for inconvenient facts: 'rhetoric'.

(v) To suppose that a hearer needs to go through an involved computation in order to figure out the meaning of *a not very expensive apartment* (404) is to deny the reality of collocations. The *OED* provides a separate definition for *not very*: 'rather un-'. One might need a bit of separate processing in *a not excessively expensive apartment*, but *not very*, *not too*, and *not so* are stored as units. (This does not invalidate my claim in note 3 about constituency. A collocation may overspread a constituent boundary, e.g. *want to* in *I don't want/to go, I don't want to.*)

(vi) L and B cite the inappropriateness of *He has a pretty inexpensive apartment* in answer to the question *How expensive an apartment does Horace have?* as resulting from a principle of parallelism that decrees that 'one should not answer a question using *expensive* with a construction using *inexpensive*' (404). The principle may be valid but the example is not. *Pretty* is the wrong intensifier--too strong. The answer *A rather inexpensive one, to tell the truth* is not inappropriate.

REFERENCES

Bolinger, Dwight. 1972. Degree words. The Hague and Paris: Mouton.

Chomsky, Noam. 1957. Syntactic structures. The Hague: Mouton.

Langendoen, D. Terence, and Thomas G. Bever. 1973. Can a not unhappy person be called a not sad one? In: A Festschrift for Morris Halle. Edited by Stephen R. Anderson and Paul Kiparsky. New York: Holt, Rinehart and Winston.

Zimmer, Karl. 1964. Affixal negation in English and other languages: An investigation of restricted productivity. Word 20 Supplement.

SUBJECT NP STRUCTURE AND VARIABLE CONSTRAINTS: THE CASE OF NE DELETION

Anne-Marie Diller
Georgetown University

Previous studies in variation have demonstrated that the syntactic structure of a subject NP, whether pronoun or full noun, influences the output of a variable rule which affects an element of the predicate. Such is the case for copula deletion in Black English, which was studied by Wolfram (1969) and Labov (1972), and for the placement of the future marker *bai* in Tok Pisin, analyzed by G. Sankoff (1973). In both cases, the same pattern was established, which could be summarized in the following manner: when the surface subject of a clause is a pronoun, unnecessary elements which could stand between the pronoun and the verb phrase tend to be excluded variably.[1]

In this paper, I present an analysis of *ne* deletion in French in negative and restrictive clauses, which shows the same syntactic constraint. Moreover, I propose than an adequate analysis of *ne* deletion must take into account the semantic structure of the pronoun.

The data used for my analysis comes from recordings which were made in 1975 during unstructured interviews of 12 speakers from a speech community of Southern France. Extralinguistic factors were controlled for the selection of the speakers who were from the same age group (older adults), same geographical and linguistic background, and who were classified into two socioeconomic classes depending on their education and profession.[2]

Ne deletion is a clear case of inherent variability in the French language, whether in France or in other French-speaking countries. The frequency of deletion varies widely according to class, age, style, etc.,[3] but my main concern here is to present an analysis of some of the linguistic constraints which trigger deletion.

Negative and restrictive forms in French are generally composed of two elements: *ne*, which precedes the verb phrase, and a second element which follows the auxiliary or the verb: *que* in the case of a restrictive clause, as in (1); *pas*, *rien*, *jamais*, *plus*, *personne*, *aucun* in negative clauses like (2) and (3).

(1) Elle (*n'*) a que trois ans.
'She is only three years old.'
(2) Sophie (*ne*) viendra *pas*. (not)
plus. (no more)
jamais. (never)
(3) Il (*n'*) aime *personne*. (nobody)
rien. (nothing)
aucun d'eux. (none)[4]

In cases like (1) to (3), it is always the second element which gives the sentence its negative or restrictive notation, whereas *ne* is not necessary to the understanding.[5]

The fact that *ne* is variably deleted in all these environments does not mean necessarily that *ne* is a purely expletive or emphatic element, as is probably the case for sentences like (4).

(4) Je reviendrai avant qu'il (ne) parte.
'I will be back before he leaves.'

There are cases, even in casual speech, in which *pas* gets deleted and *ne* gives the negative notation, as in (5) and (6).

(5) Je ne sais (pas) s'il va venir.
'I don't know if he is going to come.'
(6) Si ce n'est toi, c'est donc ton frère.
'If it is not you, it must be your brother.'

I have very briefly touched upon some interesting aspects of *ne* behavior in negative and restrictive clauses. From now on, my analysis is limited to cases like (1) to (3). In my data, there were 641 negative and restrictive sentences corresponding to these environments, in which *ne* was deleted 220 times, with a percentage of deletion of 42 for the lower class against 22 for the higher class. The main interest of these results, apart from showing that *ne* deletion is a stigmatized feature in the speech of this community, is to permit an adequate analysis of the linguistic constraints, since the relatively small number of deletions for each speaker makes it possible to consider a wider range of variable environments. Such is not the case for some speech communities in which *ne* deletion has become almost categorical.[6]

A first examination of the data shows that the first-order constraint is a syntactic one depending on the nature of the subject of the clause. The results are reported in Table 1. We see that *ne* deletion is favored when the surface subject of the clause is a pronoun, whereas a full noun phrase, which includes proper names, determiner + noun with or without adjective or another complementizer, inhibits the deletion. All the pronouns under the label Pro in Table 1 exhibit the same general features: they are monosyllabic and they cannot receive stress in subject position. This could mean that we are dealing with a phonological constraint. However, further examination of the structure of pronominal subject NPs shows that the frequencies of deletion vary considerably within that category. Furthermore, these variations cannot be described adequately if we only take into consideration the form of Pro. The most relevant factor seems to be not what the pronoun sounds like, but what it stands for in the discourse.

Table 1. *Ne* deletion in terms of subject NP.

	Pro__			Full NP__		
	Total token	Deletion	Percent	Total token	Deletion	Percent
Lower class	330	161	48	29	1	3
Higher class	217	55	25	22	1	4
Aggregated data	547	216	39	51	2	3

The five categories of subjects shown in Table 2 define the subject in terms of its 'semantic weight', which includes the notions of reference and specificity. If we posit that full NPs bear a maximum semantic weight, the semantic weight of pronouns can be described in terms of the noun they replace in discourse. I have distinguished four categories of pronouns:

(1) Pronouns with a syntactic antecedent in the sentence, i.e. the case of relative pronouns.
(2) Pronouns with a lexical reference, i.e. the case of the true personal pronouns which generally refer to a specific lexical item in the previous discourse or to a specific reality in the situational context.
(3) Pronouns with a pragmatic reference, i.e. the case of the indefinite deictic which does not necessarily have a specific referent in the previous discourse, but which corresponds to some external reality and can always be replaced by a more or less adequate paraphrase.
(4) Pronouns with no semantic weight, i.e. what I have called 'empty pronouns', also known as dummy pronouns in syntax. They take the form of the personal pronoun *il* or the deictic *ce*, but they have no reference attached to them and they cannot have any other linguistic realization.

Table 2. *Ne* deletion in terms of the 'semantic weight' of the subject.

Semantic weight		Lower class			Higher class			Aggregated data		
		Total token	Dele-tion	Per-cent	Total token	Dele-tion	Per-cent	Total token	Dele-tion	Per-cent
(–)	Empty pronoun	54	39	72	45	19	42	99	58	58
	Indefinite deictic	58	31	53	33	11	33	91	42	46
	Personal pronoun	218	91	41	139	26	18	357	117	32
	Relative pronoun	25	1	4	18	1	5	43	2	4
(+)	Full NP	29	1	3	22	1	4	51	2	3

Table 2 shows that the operation of the rule of *ne* deletion is inversely proportional to the semantic weight of the subject. The most favoring environment for the operation of the rule is the empty pronoun. Some examples from the data are given in (7) through (10).

(7) *Il* faut pas que tu viennes.
'You must not come.'
(8) *Il* s'agit pas de s'arrêter.
'There is no question of stopping.'
(9) *Il* y avait presque pas d'abonnés.
'There were almost no subscribers.'
(10) *C*'était pas la fille qui allait le faire.
'It was not the girl who was going to do it.'

The next most favoring environment is the indefinite deictic *ce*, *c'*, or *ça*. Examples are given in (11) and (12).

(11) Quand on sortait, *c*'était pas comme maintenant.
'When people would go out, it was not like now.'
(12) Ça y est, *ça* va pas.
'That's it, it doesn't work.'

In examples such as (11) and (12), the meaning of the deictic cannot be interpreted without assuming either a full-fledged knowledge of the linguistic and extralinguistic background or a good deal of guessing.

The third most favoring environment is the personal pronoun. A detailed analysis of this category is given further on in this paper.

After the third category, we observe that there is a breaking point. The deletion rule almost never applies when the subject of the clause is a relative pronoun or a full NP. Also, we must notice that both socioeconomic classes have the same frequency of deletion for the last two categories, whereas the frequency of deletion is much greater for the lower class than for the higher class in the first three categories. The fact that *qui*, as in (13), behaves like a full NP can be interpreted in at least two different ways.

(13) ... des gens *qui* sont jamais contents.
'... people who are never satisfied.'

The first hypothesis could be that a phonetic constraint due to the syllabic segment /i/ inhibits the rule operation. Such does not seem to be the case because when the subject is *il*, there is a strong tendency for all speakers to delete the liquid independently of the following environment. The second interpretation is that *qui* bears the semantic weight of its syntactic antecedent which, in my analysis, is a full NP, since pronominal weak forms cannot have a complementizer attached to them.

The third category--that is, the personal pronoun--is analyzed in more detail in Table 3. Each form was counted separately, but some forms appear together in the table when the frequency of deletion was the same. In Table 3, it is seen that a singular pronoun favors the deletion slightly more than a plural form, the first person singular *je* being the most influential. But apart from these slight differences, each form stays within the percentage limits of the third category. Therefore, the tendency to apply the deletion rule more when the subject is pronominal holds for the various forms of pronouns, given the semantic restriction on the relative pronoun.[7]

Table 3. *Ne* deletion in terms of personal pronoun subject.

Definition of pronoun	Form	Total token	Deletion	Percent
1st sg.	*je*	146	55	37
2nd address	*tu, vous*	9	3	33
3rd sg.	*il, elle, on**	88	29	32
3rd pl.	*ils, elles*	91	25	27
1st and 2nd pl.	*nous, vous*	23	5	21

*In the case of *on*, sentences like *On n'aime pas les animaux* 'People do not like animals' were set aside, since the deleted form cannot be distinguished from the form with *ne* because of nasals.

In this analysis of the deletion rule, I have not considered other possible constraints. The form of the second element in the negation clearly is influential. The rule operates much more often when the second element is *pas* than when it is another forclusive. This seems natural since *pas* gives only a negative notation, whereas *jamais, plus, rien*, etc. bring in some extra meaning. But given this restriction, the hierarchy of deletion in terms of subject is the same, as can be seen in Table 4.

Table 4. *Ne* deletion in negative clauses with *pas*.

	Total token	Deletion	Percent
Empty pronoun	63	44	63
Indefinite deictic	73	40	54
Personal pronoun	264	98	37
Relative pronoun	37	1	2
Full NP	38	2	5

Pohl (1975) points out a possible relationship between the frequency of *ne* deletion and the number of syllables that stand between *ne* and the forclusive, which he explains in terms of the functional utility of *ne*. He also gives some statistics for the rule operation in terms of the subject which seems to corroborate the basic quantitative analysis presented in this paper.

This study is not intended to propose a complete and formal description of the rule of *ne* deletion in French. However, it does identify two interesting points which such a description would have to incorporate.

First, independently of possible secondary constraints, the deletion rule obeys a syntactic constraint such that the rule operation is favored by a subject pronoun and inhibited by a full noun. On this point, there is independent evidence in French which leads in the same direction. The three categories of pronouns which favor deletion behave syntactically like clitics. They cannot occur in isolation. An adverb or some other parenthetical cannot be inserted between the pronoun and the verb, as shown in (14) to (16).

(14) *Il probablement faudra que tu abandonnes.
'You'll probably have to give up.'
(15) *Ce, paraît-il, n'est pas une blague.
'It seems that this isn't a joke.'
(16) *Je certainement pense que vous avez raison.
'I certainly think that you are right.'

This attraction of the subject pronoun to the verb is also substantiated by the phenomenon of 'liaison'. The subject pronoun undergoes liaison categorically, whereas a full NP generally does not.[8] Compare (17) and (18).

(17) Les enfants|ont mangé des pommes.
'The children ate apples.'
(18) Ils‿ont mangé des pommes.
'They ate apples.'

The second point concerns the notion of semantic weight which is proposed to account for the patterning within the Pro_category, as shown in Table 2. My interpretation is, at this point, still tentative, and the distinction made between lexical and pragmatic reference needs to be tested on a more extensive body of data. What is quite certain is that *ne* deletion rule does not operate only with phonological and syntactic constraints. In this specific case, the linguistic behavior of the pronominal system in French must be defined at the level of discourse analysis.

NOTES

1. This is a gross generalization to describe two complex and otherwise distinct phenomena.
2. See Diller (1976) for a detailed description of the criteria used in selecting the informants.
3. See Pohl (1975).
4. *Ne* also occurs when the negative marker (*personne, rien, aucun*) is in the subject NP node, as in (i). But given

the very small number of these forms in my data, and also given the fact that, for phonetic reasons, it is almost impossible to hear if *ne* is deleted or not, such cases were omitted from my analysis.

(i) Personne n'est venu.
'Nobody came.'

5. I voluntarily omit cases in which the negation is attached to an infinitive verb and in which *ne* deletion would create an ambiguity, as in (ii).

(ii) On peut (ne) pas aimer ce film.
'It is possible not to like this movie.'
'It is not possible to like this movie.'

6. David Sankoff pointed out to me that in Montreal French, *ne* almost never appears in negative clauses. See also, G. Sankoff and D. Vincent (1977).

7. In the Tok Pisin data, Gillian Sankoff found that the third person singular pronoun *em* behaves like a full NP for the operation of *bai* placement.

8. Elizabeth Selkirk, in her unpublished 1972 MIT dissertation, gives an extensive analysis of 'liaison' in French.

REFERENCES

Diller, Anne-Marie. 1978. The mute E in French as a sociolinguistic variable. In: Montreal Working Papers in Linguistics, 10. Edited by Yves-Charles Morin and A. Averido.

Labov, William. 1972. Language in the inner city: Studies in the Black English vernacular. Philadelphia: University of Pennsylvania Press.

Pohl, Jacques. 1975. L'omission de *NE* dans le français contemporain. Le Français dans le Monde 111.17-23.

Sankoff, Gillian. 1973. Above and beyond phonology in variable rules. In: New ways of analyzing variation in English. Edited by C.J. Bailey and R. W. Shuy. Washington, D.C.: Georgetown University Press.

Sankoff, G., and D. Vincent. 1977. L'emploi productif du *NE* dans le français parlé à Montréal. Le Françias Moderne 3.245-256.

Wolfram, Walter A. 1969. A sociolinguistic description of Detroit Negro speech. Washington, D.C.: Center for Applied Linguistics.

THE PATTERNING OF SONORANT GEMINATION IN ENGLISH LECTS

Charles-James N. Bailey

1. One of the most remarkable differentiations among English lects, and one of the most difficult for foreigners to become competent in, is the gemination of sonorants, particularly the liquids and the (voiced) glides. To understand what follows, it is necessary to notice that //l// is vocalized (becomes /ɫ/) before /##/, as in *sell##enough* ['sɛɫlə'nʌf] (the inserted prevocalic [l] is explained below); and that //r// is vocalized (to /ɚ/) when standing before even a single /#/, as in *gor#y*, *scar#y*, *hair#y*. In some varieties of '*r*-less' English in the Southern States, many nouns and adjectives in *-ing* have only a formative boundary, not /#/, while verb forms retain /#/. The result is that *dar+ing* (n., adjv.) and *moor+ing* (n., adjv.) do not sound the same as the verbs, *dar#ing* and *moor#ing*; these latter forms have geminated /ɚr/ and the neutralizations of diphthongal peaks normally found in diphthongs ending in /ɚ/. Thus, *moor#ing* has [oɚ] (cf. *moor* ['moə:]), while *moor+ing* retains [ʉu]. *Harry* (['hærI], without gemination) does not sound like *hair#y* (Southern States ['hæɚrI]), because denominal adjectives of this sort end in *#y*.

As will be seen, Northern States English backward-geminates liquids everywhere between vowels, so that *merry* is ['mɛɚri]. Some Northern States lects do not geminate liquids if # precedes them (e.g. *care#less*). This creates a contrast between *Jew#ry* and *jury* ['džɚri] (where N.S. /uɚ/ become [ɚ]; see Bailey 1978) and between *gay#ly* and *dai+ly* ['dɛ̌ɫli] (see Ferguson 1971:16 fn. 8). Some (not all) varieties of British English distinguish *Jew#ry* ['džʉurI] from *jury* ['džʊɚrI 'džɔɚrI]; the latter has the usual Southern British gemination of //r// after a heavy, or long, vowel; see Section 2 of this paper.

When the next segment after /ɚ/ or /ɫ/ is a vowel, /ɚ/ geminates to /ɚ~r/ where ~ is a syllabic boundary), and /ɫ/

geminates to /ɫ~l/; e.g. Northern States *jury* and *daily* above, *moor#ing* ['mʉriŋ] and *sell##enough* ['sɛɫlə'nʌf]. These are examples of a more extensive phenomenon known as 'forward gemination'. It obligatorily affects all nuclear (peak or satellite) segments in the following list if they stand between underlying vowels, replicating them with a nonnuclear sonorant at the beginning of the next syllable:

after [i I], there is inserted syllable-initial [y ɥ];[1]
after a rounded nuclear segment, there is inserted [w];
after [ɚ 'ɝ], there is inserted [r];
after [ɫ 'ɫ:], there is inserted [l];
after a syllabic nasal, there is inserted its consonantal counterpart.

Note that all nuclear peaks in the list are affected in all English lects. Examples (except for /i I/; see on *premium* below) in Southern States (S.S.) are:

(1a) laboring ['lɛⁱbɚriŋ]
(1b) gamboling ['ɟæmbɫliŋ]
(1c) situation [ˌsItšɵ'wɛⁱšən]
(1d) follower ['fɑlɵwə]
(1e) fluid (lento) ['fluwId], (allegro) ['flʏᴵd]
(1f) seasonal ['siznn̩ɫ]
(1g) botany ['bɐˀn̩nI]

The most important form of forward gemination in the teaching of English to foreigners is the insertion of 'intrusive' [w] between adjacent (heterosyllabic) nuclei when the preceding peak or satellite is rounded, as in examples (1c) and (1e).

Two (only apparent) problems should be briefly alluded to. First, geminate /y/ in lento *premium* ['phrimIəm] is deleted in English, except in the most drawled pronunciations (e.g. ['phrimI(y)əm]). But in allegro tempos, where the first of two geminates gets deleted if it is a nuclear peak (see on *degemination* in Section 3), the /y/ appears: ['phrimyəm]. Secondly, the assimilation of /n̩n/ to /m̩m/ in *open#er* ['oᵘpˀm̩nə] creates an opaque situation in which it *appears* that /m̩/ is geminated with /n/. A later, transparent rule-ordering is sometimes heard in children's or sloppy adult speech: ['oᵘpˀm̩nə].

Where a satellite [ⁱ ᴵ] or [ᵘ ᵒ] is generated out of a single long /ē ō ū/ or other vowel, it is subject to prevocalic forward-gemination, though a /y/ eventually gets deleted, as already observed:

(2a) coöperative [ˌkhoᵘˈwɑp(ɚ)rədIv ~ ˌrɛⁱdIv]
(2b) surveyor [ˌsɜ:ˈvɛⁱə səˈvɛⁱə]

(2c) paranoia [ˌphærəˈnɔᵉə]
(2d) spewing [ˈspüᵘwiŋ]

In (2c), [ɔᵉ] derives from //ṻ//, as I have shown elsewhere.

2. In Section 1, the type of gemination under discussion (except for *jury*) was forward-gemination. There is another, more varied, more complex, and more interesting kind of gemination--backward-gemination. This sort of gemination repeats a syllable-initial liquid or voiced glide as a syllable-final satellite on the preceding nucleus, provided that it is a stressed one. Cf. these Northern States (N.S.) examples.

(3a) spirit [ˈspɨᵊ˞rəˀ]
(3b) silly [ˈsɨɫli]
(3c) lawyer [ˈlɔᵉə˞] [2]
(3d) kayak [ˈchaᵉˌæcˀ] [2]
(3e) Montoya [ˌmanˈthɔᵉə] [2]

In (3c) through (3e), the geminate /y/ has been deleted. Northern States English has backward-gemination of liquids and voiced glides (but not of nasals) between nuclei of all kinds. But in Southern British, //r// (see below for the glides) is geminated only after a heavy, or long, nucleus. [3] Thus, gemination is heard in *jury* [ˈdʒʊᵊ˞rɪ ˈdʒɔᵊ˞rɪ] and *glorious* [ˈɠlɔːrɪəs]. As the last example shows, the phenomenon of gemination is made partly opaque in '*r*-less' lects by the changes of /ʌᵊ˞ ɔᵊ˞ ɑᵊ˞/ / (but not /ɔᵊ˞/ from /uᵊ˞/) to /ɜː ɔː ɑː/, even before /r/; e.g. old-fashioned Southern British *curious* [ˈkhɥ·ɜːrɪəs], contemporary *historian* [hɪˈstɔːrɪən], and (forward-geminated) *star#ry* [ˈstɑːrɪ]. Older speakers with tapped-*r* before unstressed vowels had [ᵊɾ] instead of geminate [ᵊ˞r].

Contrast *demurr+er* [dəˈmʌrə] (the result of demurring), which has short-*u* before ungeminated *r*, and *demurr#er* ('one who demurs'), which has [ɜː] from geminated [ʌᵊ˞r].

Table 1a exhibits an implicational pattern in which gemination in (c) words implies gemination in (b) words, in which group gemination in turn implies gemination in (a) words. (A temporal spread of the rule from *a* to *b* to *c* is evidently the cause of this.) Such a pattern had been predicted by the writer, but never found in all its detail until he became acquainted with Scottish English. Whereas these pronunciations for *hairy*, *various*, and *pharaoh* are due to a *lack* of gemination, Southern African (or rather, one variety of it) has [ˈheːri ˈveːrɪəs ˈfeːˌrəᵘ] *because* of gemination! Here, /ɛːᵊɾ change to [eːɾ]. In Southern African English, if [eːɾ] is heard in any (b) words, it is also heard in the (a) words.

Where gemination in Northern States English occurs in the more recent, feeding order--i.e. prior to the rule(s) neutralizing vowel peaks in the environment preceding /ᵊ˞ɫ/--one

Table 1a. //r//.

Illustrative examples	Scottish English	'r-less' Southern States	Southern British	Northern States
(a) hair#y*	['herI]	['hæ^{ə}rI]	['hɛ̨^{ə}rI]	['hɛ̨^{ə}ri]
(b) vārious	['verIəs]	['vɛ^{i}rIəs]	['vɛ̨^{ə}rIəs]	['vɛ^{ə}rIəs]
phāraoh	['fe,ro]	[fɛ^{i},rou]	['fɛ̨^{ə}ro^{u}]	['fɛ̨^{ə},ro^{u}]
(c) Hărry	['harI]	['hærI]	['hærI]	['hɛ̨^{ə}ri]
mĕrry	['mɛrI]	['mɛrI]	['mɛ̨rI]	['mɛ̨^{ə}ri]

Table 1b. //l//.

Illustrative examples	Southern (States, Britain, Africa)	Northern States
(a) hill#y	['hIlI -i]	['hɨ^{ɫ}li]
tell#it	['thɛlIʔ]	['thɛ^{ɫ}ləʔ]
(c) mellow	['mɛ̨lɵ]	['mɛ̨^{ɫ}lɵ]
Jello	['dᶻ̌ɛ,lo^{u}]	['dᶻ̌ɛɫ,lo^{u}]
(d) sell##enough	['sɛ^{ɫ}lə'nʌf]	

*Types (a) and (d) are forward-gemination. Types (b) and (c) are backward-gemination: (a) has /#/ after an internuclear liquid; (b) has //r// after a long stressed nucleus; (c) has no word boundary adjacent to the liquid; and (d) has /##/ following //l//. Different varieties of Irish English exhibit all of the patterns for *r*-gemination except the Northern States one.

hears ['fɔ^{ə}rəst^{ʔ}] for *forest*, ['sɔ^{ə}ri] for *sorry*, ['kw̥·ɔ^{ə}rɫ] for *quarrel*, and ['wɔɫləʔ] for *wallet*.[4] The reduction of the triphthong [ɔ^{e}ɫ/ to [ɔɫ:] in less cultivated Southern States pronunciations cannot occur when the lateral is prevocalic; hence, the difference between *toil* ['thɔ(^{e})ɫ:] and *toilet* ['thɔ^{e}lIʔ].

Between an unstressed vowel and a fully stressed nucleus, it does not make sense to speak of backward gemination, since a preceding unstressed /ə/ would be assimilated to a following liquid or /w/, as in these gemination-free pronunciations:

(4a) paralysis [phɚ'ræləsIs]
(4b) paralytic [,phærɫ'lIdIcʔ]
(4c) caraway ['chærɵ,wɛ^{i}]

Table 1 points to the fact that //l// is not geminated before /#/ in varieties of English other than N.S. and Canadian English; e.g. *tell#it* ['thɛlIʔ]. In these other varieties, contrast *near#est* (with gemination) and *cool#est* (not gemination).

The glides are treated in Section 7.

3. In rapid speech, the effects of forward-gemination (of a peak) are made opaque by the deletion of the syllabic sonorant:

(5a) camera ['chæm(ə́)rə]
(5b) gamboling (adj.) ['ɟæmb(ɨ)liŋ]
(5c) seasonal ['siz(n̩)nɨ]

(See Bailey 1973:239 for the reorderings of degemination heard in uncultivated *chimbley*, *fambly*, and *membry*.) Degemination is less likely to occur as the tempo is slower and as the following syllable is more heavily stressed (for further details, see Bailey 1980):

(6a) associate (noun) [ə'soᵘšɪ²]
(6b) associate (verb) [ə'soᵘš(i)ˌɛⁱ2 ə'soᵘsiˌɛⁱ2]
(6c) association [əˌsoᵘš(i)'ɛⁱšən əˌsoᵘsi'ɛⁱšən]
(6d) correct [kh(ə́)'rɛcʔtʔ]
(6e) catholic ['cæɫ(ɨ)lɪcʔ]
(6f) believe [b(ɨ)'ɫiv]

With dynamic descriptive models, degemination is characterized with $\xrightarrow{>}$ ('more likely as the time taken to say the utterance is shortened'); the (following) stress environment is: $\begin{bmatrix} V \\ <\text{accent} \end{bmatrix}$ ('most likely when the stress [of the vowel in the environment] is minus, less so when it is mid, and least so when it is plus'). The syllable preceding degemination, if any, may not be unstressed, as in *capitalist*. Some lects require degemination in *gall(e)ry, sal(a)ry, cel(e)ry, distill(e)ry, chol(e)ra, scull(e)ry*, etc. Degemination does not occur before #, as in *summer#y* (contrast *summ(a)ry*), though the # can drop out in very rapid utterances. The 'southern' lects may distinguish *battery* (an electrical device: with degemination), *batter+y* (a crime, or set of instruments or tests: degemination only in more rapid tempos, not in slower tempos), and *batter#y* ('dough-like': no degemination except in tempos which are so rapid that a # falls out, leaving only underlying //+//). Degemination does not take place when clusters of an obstruent plus two sonorant consonants would result, as in (7).

(7) mercury ['mɜ:cyə́rɪ]

Except in *every*, degemination is more likely after stops than fricatives. Laterals degeminate in slower tempos than those required for geminating other sonorants; cf. *b'líeve* with *c(o)rréct*, *corrób(o)rate*, and *s(o)náta*. (See further in Bailey 1980.)

4. A few complications to the pattern of Table 1 warrant special comment. First, '*r*-ful' Southern States English is like '*r*-less' Southern States English with respect to laterals. With one exception, '*r*-ful' Southern States is like Northern States with respect to the treatment of intervocalic //r//. Exceptionally, '*r*-ful' Southern States pronounces sequences of long vowel plus //r// plus a mid-accented (mid-stressed) nucleus like '*r*-less' Southern without gemination; examples are shown in (8).

(8) phāraoh, hēro, zēro, tīro, būreau

Exceptionally to this, however, sequences of /ɒ̄r/ plus a mid-accented nucleus (as in *chlorine*, *moron*) are treated in '*r*-ful' Southern as in the Northern States--i.e. with gemination.

As if the foregoing complications were not enough, one can hear older '*r*-ful' speakers in the Southern, New England, and Midwestern States pronounce items like *Mary* with gemination but without the vowel neutralization mentioned earlier:

(9a) ['me$^{\acute{ɚ}}$ri] (not ['mɛ$^{\acute{ɚ}}$ri]) (9b) ['fɑ$^{\acute{ɚ}}$rIst]

(This is a matter of rule-ordering. See Bailey 1973:222; sonorant gemination may be ordered prior to or posterior to the neutralization rule. '*R*-less' New Jersey lects rhyme *Mary* with *marry* ['mæri], not with *merry* ['mɛri].)

Secondly, the 'southern' varieties of English in Table 1b and Scottish English contrast with Northern States English in their treatment of a lateral after a tautosyllabic heavy rounded nucleus:

	Southern States	Northern States
(10a) mule	['mü^{u}l]	['mɥu^{ɫ}:]
(10b) school	['scʉ^{u}l]	['scu^{ɫ}:]
(10c) goal	['go^{u}l 'gω^{u}l]	['go^{ɫ}:]
(10d) drawl	['drɔl 'drɒ^{o}l]	['drɔ^{ɫ}:]
(10e) foul	['fa^{o}l 'fæ^{o}l]	['fa(^{o})^{ɫ}:]

Northern States pronounces the foregoing items to rhyme with the pronunciations of the words shown in (11), respectively; these items all end in [ɫ:] in both southern and northern pronunciation.[5]

(11) fuel, accrual, bestowal, withdrawal, towel

In the South of England, some cultivated speakers are beginning to exhibit the pronunciations on the right in (15) in unmonitored styles, the pronunciations on the left being retained in more monitored styles. The following pattern is heard in all varieties of Southern States English:

(12) mulish ['müᵘlIš]: fueling ['fɥuᶧliŋ]
(13) cowling ['khæᵒliŋ]: toweling ['thæᵒᶧliŋ]

'*R*-less' S.S. has the contrast shown in (14):

(14) sour+ing (noun, adj.) ['sæᵒriŋ]:
tower+ing, tower#ing ['thæᵒᵊ̂riŋ]

Many or most Southerners today have /#/ before *-ing* in adjectives and nouns, as well as in verb forms, as in (15a); cf. dissyllabic lento variants in (15b).

(15a) ['thæ(ᵒ)ᵊ: 'thæ(ᵒ)ᶧ:]
(15b) ['thæᵒwə 'thæᵒwɨ]

In the (15b) variants, forward-gemination is manifested in intrusive [w]. In contrast with the Southern States pattern in (14), Southern British rhymes *souring* ['saᵒᵊ̂riŋ] with *towering*, because this variety of English geminates //r// after heavy, or long, nuclei. The /#/ which is present in the verb produces the same effect; e.g. Southern States *sour#ing*.

Instead of ['fuᶧləš 'mɥuᶧləš 'hoᶧli] for *foolish, mulish,* and *holy*, many or most speakers in the Northern and Western States have a rule that deletes the lateral satellite between a (preceding) /u/ or /o/ and a (following) prevocalic /l/, so that ['fuləš 'mɥuləš 'ho(ᵘ)li] result. Note that satellite-deletion follows the rule that creates [ɥ] (through detripthongization Bailey 1973:231). In *mulish* and *dualist*, satellite-deletion follows the rule that retracts the peak vowel in each example. In lects having [ʉᵘ] in *food*, there would be no [u] in *foolish* unless a geminate /ᶧ/ (later deleted) had at some stage of the derivation followed the nucleus in question. Similarly, /ɔ/ would not be generated from underlying //ɒ// in N.S. *wallet* ['wɔləʔ] unless at some stage in the derivation the vowel had been followed by a (later deleted) /ᶧ/--the result of backward-gemination. The geminate lateral is not deleted in any lect known to the writer in instances of the sort illustrated by *fueling* ['fɥuᶧliŋ], *dualist* ['dɥuᶧlIst], where forward-gemination is involved. (See further in Bailey 1978.)

Because of the changes of /ʌᵊ̂/ to /ɜ̂/ and of /uᶧ/ to /ɨ:/ (cf. the N.S. change of /uᵊ̂/ to /ʉ̂/ mentioned above), a difference can arise between geminating and non-geminating *fur#ry* or *full#y*, even though all the lects in question have [ɜ̂] or [ɜ:] in *fur* and [ɨ:] in *full* ['fɨ:]:

	Southern States 'r-less':	Northern States (geminating):
(16) fur#ry	['fɜ:rI]	['fɝrI]
(17) full#y	['fɨlI]	['fɨ:li]

Gemination has occurred in all of these forms except ['fɨlI], where the single /#/ is not an environment for lateral-gemination outside the Northern States.

With (17) compare *hurry* in (18):

	Southern 'r-less'	Northern States
(18) hurry	['hərI]	['hɝrI] (from /'hʌ^ɚri/)

Note the absence of /#/ in *hurry*.

Lects in northern Britain having (apically or uvularly) trilled *r* do not exhibit backward gemination.

5. So far, the discussion of backward-gemination has been limited to liquids. What of the glides, concerning which it has already been noticed that /y/-gemination gets eventually undone? Consider these examples:

		Southern States	Elsewhere (vowels are Northern States)
(19a)	lawyer	['lɔyə 'lɒ^oyə]	['lɔeɚ]
(19b)	Montoya	[ˌmɐn'thɔyə -ɒ^oyə]	[ˌman'thɔ^eə]
(19c)	paranoia	[ˌphærə'nɔ^eə]	[ˌphɛ̹^ɚrə'nɔ^eə -ɔeə:] [6]
(19d.i)	roil, royal	['rɔ(e)ɫ:]	['rɔ^eɫ:] [6]
(19d.ii)	royal	['rɔyɫ 'rɒ^oyɫ]	
(19e)	Gawain	['gɑ wIn]	['gɔwən] [7]
(19f)	steward	['stʯʋ^ə:d]	['stʋ^əd], ['stʉ̽d] [8] [9]
(19g.i)	leeward	['lʋ^ə:d]	
(19g.ii)	lee#ward	['liwəd]	['liwɚd]

While older Southern British speakers have the Southern States pattern, younger Southern British speakers prefer the 'elsewhere' pattern. The Southern States pattern is in complete consistency with its pattern for laterals and with the 'r-less' Southern pattern for *r*, since gemination is absent. As for earlier *w, it combined with a preceding vowel to yield /ɔ/ in example (19e) and the output of /ü/ in (19f), (19g.i), (19g.ii). After this, no more *w* existed in the underlying representation: The [w] in present-day English is the result of forward-gemination.

Compare the following pronunciations:

	In '*r*-less' and some '*r*-ful' lects:	Only in 'northern' '*r*-ful' lects:
(20a) million	['mIlyən]	['mɨɫ:yən]
(20b) failure	['fɛilyə -ɚ]	['fɛ̃ɫ:yɚ]

The difference here is due to a different ordering of the relevant rules. One rule is the rule vocalizing //l// to /ɫ/ before a consonant; the other rules change unstressed prevocalic /i/ to /y/ and unstressed /u/ to /ɥu/.[10] The typically '*r*-less' pronunciations of (20) have the glide-creating rules posterior to the vocalization rule; this rule is therefore unable to operate. The unmarked, opposite ordering allows the vocalization rule to be fed by the glide-creating rules.

Note also *follow+ing*:

(21a) ['fɒl(ɵ)wiŋ]
(21b) ['fɑɫ:wiŋ]

As noted in Bailey (1973:241), (21a) has either no degemination or else degemination *after* the vocalization rule, while (20b) has the rules in the opposite ordering. Whether the repartition of these pronunciations agrees with the parallels in (20) is not known, though it seems to be so.

NOTES

1. This /y/ is subsequently deleted if degemination does not delete the nuclear /i I/ in fast tempos under certain conditions (see Section 3).

2. Cf. Southern States ['lɔyə 'lɒᵒyə 'chaˌyæcʔ ˌmɒn'thɔyə ˌmɐn'thɐᵒyə]. See below for *loyal* and *royal*.

3. *Story*, *glory*, etc., have [ɒ] for some speakers in the South of England and for speakers in some other British-speaking areas of the world, where *glŏry* and *gl[ɔ:]rious* may contrast. However, the [ɔ:] resulting from gemination after /ɒ/ is apparently more usual today in England in these words, which generally rhyme with *gor#y*. Southern British speakers contrast *histŏric* and *hist[ɔ:]rian*. Note that vowels become short before *-ic* and long before a consonant plus unstressed prevocalic /i/, and that /ɒᵊ/ become Southern British /ɔᵊ/ by neutralization of the peak before /ɚ/, which satellite is finally replaced by /:/. *laureate* and *aureole* have gemination for the same reason that *glorious* and *historian* have it. While *laurel* has the light vowel in both southern England and the Southern States, the following have the heavy vowel in the South of England: *laureate, oral, aura, auricle, aureole,* and *Laura*. With the exception of *oral*, these have the light nucleus in the Southern States. In both of the areas just mentioned,

Lawrence (like *laurel*), as well as examples like *warrant*, *Warren*, *wallow*, *Wallace*, and *quarrel*, have light stressed nuclei. Gemination is prevented in Southern States and Southern British *warrior* by the //rr//: Southern States ['warIə], Southern British ['wɒrIə]. Contrast Southern British *abhor#ring* (with [ɔ:] by forward-gemination) and *abhor+rent* (no gemination). Appalachian English has gemination in *barrow* and the nucleus of *bar* in this word; contrast '*r*-less' Southern States *barrow*, *barrister*, and *carriage*, where [æ] is heard before ungeminated [r].

4. Cf. Southern States ['fɐrIst 'sɐrI 'kɦʀ·*arł* 'walI?]. Southern British is similar, except that the stressed vowel is, of course, [ɒ] in all these words. It is an error of some dialectologists to suppose that the difference between [ɐ] and [ɔ] in *forest*, etc. is what is really relevant for dialectology; these nuclear differences really depend on a lectal difference in gemination. This difference in no way correlates with that between [*a*] and [ɔ] before //þ f s ŋ g//.

5. These forms result from diphthongization; see Bailey 1973:227.

6. The triphthongal pronunciations here result from diphthongization; see note 5. Diphthongization is most likely where no boundary occurs, as in *lair*, *prayer*, *mare*, *more*, *lore*, and *cure*; less likely where /+/ is present, as in *layer*, *mayor*, *mower* ('machine for mowing a lawn'), *low+er* (verb), *ewer*, *sewer*, and *steward*; and unlikely when /#/ is present, as in *(brick)lay#er*, *pray#er*, *survey#or*, *mow#er* ('a person who mows'), *low#er* (comparative of *low*), *su#er*, and *cu#er*. Note that *mayor* and *they're* are treated like *mare* and *their* in Southern England, but in the Southern States they rhyme with *bricklayer*. Both areas distinguish *lay+er* and *lay#er* from *lair*. S.B. speakers who differentiate *mayor* and *mare* also differentiate *they're* and *their*; any who keep these distinct also differentiate *layer* and *lair*, but not necessarily vice-versa.

7. Here, *aw became /ɔ/; cf. *ew ⟶ /ǖ/ in (f), (g.i), (g.ii). British has the spelling pronunciation, ['gæˌwɛ̄n], for *Gawain*.

8. Southern British ['stɥʋ^{e}:d] or ['stɥɔ^{ə}:d].

9. Southern British ['lʋ^{ə}:d] or ['lɔ^{ə}:d].

10. Unstressed /u/ becomes /ɵ/ and eventually, before //r//, /ə/; this then merges with the liquid consonant to yield /ɚ/. Both of the rules that create /y/ and /ɥ/ operate under restricted conditions which may be left out of the present discussion, as they do not bear on the exposition undertaken here.

REFERENCES

Bailey, Charles-James N. 1973. Variation resulting from different rule orderings in English phonology. In: New ways of analyzing variation in English. Edited by Ch.-J. N. Bailey and R. W. Shuy. Washington, D.C.: Georgetown University Press. 211-252.

Bailey, Charles-James N. 1975. Further observations on unmarked rule order. International Journal of American Linguistics 41:73-78.

Bailey, Charles-James N. 1978. Four low-level pronunciation rules of Northern States English. JIPA 8.24-33.

Bailey, Charles-James N. 1980. Theory, description, and differences among linguists: Or, what keeps linguistics from being a science. Appearing in: Language and Communication 1/1.

Ferguson, Charles A. 1971. 'Short A' in Philadelphia English. Stanford Occasional Papers in Linguistics 1.2-27.

II. Variation in Language Use

SYNTACTICALLY VS. PRAGMATICALLY CONTROLLED ANAPHORA

IVAN SAG
Massachusetts Institute of Technology

JORGE HANKAMER
Harvard University

0. It has long been known that certain anaphoric expressions, though generally interpreted by reference to some linguistic antecedent, do not require such an antecedent, but can be controlled by some aspect of the nonlinguistic (we will say 'pragmatic') environment. This is the case, for example, with ordinary definite third person pronouns:

(1) My brother's a doctor, and <u>he</u> says your hair will fall out if you eat that.
Sue introduced me to <u>her</u> mother.
Anyone who eats that will lose <u>his</u> hair.
If the unicorn were a possible animal, <u>it</u> would certainly be a herbivore.

(2) <u>He</u>'s saying that your hair will fall out.
<u>Her</u> hands are trembling.
I hope <u>it</u>'s a herbivore.

The examples in (1) illustrate syntactically controlled anaphora with definite pronouns. The examples in (2) illustrate instances of what we call 'pragmatically controlled' (or 'deictic') anaphora. Each of the examples in (2) is well formed in a context which, without linguistic antecedent for the pronoun, nevertheless contains enough pragmatic information to allow (more or less) unambiguous determination of its intended referent.[1]

What has not (to our knowledge) been observed before[2] is that there are anaphoric processes[3] which (with reservations to be elaborated herein) must be syntactically controlled.[4] Consider the contrast in the following utterance-context events:

(3) [Hankamer attempts to stuff a 9-inch ball through a 6-inch hoop]
Sag: It's not clear that you'll be able to.[5]

(4) [Same context]
Sag: It's not clear that you'll be able to do it.

There is a subtle but distinct difference in acceptability between these two utterances in this context: the anaphoric process which leaves a pro-form do it as anaphoric VP can more readily be pragmatically controlled than the process known as VP Deletion, which leaves behind no pro-VP, but only a bare AUX or stranded complementizer.

The utterance in (3) is fine, of course, if there has been previous linguistic context in which mention has been made of getting the ball through the hoop:

(5) Hankamer: I'm going to stuff this ball through this hoop.
Sag: It's not clear that you'll be able to.

For further illustration of the contrast we offer another example:

(6a) [Sag produces a cleaver and prepares to hack off his left hand]
Hankamer: Don't be alarmed, ladies and gentlemen, we've rehearsed this act several times, and he never actually does.

(6b) [Same context]
Hankamer: . . . he never actually does it.

Notice, however, that once the do it anaphor has appeared in a discourse, it can itself serve as controller for syntactically anaphoric VP Deletion:

(7) Hankamer: At least he never has yet.

which is well formed in the context of (6b), where do it has already been introduced pragmatically.

So it seems that syntactic anaphora can be controlled by a pragmatically anaphoric item. The difference comes out quite clearly when the two are reversed in order in the same sentence:[6]

[Sag attempts to rip Boston phone directory in half]

(8a) Hankamer: I don't think you can do it, but I know someone who can.

(8b) #I don't think you can, but I know someone who can do it.

The purpose of this paper is to investigate this difference between syntactically and pragmatically controlled anaphora, and to show that there is a class of rules which, like VP Deletion, resist pragmatic control (although we will see that various factors interfere to produce exceptions of various interesting kinds). We will argue that the class of rules which require syntactic control is just the class of anaphora rules for which evidence is available that they are syntactic deletion rules, and which produce 'null anaphors', i.e. do not leave behind a pro-form.

1. Syntactic deletion anaphora and pronominalization anaphora

1.1 Grinder and Postal (1971) have argued, on the basis of sentences like (9)-(10), that VP Deletion must be a syntactic deletion rule, relating intermediate structures like (9)-(10a) to surface structures like (9)-(10b):

(9a) I've never ridden a camel, but Jorge has ridden a $camel_i$, and he says it_i stank horribly.

(9b) I've never ridden a camel, but Jorge has, and he says it_i stank horribly.

(10a) I don't keep gerbils in my office, but Jorge keeps gerbils in his office, and $they_i$ eat holes in his books.

(10b) I don't keep gerbils in my office, but Jorge does, and $they_i$ eat holes in his books.

The essence of their argument is that the right clauses of these sentences contain a pronoun which must have an antecedent, but the surface structures of the (b) sentences contain no NP which could be the antecedent for the pronoun. Note that the instance of the NP _a camel_ in the left clause of (9b) cannot serve as antecedent for a definite pronoun:

(11) *I've never ridden a camel, and it stank horribly.[7]

On the basis of this 'missing antecedent' phenomenon, Grinder and Postal argue that an interpretive theory of VP-anaphora (and, they claim, any identity-of-sense anaphora) which attempts to generate the structures containing null anaphors directly, without deriving them from an intermediate stage where the anaphoric VP is syntactically represented, must be rejected.

Ross (1969) also gives several arguments that VP Deletion is a syntactic deletion process. In sentences like (12), if the anaphoric right clause is derived by VP Deletion, the appearance of the distributionally restricted item *there* and the plural agreement are straightforwardly accounted for; otherwise some unpleasantly ad hoc mechanisms will have to be called into play.[8]

(12) Some people think there are no such rules, but there {are. / *is}

In sentences like (13)-(14), the collocation WH+*to* and the observed restriction that the WH cannot be *why* in this collocation are accounted for directly under an analysis which derives such sentences by a combination of WH fronting and VP Deletion, since the pre-deletion versions exhibit exactly the same collocation and restriction.[9]

(13) He knows how to dress, but I don't know how to.
(14) *He knows how to get high, but he doesn't know why to.

Finally, an otherwise reducible auxiliary fails to undergo reduction before the null VP:

(15) Paul Anderson's fat, and {I am / *I'm} too.

This inability of normally reducible items to reduce has been shown (King 1970) to correlate with the presence of an immediately following deletion site.[10]

As indicated in the last three notes, there are conceivable 'interpretive' approaches which evade some of these arguments. It is not the purpose of this paper to contemplate the viability of interpretive approaches to anaphora, i.e. whether grammars can be constructed so that null anaphors are interpreted at some superficial level. What is of interest for the present is that there is a class of rules, which we will characterize as 'deletion anaphora', which give evidence of the existence of syntactic structure at some level of representation which is absent (or at least invisible) in surface structure. Any interpretive theory which is to be consistent with this kind of evidence must provide, as a substitute for the deletion relation, a system of syntactically present and active but (at least phonologically) null constituents.

1.2 Bresnan (1971) has shown that the missing antecedent arguments cannot be constructed to show that do it anaphora is a deletion process:

(16) *Jack didn't cut Betty with a knife--Bill did it, and it was rusty.
[where it = the knife Bill cut Betty with]

The judgments are delicate, but it is generally agreed there is a difference between this sentence and the corresponding one with VP Deletion, which allows control of it from the missing antecedent.

Bresnan shows, in fact, that in general sentential it anaphora--of which she assumes, probably correctly, that do it is a special case--fails to exhibit the missing antecedent phenomenon:[11]

(17) *Jack didn't get picked off by a throw to first, but it happened to Bill, and it singed his ear.
[where it = the throw to first that singed Bill's ear]

She suggests that the correct generalization should be that anaphoric processes that leave pro-forms behind do not exhibit the missing antecedent phenomenon, whereas anaphoric processes which leave no pro-form do.[12]

Notice that Ross's arguments that VP Deletion is a syntactic deletion process do not go through for do it anaphora: there are no there-insertion sentences anaphorized with do it, there is no argument on the basis of the how to/*why to contrast, since do it is manifestly a VP in its own right, and can take the relevant adverbial modifiers (do it this way, do it for this reason), and there is no argument based on the reduction prohibition. In fact, so far as we know, this is representative of the situation with respect to pronouns in general; aside from the ingenious argument of Grinder and Postal, which suggests that one(s) pronominalization involves syntactic deletion, there seem to be no arguments that pronominalization involves deletion of syntactically present constituents.[13]

1.3 We have noted that there is a correlation, for the VP anaphora rules, between the existence of evidence that the rule is a syntactic deletion and its inability to operate under pragmatic control. We advance the following general claim:

Claim: It is just those anaphoric processes which consist in syntactic deletion, leaving no pro-form in place of the deleted structure, that require syntactic control.

We thus distinguish deletion anaphora, which involves deletion resulting in an 'incomplete' surface structure, i.e. a surface structure in which a normally present constituent is absent entirely, and pronominal anaphora, where there is an anaphorically interpreted item actually present as a constituent in surface structure. Our claim is that deletion anaphora requires an antecedent in actual linguistic structure, so that 'null anaphors' produced by deletion cannot normally be interpreted under pragmatic control; but that in general, pronominal anaphors may be so controlled.

Thus, for example, as pointed out in Section 0, ordinary definite pronouns do not in general require syntactic control. Sentential it pronominalization can also occur, although less readily, with nonsyntactic control, as in the following situation:

(18) Hankamer [observing Sag successfully ripping phone book in half]:
I don't believe it.

(19) Sag [same circumstance]:
It's not easy.

When we consider nominal Identity-of-Sense anaphora, the claim appears to be borne out, although the judgments become somewhat delicate. We find nonsyntactic control of indefinite pronouns like one(s) perfectly OK:

(20) [Sag produces two apples]
Hankamer: Can I have one?

(21) [Observing Max ride by on his camel]
Daddy, buy me one.
Did you ever ride on the one Sue used to have?

But for the version of Identity-of-Sense anaphora (commonly referred to as Genitive-Head Deletion) which deletes the head entirely, leaving only a genitive modifier, nonsyntactic control is somewhat more difficult:[14]

(22) #Have you ever ridden on Sue's?

The judgment is admittedly delicate, but in the course of several presentations and discussions of this paper we have found that a majority of speakers concur in the opinion that (22) is odd in the context specified in (21) in a way that the examples given in (21) are not.

It is a fact, however, that pragmatic control is felt to be much more palatable with nominal null anaphora than with VP null anaphora. This is a troublesome and interesting fact; it seems to indicate that the size of the null anaphor determines to some extent its nonsyntactic controllability, and that this factor interacts with the independent difference between deletion anaphora and pronominalization anaphora to produce a scale of judgments fading off toward imperceptibility. It makes sense, of course, that it will be easier to interpret a missing N from pragmatic context than a missing VP; the latter case involves more guesswork.

If this is correct, then in the case of an anaphoric process which deletes almost all of a clause we would expect the requirement of syntactic control to be particularly strong. There is such a rule, the rule of Sluicing, which derives sentences like (23b) from sources like (23a):

(23a) We were looking for somebody, but I can't remember who we were looking for.
(23b) We were looking for somebody, but I can't remember who.

Ross (1969) has argued overwhelmingly that this rule must be a rule of syntactic deletion.

Sluicing, like the other anaphora rules discussed here, can be syntactically controlled from previous linguistic context, even with a change of speakers:

(24) Hankamer: Someone's just been shot.
Sag: Yeah, I wonder who.

But it cannot be pragmatically controlled, as the following example demonstrates:

(25) [Hankamer produces a gun, points it offstage and fires, whereupon a scream is heard]
#Sag: Wow, I wonder who.

We conclude, then, that our claim is substantiated at least for the cases of deletion anaphora which produce incomplete surface structures above the level of NP structure, with the larger null anaphors showing the restriction more clearly. Clause-sized null anaphors, produced by Sluicing, are almost impossible to interpret pragmatically; VP-sized ones are easier, but still pretty clearly require syntactic control; and when the null anaphor is the size of a mere N, the requirement of syntactic control, while perceptible, is considerably diminished in effect.

2. Ellipsis rules. In this section we examine the class of rules which effect ellipsis in clauses. These are the rules which delete constituents from variable locations in a clause under identity with corresponding constituents in some other clause. Their properties are discussed in Hankamer (1971), and arguments that any rule of this type must be a syntactic deletion are given in Hankamer (1973).[15]

2.1 Stripping. Stripping is a rule which deletes everything in a clause under identity with corresponding parts of a preceding clause, except for one constituent (and sometimes a clause-initial adverb or negative):

(26) Alan likes to play volleyball, but not Sandy.
(27) Gwendolyn smokes marijuana, but seldom in her own apartment.

This rule can operate across a speaker boundary. Notice that the two clauses in each of the examples can be spoken by different speakers, and the resulting discourses are well formed, as is the following:

(28) Hankamer: Listen, Ivan, he's playing the William Tell Overture on the recorder.
Sag: Yeah, but not very well.

Here the response not very well results from the application of Stripping to the full clause But he isn't playing the William Tell Overture on the recorder very well.

This stands in marked contrast to the following discourse, where the extralinguistic context might be expected to provide sufficient information to control Stripping pragmatically:

(29) [Sag plays William Tell Overture on recorder]
#Hankamer: Yeah, but not very well.

The ill-formedness of this discourse shows that Stripping requires syntactic control.[16]

2.2 Gapping. Gapping is an ellipsis rule which applies in coordinate structures to delete all but two major constituents from the right conjunct under identity with corresponding parts of the left conjunct.

(30) Ehrlichman duped Haldeman, and Nixon, Ehrlichman.

Gapping too can operate across a speaker boundary, as is shown by the following discourse:

(31) Hankamer: Ivan is now going to peel an apple
Sag: And Jorge, an orange.

Once again, we observe that although it doesn't matter whose utterance controls Gapping, it nevertheless must be an utterance, not merely a situation. Consider the following discourse:

(32) [Hankamer produces an orange, proceeds to peel it, and just as Sag produces an apple, says:]
#And Ivan, an apple.

As you can see, this discourse ranks high on the bizarreness scale. We conclude that Gapping requires syntactic control.

The rule of Gapping can also delete subjects,[17] as in

(33) Mitchell lied to the committee, and is now serving his sentence.

And, as by now should come as no surprise, subject-Gapping requires syntactic control, as the following discourse shows:

(34) [Hankamer is still peeling his orange]
#Sag: And is dropping orange peels all over my foot.

It has been suggested to us that what is wrong with examples like (32) and (34) is perhaps not the lack of syntactic control for Gapping, but the impossibility of getting an isolated conjunct beginning with <u>and</u>; in other words, that the sentences are independently ungrammatical because <u>and</u> can only occur between surface conjuncts. This, however, does not appear to be true, for there are contexts in which utterance-initial <u>and</u> is possible, with no preceding discourse:

(35) Hankamer: [observing Sag playing pretty good ragtime piano] And he doesn't even have a left hand!

Other examples are pretty easily called to mind. It seems that such cases involve essentially pragmatic omission of an understood left conjunct, which is just what would have to be possible to allow the utterance-initial and in examples like (32) and (34). And in fact, if you put the verbs back in (and the subject in (34)), the bizarreness disappears:

(36) [Same context as (32)]
And Ivan is going to peel an apple.

(37) [Same context as (34)]
And he's dropping orange peels all over my foot!

We must conclude that the strangeness of (32) and (34) is not due to the fact that the conjunction is not flanked by conjuncts, but rather to the attempt to gap under pragmatic control.

We have shown in this section that two ellipsis processes, Gapping and Stripping, can be controlled syntactically across a speaker boundary from a discourse antecedent, but cannot be controlled pragmatically. For other ellipsis rules, such as Comparative Ellipsis, it is impossible to construct examples where they apply across sentence boundaries at all, so it is impossible to test them for pragmatic control. So far as we have been able to determine, there are no counterexamples to our claim: ellipsis rules which can be shown to involve deletion cannot operate under pragmatic control.[18]

3. Conclusion. Elsewhere (Sag and Hankamer (to appear)) we argue that the claim made in Section 1.3 must be modified somewhat to take into account various instances of anaphoric processes that leave pro-forms behind but act like they don't, and vice versa. We argue, in fact, that there are two coherent classes of anaphora phenomena that must be distinguished (which we term Deep Anaphora and Surface Anaphora). The notions of syntactically and pragmatically controlled anaphora, as developed in this paper, play a crucial role in determining to which class a given anaphoric process belongs.

NOTES

1. The examples in (1) can also, with some strain, be read with pragmatic control of the pronoun--then, of course, it is not coreferent with the NP which is its antecedent on the syntactically controlled reading.

The examples in (2), and again also the examples in (1), can also be syntactically controlled in discourse, with the linguistic antecedent in a previous sentence. It is clear that this intersentential control is syntactic and not just a case of pragmatic control, for the pronoun can, as in the examples in (1), have no real-world referent:

(i) Do you know what happens to anyone who eats this stuff?
--Yeah, his hair falls out.

(ii) Is the unicorn a possible animal?
--I don't know, but if it is, it's certainly a herbivore.

2. Shopen (1972) discusses the possibility of pragmatic control of anaphoric processes in some detail, but does not note the distinction observed here.

3. We use the term 'anaphoric process' to refer to any grammatical device which allows the interpretation of an element to be chosen from an infinite number of potential values, the choice in a particular instance being determined by context. This usage is intended to be neutral as to whether the proper formulation of the grammatical device is a syntactic transformation, an interpretive rule, or whatever.

4. There are, of course, strictly sentence-internal processes, such as reflexivization, which are and always have been recognized as strictly syntactically controlled.

5. We introduce the cross-hatch (#) as an indication that the sentence so marked is incompatible with the indicated context (presuming, of course, the absence of any relevant previous linguistic context).

6. We read these with normal (noncontrastive) intonation in the first clause, so that the main stress falls on do it in (8a) and on can in (8b). If the sentences are read with contrastive stress on you in both examples, (8b) becomes for some people more nearly conceivable as a discourse-initial utterance. This is a mysterious effect, but seems to have nothing to do with pragmatic control of VP Deletion. What seems to be the case is that VP Deletion, which ordinarily (like all anaphoric processes) is reluctant to operate backwards in conjoined structures, can marginally do so if some element outside the VP in the left conjunct is contrastively stressed. Thus (8b) becomes exactly as good as (i):

(i) I don't think YÓU can, but I know sómeone who can rip phone books in half.

7. The it_i of course, may have another antecedent in discourse; then (11) is grammatical:

(i) Al, why did you refuse to ride the $camel_i$?
Al: I've never ridden a camel, and it_i stank horribly.

Sentences like (9)-(10b), however, are grammatical even in the absence of a discourse or pragmatic antecedent for the pronoun.

8. The arguments given here were designed against an interpretive theory which does not employ 'empty' nodes which can undergo syntactic rules, as proposed, for example, in Wasow (1972). Under this proposal, anaphoric or elliptical structures start out as syntactically fully developed underlying structures, except that some of the nodes are empty. These structures can then be transformed by syntactic transformations to produce elliptical derived structures, the empty parts of which get interpreted by interpretive rules which refer to other parts of the derived structure.

This proposal amounts to an admission that the anaphor is related to a syntactically real underlying representation. What distinguishes this from a deletion analysis is no longer the claim that anaphorized structures are not present at any stage in syntactic representation, but that the lexical items are never inserted.

This is not the place to go into an exhaustive analysis of the consequences of this proposal. The matter is taken up in more detail in Sag and Hankamer (to appear) and by McCawley (1974). For the moment, let it suffice to say that it is not at all clear that such an interpretive theory is distinct in any empirical way from a deletion theory, the central claim of which is that the anaphorized material is syntactically represented at some stage, and that it can be null just in case there is an identical antecedent structure.

9. This argument, however, does not go through against the syntactically active empty node version of the interpretive theory.

10. One could, of course, devise an interpretive theory employing empty nodes in 'surface structure' which would be interpreted under control from a filled node elsewhere in the structure, and say that reduction is blocked when there is an immediately following empty node. It is not clear that such a theory would differ in any interesting way from one involving syntactic deletion.

11. Postal (1972) disputes the generality of Bresnan's observation, claiming that there are cases of sentential it containing missing antecedents. The delicacy of the judgments involved makes it very difficult to evaluate the arguments in this controversy, but the fact remains that there is a difference between VP Deletion, which readily allows missing antecedent effects for all speakers, and sentential it (including do it) anaphora, which in general do not. It is this difference that we are interested in.

12. This suggestion should probably be modified to say that 'definite' pronouns do not exhibit the missing antecedent phenomenon, since Grinder and Postal show that indefinite pronouns like one can contain missing antecedents.

We also discuss, in Section 3, an anaphoric process which does not involve a pro-form (i.e. the 'anaphor' is null) and which does not exhibit the missing antecedent phenomenon. We show, however, that this process is not deletion anaphora.

13. Identity-of-Sense pronominalization with one(s) is the only anaphoric process we know of that both gives some evidence (albeit scanty) of involving syntactic deletion and appears to substitute a pro-form for the missing constituent.

14. There is another anaphoric process in NP's, closely related to the Genitive-Head Deletion discussed here but with slightly different properties (see Andrews 1974), which might be called Quantity-Head Deletion:

(ia) I asked for one orange, and she gave me three.
(ib) I asked for three oranges, but she only gave me one.
(ic) She went to look for oranges, and she found several.
(id) How many did she find?
(ie) I didn't think there were any.

The one in (ib), like the three in (ia), is a quantity expression, and must be distinguished from the pronoun one, which appears in (ii):

(ii) I asked for an orange, and she gave me one.

The pronominal one occurs only unstressed, whereas the quantity one, like other quantity expressions, may occur with stress; also the quantity one occurs before adjectives, whereas the pronoun one occurs after adjectives, and both can occur in the same NP:

(iii) Give us one blue one.

This rule of Q-Head Deletion is a deletion anaphora rule; no pronoun replaces the missing head of the NP, and missing antecedent arguments are easy to construct:

(iv) I don't own any camels that have fleas, but Bela owns three, and they keep getting in his beard.

We predict then that pragmatic control will be more difficult for Q-Head Deletion than for one(s) pronominalization, and though again the judgments are delicate, we find that this is the case:

(v) [Observing camel, no previous discourse]
My uncle owns one.

(vi) [Same context]
#My uncle owns three.

The difference, however, is disturbingly small, and the prohibition against nonsyntactic control can be overridden by various factors which we have not investigated, such as high predictability in a stereotyped environment, as when one says to a pretzel seller:

(vii) I'll take three.

15. In addition to the arguments given there, it is possible to construct Grinder-Postal type arguments based on the missing antecedent phenomenon for each of these rules. To illustrate, for the rule of Stripping:

(i) Bill took his coat off, but not Sally. She never takes if off.

In this sentence the pronoun it can refer to Sally's coat, even though the surface structure contains no NP which could control the anaphora, and the sentence is clearly good in a context where the pronoun could not be pragmatically controlled.

In order to construct a missing antecedent argument for Gapping, we must consider an idiolect such as that of only one of the authors of this paper, in which sentences are accepted which violate the No-Ambiguity Constraint proposed in Hankamer (1973). The crucial property for our purposes is the ability to gap an object NP along with the verb as in

(ii) Sally took her clothes to the laundromat, and Herman, to the dry cleaner.
[From . . . and Herman took his clothes to the dry cleaner]

Speakers who can stomach (ii) on the intended reading are also happy with (iii), showing that the gap can contain a missing antecedent:

(iii) Sally takes her clothes to the laundromat, and Herman, to the dry cleaner, even though he knows they're all wash-and-wear.

16. The possibility of pragmatic control in the following example provides a counterexample to the simple claim made in the text:

(i) Not in my wastebasket, you don't.

We have not the space here to go into the details of this very interesting phenomenon, but it appears that the requirement of syntactic control holds only for strictly declarative sentences, sentences with the illocutionary force of statements. In the case of examples like (i), the illocutionary force is clearly not declarative, but peremptory; and in imperatives and exhortatives VP deletion also can take place under pragmatic control:

(ii) [Hankamer brandishes cleaver, advances on Sag]
Sag: Don't! My God, please don't!

Similarly, if you see that an acquaintance has dyed his hair green, you can say:

(iii) You didn't!

What is clear is that in each of these cases the illocutionary force is not declarative (although what exactly it is in some cases, as in (iii), is far from clear). So far as we have been able to determine, the restriction holds perfectly (with the caveat stated at the end of Section 1) for declarative sentences. We have no idea why there should be such an effect on the behavior of anaphoric processes conditional on the illocutionary force of the utterance.

17. Arguments that such sentences result from Gapping and are not instances of VP conjunction reduction are given in Hankamer (1973).

18. There is a peculiar class of pragmatic contexts where certain of these violations lose their offensive character. In particular, when two or more people are party to a nonlinguistic event or situation, the longer the event or situation continues, i. e. the longer all parties concerned are observing a particular event without saying anything, the more 'linguistic' the context becomes. That is, once an event or situation has been observed long enough in silence, it becomes part of a tacit discourse between the observers, and it can trigger syntactically controlled anaphora, as in the following example.

(i) Sag (to Hankamer): [after watching a pygmy pole vaulter, not three feet tall, spit on his hands, rub them up and down on the shaft of his pole, eye the bar which is fixed at 19'3", take a thirty-yard running approach, and successfully clear the bar by an inch and a half]
It looks like he can!

Other related examples include the rather comic effect achieved in the Sherlock Holmes story where Watson, asleep in an easy chair, is being observed by Holmes. Watson writhes and squirms in his chair, obviously dreaming intensely. Just at the point where Watson is about to fall off onto the floor, Holmes utters a sentence like:

(ii) No she won't.

Clearly, the intended effect is that Holmes has been reading Watson's mind. The events of Watson's dream have become a common linguistic context, one which is capable of triggering syntactically controlled anaphora, as in (ii), which is an instance of VP Deletion. Although such contexts as these do permit smaller violations of control restrictions, as in the last two examples involving VP Deletion, we know of no such examples involving more severe violations.

REFERENCES

Andrews, A. 1975. One(s) deletion in the comparative clause. In: Proceedings of the Fifth Annual Meeting of the Northeast Linguistic Society. Edited by E. Kaisse and J. Hankamer. Cambridge, Mass., Harvard University Press. 246-256.

Bresnan, J. 1971. A note on the notion 'identity of sense anaphora'. Linguistic Inquiry 2.589-596.

Grinder, J. and P. Postal. 1971. Missing antecedents. Linguistic Inquiry 2.269-312.

Hankamer, J. 1971. Constraints on deletion in syntax. Unpublished doctoral dissertation, Yale University.

Hankamer, J. 1973. Unacceptable ambiguity. Linguistic Inquiry 4.17-68.

Jackendoff, R. 1972. Semantic interpretation in generative grammar. Cambridge, Mass., The M.I.T. Press.

King, H. 1970. On blocking the rules for contraction in English. Linguistic Inquiry 1.124-136.

McCawley, J. 1974. How to get an interpretive theory of anaphora to work. Unpublished paper.

Postal, P. 1972. Some further limitations of interpretive theories of anaphora. Linguistic Inquiry 3.316-399.

Ross, J. R. 1969. Guess who? In: Papers from the Fifth Regional Meeting. Chicago, Chicago Linguistic Society. 252-286.

Ross, J. R. 1972. Act. In: Semantics of natural language. Edited by Harman and Davidson. Dordrecht, P. Reidel Publishing Co. 70-126.

Sag, I. and J. Hankamer. To appear. Deep and surface anaphora.

Shopen, T. 1972. A generative theory of ellipsis. Unpublished doctoral dissertation, UCLA. Reproduced by the Indiana University Linguistics Club.

Wasaw, T. 1972. Anaphoric relations in English. Unpublished doctoral dissertation, M.I.T.

INFORMATION STRUCTURES IN DISCOURSE

CHARLOTTE LINDE

Hunter College, City University of New York

Some of the speaker's morphological and syntactic choices appear to be influenced by or determined by the nature of the information which the speaker intends to convey. With some well-known exceptions, information is thought of as being either new in the discourse and hence new to the hearer, or already mentioned in the discourse and hence known to the hearer. The subject has generally been analyzed as the position for the placement of old information, while other constituents of the sentence, which may bear the main stress of the sentence, have been seen as the position for new information (Bolinger 1972). Chafe also has noted that in the least marked instances, the old information is carried by the surface subject (Chafe 1970:212). Similarly, the article system is the morphological system which most directly reflects information status, and all other things being equal, it is assumed that the definite article is the one appropriate for old information and the indefinite for new information. Jespersen, for example, states that the definite article 'denotes one individual (supposed to be more or less familiar to the speaker or writer)' (Jespersen 1949:421).

If these familiar analyses are correct, they should be successful in predicting speakers' choice of articles and surface subjects in actual discourse. In this study, the discourses examined are a group of 72 apartment layout descriptions. They were elicited as part of a survey of attitudes on urban living, conducted in New York City. The people interviewed were not told that the interviewer was primarily interested in their language. Analysis of the apartment layout descriptions has shown that they are clearly a well-defined speech act, in Hymes' sense, and indeed are so coherent that formal rules can be written to describe the major transitions from real-world information to syntactic patterns (Linde 1974; Linde and Labov 1975).

In the sentences of this data, the subject position is occupied by locative phrases, by the dummy there, by pronouns, and by full noun phrases. It is the full noun phrase subjects which are the most suitable for a study of the informational status of the subject position.

In this body of data, there are 82 sentences which have noun phrase subjects. Of these, over half, 46, express old information, or information which has not been mentioned specifically but whose existence can be assumed from the preceding discourse. These sentences containing old information in the subject position follow the postulated unmarked distribution of information, and appear to have relatively few constraints on the nature of the information of the subject position. Examples of such sentences are (1), (2), and (3).

(1) Then there's a really skinny hallway that same width as the other hallway I described. . . . and then that hallway opens into the kitchen.

(2) And then to the left of the living room are two bedrooms. The two bedrooms are on the same side of the building.

(3) Could you tell me the layout of that apartment? The last apartment was a garden apartment.

Twenty-seven of the 46 sentences containing old information in the subject noun phrases are examples like these, in which the referent of the subject noun phrase has been directly mentioned in the preceding discourse. Similar to these are those sentences containing subject noun phrases which refer to something whose existence is entailed by the preceding discourse. An example is (4).

(4) You come into a small, uh, hallway, and one side leads to the bathroom.

Neither the specific noun phrase nor some synonym for it has appeared before in the discourse, but the existence of its referent can still be treated as known information. That is, if we know that there is a hallway, we know that it has a side. Indeed, objects and their parts are among the clearest examples of such pragmatic entailment. We may consider sentences like (1), (2), and (3), and sentences like (4) to be equivalent. In both, the speaker repeats information whose existence has been previously established in the discourse, either directly or indirectly, and uses the placement in subject position as a link with what has already been said.

However, the remaining 36 sentences with noun phrase subjects appear to contradict the postulated patterning of the information of sentences, since they contain new information in the subject position. Twenty-eight of them introduce new rooms and 8 introduce other new information. These 36 cases represent 44 percent of the sentences with full noun phrase subjects. As usual, the examination of the discourses actually produced by speakers reveals an apparently chaotic situation.

However, when we examine the interaction of the subject position introductions and the choice of article, some order begins to emerge. If the noun phrase subjects have any article, they have the definite article. This is an expected finding. The two should go together: the subject position and the definite article have both been analyzed as appropriate for the same kind of information. We may hypothesize that perhaps speakers are treating the newly introduced information as if it were already known. What this means can be made clearer by an examination of article choice for all introductions.

We will consider the introductions of all the rooms in this body of data, in every position in the sentence. The inquiry will be confined to the introduction of new rooms, since this type of information is physical, discrete, and least open to the question of whether its existence is presupposed by other elements in the discourse. We find that 38 percent of all introductions of rooms are made with the definite article. Table 1 shows the identity of rooms introduced with the definite article.

TABLE 1. Rooms introduced with definite article.

Room	Number of introductions
Kitchen	28
Living room	25
Bathroom	21
Bedroom	20
Dining room	5
Foyer	1

The introduction of rooms with the definite article is not entirely unconditioned. Most of the rooms introduced with the definite article are major rooms: only six are not. (A major room is defined as a room which an apartment may be expected to have--living room, bedroom, kitchen, and bathroom, although bathroom is a special case. A minor room is defined as a room which an apartment may or may not have--dining room, den, library, study, laundry room, etc.).

Minor rooms constitute 12 percent of all the introductions in this data, but only 6 percent of the introductions with definite articles. Thus, minor rooms are introduced with the definite article only half as often as would be predicted by their overall frequency in the data. In general, speakers use the definite article to introduce rooms which an apartment can be assumed to contain, rooms whose existence in an apartment can to some extent be treated as given. (It should be noted that the minor rooms introduced with the definite article are dining room and foyer. Although neither is a major room, they are the most frequent of the minor rooms. The rarest of the minor rooms--laundry room, library, etc.--are not introduced with the definite article. However, it is impossible to say that they would never be introduced this way, since they are so rare that the present data is not extensive enough to warrant such a claim.)

The nature of the rooms introduced in subject position is necessarily similar to that of the rooms introduced with the definite article, since there is a great deal of overlap between the two groups. Table 2 shows the rooms which are introduced in subject position.

TABLE 2. Rooms introduced in subject position.

Room	Number of introductions
Bathroom	8
Kitchen	7
Living room	5
Bedroom	4
Room	2
Foyer	1
Dining room	1

Here too, the most unexpected rooms are not introduced in subject position. That is, just as there are no sentences like (5), there are also no sentences like (6) and (7).

(5) At the end is the library.
(6) The laundry room is at the end.
(7) My den is straight ahead.

Introduction of a new noun phrase in subject position appears to be subject to the same conditions as introduction with the definite article: it is found with those rooms whose existence can be assumed.

However, the very notion of introduction with the definite article itself poses a problem. One of the best established patterns of article use is that a new noun phrase is introduced with the indefinite article and is subsequently mentioned with the definite article. That is, simple introduction into a discourse is enough to change information from new to old. Examples of this discourse pattern are (8) from Jespersen, (9) from Sorenson, and (10) and (11) from Stockwell et al.

(8) Once upon a time there lived an old tailor in a village. The old tailor was known all over the village as Old Harry.
(9) Yesterday Anderson kissed a girl with blue eyes. The girl called the police.
(10) I saw a cat in the tree this morning, but when I looked this afternoon, the cat was gone.
(11) A boy and a girl were walking down the street together and the girl was shouting at the boy.

When we examine the articles assigned to information on first and subsequent mention in the data of the present study, we find that not even this well-known pattern is categorical.

The structure of apartment layout descriptions permits us several ways to study this question. These apartment descriptions are most typically in the form of an imaginary tour, with each room and its position mentioned as an imaginary tourer would come to it. A spatial arrangement is thus transformed into a temporal one, which leads to the analysis of apartment layout descriptions as a type of pseudo-narrative. The similarity to true narratives is actually quite close. As true narratives often contain an introductory abstract, so layout descriptions optionally begin with an introductory summary which may enumerate the people living in the apartment, mention its noteworthy features, evaluate its desirability or lack of it, or list the rooms of the apartment.

Apartment descriptions which begin with an enumeration of the rooms of the layout are the clearest places to begin examining the pattern of the distribution of articles. The standard analysis of the article system would predict that speakers would use the indefinite article for mention of the room in the initial summary, and the definite article for subsequent mention in the layout description proper. But in fact speakers do not restrict themselves to this pattern. There are four possibilities: indefinite article in both summary and layout; definite article in both summary and layout; indefinite article in summary followed by definite article in layout; and definite article in summary followed by indefinite article in layout. Speakers produce all but the last of these possibilities. That is, there are sequences like (12), (13), and (14), but none like (15). (Each example contains the relevant portion of the summary followed by the relevant portion of the description.)

(12) It sort of went like this, like a fading highway, with, the living room is a little bit wider . . . You walked into the living room.

(13) It had a living room, a bedroom and kitchen and bathroom. . . . There was a kitchen off the, let's see, corridor, a living room . . .

(14) It had a bedroom, about the size of the living room, a big kitchen that could have been partitioned off into a dining room and kitchen. . . . You entered into a tiny little hallway and the kitchen was off to the left of that. And the bedroom was like, the bathroom was straight at the end of that hall and to the left again was the bedroom.

(15) *It has the big entrance hall, the living room and two bedrooms. . . . You walk into a big entrance hall and straight ahead is a living room, to the left is my kitchen, and in back are two bedrooms.

Table 3 shows the frequency of each case.

TABLE 3. First and subsequent article, summary and description.

		Subsequent article	
		a	the
First article	a	10	11
	the	0	6

It might be argued that the 10 examples of repeated indefinite article are due to error or forgetfulness, the speaker losing track of the fact that he has already introduced the room with the indefinite article and so repeating it in the layout proper. But such forgetfulness does not produce the pattern of first mention with definite article and subsequent mention with indefinite article.

Another possibility open to the speaker is to mention a room more than once in the layout description proper, usually because he needs the second mention of a room as a reference point for a direction, or because he wishes to add further information about the room. Examples are (16), (17), and (18).

(16) To your left was a hallway, leading to a bedroom which was like an L-shape. So in other words, you went to your left through a hall, . . .
(17) On the right was the kitchen, and off the kitchen, even further from the kitchen was my little maid's room.
(18) There's a long hallway which opens into a foyer. Now in back of the foyer there's the dining room.

Table 4 shows the frequency of each case.

TABLE 4. First and subsequent article, description proper.

		Subsequent article	
		a	the
First article	a	8	40
	the	3	25

This table reveals a number of interesting patterns. One striking feature is the presence of three cases in which a room is introduced with the definite article and later mentioned with the indefinite article. These are examples (19), (20), and (21).

(19) You walked into the kitchen and then there's a bathroom and a kitchen, a john, a door, you know, in the kitchen with a little john there.
(20) It has a long hallway that you walk into and straight ahead is the kitchen, there's a door and then from the hallway into I mean a big dining room and there's a big kitchen off that.
(21) You took a right down this long narrow hallway and on the right was the kitchen and off the kitchen even further from the kitchen was my little maid's room, and then keeping on going down the hall, on the right was a large bedroom and directly down the hall straight ahead down the hall was another bedroom. It was a dining room, it was turned into a bedroom, off a long hall.

This is the one pattern which is unexpected, and therefore it is not surprising that two and possibly all three of the examples involve mistakes, networks in which the speaker lost the thread.

Another interesting feature is that this table looks much more like the pattern predicted by the standard analysis of the function of the articles. The greatest number of cases use the indefinite article for first mention and the definite article for second mention. It is illuminating to compare this pattern in the two kinds of repeated mention. When the two mentions of the room are divided between the summary and the description proper, the expected pattern of indefinite article followed by definite article is no more frequent than the pattern using indefinite articles for both mentions. When the room is mentioned twice in the description proper, the expected pattern is significantly more frequent.[1]

These facts lead to a number of conclusions about the notions 'discourse' and 'new and old information'. These notions are often appealed to in discussions of syntax, but as they are currently used, they do not predict the behavior of speakers. Most discussions of information status assume that information is not known until it is introduced into the discourse, after which it becomes known. The transmission of information of this type is the main point of the discourse. In addition, there is shared knowledge, which is treated in the same way as information which has been introduced into the discourse explicitly. A clear statement of this common position is provided by Chafe (1970:211).

> Now typically, it is the case that the speaker assumes that some of the information he is communicating is new: it is information he is introducing into the hearer's mind for the first time. But typically it is also the case that some of the information in the sentence is not new. Some of it is information which the speaker and hearer already share at the time the sentence is spoken. This shared information constitutes a kind of starting point based on concepts 'already in the air', to which the new information can be related.

There are also further complications--generic noun phrases, parts of known wholes, etc. But in general, this very common conception of information appears to be implicitly based on a theory of discourse which consists of a speaker who knows something, a hearer who does not know it, and a mutual desire for its transfer.

When we actually examine conversation, it is remarkable how few situations like this there really are. There has been much discussion recently about the pragmatics of ordinary conversation--the illocutionary and perlocutionary intentions of speakers in a given social context (Gordon and Lakoff 1971, R. Lakoff 1973, Weiser 1974). However, such discussion has not yet begun to examine in a serious way the problem of information, which is still being cavalierly treated as 'the point of the discourse' or 'what the speaker intends to convey'. It is unclear, for example, how to analyze the informational status or intended force of conversations which fall under

Malinowski's heading of phatic communication, talk for the sake of something being said. These are conversations like the following.

A. Hi, how are you?
B. Fine, and you?
A. Oh, getting along.

A. This bacon is half raw. It's disgusting.
B. Yeah, I like my bacon crisp.

The information of these conversations must be analyzed as being about states of health or tastes in bacon, but clearly the point of the conversation is not to convey this information.

The apartment descriptions are equally hard to fit into a simple binary model of information transfer. The speaker does have information that the hearer does not have: he is describing his own apartment. But the hearer is not entirely ignorant. Although he does not know the details of a particular apartment, he does have a general knowledge of the nature of apartments. He knows that an apartment almost certainly has a bathroom, probably does not have a library, and certainly does not have a moat. It is this partial knowledge of the hearer which complicates the analysis of information and which permits the speaker's variation in choice of article and position of introduction of new rooms. Given the particular communicative task of describing an apartment, either article is appropriate. To introduce a kitchen or a bathroom, the speaker may decide that the room has not been mentioned before and hence is new, and may be introduced with the indefinite article. Or with equal justification, the speaker may decide that the hearer knows that an apartment normally has a bathroom and a kitchen, and hence the rooms are not new information, and may be introduced with the definite article. Both analyses of the status of information are coherent and so both choices of article are made. (It might be argued that the description of an apartment layout is a peculiarly complicated case, more ambiguous than most other types of discourse. But it is my suspicion that, in fact, the apartment description is a relatively simple discourse type, since it deals with the physical relations of objects in the real world, rather than evaluating people and events, or attempting to influence beliefs or behavior.)

In examining the patterning of information in discourse, it is also of greatest importance to clarify what is meant by discourse. In syntactic theory, this term is used to mean any string of sentences in an utterance context. Such phenomena as article choice and pronominalization are analyzed as being at least partially determined by discourse, since they may require reference to preceding sentences. But there has been little or no attempt to analyze just what a discourse is, or whether different types of discourses have different effects on the syntax of the sentences comprising them. In anthropology and sociolinguistics, there has been a more careful attempt to distinguish between different discourse types. Hymes, for example, provides a taxonomic framework for the identification of speech acts and speech events (Hymes 1972). But this theoretical orientation has not, as yet, proceeded to the study of the syntactic effects of the organization of discourse.

The results of this study show that the two kinds of research must be united. Phenomena such as article choice cannot be studied over any connected sequence of sentences. Rather, it is necessary to know the type of discourse formed by the sentences. Even within a given discourse type--in this study, apartment descriptions--the articles are patterned differently depending on whether they appear in the same section of one discourse or two different sections of the same discourse. This is direct and compelling evidence that the study of syntactic variation must rest on careful studies of the organization of discourse.

NOTES

I would like to thank Frank Anshen, Teresa Labov, and Geoffrey Nunberg for their helpful comments and suggestions.

1. The difference is statistically significant ($X^2 = 7.18$, $p < .01$).

REFERENCES

Bolinger, Dwight. 1972. Accent is predictable (if you're a mind-reader). Language, Vol. 48, Number 3.

Chafe, Wallace. 1970. Meaning and the structure of language. Chicago, The University of Chicago Press.

Gordon, David and George Lakoff. 1971. Conversational postulates. Papers from the Seventh Regional Meeting. Chicago, Chicago Linguistic Society.

Hymes, Dell. 1972. Models of the interaction of language and social life. In: Directions in sociolinguistics. Edited by John J. Gumperz and Dell Hymes. New York, Holt, Rinehart and Winston.

Jespersen, Otto. 1949. A modern English grammar on historical principles. London, Allen and Unwin.

Lakoff, Robin. 1973. The logic of politeness: On minding your p's and q's. Papers from the Ninth Regional Meeting. Chicago, Chicago Linguistic Society.

Linde, Charlotte. 1974. The linguistic encoding of spatial information. Unpublished dissertation, Columbia University.

Linde, Charlotte and William Labov. 1975. Spatial networks as a site for the study of language and thought. Language, Vol. 51, Number 4.

Sorenson, H. S. 1959. The function of the definite article in modern English. English Studies, Vol. 40.

Stockwell, Robert, Paul Schachter, and Barbara Hall Partee. 1973. The major syntactic structures of English. New York, Holt, Rinehart and Winston.

Weiser, Ann. 1974. Deliberate ambiguity. Papers from the Tenth Regional Meeting. Chicago, Chicago Linguistic Society.

HOW COME YOU ASKED HOW COME?

WALT WOLFRAM

Federal City College and
Center for Applied Linguistics

TODD D. WOLFRAM

Woodlin Elementary School

0. Introduction. This paper focuses on one relatively stable conversational frame in which a 'how come' question is asked.[1] The conversational frame typically takes the following form. (1) As part of a conversation, an individual is asked how old he/she is (i.e. 'How old are you?'). (2) The participant responds with a statement indicating his/her age (i.e. 'I'm ___ years old.'). (3) The participant who asked the original question then asks 'how come' or 'why'. (4) The participant responds to the 'how come' question in some manner.

The format is relatively simple and, as I indicated, is usually integrated into a more extended conversation that is taking place between the participants. In other words, the person who is asked the 'how come' question is not aware of the fact that a response to this question is deliberately being posed for the sake of some type of linguistic or sociolinguistic study.

At this point, you may wonder how come I decided to ask 'how come' questions of this type. First of all, I must confess, I was interested in finding out some things about my own language usage that had been noticed by others. Several of my colleagues who also qualify as friends have told me that I ask 'how come' questions in contexts that strike them intuitively as inappropriate. While I may do this unconsciously to a certain extent, I must admit that I have utilized such questions in a type of teasing or joking behavior, and in this regard, I do not consider myself all that unusual. For example, I found myself asking the following question.

(1) Wolfram: Where are you from anyhow?
Addressee: New York.
Wolfram: How come?
Addressee: Because that's where the hospital was located.

So, my first interest, then, was in looking at how I was using such types of questions, whether they were used as a form of joking behavior or simply asked in contexts that others found obtrusive.

There is, however, another reason which promulgated my interest in this type of questioning, and this relates to the types of questions that children sometimes ask. It seems to be a well-known but little studied fact that children, during certain periods of development, are 'full of questions'. Whereas the mere quantity of the questions may be impressive to some observers, there are also cases which stand out to adults as different from the types of questions adults ask each other. Children have, in fact, been known to ask 'how come' or 'why' questions in the type of frame that I set up for this study. From the home of one of my colleagues comes the following exchange:

(2) Father: Well, Judd, in a few more days you'll be five and three quarters.
Judd: How come?
Father: Well, that's just the way it works out.

A similar anecdote comes from my own home (before my wife knew I was interested in eliciting such questions). A friend was asking my three-year-old son how old he was when the following exchange took place:

(3) Friend of family: How old are you now, Terry?
Terry: Two and a half.
Mother: No you're not, you're three.
Terry: Why?
Mother: Remember, you had a birthday, so you're now three.

The only point that I'm trying to make here is that children do ask questions that fall into the frame that I have set up for my 'how come', so that an investigation of it may lead to some notions of why some of the questions that children ask may strike adults as different from the sorts of questions they feel are appropriate.

While I am concerned here with one simple question frame, I am investigating it within the broader context of question asking. What we are concerned with is the interaction of real life experience with language usage in the determination of question appropriateness. In this regard, we will see that one of the issues that becomes crucial is the distinction between what we might label 'obvious' and 'nonobvious' information. By obvious information here, I am referring to information about the real world that the speaker and hearer can be expected to have access to and each assumes such knowledge on the part of the other. Both speaker and hearer in the conversational set have acquired such knowledge and have the ability to discriminate on this basis. Nonobvious information, on the other hand, does not meet these criteria for one of the participants in the conversational set. On one level, the notion of 'obvious' and 'nonobvious' information seems to relate to the role of language as it interacts with pragmatics. That is, we use our real life experience to determine what is an appropriate and an inappropriate question. There is, however, another dimension that enters into this issue when such matters are related to age differences. What, for example, is the status of children in terms of such information? If such information is, to a certain extent, determined by culture and a child is in the process of being enculturated, it must be expected that a child may be exempt from the constraints of 'obvious' knowledge which are operative for adults. In this regard, then, the relationship of question appropriateness to real life experience may extend beyond pragmatics to ontology. Although we focus upon a particular question frame as a case in point, we are concerned with more general principles about the role of question appropriateness in language usage.

1. Asking 'how come?'. The literal reason that an object is designated to be a specific age is related to the regular divisions that are made in our culture based on the particular calendar that we have adopted. This procedure for measuring age is, of course, accepted by convention in our culture and is not necessarily that which may be accepted in another culture. For example, in some cultures, a different computation system may be devised based on a different division of a calendar. Or, the same calendar may be adopted but the year may be calculated from the inception point of the designated division rather than the completion, so that a baby may be considered to be one year old at birth rather than designating the completion of the first year as the point at which a child is one year old. Obviously, the adoption of a particular calendar system and the method for computation is something that is learned by a child as a part of his enculturation process. Typically, the type of calendar we adopt and the method for computation are accepted by

adults with little question. It is something we simply learn and accept as a part of growing up in our culture.

The traditional acceptance of this measurement of time by regular intervals seems to be an important aspect related to why certain reason questions concerning time strike adults initially as somewhat inappropriate. Thus, we do not often encounter reason questions when an individual states his current age. That is, it seems somewhat strange for a person to ask us 'how come' after telling him what our age is. This, of course, is not to say that all statements of age cannot be questioned in this way. There appear to be certain circumstances in which a 'how come' question with respect to age does not seem nearly as inappropriate.

For example, if one individual tells another individual that his dog is 63 years old, it may be appropriate to ask 'how come'. In this case, however, the reason that a 'how come' question sounds less strange seems to be related to the fact that dogs are not expected to live 63 years according to the conventional calendar adopted for human age measurement. In this case, the apparent appeal to a human equivalency time measurement (i. e. where one calendar year of a human life is roughly equivalent to seven years of a dog's life) calls the conventional calendar for measurement into question based on our real life knowledge of dog life expectancy, so that it appears to be appropriate to ask the 'how come' question. In another case, a person might declare that the Biblical character Methuselah was 900 years old and a person might ask 'How come he was 900 years old?' In this case, it seems somewhat appropriate to ask the 'how come' question since there is an obvious discrepancy between our real life expectations of a human life span and the stated age. But what the individual is really asking about is an account for the discrepancy since we all know that humans do not normally live to be over 900 years old. In this case, a person may explain Methuselah's age in terms of different calendrical calculations, the use of numbers in a figurative sense, or a justification of the literalness of the figure by explaining that God intervened.

A final example of an instance in which it might be appropriate to ask 'how come' to a person's designated age comes from the perennial age of 39 claimed by the late Jack Benny. Given our general knowledge from the real world that tells us that Jack Benny had exceeded the age of 39 by a considerable margin, we might ask 'how come'.

In all the examples just given, the legitimacy or quasi-legitimacy of a 'how come' question with reference to age seems related to the fact that our real world knowledge of age expectancies does not appear to match the designated age. In two of the cases, a dog's age and Methuselah's age, there is an expectation of life span that may call the traditional calendrical convention into question, while the third case involves a well-known refusal to accept the continuing calculation of age. The important thing in all three cases, however, is that we need some background information pointing to an apparent discrepancy in the adoption of the conventional age calculation to legitimize the question.

2. Real data on 'how come' questions. Now that we have presented some background information on 'how come' questions with respect to age, let us look at some real data that was obtained from actually asking this question of individuals after they had specified their age. Consider the following exchanges:

(4a) FW: How old are you?
INF: Twenty-six.
FW: How come?
INF: (Laughter) I don't know.

(4b) FW: How old are you?
INF: Twenty-nine.
FW: How come?
INF: (Laughter) I don't know, how old should I be?

While the responses from other adults indicate variations we shall be discussing, these exchanges indicate a very basic point. Even though the exchange usually took place within the framework of a more extended legitimate conversation, the question was invariably responded to by adults in a way that indicated it was not considered a sincere request concerning the reason for a person's age (i. e. it violated a felicity condition for questions). This, I believe, is related to the fact that the informants assumed that I knew the convention for calculating age in our society as a part of my background knowledge. I could certainly not be asking for such obvious information as a sincere question. In most cases, this was indicated by laughter, as if I had intended it to be a type of joke and the adult did not typically respond with a literal reason.

What is it that makes people laugh at this question? As a beginning point, we may say that it seems funny because the information being requested seems so obvious to the person who is being asked the question at the same time that a nonobvious reading of the question may not immediately come to mind. In this regard, it is instructive to note that there is a type of joking or riddling behavior in our society which plays on obvious information analogous to this. Riddles like 'Why did the chicken cross the road?' (to get to the other side) or 'Why do firemen wear red suspenders?' (to hold their pants up) seem to employ an analogous frame. The hearer recognizes that certain information may be so implicitly obvious that it is ruled out of consideration as a possible answer. A similar reference to obvious information comes from an interview with the ex-professional quarterback for the San Francisco Forty-Niners, John Brodie, as it was quoted by Sports Illustrated in its section entitled 'They Said It':

(5) Reporter: How come such an expensive quarterback like you holds the football for place kicks?
John Brodie: If I didn't, the ball would fall over.

Admittedly, there are cases where the appeal to obvious information may be used sarcastically, so that it is sometimes difficult to determine whether the respondent intends it to be an 'obvious information joke' or a way of evading the nonobvious response to the question (or a subtle combination of both). Thus, I am unsure of the intent of an unemployed linguist whom I happened to meet on the way to the Washington Linguistics Club one evening. As a regular attendant of such meetings it was fairly obvious that he was on his way to the meeting when I asked him 'What are you doing now?' with the intent of finding out whether he had found a job yet. His reply was 'Right now, I'm walking to the Washington Linguistics Club'.

More obvious sarcasm is found in the response of a person who has lost something when another person asks 'Where did you lose it?' and he replies 'If I knew where I lost it, I would have found it'. In this case, the nonobvious reading must interpret 'where' to refer to general rather than specific location, but the respondent chooses to interpret it as a 'stupid question' because of a potential interpretation which is out of order with the situation encountered in the real world. The main point here is that there is a type of joking behavior which may veer into sarcasm in which the distinction between obvious and nonobvious information plays an important part.

The difference between these examples and the one with 'how come' is that the play on obvious information is found in the reply of the former and in the question of the 'how come' example. This difference may, in fact, be the thing that sets it apart from the mere traditional type of 'obvious information' joke or riddle. The possible interpretation of this type of verbal encounter as a type of joking behavior is reinforced by the types of responses some informants give to the question. It seems appropriate, for example, to interpret it as a type of joking behavior which is deserving of an extension. We thus get the following:

(6) FW: How old are you?
INF: Twenty-four.
FW: How come?
INF: How come? (Laughter) How come, what do you mean how come?
FW: How come?
INF: How come? Because twenty-four years ago my parents worked something out.

In this response, we see that the informant accepted the fact that it was a question asking for obvious information, and responded to it with further obvious information which may be interpreted as an extension of the 'obvious' theme. This seems to be one type of option which a person can give besides laughter and a terminating response of 'I don't know'. (The response 'I don't know' may reasonably be interpreted as a failure to read any legitimate reason beyond the obvious information intent of the question, i.e. 'I don't know any reason besides the obvious one'.)

There are some informants, however, who attempt to read this question in terms of some aspect of nonobvious information. Typically, this is read as one where a discrepancy between the actual age and the apparent age is indicated. This is shown in the following examples.

(7a) FW: How old are you?
INF: Twenty-eight.
FW: How come?
INF: How come? (Laughter)
FW: Yeah, how come?
INF: You mean why I'm not older? I'm a genius.

(7b) FW: How old are you?
INF: Twenty-seven.
FW: How come?
INF: I'll be twenty-eight soon.
FW: How come you're twenty-seven.
INF: I don't know, my husband did it to me?
FW: Your husband did what to you?
INF: He made me this old.

It should be noted that these examples are analogous to the types of legitimate uses of 'how come' questions where the designated age does not appear to live up to the real life expectancies of age spans. In these cases, the general principle for legitimizing the question on the basis of accepted background knowledge of age spans is applied to a particular case in order to legitimize the question, even though there may be no previous general information (as a part of our real world knowledge) to suggest that there is a discrepancy between designated and apparent age. While people who tend to interpret 'how come' as a seemingly legitimate question appear to be less likely to accept it as joking behavior (i. e. they are less likely to laugh), it is not necessarily mutually exclusive with the 'obvious' information reading of the question, indicating that they may be recognizing both readings.

2.1 Adult to child. In the previous discussion, I have only mentioned cases where I, as an adult, ask another adult the 'how come' question concerning his or her stated age. Now let us turn to children and see how they respond to this question. For my purposes here, I will consider children to be age six and under, although I think ultimately the classification will be flexible with respect to chronological age and more related to developmental stages with respect to how children relate to certain types of 'obvious' information. One aspect of children's responses comes out immediately when the responses of children are compared with those of adults--they don't think the question is very funny. That is, they do not seem to accept it as a form of joking behavior playing on obvious information. In none of the 25 exchanges that I have had with children did any of them initially laugh at the question. They seem to accept it as a legitimate question which deserves a serious answer of some type. Most predominantly, this answer is given in terms of a literal justification of their cumulative years or their present age as established by their most recent birthday. The following examples are typical:

(8a) FW: How old are you?
INF: Five.
FW: How come?
INF: Cause I had five birthdays.

(8b) FW: How old are you?
INF: Five.
FW: How come?
INF: Cause my birthday was last week.

While the occasion of various birthdays seems to be the most common literal response to the question, this is not the only criterion that can be given, as the following examples indicate.

(9a) FW: How old are you?
INF: Six.
FW: How come?
INF: Because I'm in kindergarten.

(9b) FW: How old are you?
INF: Four.
FW: How come?
INF: Cause I'm this big (motions with hands his approximate height).

(9c) FW: How old are you?
INF: Three.
FW: How come?
INF: Cause I go to Sunday School.

(9d) FW: How old are you?
INF: Five.
FW: How come?
INF: Cause my tooth is out (points to missing tooth).

While none of the above examples gives a direct reference to age, it is still observed that the children have given what we might call a 'criterion-based response' (i. e. a basis which justifies their present age) and can readily be seen as an extension of the birthday criterion that other children gave. The statement that a child is six because he goes to kindergarten is related to the fact that children of this age level are found in kindergarten. And the three-year-old who stated that he goes to Sunday School is using as a criterion the fact that children are permitted to enter Sunday School when they reach their third birthday. So we see that the principle guiding the children's responses is really quite similar although the realization of the criterion-based response may be somewhat different from child to child.

There is another type of response by children we should look at briefly because it differs somewhat from the ones that we have just presented. This is the response indicating that the question was interpreted to mean something like 'why aren't you older than the age you are'. We thus get the following.

(10a) FW: How old are you?
INF: Four and three-quarters.
FW: How come?
INF: Cause I have a birthday coming up soon.

(10b) FW: How old are you?
INF: Four and one-half.
FW: How come?
INF: I'm gonna have a birthday soon.

While there are certain analogies between these children's responses and the adults' responses where the question was interpreted in terms of a discrepancy between designated and apparent age, there seem to be essential differences. Children's interpretations appear to be restricted to the immediately successive age rather than a designated and generic apparent age discrepancy.

Interestingly enough, the child's answer of this sort seem to be more typical (although not exclusively) when a child specifies fractions of an age as opposed to whole integers. In this regard, it is instructive to note that age fractions are usually given only by children and adolescents, and, in most cases, are apparently motivated by the desire to achieve the next age level. This motivation, then, may be the reason that the 'how come' question is interpreted to refer to the next successive age.

I must confess that there were several examples in my corpus where children six and under did not know how to answer the question, as typified by the following:

(11) FW: How old are you?
INF: Six.
FW: How come?
INF: Um, that's a hard question to answer. (Shrugs shoulders, indicating he doesn't know.)

These sorts of responses were, to my surprise, much less frequent than I had actually expected. Whereas I cannot explain all such cases, it may be that some children are reacting more as older children would (cf. Section 2.2), or they may be thrown off by their status relationship to me as an adult asking the question. While such cases do occasionally occur for one reason or another, their relative infrequency is striking. It is noteworthy to mention that none of the children six and under who did not answer the question laughed as if it were intended as some type of joke.

2.2 Adult to pre-adolescents. So far, I have spoken of only two groups' responses, adults and children six years old and under. There is also a group of children between seven and twelve years of age on which I have tested this question. Interestingly enough, pre-adolescents seem to respond in a way which is somewhat different from both children and adults. On the one hand, the children typically did not laugh as an initial reaction to the question (I got a couple of smiles), as if I were deliberately engaging in some form of joking behavior with them. More typically, they looked puzzled, as if they were not sure whether it was a legitimate criterion-based question. Unlike the children six and under, they rejected the criterion-based responses in terms of birthdays (e.g. 'I had eleven birthdays' or 'I just had a birthday'). Instead, there was a tendency to simply state the fact without any attempt to justify it. The following example illustrates this.

(12a) FW: How old are you?
INF: Twelve.
FW: How come?
INF: Because I just am.

(12b) FW: How old are you?
INF: Twelve.
FW: How come?
INF: How come? Because that's my age.

They seem to be caught between the adult interpretation of the question which allows for interpretation as a joke on obvious information or the apparent age and designated age discrepancy, and child interpretation in terms of a criterion-based reason. In other words, they are now at a level where they recognize that it is not legitimate to ask questions concerning obvious information. The intermediate level in which they are caught is exemplified by the hesitancies in the following examples:

(13a) FW: How old are you?
INF: Ten.
FW: How come?
INF: Because I was--I don't know.
Third party: (seven-year-old girl) Because she was born ten years ago.

(13b) FW: How old are you?
INF: Eleven.
FW: How come?
INF: Because I was born--I can't help it if I was born.

There does appear, however, to be one way in which preadolescents can legitimize the question as a criterion-based one; namely, by interpreting it as a matter of calculation from the date of birth to the present time. We thus get:

(14a) FW: How old are you?
INF: Eleven.
FW: How come?
INF: Because I was born in 1962.

(14b) FW: How old are you?
INF: Seven.
FW: How come?
INF: Cause I was born in 1966.

This sort of response seems to escape some of the 'obviousness' of a criterion-based answer such as 'I had eleven birthdays', while still retaining the criterion base. This response may be interpreted as not quite so obvious, requiring the type of arithmetic ability which might be 'nontrivial' to the pre-adolescent. Without a criterion-based interpretation that escapes the simplicity of simple counting, the question seems to be quite puzzling to the pre-adolescent who is caught between the child and adult world. One twelve-year-old youngster who happened to be present when I was asking a five-year-old how come she was five seemed to be an adequate spokesman for the pre-adolescent group when he said the following (incidentally, the five-year-old child answered the question in the typical fashion we noted earlier for her group):

(15) 12-year-old boy: That's dumb to ask her why she's five.
FW: How come?
12-year-old boy: It's just dumb.
FW: How come it's just dumb?
12-year-old boy: It just is.

The lack of option as a type of joking behavior and the inappropriateness of answering it with the type of criterion-based response that seems relatively natural for the younger child obviously makes this question most problematic for the pre-adolescent.

2.3 The child fieldworker. In the previous discussion, I think that I have demonstrated that children, pre-adolescents, and adults respond to the 'how come' question relating to obvious information in different ways. At this point in my study, however, I had a nagging suspicion that the responses by the children and pre-adolescents may have been due to a status relationship between the children and the adult fieldworker. Could it be that the different responses were simply a function of the adult-child status relationship? In other words, maybe the children really thought it was a strange question but felt an obligation to respond because I was an adult. In order to find out what influence this status relationship might have had in the data reported here, I therefore trained my six-year-old son Todd to ask this question in various contexts. My son turned out to be an excellent fieldworker, who could learn to ask the question as a normal part of the conversation without giving away the fact that the frame was being purposely structured into the conversation.

With respect to other children, the responses turned out to be quite similar to the responses that I obtained when I served as the fieldworker. We thus get the following responses from children when they are asked the 'how come' question from one of their peers.

(16a) Child FW: How old are you?
INF: Five.
Child FW: How come?
INF: Cause I had five birthdays.

(16b) Child FW: How old are you?
Inf: Six.
Child FW: How come?
INF: Cause I was born six years ago.

We see that these sorts of responses, which typify the responses from his peers, are the same types of responses that I obtained as the adult fieldworker involved in the exchange. A simple justification for age is given in terms of the number of birthdays, or the most recent birthdays.

Similarly, pre-adolescents responded in a way which matched that of the pre-adolescents when the question was asked by an adult. In some cases, there was the same hesitancy that I had experienced from members of this group, while others legitimized it by interpreting the question as a criterion-based one based on an arithmetical calculation more appropriate for their age level.

(17a) Child FW: How old are you?
INF: Seven and a half.
Child FW: How come?
INF: Because I was--I don't know--I just am.

(17b) Child FW: How old are you?
INF: Eleven.
Child FW: How come?
INF: Cause I was born in '63.

The responses of this group and the children informants leads us to the conclusion that there is a real age-grading or developmental aspect to the interpretation. That is, the differences I obtained from the groups were not simply a function of the fact that I, as an adult, was asking the question of children.

There is, however, a difference observed with a child fieldworker when we look at the exchanges between adults and a child. We previously saw that a major tendency of adults was to react to the question as a type of joking behavior (i. e. an extension of an 'obvious information joke'). This, however, does not appear to be the dominant response on the part of adults when a child asks the question. (In only one case out of ten did an adult laugh at the question and the reason for his laughter is questionable.) More typically, responses are given that indicate that the adult will accept this as a legitimate question from a child. One type of response encountered was the more sophisticated type of criterion-based interpretation that we encountered among some pre-adolescents. We thus get:

(18) Child FW: How old are you, Uncle Jerry?
INF: Thirty-seven, I think.
Child FW: How come?
INF: Cause I was born in 1936.

There are also cases where adults respond in terms of the obviousness of the question, along the same lines that some pre-adolescents did. They did not, however, appear to accept it as a type of joking behavior on the part of the child.

(19) Child FW: How old are you, Grandmom?
INF: Why do you want to know that for?
Child FW: I just do.
INF: Sixty-two.
Child FW: How come?
INF: Cause that's when I was born.

Or, an adult may interpret the question as legitimate by extending the reading beyond the realm of obvious information. In these cases, it seems to be interpreted something like 'How did you ever get to be so old?'

(20a) Child FW: How old are you?
INF: I'm about four times older than you, forty-two.
Child FW: How come?
INF: The years just fly by so fast, they're like birds the way they fly.

(20b) Child FW: How old are you?
INF: Thirty-seven.
Child FW: How come?
INF: I don't know why I'm so old, do you know why I'm so old?
Child FW: No.

While the cultural reasons for this sort of extension may be interesting (given how adults and children differ in terms of their outlook on age), the important aspect of these adult responses is that the question asked by a child was considered to be deserving of some type of legitimate or quasi-legitimate response. We may suggest that the responses by the adults typify a certain cultural regard for the necessity of answering a child who asks a question. It is, however, interesting to note the difference between these responses by adults to the child fieldworker and the qualification that children give for their age. The information considered obvious by the adult is eliminated from consideration even though this is how children typically respond. In this regard, it might be interesting to compare how adults responsible for child rearing respond to such questions by their child as opposed to the adults who served as informants in this study. Although I have only several examples of parents actually being asked such a question by their children (cf. example (3)), it may certainly be the case that the question would be answered differently by an adult in a child-rearing relationship, but this will have to await more data. What we have evidence for here is the important difference between the response of adults when a child asks the question and when an adult asks the question. Interestingly enough, in several cases where I later asked the adult informants what they thought of the question by the child, they said that it seemed a little silly, but that they felt obligated to answer it because the child deserved an answer when asking a question.

3. Conclusion. In the previous sections, the responses of several different groups have been examined in the context of one simple question frame. It has been seen that children, pre-adolescents, and adults tend to interpret the question in different ways, and I have suggested why this might be the case. It has also been seen that the age of the person asking the question may alter its reading for the adults.

Ultimately, I would like to look at this question in terms of the broader framework of language and pragmatics. As a part of such real life experiences, one may say that there is an important distinction between what may be called 'obvious' and 'nonobvious' information. Questions for which one of the readings may involve obvious information would appear automatically to reject this reading unless it is considered acceptable as a type of joking behavior related to the notion of obvious information. It is, of course, important to note that the distinction between obvious and nonobvious information is determined by the particular culture, although the basic distinction appears to be a good candidate for a universal of language as it relates to pragmatics. Thus, one culture may not consider the rationale for an individual's age to be a matter of obvious information, whereas another culture (in the absence of birth certificates, conventional attention paid to calculating age by a particular calendrical system, etc.) may consider it as nonobvious information. On the other hand, another culture may consider certain types of information that we classify as nonobvious to be obvious information.

Because of the peculiar experiences of children in acquiring the expertise to discriminate between obvious and nonobvious information, I would also like to maintain that they are, in some sense, exempt from the norms of questioning that are operative among adults. That is, it may be all right for a child to ask an obvious information question while adults would have to avoid it. In this regard, I would like to suggest that the use of obvious information as a type of riddle or joking behavior may be beyond the capabilities of children because of their real world experiences. I am now convinced that children who tell obvious information jokes (e.g. 'Why did the chicken cross the road?') really may not understand why it is a joke. They may tell it because an older person related it to them as a joke, but I really don't think they understand why it is funny. In other words, this type of verbal exchange is a joke for a child because someone classified it as a joke, but the reason that it is funny escapes him. I have long held this suspicion about some of the jokes that children tell, but the bit of information I have uncovered in this study now gives me a principled basis for making this claim.

Before concluding, I should mention something about the type of methodology that was utilized in this investigation. Essentially, I have used what I considered to be a questionable verbal exchange as a basis for making decisions about what can and cannot be subjected to a reason question. In a sense, this appears to be a sociolinguistic analogue to the determination of grammatical and ungrammatical sentences that has been utilized to great advantage in linguistics for some time now. The main difference, however, is that instead of simply asking people how they would react to such a question, I have placed them in a real life situation in which they were forced to react in some way. This seems to be more appropriate for certain types of verbal exchanges, and I think it is more reliable than asking people to intuit in terms of certain questionable hypothetical sociolinguistic occasions. Adding the dimension of child fieldworkers allows one to observe an important difference in terms of an age variable that would be difficult to hypothesize about in the absence of such a technique. While I may be wrong in some of my conclusions, and need more quantitative data to be certain of others, the study is readily replicable for anyone who questions my conclusions.

Utilizing this methodology, I must admit, has had two deleterious effects. One is that people whom I have told about this study have become suspicious whenever I ask a 'how come' question. This is compounded by the fact that I have, as mentioned earlier, a tendency to ask 'how come' questions that people consider inappropriate as a part of my peculiar style of verbal exchange. The second effect is that people have been giving me some of my own medicine and have been asking me strange sorts of 'how come' questions so that I don't know whether they're serious or not. Both of these I can learn to live with if I can get some more good data.

In a series of lectures given by Charles Fillmore (1973:15), he is drawn to a particular problem of deixis which he feels might be resolved by an experiment in which he walks around with a dirty face to see whether people are willing to talk about it. As it turns out, he is unable to resolve his problem because he is 'naturally . . . unwilling to do that'. While I can certainly not argue with someone else's desire to avoid certain social inconveniences for the sake of ferreting out interesting linguistic facts, it would appear that a willingness to talk with a certain degree of 'sociolinguistic smudge' on our faces may be the price we have to pay in order to get at some of the most interesting problems in the area. Smudged faces may be the coming thing in sociolinguistics.

NOTE

1. The precise relationship of _how come_ to _why_ is still in some dispute. Bolinger (1970:66) notes that _how come_ is a reduction of _how comes it that_ which asks about something previously established, but _why_ is neutral in this respect. Zwicky and Zwicky (1973:926) observe that _how come_ and _what for_ divide the semantic domain of _why_ on the basis of a cause/purpose distinction. In most cases, it appears that _why_ is interchangeable with _how come_, although there are several grammatical frames (e.g. responses to commands, which are not factual) in which they operate differently (cf. Bolinger 1970:67). These differences, however, do not appear crucial to the questions I am investigating here.

I am not concerned here with the whole range of _how come_ questions which are considered appropriate reason or cause requests. That is, they meet the type of conditions for appropriate questions elaborated by Lakoff (1973).

REFERENCES

Bolinger, Dwight. 1970. The lexical value of it. Working Papers in Linguistics, University of Hawaii, Vol. 2, No. 8.

Fillmore, Charles F. 1971. Lectures on deixis. Unpublished manuscript, Linguistics Department, University of California, Berkeley.

Lakoff, Robin. 1973. Questionable answers and answerable questions. In: Issues in linguistics: Papers in honor of Henry and Renée Kahane. Urbana, University of Illinois Press.

Zwicky, Arnold M. and Ann D. Zwicky. 1973. How come and what for. In: Issues in linguistics: Papers in honor of Henry and Renée Kahane. Urbana, University of Illinois Press.

THE UNIVERSALITY OF CONVERSATIONAL IMPLICATURES

ELINOR O. KEENAN

University of Southern California

In the past several years, linguists interested in the interpretation of whole utterances have made use of a number of concepts developed by philosophers--concepts such as speech act, illocutionary force, and performative. More recently, some linguists (Gordon and Lakoff 1971, Lakoff 1973, Heringer 1972, among others) have shown interest in philosophical ideas concerning the organization of conversation. In particular, there has been a great deal of discussion centering around ideas of Paul Grice as set forth in lectures entitled 'Logic and Conversation' (1975). In developing such notions, philosophers probably reflect on conversational conduct as it operates in their own society. The qualification is not explicit, however, and principles of conversational procedure are presented as universal in application. In this paper, I examine the validity of this assumption, focusing on the work of Grice, in particular on his notion of conversational maxim and conversational implicature. I examine these concepts in regard to a non-Western society, that of the plateau area of Madagascar.[1]

Conversational maxim and conversational implicature. In Lecture 2 of 'Logic and Conversation', Grice presents the idea that certain inferences we make from utterances arise from our expectations concerning everyday conversational behavior. There is a certain code of behavior we expect interlocutors to follow. We expect them to conform to certain 'conversational maxims'. One such maxim is 'Be relevant'. That is, interlocutors are expected to make their utterances relevant to the topic or direction of the conversation at hand. When interlocutor A makes a comment or asks a question, he expects his conversational partner to attend to that remark and respond in a relevant manner, and he makes certain inferences based on this expectation. For example, if A says, 'The football match is cancelled', and B responds, 'There is an energy crisis', A, assuming that B is following normal conversational practice and has addressed his remark to the topic proposed, may interpret B's utterance as providing a reason why the football match is cancelled. Another way of putting this is to say that in the wake of A's utterance, B's utterance implies that the energy crisis is in some way related to the cancelling of the football match. Implications based on our expectation of normal conversational conduct are referred to as 'conversational implicatures' in Grice's analysis. They contrast with implications based on the truth conditions of utterances. That is, the notion 'conversationally implies' is contrasted with the notion 'logically implies'. We say that certain utterances 'logically imply' others just in case the truth of these utterances guarantees the truth of the others. For example, if an utterance A: 'All public events require an admissions fee' is true and an utterance B: 'Football matches are public events' is true, then Q: 'Football matches require an admissions fee' is true. That is, A and B logically imply Q. The implication does not depend on conversational procedure.

One characteristic of logical implication as used in standard logic (not various modal logics) is that it is not culture-dependent or situation-dependent. The implications hold wherever individuals agree on the conventional meanings of the logical words (e.g. all, not, some, and, if-then, etc.). The same cannot be said for conversational implicatures. It is an empirical question as to whether in all societies and in all situations, independent observers agree on the conversational implicature of a given utterance, since the implicature depends on how the utterer is expected to behave with respect to conversational maxims, and these may vary situationally and cross-culturally.

Conversational maxim: Be informative. In this section, I focus on one particular maxim suggested by Grice as basic to the exchange of utterances in conversation. Grice suggests that participants in a conversation are expected to make their utterances as informative as required by the exchange at hand. The maxim as it stands is not helpful, for it can never be violated. The constraint 'required by the exchange' can be stretched to justify the kind or amount of information in each given case. For example, a speaker may provide information that intentionally confuses or misleads the hearer, but one could include the speaker's intention to deceive as part of the definition of the exchange. The speaker, conforming to the requirements of the exchange so defined, would not be violating the maxim: 'Be informative'.

Likewise, one can build into the definition of the situation, intentions of speakers to provide no information or to allude subtly to certain information (Albert 1964). The speaker in each case would be conforming to the requirements of the exchange as defined by himself or by social convention.

When Grice later illustrates the maxim (1975:45), he presents a more precise interpretation: interlocutors are expected to meet the informational needs of their interactional partner(s). That is, if a speaker has access to the information required by the hearer, then he is expected to communicate that information to the hearer. This is, in part, what it means to 'cooperate' (Grice 1975:45) in talk. The maxim thus leads one to expect that when one interlocutor requests specific information, the conversational partner will provide that information, insofar as possible. The verbal response to such a request may conversationally imply what the utterer knows about the material requested. Thus, for example, if speaker A asks 'Where is your mother?' and B responds 'She is either in the house or at the market', then B's utterance conversationally implies that he does not know specifically where his mother is located. He knows only that she is located in one of two places. If speaker B in fact does know at which of the two locations one could find his mother, he has misled the co-present interlocutor and so violated the maxim.

Almost as soon as one presents this interpretation, members of this society[2] can offer cases in which interlocutors do not abide by the maxim. One does not conform to the maxim if to do so would be indiscreet, impolite, unethical, and so on. Grice might argue that interlocutors generally expect the maxim to hold in social interactions. This contention is supported by the social fact that underspecification of information usually implies that the speaker is not able to offer more specific information. At times, however, conforming to the maxim may 'clash' with other interactional maxims (Grice 1975:49); in certain situations, other maxims may take precedence, leading the speaker to violate the maxim 'Be informative'.

In testing this maxim cross-culturally, one does not expect to find that in some societies the maxim always holds and in some societies the maxim never holds. It is improbable, for example, that there is some society in which being informative is categorically inappropriate. Differences between societies, if there are any, are more likely to be differences in specification of domains in which the maxim is expected to hold and differences in the degree to which members are expected to conform to this maxim (Dell Hymes: personal communication). In some societies, meeting the informational needs of a conversational partner may be an unmarked or routine behavior. In other societies, meeting another's informational needs may be an atypical or marked behavior. Let us consider the way in which this principle operates in Malagasy society, first, with respect to its markedness and secondly, with respect to its domains of application.

Conversational practice in Madagascar. To what extent does the maxim 'Be informative' hold for interlocutors in Malagasy society? Despite certain clashes with other maxims, are members generally expected to satisfy the informational needs of co-conversationalists? No. Interlocutors regularly violate this maxim. They regularly provide less information than is required by their conversational partner, even though they have access to the necessary information. If A asks B 'Where is your mother?' and B responds 'She is either in the house or at the market', B's utterance is not usually taken to imply that B is unable to provide more specific information needed by the hearer. The implicature is not made, because the expectation that speakers will satisfy informational needs is not a basic norm.

There are two reasons for this. The first is related to the status of new information in this society. New information is a rare commodity. Villages are composed of groups of kinsmen whose genealogical backgrounds and family lives are public knowledge. Their day-to-day activities are shaped to a large extent by the yearly agricultural cycle. Almost every activity of a personal nature (bathing, play, courtship, etc.) takes place under public gaze. Information that is not already available to the public is highly sought after. If one manages to gain access to new information, one is reluctant to reveal it. As long as it is known that one has that information and others do not have it, one has some prestige.

When one member of the community requests specific information from another, the addressee is usually reluctant to part with that information for this reason. It is unlikely, therefore, that the informational needs of the requester will be immediately satisfied. In fact, interlocutors are generally aware of the reluctance to give up requested information. They expect the response of the addressee to be less than satisfactory. Normally, if the information requested is not immediately provided, the two interlocutors enter into a series of exchanges whereby the one tries to eke out the new information from the other.

A second and perhaps more significant motivation for revealing less information than would satisfy the addressee is the fear of committing oneself explicitly to some particular claim. Individuals regularly avoid making explicit statements about beliefs and activities. They do not want to be responsible for the information communicated. For example, if someone asks 'Who broke the cup?', hardly any speaker would want to be the one to specify the culprit. Such a statement may have unforeseen unpleasant consequences for the speaker and his family, and he alone would have to shoulder the tsiny 'guilt' for uttering such a claim. Only if the individual is assured that his statement will not bring tsiny will he make the statement.

Even if someone were caught in the act of doing something wrong, one could not directly point at this person to dishonor him directly. One must use special expressions or go about it in a roundabout way. But if by chance there are people who demand that this wrong-doer be pointed out directly, then the speaker must say directly in his talk who the person is. But because he must speak directly, then the speaker must ask the people to lift all tsiny from him. If there is someone in the audience who wants to know more, who does not understand, then he may respond during a break in the talk:

> It is not clear to us, sir. It is hard to distinguish the domestic cat from the wild cat. They are the same whether calico or yellow or grey. And if it is the wild cat who steals the chicken, we cannot tell him from the others. The wild cat steals the chicken but the domestic cat gets its tail cut off. So point directly to the wild cat.

It is not only to past events that individuals are reluctant to make explicit reference. There is a clear tendency to avoid making a specific commitment to some future event. Thus, if a member of household X asks a member of household Y when the turning of the ancestral bones is to take place, he will likely get an answer such as 'I am not certain' or 'In a bit' or 'Around September', but no precise date will be specified even if such a date has been set. Individuals do not wish to commit themselves publicly to a precise date until they are absolutely certain the event will take place at that time. They may suffer tremendous loss of face if the event does not take place as specified. They will be guilty of premature or faulty judgment. Consequently, those outside the family are told details of time and place only at the last moment.

This same fear of committing oneself to some future event taking place leads one to hold back certain information when warning, advising, and giving directions. Thus, if speaker A asks speaker B 'How does one open this door?', speaker B may respond with the instruction 'If one doesn't open it from the inside, the door won't open'. That is, speaker B tells speaker A that if he doesn't do X, then Y will not take place. He is not making the stronger commitment and stating that if A does do X, then Y will take place: if you open it from the inside, the door will open. Again the speaker is unwilling to commit himself to the stronger statement, as he cannot guarantee that the action will take place as instructed. He makes a weaker statement using the double negative 'If not X, then not Y'. The double negative is used in response to many questions seeking information. Thus, when I once asked an elderly woman when I might find her brother at home, she gave me this answer, 'If you don't come after five, you won't find him'. She did not say that if I did come after five, I would find him. She simply told me what would lead to my not finding this man. In both of these situations, the speaker has not made his contribution sufficiently informative to meet the purposes of the interlocutor.

The hesitation to make explicit statements concerning the actions and beliefs of individuals affects a wide range of speech behaviors. One finds, for example, that speakers regularly avoid identifying individuals in their utterances. Many villagers feel that in identifying an individual, they may bring his identity to the attention of unfriendly forces. Someone in the world of the living or dead may overhear the utterance and take note of the individual referenced. Something unpleasant may befall the individual as a consequence of this specification. The tsiny would rest with the utterer. Consequently, terms of personal reference that specify individuals as distinct from other members of the community are avoided in favor of terms that do not make this distinction. For example, speakers generally avoid referring to individuals by the personal name given to them at birth. This practice is a virtual taboo in the case where the individual referenced is a child. It is felt, for example, that such a practice can lead to malevolent ancestral forces taking the child away from the living. Every effort is therefore made to obscure the child's identity and to make the child as unattractive to these ancestral forces as possible. Normally, after an official Malagasy name is given to the child, a second name is given as well. This name is usually a term referring to some unpleasant item--for example, a small child may be called 'Garbage Girl' or 'Garbage Boy', 'Dung Heap', 'Dwarf', 'Dog Face', 'Red Face', and so on. Furthermore, this name is usually shared by a number of children. When a speaker refers to a child as 'Dwarf', he could be talking about any of several children. The addressee is to identify the referent from other cues. In highly missionized areas and in areas where children regularly attend school, a third name is given. This name is a French Christian name--Suzanne, Jean, Marie, Philippe, and so on. This name, however, operates in much the same way that the Malagasy nickname does. Like the nickname, the French name is usually adopted by several children in a village. Thus, a village could have half a dozen boys named Jean and several girls with the name Marie. When one speaks of individuals using these names one is not marking out one individual as distinct from others.

The sensitivity towards one's personal name decreases as one grows older. However, even when one is an adult, one does not like one's name to be casually handled. There remains a strong feeling that unfavorable events that befall an individual are associated with the meddling of malevolent forces. It is not unusual for an adult to change his name following some unpleasant circumstance. In fact, in the past, name-changing was a frequent occurrence (six or seven times in a lifetime). At present a national law exists that limits to three the number of name changes per person.

If one avoids the use of personal names, what are the preferred alternatives of personal reference? One alternative is to refer to the individual by some generalized animate noun. A noun referring to some social category of which the referent is a member is used. For example, members of a village may refer to one another as olona 'person', zazavavy 'girl', zazalahy 'boy', ray aman-dreny 'elder', and so on. Thus, a mother once asked her son Mbola mator y ve ny olona? 'Is the person still sleeping?' in reference to her husband. And another mother once asked her daughter to fetch ny kulatin'ny olona 'the person's pants', where 'person' referred to the daughter's sister. Likewise, a young boy once said to me, Misy zazavavy ho avy 'There is a girl who is coming' and 'girl' referred to the boy's sister.

This use of personal reference is clearly distinct from the use of personal reference in our society.[2] When someone in our society says There is a girl coming, I see a girl, or I see a person, the hearer infers that the speaker is not intimately associated with the referent. In fact, Grice brings up this precise usage (1975:56, 57) as an example of a conversational implicature that may hold in all contexts. He states:

> Anyone who uses a sentence of the form 'X is meeting a woman this evening' would normally implicate that the person to be met was someone other than X's wife, mother, sister, or perhaps even close platonic friend. . . . The implicature is present because the speaker has failed to be specific in a way in which he might have been expected to be specific, with the consequence that it is likely to be assumed that he is not in a position to be specific.

In this society, we ordinarily distinguish in speech individuals with whom we have an intimate relationship from others with whom we do not share this kind of relationship. We expect speakers to note in their utterance intimate relationships such as kin ties, friendship ties, and so on. We infer from the absence of such specification that such ties do not hold between speaker and referent. However, the same cannot be said of speakers and hearers in Malagasy society. When someone in a Malagasy village says I see a person, those listening do not infer that the speaker is not closely associated with the referent. Such a format is simply a conventionalized mode of personal reference. It is a way of referring to an individual without bringing harm to him or shame to the speaker himself.

This difference in conversational implicature is seen in the other alternatives of personal reference as well. For example, a second mode of personal reference that is preferred is the use of agent nouns. Thus, a speaker may refer to a closely associated person as 'cow watcher' or 'house builder' or 'teacher' or 'student', etc. A woman could refer to her husband as 'cow watcher', as in the utterance The cow watcher is coming. Or a young boy could refer to his father as a 'house builder', as in the utterance The house builder is hungry. Normally, in our society, speakers do not refer to intimate relationships in this manner. If a young child were to utter this same sentence in our society, we would infer that no special relationship held between the child and referent.

Another preferred mode of personal reference is the use of the indefinite pronoun someone. No lexical item corresponding to this term actually exists in Malagasy. The indefinite is implied but not specified in the utterance. For example, the utterance Misy mitady translates literally as 'There is looking'. However, it is loosely understood as 'There is someone looking'. Again, the suppressed indefinite is used to refer to those intimately related to the speaker as well as to those remotely known to the speaker. Thus, a speaker may be speaking of his brother or wife or close friend in the utterance cited. In our society, however, a speaker who says There is someone looking implicates that he does not know who that someone is.

It is clear from these examples that speakers regularly mask the exact identity of individuals in their utterances. If they must specify an individual, they do so in the least specific sense. In fact, if at all possible, they try to omit any reference to individuals in their utterances. The deletion is made possible by a careful selection of verb voice. In Malagasy, there exist three voices in which a speaker may couch his utterance. Like Indo-European languages, Malagasy has an active voice in which the performer of an action is the subject of the sentence. For example:

Nanasa ny vilia tamin'ny savony iBozy.[3]
washed the dishes with the soap Bozy
'Bozy washed the dishes with the soap.'

Secondly, like Indo-European languages, Malagasy has a passive voice in which the object of the active sentence is made the superficial subject. For example, it is possible to take the direct object ny vilia 'the dishes' and make it the subject of a passive sentence:

Nosasan-iBozy tamin'ny savony ny vilia.
Washed-by-Bozy with the soap the dishes.
'The dishes were washed by Bozy with the soap.'

Furthermore, in the passive voice, it is possible to delete the personal agent of the action entirely. For example:

Nosasana tamin'ny savony ny vilia.
Washed with the soap the dishes.
'The dishes were washed with the soap.'

Given the prevalent attitude towards personal reference, it is not surprising that passive sentences are preferred over the active form. Passive sentences allow the speaker to omit certain critical information, namely, individual agents of actions. Active sentences do not provide this option.

The option of deleting the personal agent is available in yet another voice, the circumstantial. In this voice, some circumstance of the action taking place is made the superficial subject. For example, the time or place of an action, the instrument with which an action is carried out--any such complement may be made the subject. Thus in the sentence given, it is possible to take the instrument with which the action is carried out, ny savony 'the soap' and make it the subject of a circumstantial sentence:

Nanasan'iBozy ny vilia ny savony.
Washed-with-by-Bozy the dishes the soap.
'The soap was washed-with the dishes by Bozy.'

It is possible to restate this sentence with the personal agent deleted:

Nanasana ny vilia ny savony.
Washed-with the dishes the soap
'The soap was washed-with the dishes.'

Whenever speakers wish to avoid specifying individual agents of actions and whenever it is grammatically possible, the passive and circumstantial voices are used.

This preference for passive and circumstantial forms is not well understood by local Europeans. Most grammars of Malagasy written for Europeans begin with an explanation of the active voice. Somewhere around the middle follows a description of the passive form. The last pages may make mention of the circumstantial voice. Many of the grammars are written by Europeans who have assumed that the active voice plays the same role in Malagasy as it does in Indo-

European languages. Consequently, many European residents learn only the active sentence form. Malagasy villagers who come into contact with these Europeans find their speech offensive and much too direct. European speech is generally stereotyped as brusque and impolite. It is clear that in many cases Malagasy speakers provide less information than a European speaker would provide. If a European knows the name of an individual, or the time or place for an event to take place, he normally specifies this in his utterance. A Malagasy speaker normally does not specify these things. The expectations of interlocutors, then, differ in the two societies. And consequently, conversational implicatures differ in these societies.

Situational constraints on the maxim. It would be misleading to conclude that the maxim 'Be informative' does not operate at all in a Malagasy community. We would not be justified in proposing the contrary maxim 'Be uninformative' as a local axiom. Members of this speech community do not regularly expect that interlocutors will withhold necessary information. Rather, it is simply that they do not have the contrary expectation that in general interlocutors will satisfy one another's informational needs.

One can point to certain features of the speech situation that do influence the direction of one's expectation. The expectation that a speaker will observe such a norm varies according to context. Three dimensions of the speech situation influence adherence to or abandonment of the maxim.

(1) The significance of the information communicated. A speaker is more likely to withhold information when that information is significant than when it is not significant. Significance has to do first with the independent access of the hearer to the information. Information which the hearer can easily obtain independently of the speaker is not significant. For example, a pot of rice cooking on a fire is open to inspection by any member of the community. Information relevant to its cooking can easily be obtained and hence such information is not significant. Its relative insignificance means that it is likely to be discussed openly and explicitly. If someone asks, Is the rice cooked?, a straightforward response is likely to be provided. That is, it is likely that members of the community will follow the maxim 'Be informative'.

Information to which the hearer has no independent access becomes thereby more significant. For example, if only two members of a village of fifty inhabitants go to market one day, then those two alone have information relating to market events that day. Possessing significant information, they may well be reluctant to impart details to those who do not have it. If some member of the community asks a returning villager, What's new at the market?, he is likely to get an informationally unsatisfactory response. For example, one is likely to respond There is nothing new or There were many people (there are always many people at the market). In this context, then, the maxim is likely to be disregarded.

A second dimension of significance has to do with the consequences of imparting information. If imparting certain information may incur unpleasant consequences for speaker or referent, then that information is significant. For example, any information whose communication may bring tsiny 'guilt' to the speaker and henatra 'shame' to the speaker's family is significant. Information relating to the misdeeds of individuals falls into this category. Consequently, speakers are generally reluctant to speak openly on such a topic. If certain information is not likely to lead to unpleasant consequences, then that information can be considered relatively insignificant. When communicating this latter kind of information, interlocutors tend to be more open and specific. When the utterance precludes the possibility of tsiny, then the speaker is more likely to satisfy the informational needs of the addressee.

(2) The interpersonal relationship obtaining between interlocutors. Speakers are more likely to satisfy the informational needs of the hearer if speaker and hearer stand in some socially close relationship with one another than if they are not familiar with each other. Those who are close kinsmen and neighbors (havana) are more likely to provide explicit information to one another than would distant kinsmen (havan-davitra) or strangers (vahiny). Thus, for example, a havana of the speaker is more likely to satisfy the question Where is your mother? than someone who stands in a vahiny relation to the speaker. (This is not to say that it is likely that the havana will answer explicitly, only that the probability of his doing so is greater than if the addressee were a vahiny.)

Havana are tied by a network of moral and social bonds. They are ritually and economically obligated to one another in a way vahiny are not. It is felt that havana can be more trusted than vahiny. Thus, there is a feeling of mutual mistrust among villages in regional cooperative enterprises, because these organizations include vahiny as well as havana. For this reason among others, cooperative enterprises have not been successful. One verbal expression of the attitude is the reluctance of an interlocutor to meet the informational needs of a co-present vahiny. Speakers are reluctant to specify details of agents and activities, because they are not certain what the hearer will do with the information. The speaker cannot guarantee that the hearer will not use that information to damage the reputation of speaker or referent. This difference in attitude influences the use of personal reference terminology. Interlocutors are more likely to use terms that distinguish individuals (e.g. personal names) if speaker, addressee, and referent stand in a havana relationship than if a vahiny relationship obtains between any two. The tendency to mask the identity of the referent (general animate nouns, agent nouns, indefinite pronouns) increases as the social distance between interlocutors (and referent) increases. Speakers are careful that they do not bring the identity of an individual to the attention of those they mistrust.

(3) The sex of the speaker. The conversational principle 'Make your contribution informative' is more likely to be upheld by women than by men. Women are more likely to satisfy the informational needs of hearers. They are more likely to reveal details of events of the past or future. This behavior is not, however, well regarded by members of the speech community. Both men and women say that women have a lavalela 'a long tongue'. This long tongue may reveal things which should not have been revealed. Statements which women make may offend others and bring shame and loss of face to the family. In general, women are not trusted to communicate information in formal social situations. They are never recruited as principal spokesmen to represent the family on ritual occasions. These occasions require careful speech, speech which will not offend or bring tsiny 'guilt' to the family. Men pride themselves on their ability to speak cautiously and inoffensively. They feel that they alone can be speechmakers. The status of speechmaker is highly regarded in the community. Men who are good speechmakers are considered tena ray-amn-dreny 'high elders, knowledgeable individuals'. Men, then, strive to achieve this position. To be recruited, a man must use language in the manner demanded of oratorical situations. That is, he must use language that does not injure the reputation of any individual.

Women are excluded from this respected position, and their style of speaking is not motivated by the possibility that they might qualify for it. In this sense, they have less to lose by speaking explicitly and offensively. In fact, they often have something to gain by speaking in a less than ideal manner. They are able to make accusations (e.g. to answer the question Who broke the cup?), to gossip, to criticize others. In short, they are able to gain considerable power from the fact that they are able to hold others accountable for their actions.

In Malagasy society, then, the same utterance may have different conversational implicatures, depending on whether the speaker is a man or a woman. For example, in response to an information question When are you going to market?, a response such as Either today or tomorrow may be interpreted differently depending on the sex of the speaker (as well as on other features of the nonlinguistic environment). If the speaker is a woman, the response may conversationally implicate that the speaker does not have further knowledge of the matter at hand, for a woman may be expected to answer the question fully if she has the information desired. This is not the case with a man.

Grice tantalizes the ethnographer with the possibility of an etic grid for conversation. However, no ethnographer can be happy with the paradigm as expressed in Grice (1975:48). The conversational maxims are not presented as working hypotheses but as social facts: 'It is just a well-recognized empirical fact that people do behave in these ways, they have learnt to do so in childhood and have not lost the habit of doing so.' Serious research into conversational practice has only recently gotten underway. At best we have restricted analyses of certain dimensions of conversation (illocutionary force, sequencing, situated meaning, etc.). It is difficult for those with experience in the analysis of conversation to accept Grice's proposal by fiat.

But Grice does offer a framework in which the conversational principles of different speech communities can be compared. We can, in theory, take any one maxim and note when it does and does not hold. The motivation for its use or abuse may reveal values and orientations that separate one society from another and that separate social groups (e.g. men, women, kinsmen, strangers) within a single society.

More importantly, Grice's paradigm orients us to pursue the stronger goal of assessing universal conversational principles. Many of those carrying out research in language use are ethnographers. Their work by tradition focuses on speech interaction in a particular ethnographic area. The value of Grice's proposal is that it provides a point of departure for these ethnographers to pool their observations. That is, it invites ethnographers to propose stronger hypotheses related to general principles of conversation.

NOTES

1. From June, 1970 to September, 1970 I carried out anthropological fieldwork in a small village in Vakinankaratra, Madagascar. This research was supported by the National Institute for Mental Health.
2. Western European, academic society.
3. Underscore in the examples indicates subject of sentence.

REFERENCES

Albert, Ethel M. 1964. 'Rhetoric', 'logic' and 'poetics' in Burundi: Cultural patterning of speech behavior. American Anthropologist 66.6, Pt. 2, 35-54.

Gordon, David and George Lakoff. 1971. Conversational postulates. In: Papers from the Seventh Regional Meeting. Chicago, Chicago Linguistic Society. 63-84.

Grice, H. Paul. 1975. Logic and conversation. In: Syntax and semantics: Speech acts, Vol. 3. Edited by Peter Cole and Jerry L. Morgan. New York, Academic Press. 41-58.

Heringer, James T. 1972. Some grammatical correlates of felicity conditions and presuppositions. Ohio State University Working Papers in Linguistics, No. 11:1-110. Columbus, Ohio, Ohio State University Department of Linguistics.

Lakoff, George. 1973. Fuzzy grammar and the performance/ competence terminology game. In: Papers from the Ninth Regional Meeting. Chicago, Chicago Linguistic Society. 271-291.

THE CHANGING DISTRIBUTION OF INDEFINITE PRONOUNS IN DISCOURSE

Suzanne Laberge
Université de Montréal

In Montreal French, the pronoun *on* has almost completely (about 98 percent) replaced *nous* in subject position for the first person plural. This leads naturally to the question of how the ambiguity is resolved between this usage of *on* and its more standard indefinite function (= 'one'). I claim that this question is partially circumvented by the use of other subject clitics for indefinite referents, namely, *tu* and *vous*, which in their standard uses indicate second person singular and second person plural (or formal), respectively. An exhaustive examination (Laberge 1977) of the linguistic contexts of usage of the indefinite referent shows that the *tu* (or *vous*) realization is in variation with *on*; that is, these variants have come to be synonymous and are now usable in identical contexts. The only exceptions involve a small number of invariant contexts where the use of one or other of the variants is obligatory in order to render the indefinite meaning. Note that just as the use of *on*, when an indefinite referent is intended, risks a first person plural interpretation, the use of *tu* (or *vous*) risks a second person interpretation, if the context is not sufficiently disambiguating. I am not going to dwell on the categorical contexts, but rather proceed directly to an analysis of the variable. I do not discuss here the factors influencing the choice of *tu* versus *vous*, nor the exclusive indefinite referent, for which *on* and *ils* are in variation.

The data were extracted from the Sankoff-Cedergren corpus of Montreal French gathered in 1971. All 120 interviews were listened to, and coded for each occurrence of an indefinite pronoun subject, as function of the linguistic constraints which I discuss next.

Syntactic and lexical constraints. The indefinite referent can be identified in discourse by one or more of a large number of possible lexical markers or syntactic properties. Thus, in every case there is a generalization involved, or statement of a general fact by the speaker. To illustrate just two such indications, consider (1) and (2).

(1) J'en ai peut-être regagné un peu ... A part ça, *à travailler* puis *à lire* ON s'améliore toujours un petit peu. (30:40)
'I've perhaps made a little progress ... Besides, in working and in reading *one* always improves somewhat.'

(2) Disons quand j'ai mis les pieds dans le vrai monde là, dans *le monde* où TU rencontres toutes sortes de gens ... (58:5)
'Let's say that when I stepped into the real world, into the world where *you* meet all sorts of people ...'

In (1), the use of the infinitive renders the verbs atemporal and hence leads to a general proverb-like statement. In (2), the speaker explicitly evokes the general situation 'the world where'. These examples also contain other evidence of the indefinite referent. They are both first person accounts and the *on* in (1) can hardly be confused with 'we', nor can the *tu* in (2) be interpreted as 'you'. The atemporal adverb *toujours* 'always' in (1) and the change to the present tense in (2) are further indication of the generality of the utterances.

I do not list here all the markers and types of sentence which can express generality, of which there are dozens. There are, however, two types of utterance which are particularly frequent and which seem to form natural classes.

Implicative constructions. These consist of two sentences (either juxtaposed, or embedded one in the other) between which there is a semantic relation of cause and effect, the first setting up a supposition and the second furnishing the implications. Examples (3) and (4) illustrate this.

(3) Bien si *on* laisse faire les hommes c'est tout' des grosses bêtes. (79:17)
'Well if *one* lets men do what they want, they're all big brutes.'

(4) *Tu* vas être en maudit, *tu* vas parler joual. (4:42)
'*You*'re madder than hell, *you*'re gonna talk *joual*' ('bad' French).

It is clear that the hypothetical nature of such sentences diminishes the possibility of ambiguity with the second person referent when *tu* (or *vous*) is used. This would lead us to expect the *tu-vous* variant to be numerous in this class.

Propositions headed by a presentative construction. In this case there is a presentative clause introducing the sentence in which the variable occurs. This presentative clauses constitutes an overt means for indicating the generality of the following proposition. The syntactic forms it may take are numerous but they all have the same goal of notifying the hearer that what is coming next is a generally admitted truth, or a personal opinion which the speaker hopes is shared, if not universally, at least by the hearer.

It is important to note that the variable does not occur in the presentative clause itself, but rather in the following sentence. In (5) I list some of the presentative forms found in the corpus.

(5) il me semble 'it seems to me'
{il / c'} est vrai 'it is true'
faut dire 'it must be said'
disons 'let's say'
je dis 'I say'
je pense 'I think'
je trouve 'I find'
d'après moi 'according to me'

Following are examples of occurrences of the variable in propositions headed by presentative constructions.

(6) Puis ça, moi j'ai pour mon dire, *on* peut pas se mettre dans la peau d'un autre. (42:12).
'There's this, I would say, *one* cannot put oneself into the skin of another [another person's shoes].'

(7) D'après moi, c'est pas avec des guerres que *tu* réussis à faire un pays, *tu* t'assis puis *tu* discutes. (6:17)
'According to me, it's not with wars that *you* succeed in making a country, *you* sit down and *you* discuss.'

The metalinguistic quality of such constructions would seem to be concurrent with an inherent formality or distance which the speaker adopts with respect to his own views. It serves as well to dissociate the speaker from the referent of the subject of the sentence. These two factors would lessen the possibility of ambiguity between indefinite *on* and first person plural *on*, leading us to expect the variant *on* to be numerous in this class.

For the quantitative analysis, then, all occurrences of the variant were coded either as implicative, as presentative, or as other (usually lexically marked) generalization.

Pragmatic considerations. In addition to the use of syntactic or lexical devices to indicate a general statement, there are other factors not necessarily marked on the surface and situated at what must be called the pragmatic level; these factors appear to be just as influential in the choice of the variant. Thus they must be taken into account, in a crossclassification with the syntactic and lexical factors discussed earlier.

The pragmatic factors relate to speaker strategies which allow hearers to make inferences regarding speaker intentions. These factors can be categorized in terms of their discursive effects. Two types of discursive effect seem to be relevant for the variable in question.

Situational insertion. Insofar as the sentences containing the variable are effectively generalizations involving an indefinite person, they have the effect of situating this person in some sort of repeatable activity or context, which may stem from the experience of the speaker, the hearer, or some other party. Consider examples (8) and (9).

(8) J'aime mieux boire une bonne brosse, c'est mieux que fumer de la drogue, je trouve. Le lendemain matin *tu* as un gros mal de tête mais ça fait rien, *tu* es tout' là, tandis qu'avec la drogue *tu* sais pas si *tu* vas être là le lendemain. *Tu* peux te prendre pour Batman ou Superman puis *tu* te pitches dans les poubelles. (62:11)
'I prefer to drink myself stoned, it's better than smoking dope, I feel. The next morning *you* have a bad headache but that's no big deal, *you* are all in one piece, whereas with drugs you don't know if you will be there the next day. *You* might decide you're Batman or Superman and take off into a garbage can.'

(9) Ben *on* a qu'à prendre l'autobus puis *on* se rend compte comment les jeunes parlent; disons ça c'est le mauvais langage. (3:30)
'Well, *one* only has to take the bus and one realizes how young people talk. Let's say it's poor language.'

In (8) we can see that the use of *tu*, which refers in reality to the experience of the speaker, serves to embed him in a much wider class of people by assuming that it is only incidentally his experience, but in fact, could or would be anybody's.

In (9) we have an example of a hypothetical activity, 'taking the bus', which anybody may experience; it turns out that the speaker's use of an indefinite pronoun functions to claim that her assertion is verifiable by anybody. The discursive effect is again the insertion of an indefinite agent into a hypothetical situation.

Moral. A second type of discursive effect is achieved in cases where the speaker tries to transcend the specificity of a situation in order to present his or her evaluation of it as a truism or what may be labeled a 'moral'.

(10) Ça sert à rien de savoir compter de nos jours, ou *tu* es bien riche puis *tu* as un comptable qui compte pour toi, ou *tu* es très pauvre puis *tu* as pas d'argent à compter. (6:24)
'It's no use knowing how to count these days. Either *you*'re good and rich and *you* have an accountant do your counting, or else *you* are poor and *you* have no money to count.'

(11) Mais à ce moment-là je pense bien qu'ils devaient peut-être pas souffrir parce qu'ils connaissaient pas mieux. Naturellement c'était pas inventé alors, *on* peut pas rêver d'une chose dont *on* ne connaît pas ni en souffrir. (61:11)
'Well, at that time, I think that maybe they couldn't have been suffering because they didn't know any better. Naturally, it wasn't invented so *one* can't dream of a thing of which *one* doesn't know, nor suffer because of it.'

It should be reemphasized that a sentence which presents a moral is neither syntactically nor lexically characterized as such, but is essentially perceived in that way because of its particular relation to the totality of the discourse. What distinguishes a situational insertion from a moral is that the latter constitutes a kind of reflection based on conventional wisdom; it is, of course, inherently the evocation of a situation but it usually possesses an evaluative connotation in the sense that it refers to socially conditioned custom. This is evident when the sentence is a saying or proverb overtly borrowed from oral tradition of the community, as in example (12).

(12) Mon père disait tout le temps, 'Bien, quand *on* est valet *on* est pas roi'. (65:6)
'My father always used to say, "Well, when *one* is a valet [jack], *one* is not a king".'

A moral usually appears at the end or the beginning of a narrative or of a description (cf. Labov's 'coda', 1972:365).

The fact that a moral is a sort of considered pronouncement, and somewhat removed from running discourse, leads us to postulate that it would favor the preservation of the more formal variant *on*, in comparison with the bulk of situational insertions.

To conclude this discussion of pragmatic constraints, I present a tabulation of the occurrence of indefinite clitics, classified according to the number of *on* and *tu-vous* in the context of each of the three utterance types and two pragmatic effects discussed earlier.

Table 1. Occurrences of the variants according to linguistic and pragmatic context.

Pragmatic effect	Generalization *on*	Generalization *tu-vous*	Implicative *on*	Implicative *tu-vous*	Presentative *on*	Presentative *tu-vous*
Situational insertion	48.6%	52.0%	36.5%	63.5%	64.7%	35.2%
	(N=1850)		(N=1383)		(N=360)	
Moral	63.0%	37.0%	61.1%	38.9%	68.1%	31.9%
	(N=254)		(N=360)		(N=160)	

An examination of the values of N in each cell of Table 1 shows which utterance type is preferred to obtain a given discursive effect. It is noted first that situational insertion, the most common discursive effect involving this variable, seems to favor neither of the special syntactic constructions I have discussed, but rather the residual category of largely lexically marked indices of generalization.

The category 'moral', however, doubles the rate of use of propositions headed by presentatives, and shows a marked increase of implicative constructions, with a concomitant decrease in the proportion of utterances with other markers of generalization.

Table 1 shows that in the context of a 'moral', *on* is clearly preferred to *tu-vous* in all utterance types (63.0% vs. 37.0%, 61.1% vs. 38.9%, and 68.1% vs. 31.9%). In the context of situational insertion, the indefinite *tu-vous* is more frequent (52.0% vs. 48.6% and 63.5% vs. 36.5%), except for the presentative type where *on* is still dominant (64.7% vs. 35.2%). These figures do not, however, enable us to precisely evaluate the contribution of each utterance type to the use of one or the other variant.

Variable rule analysis. To carry out a statistically rigorous analysis of factor effects, we undertook a variable rule analysis according to the methods described by Rousseau and Sankoff (1978). There were three factor groups to be taken into account, namely, (1) type of utterance: implicative, presentative, or other marker of generalization; (2) discursive effect: situational insertion or moral; (3) identity of speaker (120 individuals). The model of analysis is summarized in (13), where the *p*'s are parameters to be estimated by computer methods.

$$(13)\quad \frac{\text{Prob (ON)}}{\text{Prob (TU)}} = \frac{p_{input}}{1-p_{input}} \times \frac{p_{speaker}}{1-p_{speaker}} \times \frac{p_{syntax}}{1-p_{syntax}} \times \frac{p_{pragmatic}}{1-p_{pragmatic}}$$

I first discuss the results for the first two factor groups and then examine the distribution of individual speaker parameters.

The linguistic factors. The values of the linguistic and pragmatic factors are listed in (14).

(14)		
p_{syntax}:	Presentative	0.75
	Other marker	0.65
	Implicative	0.43
$p_{pragmatic}$:	Situational insertion	0.37
	Moral	0.63

These results accord with the hypothesis formulated earlier in the discussion of the constraints. Syntactic structures headed by a presentative construction are the most favorable for the conservation of the *on* form. The most favorable for the use of *tu-vous* is the implicative structure.

Concerning the discursive effects, the enunciation of a moral strongly favors the use of *on*.

I should mention that another linguistic dimension of the context of usage of the indefinite clitic had no effect on the choice of variant. This was the tense of the verb whose subject is the indefinite referent. The present tense is used overwhelmingly in utterances involving such generalizations. However, in the few dozen cases of imparfait and passé composé which occurred in the data, this fact did not statistically seem to affect the use of *on* versus *tu* or *vous*.

The social factors. The variable rule analysis results in a list of values, one for each speaker, expressing his or her tendency to use *on*, taking into account the proportions of the various linguistic contexts in the data input. I did not include any social factors, other than the identity (interview number) of the speakers, in the variable rule analysis. However, by statistically comparing the individual values with the social characteristics of each speaker, one can investigate how an individual's place in society relates to his production of *on/tu-vous*.

This investigation shows that an individual's sex is an important factor in conditioning the variable, especially among young speakers. Figures 1 and 2 show the distribution of men and women as a function of age and of their tendencies to use one or the other of the variants.

Figure 1. Tendency among men to use *on*, as a function of age.

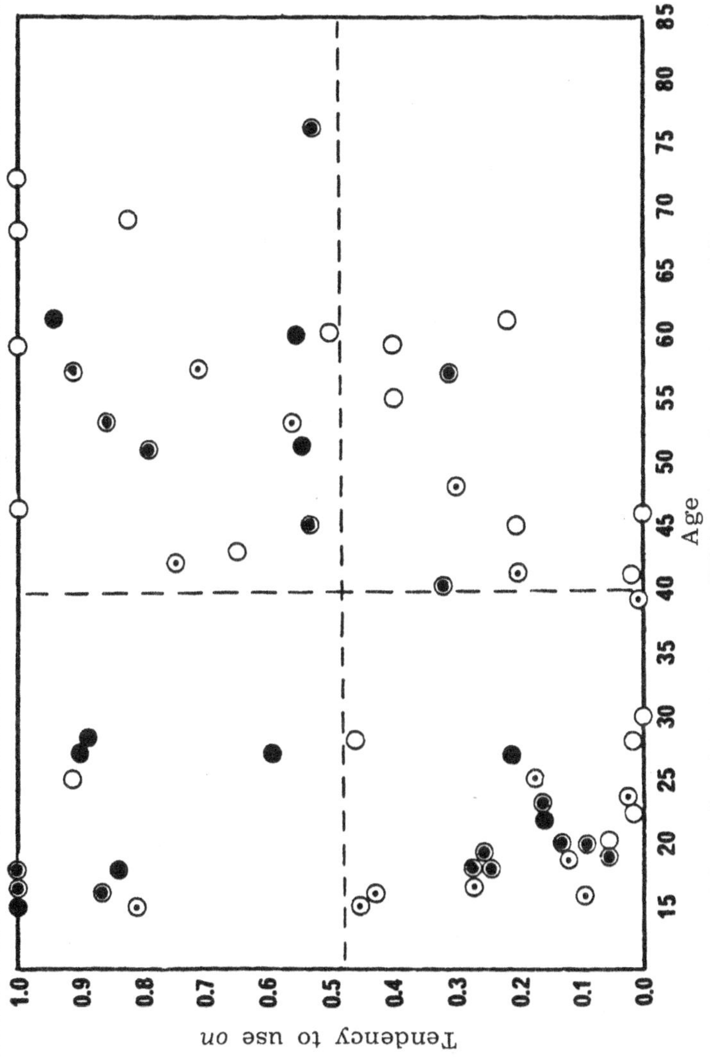

Legend (Index of participation in the linguistic marketplace): Filled circles - 0.80-1.00; mostly filled circles - 0.43-0.79; dotted circles - 0.12-0.42; empty circles - 0.00-0.11.

Figure 2. Tendency among women to use *on*, as a function of age.

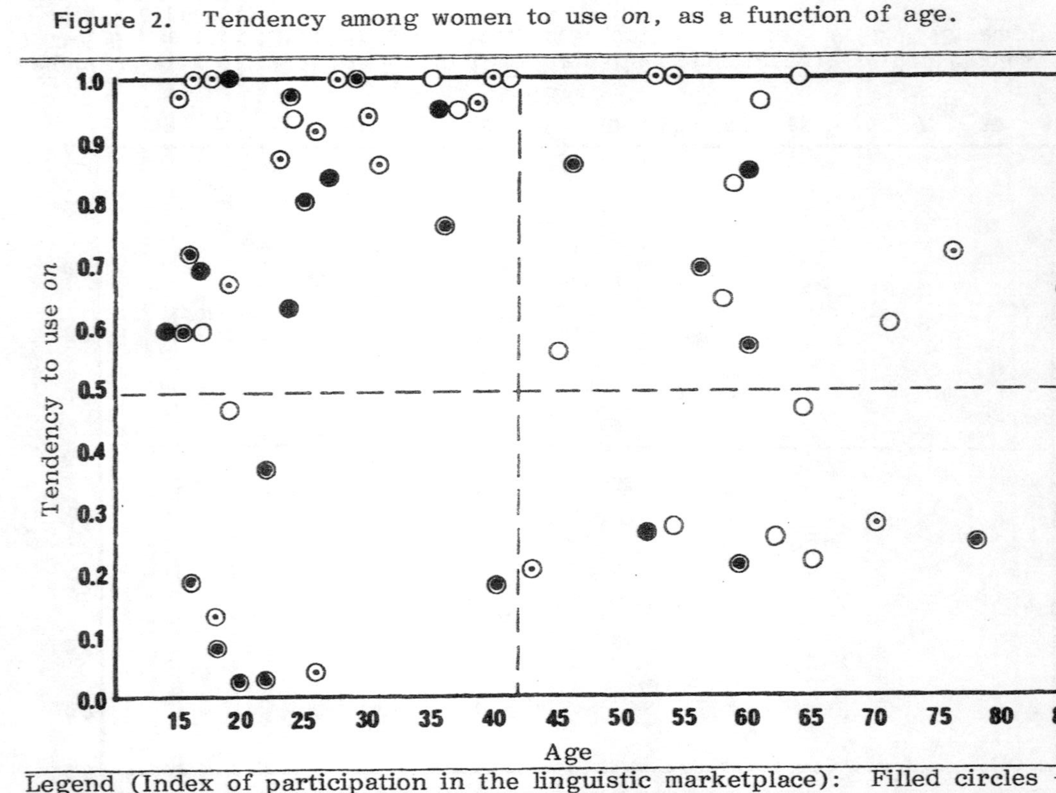

Legend (Index of participation in the linguistic marketplace): Filled circles - 0.80-1.00; mostly filled circles - 0.43-0.79; dotted circles - 0.12-0.42; empty circles - 0.00-0.11.

The marked differences between the two figures can be summarized in tabular form. Grouping speakers according to whether they are 40 years old or less, or more than 40, and according to whether their tendencies to use *on* are greater or less than 0.5, results in Tables 2a and 2b.

Table 2a. Preferred variant for indefinite clitic as a function of age and sex: Men (N=60).

	Age	
Tendency to use *on*	40 and under	over 40
0.5 and up (favors *on*)	28.1%	65.8%
less than 0.5 (favors *tu*)	71.9%	34.2%
Total	100% (N=32)	100% (N=28)

Table 2b. Preferred variant for indefinite clitic as a function of age and sex: Women (N=60).

	Age	
Tendency to use *on*	40 and under	over 40
0.5 and up (favors *on*)	75.6%	68.7%
less than 0.5 (favors *tu*)	24.4%	31.3%
Total	100% (N=37)	100% (N=23)

In Table 2a, it is seen that the older men have a clear preference for the *on* form, while the opposite is true for the younger men. In Table 2b, on the other hand, one notices that while the older women behave similarly to the older men, the younger women do not parallel the younger men in a tendency to use *tu-vous*. In fact, the younger women use *on* more often than any other group in the tables.

Tables 2a and 2b suggest not only that a change in patterns of indefinite subject pronoun usage has been in progress over the last generation, but also that this change involves the linguistic differentiation between men and women.

What of the socioeconomic factor? In Figures 1 and 2, it is seen that there is little systematic differentiation of speakers according to the role they play in the linguistic marketplace, an index which has been designed (cf. Bourdieu and Boltanski 1975) to be most sensitive to any social class effect on linguistic variation (cf. Sankoff and Laberge 1978).

There is a cluster of young men, however, who differ from the tendency shown by their age peers in using a great deal of *on*. This group consists largely of persons who are highly integrated into the linguistic marketplace.

Summary and conclusion. It should be abundantly clear that *on* and *tu-vous*, in the contexts in which I have studied them, are surface variants fulfilling identical semantic functions. This is clear both from an examination of their linguistic and pragmatic contexts of interchangeable use, and from their socially conditioned distribution in the population. Any analysis claiming that the use of *tu* or *vous* is tinged by the definite second person origins of these clitics, is not only thoroughly unfounded distributionally and behaviorally, but also falls necessarily into the trap of espousing such discredited notions as that working-class speakers are less capable of abstract discourse, not having access to genuinely indefinite forms. Additional evidence against the validity of such intuitions is provided by the results of our quantitative analysis, which shows that it is precisely when the use of *tu* or *vous* is least likely to be misinterpreted in their determinate senses, namely in implicative constructions, that this use is most widespread.

The quantitative analysis, or rather its results, provide justification for another aspect of my methodology. The class of utterance types I have called implicative contains various constructions which, though they share an overall surface similarity, must be derived by rather diverse syntactic processes. The same holds for presentatives. When it comes to the pragmatic category I have labelled moral, there is no surface indication whatsoever on which to base this categorization. Nevertheless the fact that all these classes have strong, distinct effects on the choice of variant for the indefinite clitic proves that they are meaningful and natural groupings with important linguistic ramifications, and not arbitrary or ill-defined constructs. This points out the necessity, in analyses such as mine, for interpretatively defined constraints as well as distributionally based ones.

The results document the pattern of spread of *tu* and *vous* into indefinite or general contexts. This spread is most advanced in contexts where there is little danger of ambiguity with second person interpretations, and is least advanced where *on* is not likely to take on its definite interpretation as first person plural. In addition, it is noted that an evaluative pragmatic effect can be achieved by use of *on*.

As for the differentiation within the population, one detects the emergence of distinct behaviors with respect to the variable, between the sexes, at least in the interview situation where the corpus was collected. Except for a minority of young men whose social position requires a competence in the standard variety of French, the younger generation of men is the focus of the change in indefinite clitic usage. This change is resisted by the great majority of younger women, irrespective of social class considerations.

NOTE

The contents of this paper are drawn largely from my Ph.D. dissertation. I would like to thank David Sankoff for his help in translating and adapting this material, and in supervising the preparation of the manuscript.

REFERENCES

Bourdieu, P., and L. Boltanski. 1975. Le fétichisme de la langue. Actes de la Recherche en Sciences Sociales 4.2-32.

Laberge, S. 1977. Etude de la variation des pronoms sujets définis et indéfinis dans le français parlé à Montréal. Unpublished Ph.D. dissertation. Université de Montréal.

Labov, W. 1972. The transformation of experience in narrative syntax. In: Language in the inner city: Studies in the Black English vernacular. Edited by W. Labov. Philadelphia: University of Pennsylvania Press.

Rousseau, P., and D. Sankoff. 1978. Advances in variable rule methodology. In: Linguistic variation. Edited by D. Sankoff. New York: Academic Press.

Sankoff, D., and S. Laberge. 1978. The linguistic market and the statistical explanation of variability. In: Linguistic variation. Edited by D. Sankoff. New York: Academic Press.

WHAT DO YOU MEAN BY REQUEST FOR CLARIFICATION?

Donna Christian
Center for Applied Linguistics
and Georgetown University

The question of deciding what to count is a basic one in identifying a phenomenon for a linguistic study. Too often, it seems, investigators allow hazy notions to guide them in classifying instances of language behavior, particularly when it is the intersection of that behavior with other variables (age, social class, etc.) that is of main interest. When a certain uneasiness is felt in including or excluding what seem to be borderline cases, the investigator is forced either to make some arbitrary decisions or to take a closer look at the behavior in question. The present discussion is the result of trying to count instances of a particular use of language, requesting clarification. A search of some videotapes for examples of this behavior made it clear that a closer examination was required in order to make principled decisions about what should be included and excluded. It also became clear that evidence from a variety of levels of language was needed in order to address the problem.

A request for clarification, as defined here, is a special type of request for information, one which seems to indicate a problem in processing the previous utterance. It is both a contingent query in Garvey's (1977) sense and part of a side sequence as described by Jefferson (1972). Clarification requests most often take the form of questions, and this discussion is restricted to these forms. Some easily recognizable instances of this function are given in (1).[1]

(1a)	(I)	Michael:	I'm on it. I'm on your team.
		Duncan:	*What?*
		Michael:	I'm on your team, Duncan.

(1b) (K) Barbara: ... You get to put the chapstick on.
Joyce: *On what?*
Barbara: On her lips.
(1c) (II) Teddy: How do you spell 'early'?
Julia: *Earling?*
Teddy: 'Early'.
(1d) (I) Ben: You guys, we have to push these back some.
John: *Put, push what back?*
Ben: These. (pointing)

However, other instances that occurred in the data were not as clearly 'countable' and it became evident that a more rigorous set of defining criteria was needed. For example, Eric's second 'question' underlined in (2) resembled in form a request for clarification, but did not seem to be acting like this function in other ways.

(2) (II) Eric: How much is this all gonna cost?
Steven: Oh, I would say, about a hundred dollars.
Eric: *A hundred dollars?* You're crazy!

What follows is the result of taking a closer look at requesting clarification and finding some language events, like (2), which resemble them but should be excluded for specific reasons. The process of deciding what to count is described as three steps in the following sections, but these three activities naturally overlapped and intersected tremendously during the course of the investigation. The first step is to review the literature.

1. Looking at the literature. Studies of types of requests have not typically dealt with requests for clarification. The literature within linguistics has dealt for the most part with requests for action of some kind (for example, Green 1973). Treatments of requests for information do not specifically mention the special class of clarification requests. They either implicitly include it within the broader category or do not consider it at all. (See, for example, Sadock's 1974 discussion of whether or not questions are semantically requests to tell.) The formal aspects of the questions that may serve as requests for clarification have not received much attention either. When such question forms are discussed, they are typically used as examples in treatments of different issues. For instance, in the discussion of question intonation in Pope (1975), she considers certain kinds of clarification questions as 'echo' questions, because of their intonational properties.

Discussions which are more directly related are found in developmental and conversational work. Brown (1968) investigates the development of WH questions in children and notes what he calls 'occasional questions', which are uninverted forms such as *You want what?* He then speculates on the role such questions can play in children's language development when adults in their environment use them. Cherry (1976) also treats the role of adults' requests for clarification in child development, giving a more detailed presentation of this function. She calls such a request 'a conversational device which functions to allow either speaker to bring a misunderstanding in the conversation to the attention of the other' (Cherry 1976:2), and observes that a sequence including this type of request does not affect the topic or change the turn-taking sequence. Her discussion is limited to questions involving repetition, either where the hearer requests repetition, or where the hearer repeats the utterance or some part of it, seeking confirmation of the correctness of his rendition. (A third category, repetition with syntactic expansion, is not pertinent to the present discussion.)

Jefferson (1972) concentrates on repetition from a conversational perspective, in discussing certain questions and other kinds of utterances that initiate what she calls a 'side sequence' in a conversation. This is an occurrence which 'constitutes a break in the activity', in this case a conversation, after which 'the on-going activity will resume' (Jefferson 1972:294). Requests for clarification can be characterized as initiating such side sequences, since once the needed clarification is provided, the ongoing conversation can resume. Her description of different ways of using repetition, including questions, contributes to the separation of those which are truly requests for clarification from those which serve different functions. For example, she distinguishes between questioning repeats that carry a feeling of surprise, as in (2), *A hundred dollars? You're crazy!*, and those that do not, calling the latter 'more nearly straight requests for information' (Jefferson 1972:303). Her observations about questioning repeats will be useful later in the discussion of excluding certain cases from the class of requests for clarification. Merritt (1976) considers requests for repetition, or 'calls for replay', as one type of question that can immediately follow another question in her treatment of questions sequences in service encounters.

Finally, Garvey (1977) also describes a type of language event which subsumes requests for clarification but includes questions which function in other ways as well. She presents a detailed study of what she calls 'contingent queries', providing an analysis of that category and a discussion of certain aspects of its development in children. The contingent query is characterized as a speech act which is dependent on the prior utterance in the conversation and which does not alter the ongoing conversation (i.e. a side sequence, in Jefferson's terminology). Included in this category of speech acts are questions used to seek clarification, but these are not clearly distinguished from the other kinds of contingent queries.

Other types of contingent queries mentioned include the indication of surprise (not further discussed due to a small number of tokens) and 'solicited' contingent queries which will be treated in a later section. For the most part, her discussion of 'unsolicited' contingent queries deals with clarification questions, although she refers to them only as a more common kind of contingent query. For example, she maintains that

> the intended illocutionary force of a contingent query is that the addressee understands that the speaker has made a request for information of some sort and that the intended perlocutionary effect is that the addressee attempts to comply with the particular request (Garvey 1977:67).

This is true of clarification requests, but does not hold, for instance, in the case of queries used to indicate surprise, where no request for information is intended. Much of the remainder of this paper is concerned with isolating those questions which may properly be considered requests for clarification from the larger set of contingent queries.

2. **Developing the criteria.** The major defining characteristic of a request for clarification as it is viewed here is that it signal some problem in processing a prior utterance, either in hearing or fully understanding it. Its role in conversation is that of a side sequence, as discussed by Jefferson (1972), in that it initiates a break in the ongoing activity which can then resume with no alteration of topic or turn-taking sequence. In a simple version, its form within a conversation can be seen in (3a) and exemplified in (3b).

(3a) X: utterance
    Y: request for clarification
    X: clarification
Y: response to X's first utterance
(3b) (K) Teacher: Two and one is--?
    Robin: *Two and one?*
    Teacher: Yes.
    Robin: Three.

Y's response to X's first utterance need not be verbal, of course. For example, if X issued a directive, after which a clarification sequence occurred, Y's response could be carrying out the directive. If X's utterance was an assertion, after clarification Y's response could be simply a nonverbal acknowledgment of understanding and X might immediately continue the narrative.

As a contingent query, in Garvey's sense, the request for clarification is dependent on a prior utterance and so its placement within a discourse is restricted. The intent of the issuer is to obtain the desired clarification before continuing with the conversation. This is not always the result, particularly in conversations with more than two participants, and, depending on a variety of factors, such as the degree of urgency involved in the clarification, the requester may persist or drop it. If he chooses to persist, the nature of the question may change, depending on how far the conversation has advanced. The clarification question may relate to the previous utterance by indicating a need for repetition of all or part of it or a need for some specific information needed to fully understand it (such as the referent of a pro-form). The WH form question asks specifically for the information (*A what?*), while a yes-no question asks for confirmation or denial of the correctness of a proposed version of the information (*A shark?*).

2.1 **Differences between requests for clarification and other requests.** Requests for clarification share certain properties with other requests but differ in certain respects which lead to their being grouped together in a separate class. Like requests in general (Gordon and Lakoff 1971; Green 1975), for example, they operate under the condition that the speaker desires the request to be carried out. Like requests for information (Sadock 1974), the desired action is in most cases a verbal response which gives certain information. However, as a result of their dependence on the previous utterance, requests for clarification are a special class of requests for information in three respects. First, requests for information can be placed fairly freely within a discourse, with certain limitations on appropriateness (topic and turn restrictions, and so on). On the other hand, requests for clarification are much more restricted since they must immediately follow the utterance being questioned. Second, in making a request for information, the speaker assumes that the addressee is able to provide the information on some grounds, usually unspecified. In requesting clarification, the assumptions about addressee knowledge are specific and directly based on the fact that the addressee issued the utterance being questioned. (Of course, there are exceptional cases where the addressee does not have the information.)

Finally, there is a functional difference with formal consequences that distinguishes requests for clarification from other requests. Indirectness is commonly used when issuing requests, and politeness is a major concern. Requests for information can be couched in terms like *Do you know what time it is,* when information about the time, not addressee knowledge, is of direct concern. Requests for clarification do not involve this kind of indirectness because the addressee can be assumed to be willing to answer questions about his utterance since he just issued it and presumably intended it to be understood. In such a situation, the best way a hearer can be cooperative is by making his request for clarification direct. Consider, for example, certain alternative forms for requests for clarification that one might expect if indirect requests were appropriate. Given an utterance such as *Jane wants you to call her as soon as possible*, some of these alternative forms might include:

(4a) *Can you tell me who (wants me to call)?
(4b) ?*Could you please repeat who (wants me to call)?
(4c) ?*I'd like you to repeat who (wants me to call).
(4d) Would you please repeat what you just said?

The first response, (4a), appears to be completely inappropriate as a request for clarification. Items (4b) and (4c) might work as responses to the utterance given, which could, in fact, accomplish the goal of finding out the information needed. However, they are at least not very cooperative and would be regarded as somewhat odd. Because of this indirectness, the speaker is forced to specify overtly what information is needed and the question form no longer is limited by the placement-in-the-discourse restrictions on requests for clarification. Hence, such questions are excluded from this category. A simple *Who?* would accomplish the same end and would be the cooperative response in an informal conversation, and would be considered a request for clarification. Item (4d) is a possible alternative to the request for clarification *What?*, but again would not be as cooperative a response in the conversation as the more direct form, and because of considerations such as placement in the discourse due to its explicitness, it would not fit the category of request for clarification. The importance of this difference between requests for clarification and requests, including requests for information, is major. A class of forms, indirect questions, will not be expected to occur here.

It is possible to attach *please* to requests for clarification, as in (5), but this too is rare.

(5) Buyer: I'd like a ticket to New York.
Seller: *To where, please?*
Buyer: New York.
Seller: All right. The train will be leaving in 10 minutes.

One way of being more polite is the substitution of certain forms for *what?* or *huh?* in requesting repetition. These include *Excuse me?, Pardon?* and so on. None of these politer forms were found in the corpus of children's language, although they have been heard fairly frequently in use by adults. This suggests that the children may not yet have learned some of the social rules surrounding requests for clarification (or, at least, requests for repetition), although they certainly have acquired the basic strategies and use them appropriately. What appears to be happening in this set of polite forms relates to the observations made earlier about indirectness and can be described by using the distinction between 'constitutive' and 'regulative' rules made by Searle (1971). He defines these types of rules as follows:

> Regulative rules regulate a pre-existing activity, an activity whose existence is logically independent of the existence of the rules. Constitutive rules constitute (and also regulate) an activity the existence of which is logically dependent on the rules (Searle 1971:617).

There is a constitutive rule for requesting clarification involving the avoidance of indirectness in the form used. This property in part defines requests for clarification. At odds with this, however, is a more general rule in conversation, a matter of 'etiquette', that calls for finding a way to be polite. This combination of rules leads to the polite forms mentioned earlier (*Excuse me?* and so on) used by adults. However, with the children, it appears that they may not yet have developed the regulative rule. They know how to use requests for clarification, they know the constitutive rules, but they do not indicate an awareness of the ways to implement the regulative rule and/or the times when this 'etiquette' is appropriate.

2.2 **Formal properties.** Formally, the questions used to request clarification may be either the WH or the yes-no type. Within each type, however, there are certain differences in form between clarification questions and most other kinds of questions that set them apart. (Certain questions that resemble clarification questions in form but differ in function are discussed in the next section.) There are also some interesting intonational properties, but these are not dealt with here. (See Pope 1975 for some discussion of these properties.)

In the WH type of clarification question, the WH form itself specifies the information desired, in reference to the previous utterance. In other WH questions, what is being asked for must be more fully specified, since the special relationship to the previous utterance is not applicable. For example, the utterance *Put the can over there* might be met with the clarification question *Where?* If the directive had not been the previous utterance, or if it had been part of a more general directive, something like *Clean off the table*, a fuller question would be needed to get the same information, i.e. *Where should I put the can?* Also, WH word and subject-verb inversion is not necessary in clarification questions. *You went where?* is appropriate in response to *I went to the movies*, whereas *Where did you go?* is the comparable form for an information question. In yes-no clarification questions, inversion is also unnecessary, since a version of the previous utterance is being offered. A question response to *He was late for the meeting* might be *John was late?* rather than *Was John late?* These kinds of formal differences set clarification questions apart from many other kinds of questions, but, as we shall see, they are not sufficient to define the class uniquely. They must be used in combination with the other functional and conversational properties discussed earlier.

3. **Deciding what should be excluded.** Forms which structurally resemble clarification questions and which are placed within a discourse in a similar way can be used for different functions. However, since they are not being used to obtain clarification, they need to be separated out when instances of these requests are being collected. In this section, I examine some question forms which resemble requests for clarification but are used to do other things. These examples fall into two main categories. First, I look at how the addressee of an utterance can use such questions to make a comment on the utterance, not actually seeking an answer to the question. Second, I examine how the issuer of an utterance can manipulate the addressee into responding with this type of question. The speaker can design an utterance so that the hearer is practically obliged to respond with what looks like a clarification question. This then gives the speaker the license to continue. In both cases, the reasons why these questions should not count as requests for clarification are discussed.

The addressee of an utterance can use question forms to indicate surprise or disbelief at what the speaker has just said, as in (6).

(6a)	(I)	Michael:	We're almost done making our special secret base.
		Duncan:	*What?* I'm allowed to go in it.
(6b)	(III)	David:	The 'E' is an inch away from the 'A'. How can you make--
		Robin:	*It is?* (picks up ruler to measure).
(6c)	(K)	Teacher:	Drew's going to hang up his clothes and Joyce is going to talk.
		John:	*His clothes?*
		Teacher:	His coat.

In (6a), Duncan is surprised that the base is labeled *secret*, and goes on to maintain that he can still go into it. Robin in (6b) expresses doubt about the measurement figure David has offered and decides to check the figure by measuring the distance herself. In (6c), the teacher is trying to get a class meeting going, and Drew has just come in late. John questions the teacher's indication that Drew will hang up his clothes. He does not seek confirmation of his version of part of what the teacher has said, but rather he expresses doubt as to its accuracy. The teacher responds to this by modifying her original utterance. If she had taken the question as a clarification question, she would have responded differently. Jefferson (1972), in her work on side sequences, talks about examples like (6b) and (6c) as questioning repeats which demonstrate disapproval. She does not mention the use of WH forms in this way, since she is concentrating on the use of repetition of all or part of a previous utterance. However, the WH forms that can signal a request for repetition work in the same way, with their use indicating surprise or disbelief, as in the two alternative responses shown in (7).

(7) X: I saw a camel on Broadway this morning.
  Y: *You what?* That's impossible.
  Or: *You saw a camel?* That's impossible.

Jefferson's observations on how these forms work in a conversation point out where they differ from real requests for clarification. She notes (1972:299) that 'This type of repeat characteristically signals that there is a problem in its product item, and its work is to generate further talk directed to remedying the problem.' Unlike real requests for clarification, the question is not intended to provoke an answer that provides some missing information. It is instead an expression of some kind of disbelief and further discussion can be initiated by either party. Thus, these forms are distinct because a direct answer is not desired and the shape of the following discourse is different. The person responding with such a question may continue talking or the original speaker may go on to justify his utterance, and so on. Any number of things can happen, but characteristics of discourse that include a real request for clarification are lacking, since the course of the conversation is usually altered.

Such question forms can also be used in an opposite way, that is, to indicate some form of approval or appreciation, with similar characteristics distinguishing them from requests for clarification. Garvey (1977) discusses these as appreciation sequences. These occur frequently in interactions, as shown in (8).

(8) X: I bought a new car yesterday.
  Y: You bought a new car? That's great!

In these cases, however, WH forms would not appear to be appropriate. They also differ from similar expressions of disapproval in that they are less likely to generate further talk about the utterance, since they indicate that it has been accepted and the conversation can move on.

In the second category, there are cases where the speaker of the original utterance makes use of forms made available from requests for clarification. In doing this, the speaker arranges his utterance so that the hearer may or must respond with one of these forms, which then shifts the floor back to the speaker with permission to continue. These kinds of uses are mentioned by Garvey as 'solicited contingent queries', about which she concludes: 'In effect, Y has maneuvered X into asking him just what he wanted to say anyway' (Garvey 1977:81). One of the simpler situations in which this is found is in summons-answers sequences, as in (9).

(9) (I) Sophia: Hey Julie, Julie!
Julie: *What?*

These are distinct from requests for clarification in that the question is itself a response to the utterance rather than initiating an embedded sequence after which the conversation advances. The question in the role that it plays serves to advance the conversation.

A more complex situation exists in cases where the speaker uses a postverbal WH embedding, illustrated in (10).

(10a) I know what you're getting for Christmas.
(10b) Do you know what the answer is?
(10c) Betcha don't know what Felix said about you.
(10d) Guess what we're having for dessert.

(I am purposely avoiding the controversial distinction between embedded questions and free relatives. See arguments in Griffin 1974.) Each of the foregoing utterances could be responded to by the question form *what?*, but in each case the speaker who intended that to happen would be using this conversational device to ensure another turn at talk. (That statement is qualified since the intention could be different in (10b), where the speaker could be issuing a direct or indirect request for information, if the question concerns the hearer's knowledge or the answer).

This conversational device available to the speaker to ensure a further turn at talking can take a variety of forms, but they all share one thing: the notion of some unspecified knowledge which the speaker has. The degrees of certainty about this knowledge can vary, making the question form response more or less appropriate. This becomes clearer after some more examples. In assertions like (10a), the speaker asserts that he has a certain knowledge so the hearer has no doubt about it. In (11), the hearer cooperates and asks the speaker for the information.

(11) (K) Katie: I'm going to make a little bunny.
Caroline: *I know what I'm going to make.*
Katie: *What?*
Caroline: My kitty cat.

There seems to be little point in Caroline's first utterance here, other than to provoke Katie into asking for the information she has so far held back. The conversation advances because of the question and its response, rather than resuming its progress after the sequence. This type of statement is also often used in teasing, particularly by children; the information is then withheld even after the question response is provided (the common 'I know what you're getting for your birthday and I'm not telling!'). Another version of this is stating that the hearer does not have the knowledge, implying that the speaker does, as in (12).

(12a)	(K)	Jennifer:	I'm making a Mexican girl. *You don't know what her name's gonna be.*
		Caroline:	*What?*
		Jennifer:	I'm not gonna tell.
(12b)	(N)	Scott:	... and *you don't even know my middle name.*
		Sara:	You don't know my middle name!
		Scott:	Why don't you try to guess?
		Sara:	*I know what it is!*
		Scott:	*What?*
		Sara:	Stiltskin!

Example (12a) clearly involves teasing, judging from Jennifer's response to Caroline's question. In (12b), Scott is forced to make more explicit the intention of his first utterance when Sara fails to respond the way he wants her to. Then Sara reverses the game, using an assertion of her knowledge to provoke Scott into asking a question. These statements about an addressee's lack of knowledge can also function as a sort of challenge, more obviously when they take a form like (13).

(13) Betcha don't know what her name's gonna be.

The 'betcha' form would clearly invite either the question response or a guess at the unspecified information. An incorrect guess (or guesses) could then be followed by the question form in an attempt to get the correct information, as in (14), which is yet another device a speaker can use.

(14)	(III)	Gary:	If I told you what movie I was going to, with my brother, you'd probably say I was cuckoo.
		Albert:	*Bambi?*
		Gary:	*No.*
		Albert:	*What?*
		Gary:	Snow White and the Seven Dwarfs.

Another version of this conversational device involves asking a question about the hearer's knowledge, with various aspects of the context contributing to the certainty implied about the speaker's knowledge. Examples of this are given in (15).

(15a) (III) Charles: *You know what that diagram's of?*
John: *What?*
Charles: The troop at rest, no, the troop on the move.

(15b) (N) Sara: *Do you know what my mother's name is?*
Catherine: No.
Sara: I do.
Catherine: *What?*
Sara: Gail.

(15c) (III) Teacher: Now, Laura, *do you know what you're being now?*
Laura: *What?*
Teacher: What?
Laura: Silly?
Teacher: Yes.

In (15b), Sara persists in trying to provoke Catherine to ask her the question, even after Catherine resists a first time. Sara does this by moving from a question about addressee knowledge to an assertion about her own knowledge, a stronger form. In (15c), Laura reasonably assumes that the teacher knows the answer to her question, even though the teacher goes on to insist that the child verbalize it. This brings up a special feature of the social context in the school that is relevant here. Teachers, because of their special role in the school, are allowed to ask questions that they already know the answer to, and children, their students, realize this. In fact, it is probably the marked case when teachers ask questions they *do not* already know the answers to, particularly from the child's viewpoint. This leads to occasional conversational problems, as in (16), where Peter assumes that the teacher knows the answer and is eliciting a question response, when in fact, it seems the teacher does not know.

(16) (N) Teacher: You said the sign should say what?
Peter: It should say, 'Here lies a dead bird'.
Teacher: ... You say, 'it should say'. *Do you know why it should say that?*
Peter: Why?
Teacher: I don't know. I was wondering why you were so emphatic about it.

Finally, there are cases where the hearer can be virtually certain that the speaker has the information that is left unspecified and wants to elicit the question response. These are the forms *Guess what X*, as in (17a), with the nature of the information specified, and the forms *You know what?* or *Guess what?* as in (17b), which are totally unspecified.

(17a) (N) Becky: *Guess what we're having for dessert?*
Teacher: What?
Becky: Apples.
(17b) (K) David: Hey, *you know what?*
Teacher: What?
David: I was pretty quick on this.

In the case of (17a), the hearer can assume that if the speaker is asking him to guess, he will also be able to evaluate the correctness of the guess and so must have the information. In (17b), there is very little ground on which the hearer can even speculate on the information, since the possibilities are potentially infinite, and the speaker must then have some information to convey, or the utterance is pointless. This last set of examples, then, are clearly and probably almost exclusively used as conversational devices to ensure another turn, using the forms made available by the function of requesting clarification. This may provide some explanation for why they are so popular and so frequently used by children. Children may be unsure about how to get a turn with each other, or may feel--or understand correctly--that it is hard for them to get a turn with adults. However, answering someone else's question is something that they do a lot, it is polite, and it may seem attractive as a way of getting turns. It at least is a way of legitimizing their presentation of some information they want to get out, and so they get the other speaker to ask them for it. This may help account for the high frequency of *Guess what?* observed in children's language use.

The point of the preceding discussion is that there are a variety of question responses which look, on the surface, like requests for clarification, but when they are seen as conversational devices a speaker can use to ensure another turn at speaking, they can be excluded in a principled way. The facts about their usage are quite complex, with the certainty about speaker's knowledge depending not only on such factors as the use of negation (12), conditionals (14), or questions (15), but also the pronominal forms employed (i.e. *you* vs. *I*), the type of verb (*know* vs. others), and probably many others that cannot be dealt with here. And naturally, the nonlinguistic context is important, including such features as the special teacher role in the school situation examined here.

While this discussion has not exhausted the problems encountered in attempting to identify instances of the language function of requesting clarification, some of the cases that need to be excluded have been pointed out and reasons given for their exclusion. It is clear that both form and function must be considered, and examination of the data must include the prior utterance, the request for clarification itself, and subsequent utterances. If we want to look at requesting clarification as it intersects with other variables, such as cross-sectional age variations or variations that correlate with social setting, we must first answer the question, what is a request for clarification?

NOTES

This research was supported by a grant from the Carnegie Corporation of New York to the Center for Applied Linguistics. I would like to thank Peg Griffin, Bruce Fraser, and Stephen Cahir for their comments on earlier versions of this paper.

1. The corpus I am discussing was collected from videotapes of classroom interactions involving children four to nine years of age, in nursery, kindergarten, first, second, and third grade. The number in parentheses preceding each example identifies it as a member of this corpus and indicates the grade level of the children involved. A variety of situations was represented in the videotapes, including whole group and small group sessions with the teacher and small groups with no teacher present. Thus some of the interactions include an adult, the teacher, while others do not. Approximately 40 hours of videotape were searched in all. The original objectives of this study were to investigate requesting clarification cross-sectionally, by age, sex, and other groupings of the children, and to see what differences, if any, existed between interactions with the teacher as opposed to those with other children. The results of this investigation are reported elsewhere (Christian and Tripp 1978).

REFERENCES

Brown, Roger. 1968. The development of WH questions in child speech. Journal of Verbal Learning and Verbal Behavior 7.279-290.

Cherry, Louise J. 1977. The role of adults' requests for clarification in the language development of children. In: Discourse production and comprehension. Edited by R. O. Freedle. Norwood, N.J.: Ablex.

Christian, Donna, and Rosemary Tripp. 1978. Teachers' perceptions and children's language use. In: Children's functional language and education in the early years: A final report to the Carnegie Corporation. Arlington, Va.: Center for Applied Linguistics.

Garvey, Catherine. 1977. The contingent query: A dependent act in conversation. In: Interaction, conversation, and the development of language: The origins of behavior, Volume 5. Edited by M. Lewis and L. Rosenblum. New York: Wiley.

Gordon, David, and George Lakoff. 1971. Conversational postulates. In: Papers from the Seventh Regional Meeting of the Chicago Linguistic Society. Chicago: Chicago Linguistic Society.

Green, G. M. 1973. How to get people to do things with words: The question of whimperatives. In: Some new directions in linguistics. Edited by R. W. Shuy. Washington, D.C.: Georgetown University Press.

Griffin, Peg. 1974. Their leaving usage alone is important. Paper presented at the Linguistic Society of America Summer Meeting.

Jefferson, Gail. 1972. Side sequences. In: Studies in social interaction. Edited by D. Sudnow. New York: Free Press.

Merritt, Marilyn. 1976. On questions following questions in service encounters. Language in Society 5.315-357.

Pope, Emily. 1975. Questions and answers in English. Unpublished Ph.D. dissertation. Massachusetts Institute of Technology.

Sadock, Jerrold M. 1974. Toward a linguistic theory of speech acts. New York: Academic Press.

Searle, John. 1971. What is a speech act? In: Readings in the philosophy of language. Edited by Jay F. Rosenberg and Charles Travis. Englewood Cliffs, N.J.: Prentice-Hall.

WHICH

Jennifer Greene
Montgomery County Public Schools (Md.)

1. This paper is concerned with the use of *which* as a relative marker in nonrestrictive relative clauses. It investigates sentences where *which* stands for some structure other than an identical surface level NP antecedent. The data examined comes from three sources, each of which represents the speech of white middle-class Americans, those people whose speech is understood to be Standard English. The first source, and that which initially inspired the study, is audio tapes from the Detroit Dialect Study conducted by Roger Shuy in 1966. (Sentences from this source are identified in brackets by *D* followed by the number of the tape from which they were extracted.) The second source consists of sentences heard by or reported to the investigator. (These are identified by an *I* in brackets.) And the third source is sentences constructed by the investigator for the purpose of controlling some factors in order to discover principles at work in others. (These sentences are left unmarked.)

As it turns out, nonrestrictive *which* frequently does not have a fully specified structural antecedent. Rather, traditional identity requirements are often so ignored that the antecedent provides just the structural basis for something that is inferenced in *which*.[1] By examining how a number of these inferences are set up in topic and structure, this paper attempts to establish some of the principles at work in making such inferencing possible.

Since inferencing is a ubiquitous process in language use, it is important to identify at the outset what is meant here by an 'inferenced' *which*. It is possible to identify two general kinds of inferencing with *which*, distinguished by the extent to which the inference is more or less essential for an understanding of the intended meaning of the sentence. On the one hand, while an inference may be involved in the way a sentence is understood, it may not be a necessary part of *which*. For example, in (1), where the speaker is describing the worst trouble she ever got into in school, while the *which* clause is literally about where the side chalk board was, the speaker is more concerned with where the teacher was. (The content of *which* appears in parentheses following each example.)

(1) She had moved to the side board, which was of course right by my desk. (the side board) [D: 43]

The function of the sentence is to tell how it happened that the teacher was right by her desk. This information is part of the intended meaning of the sentence, but it need not be understood as contained in *which*. The inference is in a sense outside the structure of the sentence. Example (2) provides another illustration.

(2) And then if you were punished, you would be sitting with the boys, which didn't bother me at all. (sitting with the boys) [D:151]

While the most literal interpretation is that it was simply 'sitting with the boys' that did not bother her at all, the more accurate understanding includes the inference (stated only approximately here) that being punished was not so bad, since it resulted in sitting with the boys. That is, although the notion of punishment is not an essential part of *which* in the sentence structure, it is a part of what the *which* clause is about. The inference is set up in the sentence, but the thing *which* stands for does not actually contain the inference.

Examples (1) and (2) contrast with (3), where *which* is inferenced.

(3) Roland is a philosopher, which has always been a tough field to find a job in. (philosophy)

Here the inference of the field of study (philosophy) from mention of the person in the field (a philosopher) is essential to the topic and structure of the *which* clause. In (4), the inference is not as forcibly pushed through as it is in (3), but it is nevertheless as obviously set up.

(4) Andy can add 15 and 15 and 15 on a calculator, which is higher than he can count to. (45) [I]

Clearly 45 is the number referred to in the *which* clause. The only question that might be raised is whether the result of adding 15 and 15 and 15 is actually contained in *which*, meaning that it is inferenced as in (3), or whether the whole is represented by its parts in *which* and the addition takes place outside the structure of the sentence, making it more like the inferencing in (1) and (2). Because the inference in (4) is more essential to an understanding of the sentence than it is in (1) and (2), the first view is the one represented here.[2] This paper, then, is about the kind of inferencing involved in (3) and (4), with the balance heavily tipped in the direction of (3).

1.1 To understand how inferences are set up in *which*, several interacting factors must be examined. The first, upon which everything else hinges, is the conceptual relationship between the antecedent and the inferenced *which*. For example, as (4) illustrates, if the antecedent is the parts of a thing, the inferenced *which* can stand for the whole. In an important sense, the existence of the conceptual relationship as common knowledge between speakers of English makes it possible for antecedents to be only the structural bases for inferences. That is to say, the fact that generally shared understanding is involved makes it possible for the information to be implicit rather than explicit. Several categories of conceptual relationships have emerged from the sentences that have been studied. These categories are to be understood as representative rather than complete. They provide the organizational framework for the paper, due to the fact that the other factors involved in setting the inferences up are at work in all of the categories of conceptual relationships.

A second major factor to examine is the structure of the *which* clause as it constrains what *which* can stand for. In some cases, it tells what the syntactic function of the thing *which* replaces has to be, as in (5).

(5) My father is an excellent cook, which few men of his generation enjoy doing. (cooking)

Doing requires a more predicative word in the *which* clause than the NP *cook* in the antecedent. In other cases, the *which* clause actually specifies the particular kind of a noun or verb that is needed to complete it, such as the word *field* in (3).

When the structure of the *which* clause does not actually push an inference through, background information often helps to set the inference up, as in (6).

(6) What you do is mix three parts of gin with one part vermouth, and drop in an olive or two, which is sort of the classic American drink. (a martini)

While it is possible to stop at the mixture of the ingredients without supplying the name, anyone who knows the name will supply it. Background information, then, is a third factor to consider in investigating how these inferences are set up.

A fourth factor is what the sentence is about, apart from the antecedent. This can involve part of the main body of the sentence, as in (6), where the word *mix* indicates that the ingredients are to be put together; or it can involve part of the *which* clause, as with *field* in (3). In the latter example, topic and structure seem to work together inseparably.

A fifth factor to examine is the morphological relationship between the antecedent and the inferenced structure in *which*. Morphological similarity is not a necessary condition, but it often seems to help. And, as (7) suggests, the process need not be lexical decomposition.

(7) Anne is a linguist, which is a field she didn't even know existed when she was thinking about what she might want to study in college. (linguistics)

Figuring out the rules that govern when an inferenced *which* can be morphologically more complex than the structural antecedent would involve an understanding of the interaction of all the factors at work, and that is somewhere in the future.

A sixth factor is the function of the *which* clause, that is, the degree to which it is attached to the main body of the sentence and the reason the person had for attaching it. Because this raises the complex issue of intonation, any kind of careful analysis of it is beyond the scope of this paper, but in general it can be said that the more parenthetical the speaker makes the *which* clause, the lighter the constraints are on inferencing. The decisions about starring sentences further on in this paper were based on intonation patterns that gave the *which* clauses relatively important status in the sentence. Were they to be understood as more parenthetical, many of these sentences would be considered acceptable.

2. Five general categories of conceptual relationships between the antecedent and the inferenced structure replaced by *which* are discussed in Sections 2.1 through 2.5. Some of them are quite small and neat; others are larger, with more internal variation. This may be reflective of a sample that is biased because it is small, or it may be a realistic representation of the way things are. At any rate, this analysis is to be understood as neither final nor complete.

2.1 One category of conceptual relationship that has been identified is the relationship of the result of an action to the action that brings it about. If the antecedent is the result, what *which* stands for can be the state of affairs of that coming about, as in (8) and (9).

(8) Alice claims she still wants to be a general practitioner, which her advisor hopes she'll do. (become a general practitioner) [I]

(9) I just think that if we can get a negotiated settlement, even with the Vietcong as part of the government, which, you know, will probably happen anyway, we can get out of there and not lose all our allies. (the Vietcong becoming part of the government) [D:618]

The inferenced action can also be more specific than the general coming about of something, as in (10) through (12).

(10) I like to wear socks because they soak up sweat, which happens inside these boots. (sweating) [I]

(11) Those are my initials there in the top right-hand corner, which is about all I do in this damned place. (put my initials in the top right-hand corner) [I]

(12) Finally, what issues from it is an audit report called the certified opinion. Well, along with the certified opinion, which is really our main function ... (writing the certified opinion) [D:161]

In (10), the morphological similarity between the NP *sweat* and the more predicative NP *sweating* that is needed in the structure to complete the *which* clause seems to push the inference through smoothly. Examples (11) and (12) reveal, however, that more complex work can be accomplished with *which*: in both cases, a verb naming the action that produces the result is needed for completion of the clause. The *do* in (11) makes a verb primarily a syntactic necessity, while the word *function* in (12) makes a verb primarily a semantic necessity.

It is also possible for the inference to be in the opposite direction: from the action in the antecedent to the result in *which*. In (13) and (14), morphological similarity helps push the inference through when the syntax and semantics of the *which* clause call for a particular noun.

(13) Erica Jong reviewed that book, which appeared in last Sunday's *Book World*. (the review) [I]

(14) I could report on the dog show, which would be a story some of our readers would like. (the report) [I]

But (15) and (16) show that morphological similarity is not necessary, probably if the conceptual relationship is unambiguously close enough.

(15) Harry threw up on the way home, which got on the side of the car. (the vomit)[3]

(16) He wrote me last week, which just arrived today. (the letter)

With respect to (15), throwing up can always be relied upon to yield vomit. Example (16) is a little more complex. While writing can result in other things than letters, writing to a person generally does not. That is, the fact that *write* has an indirect object in the main body of the sentence is part of what sets up the inference. Then background information supplies *letter*, ruling out other things that one person can write to another, such as postcards, invitations, etc., that would have to be specifically named.

In (13) through (16), the structure of the *which* clause, by needing an NP for completion, pushes the inference through. Example (17) is interesting because, while the syntax would permit a noninferenced understanding of the *which*, semantic factors force at least the inference of a noun from a verb.

(17) We've reserved a cabin in the woods at Cacapon for a week-end around Christmastime, which I'm really looking forward to. (being in the cabin ...) [I]

Since it is not possible to look forward to something that has already happened, the inference of *reservation*, from *reserved* in the antecedent, is needed for the sentence to be intact semantically. But the logical result of having a reservation is doing the thing reserved, in this case being or staying in a cabin in the woods, and that seems to be the most natural understanding of the sentence. Examples (18) and (19) provide additional illustrations of result inferences that are set up but not forced by the structure of the *which* clause.

(18) Fred covered a series of plant shows, which won him a journalism award. (the report) [I]

(19) Malcolm likes a cigar now and then, which stinks up the apartment for days. ('smoking the cigar' or 'the smoke from smoking it') [I]

In (18), background information about what kinds of things are capable of winning journalism awards in part sets up the inference that it was the story or report he wrote, rather than the covering of the plant shows, that won. And it is the topic of the *which* clause that calls for the use of background information.

There are two stages of inferencing in (19): first, that the liking of a cigar now and then results in the smoking of one every so often, and second, that smoking one results in the presence of strong smoke. Either stage is a reasonable understanding. The important point is that the *which* clause is about the result of what is said in the main body of the sentence, i.e. that the topic of the clause helps to set the inference up.

The inferencing in (20) works much more smoothly than in (21), if indeed it works at all in the latter.

(20) We put blueberries in the waffle batter, which tasted delicious. (the blueberry waffles)

(21) We put blueberries in the waffle batter, which were delicious. (?)

Tasted in (20) sets up the inference that *which* stands for what was eaten, and background information supplies what is needed with respect to waffle batter becoming waffles. In (21), while the past tense of *be* also implies that *which* stands for something that was eaten, and background information encourages the inference that the waffle batter was transformed to waffles, the plural verb seems to permit the separating out of *blueberries*, so that it is the (structural) antecedent. While the inference of cooking the batter can be part of the way the sentence gets understood, *which* itself is not inferenced.[4]

2.2 A second category of conceptual relationship is that of one or more parts of a thing to the whole, or of one or more members of a set to the set as a whole. If the antecedent structure is part, the whole or the set can be inferenced in *which*. The example provided in (4) involved naming all the parts (15 plus 15 plus 15) to get the whole. This need not be the case, as (22) illustrates.

(22) My idea at that time was that I would go to the University of Michigan for two years and then become a service representative for the telephone company, which was what their requirement was at that time. (two years of college) [D:43]

Knowledge of the real world supplies the information that a telephone company would not specify which college a prospective employee must attend. This sets up the inference that two years of college, not two years at the University of Michigan, was required. Again, it is the topic of the *which* clause that says to call on background information.

Making the inference in (23) involves knowing what two somewhat different things have in common and putting them into the appropriate set.

(23) I would never give anyone a canary or a parakeet for a wedding present, which is what happened to me. (someone's giving me a pet bird) [I]

And it appears that quite complex tasks of extracting common features can be done, as shown in (24).

(24) Henry wants a tarantula or a baby cobra or a pygmy rattler, which is the last kind of pet in the world his mother wants to have in the house (a disgusting poisonous one) [I]

At least two bits of background information go into the formation of the set that is inferenced in *which*: first, that people are generally repelled by spiders and snakes; and second, that the particular ones named are poisonous. The structure of the *which* clause, with its assertion that the animals named can be classified as a kind of pet, is a major factor in pushing the inference through.

The factors which set up the inference in (25) are also very complex.

(25) It's only Wednesday and Fred has gotten his fifth parking ticket, which is a new record for him. (five parking tickets in less than three days) [I]

Here the inference is not of the whole from the naming of a part, but rather a calculation based in part on knowledge of how the whole is constructed. In addition, the information that parking meters do not need to be fed on Sunday is called upon, indicating that the counting begins on Monday. Example (26) works much as (25) does, only more so.

(26) Gabrielle got a job as a receptionist at a technical school at the beginning of September, and by the first of October she was doing graphic art for the brother of the head of the technical school instead, which has to be a record, even for her. (working at two such dissimilar jobs within the space of a month)

Here the inference not only involves the calculation of a period of time, but also something about Gabrielle's seductive powers and occupational versatility.

Another kind of membership inclusion involves the association of a person with such things as an organization or a place or a field of study. If the antecedent names the person, the thing he or she is associated with can be inferenced in *which*, as in (27) through (30).

(27) Most Detroiters, which is where I am from, are still buying big American cars. (Detroit) [I]

(28) Rich is a native Californian, which is where his wife is from too. (California) [I]

(29) Joe is an Elk, which is a national club. (the Elks Club) [I]

(30) Ave is a Rotarian, which is better than the Lions Club. (the Rotary Club)

In (27) and (28), *where* provides instructions to pick out a place, as *club* in (29) and (30) says to pick out one of those. And morphological similarity no doubt helps to push the inferences through smoothly.

The conceptual relationship of a language to the country in which it is spoken involves a kind of membership, or belonging, too. It appears that the language is understood as belonging to the country, rather than vice versa, and that as a result, the direction of the inference can only be from the name of the language in the antecedent to the name of the country in *which*. Compare (31) and (32).

(31) Helen is taking an intensive course in German, which is where she plans to spend the summer. (Germany)

(32) *Next summer Helen plans to go to Germany, which she is studying in school this semester.[5]

Examples involving the relationship between a language and the country in which it is spoken provide clear evidence against a lexical decomposition analysis of inferenced *which*es. While the name of a language can be morphologically more complex than the name of a country, it can also be less so; Italian is more complex than Italy, German, less complex than Germany. And notice, too, that similar constraints on direction of inference hold for a person and the place he comes from.

(33) Christine is Polish, which is where her husband is from, too. (Poland) [I]

(34) *Christine comes from Poland, which her husband is, too. (Polish)

(35) I've noticed that many Latin Americans, which is where Carlos is from, invade my personal space. (Latin America) [I]

(36) *I've noticed that many people who come from Latin America, which is what Carlos is, invade my personal space. (a Latin American)

Why this should be true is not at all clear. It is not the case with at least some other kinds of belongings, as illustrated in (37) and (38), where a faith and the holder of the faith are involved.

(37) Susan plans to convert to {Judaism / Catholicism}, which is what her financé is. (a Jew/Jewish; Catholic)

(38) Suri became a Christian which is the most prevalent religion in the world. (Christianity) [I]

Inferencing involving the relationship between people and their fields of study is, with respect to the direction it can go, less constrained than when it involves people and their countries, and more constrained than when it involves a faith and the holder of the faith. Observe the difference of acceptability between (39) and (40).

(39) Today Helen is a chemist, which (is a subject) she was afraid to study in high school. (chemistry)

(40) *Helen is interested in chemistry, which she hopes to become some day. (a chemist)

The presence of 'is a subject' in the *which* clause of (39) certainly helps to push the inference through, but it also seems to work all right without the obvious structural/topical push. Example (40), on the other hand, does not work at all. Notice, however, the acceptability of (41), in which the direction of the inference is the same as in (40).

(41) I have a male friend who's studying nursing, which few men want to become. (nurses)

Part of what makes (41) work may be the conceptual similarity between studying nursing and becoming a nurse, i.e. that in neither case has the person achieved his goal. It may be that a mere interest in a field of study, as in (40), is not sufficient to set up an inference of a person in the field, while actually studying the field, as in (41), is. Or it may be that chemists are not to chemistry as nurses are to nursing, and that this difference in the conceptual relationships involved can account for the difference in acceptability between (40) and (41). Running through a long list of fields of study to discover the principles at work is beyond the scope of this analysis. For the present purpose it is enough to demonstrate that the factors at work in setting up these inferences as *which* are extremely sensitive and complex, and to suggest in what direction further analysis of the phenomenon might go.

In the final illustration of inferencing in this category, the precise wording of the content of *which* is left to the imagination. It appears that where stereotyped associations are very strong and structural clues in the *which* clause impose a firm constraint, a great deal of information can be left out.

(42) Albert said all the right things to all the right people and finally managed to get into the most prestigious country club in town, which is the sort of person I can't stand.

2.3 A third category of conceptual relationship is that of the doer of something to what he characteristically does, or vice versa. In the first part of this category are sentences like (43), where the antecedent is the activity and the inferenced *which* stands for the person who does it.

(43) Fred gave up his academic career in order to write, which is what he always wanted to be. (a writer) [I]

Be in the *which* clause constrains the antecedent structurally, but the introduction of the notion of a career in the main body of the sentence also helps to set the inference up. If (44) works, it suggests that the conceptual relationship is more important than the morphological one in this case.

(44) Fred gave up his academic career in order to repair cars, which is what he has always wanted to be. (a mechanic)

For some people, the inference in (44) may stop at car repairman, but if the word *mechanic* is readily available, *which* is set up to stand for it. The fact that (45) does not work implies that there has to be a word that really captures what the person is.

(45) *Fred gave up his academic career in order to travel, which is what he has always wanted to be. (a traveler)

If one gives up an academic career to do something he has always wanted to do, it implies that he is going to do it in some serious way that is not connoted by the word *traveler*. Such an example suggests that morphological similarity must be accompanied by logical similarity in order for an inference to work. Further support for this hypothesis is given later on in this paper.

A related phenomenon is illustrated in the difference between (46) and (47), where the direction of the inference is reserved.

(46) Most teachers, which is an underpaid profession, don't belong to unions. (teaching) [I]

(47) *Most professors, which is an underpaid profession, don't belong to unions. (?)

While teachers teach, professors do not profess, and the things a professor does cannot be bundled into a single word; hence, the problem, and it is compounded by the morphological similarity of *professors* to *profession*, which misleads people into expecting a logical similarity. Example (48) again suggests that morphological similarity is not a necessity in this category of inferences.

(48) My sister is an excellent ventriloquist, which I can't do at all. (throw my voice)

It appears that inferencing the activity from naming the person who does it in the antecedent structure may work more smoothly if the *which* clause forces the inference of a verb from a noun by virtue of its structure, rather than just asking for the inference of a verb on the basis of what it is about. Compare (49) and (50).

(49) After years of playing in the local symphony, my uncle took over as its conductor, which he really loves doing. (conducting (it)).

(50) *Most symphony conductors, which is known to be excellent exercise, live to a ripe old age. (conducting a symphony)

The presence of *doing* in the *which* clause of (49) seems to make the inference more palatable than it is in (50).

2.4 A fourth category of conceptual relationships involves the notion of using something. If the antecedent is the thing that gets used, the using of it can be inferenced in *which*, as in (51) through (53).

(51) His grandmother bought him a finger painting set, which shot the laundry bill way up. (finger painting) [I]

(52) I got a wok and a Chinese cook book last Christmas, which is now one of my favorite ways of cooking. (Chinese cooking) [I]

(53) Hula hoops, which I was pretty good at when I was a kid, are now made out of cheap plastic. (using a hula hoop) [I]

Or the inference can be in the opposite direction, from use to the thing used, as in (54).

(54) Yesterday our four-year-old decided to polish his shoes, which he managed to get on everything within his reach. (the polish) [I]

Example (55) illustrates an inference being set up in a way not seen up to this point. Compare (55) with the unacceptable (56).

(55) I'm gonna use the money to buy fertilizer and gardening supplies, which is a new source of pleasure for me. (gardening) [I]

(56) *I'm gonna use the money to buy fertilizer, some seeds, and a hoe, which is a new source of pleasure for me. (?)

While there is an uninferenced antecedent structure available in both cases, the strangeness of (56) indicates that buying the things named does not in and of itself qualify as something that could be a new source of pleasure for someone. Using them as they are meant to be used, however--i.e. for gardening--does so qualify. In (56), there is nothing in the structure to push the inference through, while in (55), the word *gardening* is right there in the antecedent. What happens in (55) is not that the word *gardening* alone, as it occurs in the sentence, is the real antecedent (i.e. that it is pulled out of the larger structure in which it occurs), but rather that its presence there in the antecedent 'buy fertilizer and gardening supplies', sets up the inference. The inference does not go through in (56), in spite of the obvious logical relationship between the purchase of the particular items mentioned and their use in gardening, because the morphological helper is not there.

The next set of examples addresses the question of what sort of balance, if any, there needs to be between logical similarity and morphological similarity of the antecedent and the thing inferenced in *which*. When both logical and morphological similarity are present, the inference works smoothly, as in (57).

(57) He is violinist, which is my favorite instrument. (the violin) [I]

With logical similarity only, the sentences are a trifle strange, as (58) and (59) illustrate.

(58) She is an equestrian, which is an animal I'm afraid of. (the horse)

(59) I've noticed that most carpenters, which is my favorite building material, live in brick houses. (wood)[6]

And with morphological similarity only, the result is decidedly bad, as (60) shows.

(60) Paul claims to be a vegetarian, most of which I know for a fact he can't stand. (vegetables)

The difficulty here, of course, is that being a vegetarian is more closely associated with not eating meat than with eating vegetables. Clearly there are other factors at work affecting the goodness or badness of these sentences, but given what is now known, the foregoing generalizations are certainly reasonable hypotheses.

2.5 In the last category of conceptual relationships investigated here, the inference includes the antecedent with some sort of comment on the saying of it. The inference can be straightforward 'my saying X', where the *which* clause then tells why the thing was said, as in (61).

(61) Well, diet schmiet, which means I'd like you to start acting like a human being again. (my saying 'diet schmiet')

Example (62) works in much the same way, except that here people are called upon to use some background information about what is special in the saying of the antecedent, namely, that it is the giving of the publisher, in addition to the author and title of the books, that makes it a recommendation.

(62) I've been reading Doris Lessing's four-volume work, *Children of Violence*, published by Plume, which means that I'm recommending it to you. (my saying the author, the title, and the publisher) [I]

The next two illustrations show that it is possible to inference other kinds of illocutionary force than a declarative. In (63), an interrogative is involved.

(63) He wanted to know if she was busy Saturday night, which was a painful question for him. (asking if she was busy Saturday night) [I]

And in (64), the inference involves filling in some information missing from a familiar adage and then acknowledging its imperative force.

(64) You know the old saying about sleeping dogs, which is my advice to you right now. (let sleeping dogs lie) [I]

Examples (65) and (66) involve a slightly different kind of conceptual relationship, although it is clearly analogous to the kind that has been the topic of this section so far. In this case, the inference is of the literal meaning of a proper name given in the structural base.

(65) I gave my brother a subscription to *Organic Gardening*, which is something he's been wanting to get involved in. (organic gardening)

(66) Frank got a subscription to *Playboy*, which is what he's always wanted to be. (a playboy)

And, as (67) illustrates, the inference can work in the opposite direction.

(67) Frank fancies himself as quite a playboy, which, by the way, just happens to be his favorite magazine. (*Playboy*)

3. The variety of the examples cited in Section 2.5 is a testament to something that is true of the entire investigation of inferenced *which* at this stage: it is tentative and incomplete. Five categories of conceptual relationships between the antecedent and the content of *which* emerged from the data examined in this paper. No doubt there are others that have not yet become apparent. And, quite obviously, an understanding of how all the factors at work in setting up inferenced *which*es interact is also somewhere in the future.

This is not meant, however, to minimize the importance of what has been done. With respect to linguistic research alone, this investigation provides further evidence of the necessity of finding out how inferencing in language works in order to understand how language works. And with respect to the investigation of human cognition, this study makes it abundantly clear that in order to understand what people do when they make inferences, the instructions they are getting from the language need to be understood. People and language are inextricably bound together, with the effect that looking at the latter without attention to the former yields very limited information. Sentences are manifestations of people in the process of communication. They take place in time, not only from one to the next, but from the beginning of one to its end. Looking at a sentence without taking into account the movement within it is very much like looking at a dead body. There is a considerable amount of structural information to be had, but very little of the living organism.

The use of *which* thus points to the need for a linguistics that is concerned with human cognition, a linguistics that investigates language as reflective of the activities in which people's minds are constantly engaged.

NOTES

1. I am grateful to Don Larkin, in part for providing me with examples, but especially for helping me begin to make some sense out of them.

2. There are cases where a summing up of what is said in the antecedent is clearly part of the intended meaning of the sentence, but where the antecedent itself is not actually inferenced. Observe, for example, (i).

(i) So I had this one group that I stayed friendly with at the public school, and I had this other group of friends from the Catholic school, and then at one time we lived in the St. John's parish and I knew those kids too, which was kind of nice--I mean I was at home most any place. [D:43]

3. Corum (1973) suggested some places to look for instances of possible inferencing with *which*.

4. Example (21) works very much like (ii).

(ii) We put chopped almonds in the cake batter, which were delicious.

The only possible understanding is that *chopped almonds* is the uninferenced antecedent. While waffle batter generally produces more than one waffle, cake batter is usually assumed to produce one cake; thus the plural *were* prohibits an inferenced antecedent. Now observe (iii) and (iv).

(iii) We put chopped almonds in the cake batter, which was delicious. (*the cake)

(iv) We put chopped almonds in the carrot cake batter, which was delicious. (the carrot cake)

In (iii), since the singular *was* blocks *chopped almonds* from being the antecedent, and since an inference of *the cake* is not at all natural, the tendency is to look for another antecedent in the structure; *putting chopped almonds in the cake batter* thus becomes the (structural) antecedent, with the inference then being made that it is the result of the action that was delicious. With respect to (iv), it seems that specifying the kind of cake, with stress on the word, helps to push the inference through in the antecedent. I am sure that some people would disagree. All that is certain is that the phenomenon is very complex.

5. It appears that while sentential constraints do not permit the inference of a language from the place where it is spoken, a larger discourse context can let such an inference through, as in (v).

(v) First we went to France, where I could get along with the French I studied back in college. But then we went to Italy, which I can't speak at all. (Italian)

The introduction of language as a topic in the first sentence makes the inference in the second sentence possible. (Admittedly, this is one of those borderline cases where intonation can make the *which* clause very parenthetical, and thus palatable.)

6. A reasonable explanation for the sentence following the second *which* clause in (vi) is that the speaker realized that the lack of morphological identity between *drafting* and *engineer* was a problem and tried to fix it up.

(vi) I majored in, ah, which is a bad subject to major in--drafting--will--which I am now though--I'm an engineer. [D:126]

REFERENCES

Aissen, Judith. 1972. Where do relative clauses come from? In: Syntax and semantics, 1. Edited by J. Kimball. New York: Seminar Press.

Bach, Emmon. 1968. Nouns and noun phrases in English. In: Universals in linguistic theory. Edited by E. Bach and R. R. Harms. New York: Holt, Rinehart and Winston.

Bolinger, Dwight. 1970. The meaning of *do so*. Linguistic Inquiry 1.140-144.

Bolinger, Dwight. 1972. That's *that*. The Hague: Mouton.

Cantrall, William. 1972. Relative identity. In: Papers from the Eighth Regional Meeting of the Chicago Linguistic Society. Chicago: Chicago Linguistic Society.

Chomsky, Noam. 1968. Remarks on nominalizations. In: Readings in English transformational grammar. Edited by R. A. Jacobs and P. S. Rosenbaum. Waltham, Mass.: Ginn/Blaisdell.

Coleman, Linda. 1973. Why the only interesting syntactic dialects are the uninteresting ones. In: Papers from the Ninth Regional Meeting of the Chicago Linguistic Society. Chicago: Chicago Linguistic Society.

Corum, Claudia. 1973. Anaphoric peninsulas. In: Papers from the Ninth Regional Meeting of the Chicago Linguistic Society. Chicago: Chicago Linguistic Society.

Darden, William. 1973. On confirmative tag sentences in English. In: Papers from the Ninth Regional Meeting of the Chicago Linguistic Society. Chicago: Chicago Linguistic Society.

Davidson, Donald, and Gilbert Harman, eds. 1972. Semantics of natural language. Boston: D. Reidel.

Drake, James A. 1960. How *which* is used in America today. American Speech 35.275-279.

Drubig, Bernard. 1968. Some remarks on relative clauses in English. Journal of English as a Second Language 3.23-40.

Fillmore, Charles J., and D. Terence Langendoen, eds. 1971. Studies in linguistic semantics. New York: Holt, Rinehart and Winston.

Geis, Michael. 1970. Adverbial subordinate clauses in English. Unpublished Ph.D. dissertation. Massachusetts Institute of Technology.

Geis, Michael, and Arnold Zwicky. 1971. On invited inferences. Linguistic Inquiry 2.561-566.

Gleitman, Lila R. 1965. Coordinating conjunctions in English. Language 41.260-293.

Greene, Jennifer. 1977. The use of *which* as a nonrestrictive relative marker in Standard English. Unpublished Ph.D. dissertation. Georgetown University.

Grinder, John, and Paul Postal. 1971. Missing antecedents. Linguistic Inquiry 3.269-312.

Hankamer, Jorge, and Ivan Sag. 1976. Deep and surface anaphora. Linguistic Inquiry 7.391-426.

Jesperson, Otto. 1928. A modern English grammar on historical principles, Part III, Syntax. London: Allen and Unwin.

Labov, William. 1966. On the grammaticality of everyday speech. Paper presented at the Annual Meeting of the Linguistic Society of America, New York.

Lakoff, George, and John Robert Ross. 1972. A note on anaphoric islands and causatives. Linguistic Inquiry 3.121-125.

Lakoff, R. 1971. *If*'s *and*'s and *but*'s about conjunction. In: Studies in linguistic semantics. Edited by C. J. Fillmore and D. T. Langendoen. New York: Holt, Rinehart and Winston.

Lakoff, R. 1974. Remarks on *this* and *that*. In: Papers from the Tenth Regional Meeting of the Chicago Linguistic Society. Chicago: Chicago Linguistic Society.

Loetscher, Andreas. 1973. On the role of nonrestrictive relative clauses in discourse. In: Papers from the Ninth Regional Meeting of the Chicago Linguistic Society. Chicago: Chicago Linguistic Society.

Morgan, Jerry L. 1975. Some remarks on the nature of sentences. In: Papers from the Twelfth Regional Meeting of the Chicago Linguistic Society, Parasession on Functionalism. Chicago: Chicago Linguistic Society.

Peranteau, Paul M., Judith N. Levi, and Gloria C. Phares, eds. 1972. The Chicago *which* hunt: Papers from the Relative Clause Festival. A paravolume to Papers from the Eighth Regional Meeting of the Chicago Linguistic Society. Chicago: Chicago Linguistic Society.

Poutsma, Hendrik. 1916. A grammar of late modern English, Part II, Section 1.B. Groningen: Noordhoff.

Quirk, Randolph, Sidney Greenbaum, Geoffrey Leech, and Jan Svartvik. 1972. A grammar of contemporary English. New York: Seminar Press.

Rosenberg, J. G., and Charles Travis, eds. 1971. Readings in the philosophy of language. Englewood Cliffs, N.J.: Prentice-Hall.

Ross, John R. 1967. Constraints on variables in syntax. Unpublished Ph.D. dissertation. Massachusetts Institute of Technology.

Ross, John R. 1971. The superficial nature of anaphoric island constraints. Linguistic Inquiry 2.599-600.

Ross, John R. 1972. Act. In: Semantics of natural language. Edited by D. Davidson and G. Harman. Boston: D. Reidel.
Sadock, Jerrold. 1974. Toward a linguistic theory of speech acts. New York: Academic Press.
Staal, J. F. 1970. Performatives and token reflectives. Linguistic Inquiry 1.373-381.
Stahlke, Herbert F.W. 1975. Which that? Unpublished MS.
Stockwell, Robert P., Paul Schachter, and Barbara Hall Partee. 1973. The major syntactic structures of English. New York: Holt, Rinehart and Winston.
Taglight, J. 1972. A new look at English relative constructions. Lingua 29.1-22.
Thompson, Sandra Annear. 1971. The deep structure of relative clauses. In: Studies in linguistic semantics. Edited by C. J. Fillmore and D. T. Langendoen. New York: Holt, Rinehart and Winston. [Reprinted in: Syntactic argumentation. Edited by Donna Jo Napoli and Emily Rando. Washington, D.C.: Georgetown University Press. 109-126.]

ON THE USE OF OK IN SERVICE ENCOUNTERS

Marilyn Merritt
Center for Applied Linguistics

In this paper I would like to do two things. First I would like to report on my observations of some patterns in which *OK* is used. The patterns given are not, of course, exhaustive. Secondly, I would like to suggest an analysis that makes use of interactional concepts. I suggest that the implication is that such social interactional concepts need to be considered in the development of a viable way of talking about language use.

The analysis I am presenting here is based upon naturalistic observations of dialogic speech in one type of social context or situation. This is a context which I identify by the term 'service encounter'.[1] Briefly, by a service encounter I mean the situation of interaction between a 'posted' server and a second party (a customer) who invokes the server's participation as an operator of a 'serving post'. The serving post--in many cases, the cash register counter--is typically part of a larger 'service area' such as a store or a shop. Thus a buying and selling encounter between a customer and a server is a typical instance of a service encounter.

In looking at what people say in service encounters, it has been natural to focus on questions and responses to questions, as these comprise much of what goes on in service encounters. In doing so, I came to notice the occurrence of the word *OK*.

OK was referred to by Bolinger (1957) as an 'approbative'--defined in the dictionary as an act that is approving or assenting to the propriety of a thing with some degree of pleasure or satisfaction. *Webster's New International Dictionary of the English Language* (1928 edition) gives under the entry for *OK*: 'Correct; all right--chiefly put or indorsed on documents, bills, etc. to indicate approval'. The entry also suggests that the word is probably derived from the Choctaw *Okeh*, meaning 'it is so and not otherwise'.[2] *Webster's Third*

International Dictionary of the English Language (1971 edition) makes no mention of the origin of the word. The entry lists its use as an adverb, synonomous with *all right* and *yes*, as in the sentence 'OK Doctor, I'll let you know'; and as a transitive verb, synonomous with *approve*, *authorize*, and *sanction*. Both these definitions corroborate Bolinger's designation.

My observations of the use of *OK* in service encounters are also largely corroborative. However, a closer look has led me to believe that a sense of approval or acceptance is often only part of what is being conveyed when the term *OK* is used. In particular, I argue that use of the term is attuned to punctuating interactional units within the encounter: move, turn, and stage.

I first noted that *OK* occurred in a particular position within the service encounter sequence, thereby characterizing what might be thought of as a pattern of usage. This pattern relates to the customer's initial request--occurring in the conversational slot I have elsewhere (Merritt 1976a:66, 70) called the 'customer start'--and the server's response or response slot.

The English language provides a number of lexical items with which to express affirmative response: *yes, yeah, yeh, yep, all right, OK, fine, right*, and so on. The differential use of these items in different contexts undoubtedly reflects degree of formality. However, at least in service encounters, there are patterns of variation that suggest another kind of distinction. As I have suggested elsewhere (Merritt 1976a,b) there are at least two major types of 'customer starts': requests for information (as in 'Do you sell bathing caps?') and requests for action (as in 'Can I have a pack of Marlboros please?'). Correspondingly, there seems to be a dichotomy in the affirmative responses between *yes* items (*yes, yeah, yeh, yep, Umhmm*) and *OK* items (*all right, OK*). In particular, items seem to operate primarily as affirmative responses to requests for information, while *OK* items seem to operate more as affirmative or 'granting' responses to requests for action. Compare (1) and (2), for example, in which *yes* items occur, with (3), in which the server responds with an *OK* item.

(1) Library:
C: Do I reserve a book here?
→S: Yes.
(2) Gift shop:
C: Do you have lighters?
→S: Yes. Over on the other side of the showroom.
(3) Notions:
C: C'n I have two packs of Vantage Green?
→S: OK (turns to get).

Frequently, if not typically, of course, these kinds of interchanges occur in sequence, as in (4), (5), and (6).

(4) Snack truck:
C: Do you have Marlboros?
→S: Yeah. Hard or soft pack?
C: Soft please.
→S: OK (turns to get).

(5) Notions:
C: Hi, do you have uh size C flashlight batteries?
→S: Yes sir.
C: I'll have four please.
S: Do you want the long life or the regular? See the long life doesn't last ten times longer than the regular battery. Usually lasts three times as long. Cheaper in the long run. These're eighty-eight. These're thirty-five each.
C: Guess I better settle for the short life.
S: How many you want?
C: Four please.
→S: OK (picks four and puts on counter). That's a dollar forty and nine tax, a dollar forty-nine.

(6) Photography store:
C: Do you stock polycontrast paper?
→S: Yes we do. What size and quantity do you want?
C: Twenty-five sheets, eight by ten, double weight.
→S: OK (puts box on counter).

It may be that the *yes* items do occasionally occur in the response slot after requests for action (when they are accompanied by appropriate action). An example is given in (7).

(7) University cafeteria:
C: Can I have one large cup of coffee black and one large cup of coffee with cream?
→S: Um Humm. (starts fixing)

However, I have observed no instances of *OK* in the response slot to a question of the 'Do you have ____?' type. Rather, in the slot that is a response to the customer start, *OK* seems to be specialized as a response to a request for action. The actual satisfaction of a request for action, of course, is not a verbal response but the requested action itself (such as getting the pack of cigarettes, preparing the cup of coffee, etc.). This suggests that *OK* may have some special function as a signal or cue that the requested action is about to take place.

Initially, I hypothesized that *OK* might operate generally as an acknowledgement that it is the speaker's (that is, the person who said *OK*) 'turn' (or present obligation) to take some action (getting the cigarettes, getting out the paper requested, etc.). In other words, the *OK* might signal approval of the request and intention to act on the request. It seemed, too, that the word *OK* might have a special role in bridging the transition from a verbal to nonverbal mode of interaction, much as the passing of a baton in a relay race bridges the transition from one person's running the race to a second person's running the race.

I began to notice, however, that the move immediately following the uttering of *OK* was not always nonverbal. This is illustrated in examples (8) through (11).

(8) Savings bank:
C: Do you sell government bonds?
S: Yes, we do.
C: I'd like one for fifty dollars please.
→S: OK. Would you please fill out this application completely, sir.

(9) Ticket booth, movies:
C: Two please (pushing bill through window)
S: Which picture?
C: *American Graffiti.*
→S: OK. That's five dollars.

(10) Department store, hosiery:
C: (approaches S with stockings, hands them to S)
S: OK hon. That'll be one--
C: (hands bill to S)
S: --out of five.

(11) Snack truck:
C: (stands at window, S is turned away)
→S: (S turn to C) OK. What do you want?
C: Hot dog.

In every case, however, the next move (whether nonverbal or verbal) was made by the same speaker who said *OK* (in all these examples, the server), as predicted. Thus I modified my hypothesis to wit.

> **Revised hypothesis.** In my materials *OK* items seem to operate generally as an acknowledgment that it is the speaker's (that is, the person who said *OK*) turn (or present obligation) to take some action--whether verbal or nonverbal--that is, to make the next move in the interaction. In cases where the next move is a nonverbal act, the *OK* item can be seen to be doing a kind of 'bridging' between the verbal and the nonverbal. It anchors the nonverbal action in what has already gone on verbally, at the same time as it provides an expectation of something to follow.

The two patterns of use that have been examined so far involve the server's use of the term *OK* and its relation to the server's providing a requested service. Now let us consider examples in which it is the customer who says *OK*, as in (12) and (13).

(12) Jewelry:
(S has just shown C a necklace)
C: Can you show me something else in that price range?
S: Let me see what else I have (looking down). Here are two other pendants.
→C: OK. I'll take these two (pointing).

(13) Department store, cosmetics:
C: Can I have a bottle//o' the mint?//
S: // What? // What shampoo?
C: The green.
S: Which?
C: The mint protein. Can I also see the conditioner?
S: Which?
C: The cucumber. Can I smell it?
S: Sure (placing on counter).
→C: OK. I'll take both. That'll be charge.

In both cases, the customer seems to be not only expressing approval of the requested commodity, but also to be expressing satisfaction with having examined it. That is, he is expressing his having completed examination and his readiness to take the next move (in these cases, to decide whether to take the commodity or not, though in other cases the customer may defer this move pending examination of other commodities).

Now consider (14).

(14) Notions:
(C has been looking in rear of store at a selection of hair ties.)
C: These're the only ones you have, right?
S: Right.
→C: OK. Guess not. Thanks just the same.
S: You're welcome.

Here the customer is expressly not approving of the requested commodity, but is satisfied with his examination of it. He then takes the next move to state his decision not to buy. By expressing his satisfaction with his examination of the commodity, he in a sense releases the server from any further obligation to continue to provide the requested commodity.

The use of *OK* to release the other party from the current obligation occurs also in examples (15), (16), and (17). In these examples, the requested commodity is not provided by the server but a reason is given. When the customer replies with *OK*, he gives an acceptance of that reason or account.

(15) Delicatessen:
C: Do you have two dimes and a nickel for a quarter?
S: (rings cash register, opens drawer) We don't have any dimes left.
→C: OK. Thank you.

(16) Drug store:
C: Excuse me, I'm looking for Phisohex--do you have any?
S: Should be over in aisle three under skin care.
C: I already looked there. You wouldn't have any in stock, would you?
S: No. If it's not on the shelf, we must be out.
→C: OK. Thanks anyway.

(17) University cafeteria:
(the complete sequence of which example (7) is a segment)
C: Can I have one large cup of coffee black and one large cup of coffee with cream?
S: Um Humm. (starts fixing)
C: Make that black with sugar.
S: You'll have to put your own sugar in. It's out.
→C: Oh. OK. Fine.

In these cases, in which *OK* seems to be used by one participant to release the other participant, the release function can be interpreted as a special case of general or 'ordinary' use of *OK*, as tentatively suggested in the 'revised hypothesis' I have given. That is, since the *OK* speaker thereby obligates himself to take the next necessary move in the encounter, by so obligating himself he necessarily releases the other participant from any current obligation to continue his turn. Example (18) is another example of a 'releasing' *OK*. In this case, it is not a commodity that has been requested but rather information as to its whereabouts.

(18) Notions:
C: Do you have Chanukah cards?
S: Yeah, right back against the wall there. See the sign--Chanukah cards?
→C: OK.

OK may also be used by the server to release the customer--in many cases, to express satisfaction with payment, as in (19).

(19) Notions:
S: OK. That'll be fifty, seventy-five, ninety cents altogether.
Coin
Cash register
Change
→S: OK. Thank you.

Note that in (19), *OK* occurs twice. In (20), a similar term *all right* occurs in almost the identical pattern.

(20) Notions:
S: All right. That's twenty-five and two tax--twenty-seven.
Sound of money
→S: All right. Thank you.

The words *OK* and *all right* seem almost to punctuate the sequence. If they were in some sense punctuating or marking transition, the question arises as to what they would be marking transition between. I propose that the use of *OK* (and other *OK* items like *all right*) may signal a transition in stages or something like stages (perhaps 'phase' is a better word). Elsewhere (Merritt 1976a) I have suggested that service encounters typically are composed of four different stages: access, selection, decision, exchange, and closure. In (19) and (20), *OK* items are used twice in each sequence: first, at the point at which transition is being made from selection decision to exchange; and second, at the point at which transition is being made from exchange to closure. This suggests that *OK* does indeed function as a kind of bridging device, as proposed in the revised hypothesis. However, it does not necessarily perform this function only between verbal and nonverbal phases of the encounter, but rather may occur at other possible transition points as well.

As a result of these observations I offer the following generalization. Use of the term *OK* has at least two possible functions: (1) that of signifying approval, acceptance, confirmation; (2) that of providing a bridge, a linking device between two stages or phases of the encounter. In these cases, use of the term *OK* seems to signify that the speaker suggests the termination of the phase that has just preceded and agrees to take the initiative in continuing with the next phase (or be satisfied with termination (as in (15) through (18)).

There are cases in which only the first, more traditionally assigned function seems to be operating, as in example (21).

(21) Notions: (midway through the encounter)
C: Yeah, but I wantta get//
S: Yeah
C: I wantta get colors--
→S: Yeah you can mix the papers. OK. Whatever you wantta do.

But very frequently, as has been shown, both functions seem to be operating.[3] Consider the many occurrences of *OK* in the following service encounter (which is the entire sequence of which (21) is a part).

(22) Notions:
S: Whattaya lookin' for Miss? Cough ((maybe)) I can help you?

C: Uh yeah. Christmas wrapping paper.
S: All right. We'll show you. (Cash register slam.)
Here you are. Right around here, Miss, look.
C: Oh. OK.
S: Around here.
C: Oh I see.
S: Here's this ((inaudible)) and then we got uh
different boxes here.
C: ((You don't carry)) the individual sheets.
S: All right.
C: Hmm.
S: And if you don't see anything individual, we'll
sell these rolls, we'll break // a box for you.
C: Oh really?
S: We'll sell you one--you know what I mean. In other
words, this is a dollar and a quarter for three,
forty-five cents for one. Of course, this is Christmas wrap individual.
C: Yeah. OK. Good.
S: You can buy any of these individually. In other
words, like--like one of these rolls you can have//
C: Un Hunh.
S: ... for forty-five cents a roll.
C: OK. Thank you.
(S goes back to serving post; C looks at paper)
S: You can break any of those boxes OK. Just take
one roll out you want it.
C: ((OK)).
(S attends to other customer, a few minutes elapse)
C: You don't have any *yarn* ribbon, do you?
Ring
S: Yarn ribbon?
C: Unh Hunh.
S: No. No yarn ribbon. Just uh--I forget--for
wrapping packages?
C: Unh Hunh.
S: No--we have what you see over here (walking away)
C: OK.
(a few seconds pass)
C: Is it ever possible to *mix* these tt-
S: Yeah. You can do whatever you want. You
wantta--you can mix-em--whatever you wantta do.
C: The problem being that if I get one of these little
boxes of bows I gotta make'em match (huh huh) same
((amount of)) paper.
S: Well--we're not breaking up the bows you know.
'Nother words you wantta take--a package of bows?
C: Yeah. But I wantta get//
S: Yeah.
C: I wantta get colors--

S: Yeah you can mix the papers. OK. Whatever you wantta do.
(several minutes go by, then C approaches the serving post)
C: (putting selections on counter) Two rolls.
S: All right. Ninety and forty-nine is//
C: Oh and I need some hair spray too.
((inaudible few seconds))
C: I'll come down and look. Go ahead and take his. (referring to next customer)
(after a few minutes)
S: OK. Anything else?
C: That's all. Thank you.
S: ((inaudible))
C: Three o seven, three ten, three twenty-five. I'll put it in a bag for you.
Rattling
S: OK. Thank you.

The notion that discourse and the significance of words as used should be studied within an interactional framework (utilizing interactional concepts such as move, turn, and stage (or phase)) has been suggested by Goffman (1964, 1971), Labov (1972), and others. The findings presented here about the use of *OK* in service encounters corroborate this notion, and hopefully contribute to a general understanding of the use of the word *OK*.

NOTES

This is a slightly revised version of the paper presented to the Fifth Annual Conference on New Ways of Analyzing Variation, Georgetown University, October, 1976. I am grateful to Dwight Bolinger and William Labov for useful comments. Correspondence to the author should be directed to 2706 Key Boulevard, Arlington, Virginia 22201.

1. The notion of a service encounter is developed more fully in Merritt (1976a, Chapters 1 and 3). See Chapter 4 or Merritt (1976b) for a discussion of service encounter as it relates to the notions of discourse and speech event generally. Chapter 2 of Merritt (1976a) describes in detail the corpus from which the examples in this paper are drawn.

2. This suggestion is not supported by the well-known papers of Read (1963a,b) on the origin of *OK*. Read argues that *OK* began as a linguistically 'faddish' way of abbreviating *all correct* (*oll korrect* = *OK*) in the late 1830s, and was later 'boosted' by its association with the phrase *Old Kinderhook*, used in the political campaigns of 1840. Another researcher, Heflin (1962), argued against such an etymology of the word. The origin of *OK* is apparently not clearly resolved.

Though I shall not be concerned with word origin in this paper, it is interesting that the properties that have obscured the origin of *OK* are the very ones that make it interesting in terms of language use: '... It has been urged that *OK* was used in such a loose sense that it must have stood for something else besides *all correct*. But slang expressions are notoriously loose, and it should not be expected that either *OK* or *all correct* would be used in a strict sense ...' (Read 1963a: 13-14).

3. This raises, of course, the possibility of ambiguity of function for any given occurrence. In talking with servers, I have been told that in some service encounters there can be, indeed, ambiguity from this source. For example, one server, who sold jewelry and had to take stock out of a display case in order to show it to a customer, told me that when she had displayed an item and the customer said *OK*, it was not always clear whether the customer meant 'Yes, I'll take that one' or 'I'm finished looking at it (show me the next one'. In a much more serious vein, an airline disaster of May, 1977 has been linked to the possible misunderstanding by one pilot of *OK* to mean 'confirmed; approved; go ahead and take off' rather than the intended 'that's all for now; I'll get back to you (when there is more information, when you're cleared for take-off').

This area of ambiguity is one that I hope to explore further in future research.

REFERENCES

Bolinger, Dwight. 1957. Interrogative structures of American English: The direct question. University, Ala.: University Press.

Goffman, Erving. 1964. The neglected situation. In: The ethnography of communication. Special publication of the American Anthropologist, 66. Edited by John J. Gumperz and Dell Hymes.

Goffman, Erving. 1971. Relations in public: Microstudies of the public order. New York: Basic Books.

Heflin, Woodford A. 1962. 'OK' and its incorrect etymology. American Speech 37.243-248.

Labov, William. 1972. Rules for ritual insults. In: Studies in social interaction. Edited by David Sudnow. New York: Free Press.

Merritt, Marilyn Wilkey. 1976a. Resources for saying in service encounters. Unpublished Ph.D. dissertation. University of Pennsylvania.

Merritt, Marilyn Wilkey. 1976b. On questions following questions (in service encounters). Language in Society 5.315-357.

Read, Allen Walker. 1963a. The first stage in the history of 'OK'. American Speech 38.5-27.

Read, Allen Walker. 1963b. The second stage in the history of 'OK'. American Speech 38.83-102.

Webster's New International Dictionary of the English Language. 1928. Springfield, Mass.: Merriam.
Webster's Third New International Dictionary of the English Language. 1971. Springfield, Mass.: Merriam.

PSYCHOANALYTIC DISCOURSE AND ORDINARY CONVERSATION

Robin Tolmach Lakoff
University of California, Berkeley

The grammar of a language, a system of rules distinguishing utterances permissible in a language from those that are not, can be thought of as a species of social contract, in the sense that its rules are recognized and followed by all speakers of the language as shared knowledge and by mutual consent. This knowledge and consent are more implicit than explicit: we mark violations but not normal utterances. The grammar is seen as a continuum, from the strictly linguistic rules of phonology, morphology, syntax, and semantics to the contextually bound rules of the pragmatic system. Speakers of a language, although they treat violations of different levels of the grammar differently (thus, a phonological violation on the part of an obvious native speaker, is viewed as a physiologically based defect; a syntactic error, typically, as a mark of intellectual deficiency and a pragmatic error, as an indication of character defect), nonetheless know what is in keeping with the rules and what is not, just as they do for the rest of their social structure. Thus it is appropriate to think of the grammar as part of a set of descriptive rules covering both the norms of social behavior and the assumptions of a cognitive system.

For an explicitly recognized rule system, it is easy to demonstrate the existence of a system of rules. If we ask a traditional poet how to write a Shakespearean sonnet, he will oblige us with the set of rules he follows. But implicit knowledge is more difficult to prove: we must infer it from other behavioral clues.

The difficulty of justifying the postulation of an implicit grammar as a representation of the native speaker's linguistic competence has been discussed at length in the literature; I consider the existence of such a grammar conclusively proved. But the proof has involved only purely linguistic aspects of communicative behavior: the phonological and syntactic components of a grammar have received the lion's share of the efforts to construct and justify the notion of an implicit formal grammar. We may, however, conclude that the ability of a human being to learn certain forms of behavior through the intuitive development of systems of rules has been established to the satisfaction of the majority of scholars in this area.

It is still something of an open question, however, how much of human social behavior is rule-governed in the way purely linguistic behavior is. Can we speak in terms of a grammar covering all social interaction? Is the linguistic grammar, in fact, just one component of a larger, all-inclusive grammar of social and cognitive behavior? If so, what would the formal system look like? These are tantalizing questions that cannot be answered for some time.

But one thing that can be done in the direction of exploring such questions is to examine the area of intersection between purely linguistic and social behavior, to see if it is amenable to formal description. In particular, the investigations of pragmatic theory--dealing as it does with the use of language by speakers as it influences and is influenced by the real-world situation of the discourse--seem a good way to approach the larger problem. We might ask, then, to what extent conversational strategies are describable in terms of a system of rules, a 'grammar'. Since conversation is of course linguistic, we may feel justified in utilizing some of the theoretical assumptions made in other branches of the field. And, since a conversation is social, if we can establish the existence of a grammar of discourse, we have taken a first step toward writing grammars for social interactions more generally.

I have described preliminary work on this question at length elsewhere (cf. Lakoff 1973 and 1977). Here I shall briefly review this work in order to provide a context for what I am going to say. I assume that one argument for the existence of a grammar is the recognition by its users of violations of the rules by other users and themselves; and so in the bulk of this paper I describe a system that is recognized as being in violation of the normal rules of discourse, in order to examine how participants cope with such a situation.

One justification for the existence of a grammar has resided in the fact that native speakers agree, by and large, about the limits of rule applicability. One can construct ungrammatical sentences and show that they are ungrammatical in that they involve the misapplication of one or more rules. In the same way, one way to approach a proof of the existence of a grammar of discourse would be to show that deviant systems can be constructed and recognized by participants as deviant. This is the task I propose to attempt here.

That is to say, I want to see whether there exist systems of communication that are considered, by those who encounter them, beyond their capacity to understand, or as in any event not working by the same system as does their normal mode of discourse. What do speakers do, if and when they are confronted by such a situation? Do they assume that they are faced with a whole new set of rules, so that everything they know is useless, and communication must fail? (The analog is the monolingual speaker of English confronting for the first time a speaker, say, of French. No simple adaptation of his rules will render the other's communication intelligible to him, nor his to his interlocutor's. No communication is possible for them.) Or do they assume that what they are encountering is but a variant of their own system, and by making certain principled modifications, they can understand and be understood? (For instance, this is what might be concluded by a speaker of English encountering Pig Latin for the first time.) He might, of course, finally conclude that the other speaker was producing pure gibberish, utterances not governed by rule, and that therefore he could not make hypotheses of predictions, and nothing he could do would render the other's contribution intelligible.

Even if the second situation were the one assumed by our imaginary participant, he might still be unable to devise a mode of mutual intelligibility if the modifications to the normal system were too thoroughgoing, too extreme, or too idiosyncratic. So simple difficulty in arriving at successful communication does not necessarily entail that we are dealing with the more profound communicative problems of types (1) or (3), rather than (2).

Of course, all this remains purely speculative until we find and examine such deviant systems. That is why I propose to do just this in the remainder of this paper, and present evidence for the following hypotheses: (1) Since participants can recognize deviation from expected communicative principles, there exists a system of rules of communicative competence. (2) Some forms of deviation from this code are more acceptable to other participants in a discourse than others. This is suggestive that we are dealing with rule-governed behavior. (3) Participants learn to engage in special forms of communication by mutual consent and in a well-defined context. Under these circumstances, deviations from the norm are countenanced and employed, where otherwise they would not be.

One can think of the language of a schizophrenic as rule-governed deviance of the sort I am talking about, but produced under conditions other than those indicated in (3), so that other participants cannot or will not learn the new system. Hence schizophrenic communication normally remains unintelligible to everyone but the schizophrenic. On the other hand, the communicative assumptions involved in psychotherapy furnish a clear example of a system which, while deviant, is nonetheless engaged in by the participants with mutual knowledge and consent, in a well-defined context. Participants learn to communicate in this special system when it is in effect, learning both the difference between the new and the normal system, and the range of permissible behavior that is within the new system. That is to say, they devise--unconsciously, of course--both a comparative grammar contrasting their normal communicative system with that employed in psychotherapy, and a descriptive grammar of the therapeutic language itself.

In first attempting to test a new theoretical system, the clearest cases are the ones to look at, and the best-defined examples the ones to use. For this reason, in this paper I propose to look at psychoanalytic discourse as a model of psychotherapeutic discourse, although--or, more accurately, because--it is an extreme instance of deviation from the normal rules. The procedure has been more fully and rigorously defined and justified in psychoanalytic theory than in that of any other therapeutic model; and further, virtually any therapy dependent on verbal communication is based on psychoanalysis, however indirectly. For these reasons I am confining my comments to the assumptions made within this theoretical framework. What is required of a theory of communicative competence--such as the one to be summarized here--is that it be able to account for both our understanding and use of normal discourse, and our ability to transcend the assumptions of normal discourse in a principled and replicable way in specified situations.

In a normal discourse, participants make two overriding assumptions: (1) the participants are rational; (2) all contributions benefit the participants.

With regard to (1), the 'rationality' of a participant is indicated by the ability and willingness of other participants to identify with him in his role as speaker; each can conceive of himself saying the same thing in the circumstances of the discourse. The Principle of Rationality (PR) thus implies that participants assume that one another's contributions are intelligible, and that a failure in intelligibility tends to be perceived by the addressee as *his* fault; and from this follow the well-known facts that speakers will go to great lengths to make sense of each other's contributions, and that the suggestion that either a contribution itself, or the reasons for making it, are not clear to another participant is perceived as an affront to the speaker whose contribution is thus called into question.[1] In a sense, questioning a speaker's meaning or motivation implies that the questioner no longer is able to maintain a sense of identity with the other, and (implicitly) considers him not a member of the community to which the questioner belongs. When this non-belonging can be attributed to natural causes, such as being a foreigner, then the affront is much less, and explanations may be much more freely asked and given. But if the speaker is one who by rights should be a member of the community, any imputation to the contrary is threatening.

With regard to assumption (2), that all contributions benefit the participants, the notion of 'benefit' here is to be construed a bit loosely. Perhaps it might be clearer if we were to state this postulate negatively, i.e. 'No contribution shall be made that is injurious to either participant'; but I feel that the positive injunction is more nearly correct: people engage in discourse, this postulate says, because they expect to and do get something out of it. 'Something' may be useful factual information; it may just be an emotional feeling of acceptance or well-being; most often it is a combination of the two. Actually, the Principle of Benefit (PB) follows from PR to some extent, since each speaker judges what sort of contribution is apt to be perceived as beneficial by the other, on the basis of what he himself would construe as beneficial under the circumstances --that is, through identification with his interlocutor. And therefore it is likely that a contribution that fails to be beneficial is perceived as hurtful by its receiver on two grounds: first, that it does not benefit and may actually hurt; and second, that he has not been correctly perceived by the other, that therefore a relationship of identification does not exist between the other person and himself. Depending on individual character, this discrepancy may be interpreted as due to his own inability to be a regular member of the community, or as due to a fault of the other participant; but in any case, it is troublesome.

Participants in a normal conversation take turns at the roles of speaker and addressee. Holding the role of speaker is one of the principal direct benefits to be gained from a conversation, and a participant who monopolizes a conversation is thus in violation of PB.

The determination of how participants are to benefit each other rests upon two sets of lower level rules. Adherence to one of these, the Rules of Clarity, entails maximally informative communication: its purpose is the optimal expression of content. The other, the Rules of Rapport, concerns meeting the emotional needs of the participants, making them comfortable in the discourse. Stylistic choices tend to express Rapport considerations, while pure content is dictated by Clarity. It is also generally true that Clarity communications are largely verbal in nature; rapport-oriented communication may at least as often be nonverbal. Emotional satisfaction appears to be a higher benefit than the gaining of information: if one must choose between maximal Clarity and optimal Rapport--between transmitting necessary information most clearly and interfering with someone else's feelings of well-being--the latter supersedes. Hence one reason we relatively seldom express things as clearly as we might, is that we fear we might thereby violate Rapport. We tend, I think, to be overly generous on the side of Rapport, to be indirect where there is even a slight threat of offense. Other participants in a dialog will be upset if either of these principles is invoked where it would not be by him: if the speaker uses Clarity where indirectness would be more tolerable, and also if he is indirect where there is no perceived need to be so. This follows from the Principle of Rationality. These Principles of Communicative Competence that I have enumerated are shown in diagrammatic form in Figure 1.

Figure 1.

Principle of Rationality of participants (PR)

Principle of Benefit to participants (PB)

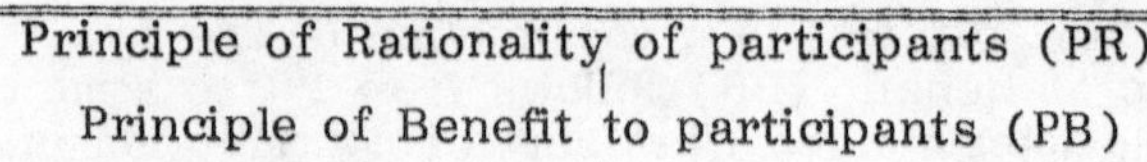

Rules of Clarity	Rules of Rapport
1. quality: be truthful	1. distance: remain aloof
2. quantity: say only what is necessary	2. deference: give the other options
3. relevance: be relevant	3. camaraderie: make the other feel comfortable
4. manner: be clear	

It should be noted, too, that the Rules of Clarity express the relationship between the speaker and his message; the Rules of Rapport, between speaker and addressee. The Rules of Clarity, moreover, are all applicable at once. Observing one does not necessarily entail infringing another. But the Rules of Rapport are in part mutually incompatible: while the second is applicable along with either of the others, it appears necessary to make a choice between the use of 1 and 3. Different societies, as well as different individuals, make this determination at various points in a relationship, or under various social circumstances: this difference constitutes much of what we consider 'character'. Similarly, the decision as to whether one is in a Clarity- or a Rapport-relevant discourse may differ among cultures and speakers. But a decision on the part of a speaker that is not normal for one in his culture tends to be perceived as a more serious characterological defect than do wrong choices within the Rapport system: it seems that the higher up in the diagram violations are made, the more seriously will they be perceived. (For discussion, cf. Lakoff in preparation.)

Having set forth this outline, it is time for me to return to the question I posed earlier: to what extent and in what ways is psychoanalytic discourse a deviation from this model of ideal communication? How is the deviation perceived, how learned, and how is it to be formally integrated into a general theory of communicative competence?

As normal discourse has its Principles of Communicative Competence, so analytic discourse has its, in the form of the Basic or Fundamental Rule, first enunciated by Freud, about 65 years ago, in his paper, 'On beginning the treatment'. I shall cite his discussion in full and then consider this presentation of the analytic mode of discourse as a form of communication, to see how adherence to it corresponds to adherence to the usual Principles of Communicative Competence.

> What the material is with which one starts the treatment is on the whole a matter of indifference--whether it is the patient's life-history or the history of his illness or his recollections of childhood. But in any case the patient must be left to do the talking and must be free to choose at which point he shall begin. We therefore say to him: 'Before I can say anything to you I must know a great deal about you; please tell me what you know about yourself'.
>
> The only exception to this is in regard to the fundamental rule of psychoanalytic technique which the patient has to observe. This must be imparted to him at the very beginning: 'One more thing before you start. What you tell me must differ in one respect from an ordinary conversation. Ordinarily you rightly try to keep a connecting thread running through your remarks and you exclude any intrusive ideas that may occur to you and any side-issues, so as not to wander too far from the point. But in this case you must proceed differently. You will notice that as you relate things various thoughts will occur to you which you would like to put aside on the ground of certain criticisms and objections. You will be tempted to say to yourself that this or that is irrelevant here, or is quite unimportant, or nonsensical, so that there is no need to say it. You must never give in to these criticisms, but must say it in spite of them--indeed, you must say it precisely *because* you feel an aversion to doing so. Later on, you will find out and learn to understand the reason for this injunction, which really is the only one you have to follow. So say whatever goes through your mind. Act as though, for instance, you were a traveler sitting next to the window of a railway carriage and describing to someone inside the carriage the changing views which you see outside. Finally, never forget that you have promised to be absolutely honest, and never leave anything out because, for some reason or other, it is unpleasant to tell it' (1958 (1913):134f.).

In this quotation we find a statement approximating our Rules of Communicative Competence, a statement of the psychoanalytic Basic Rule, and various implications about their interrelationship. Freud suggests that--with the exception of the additional imposition of the Basic Rule--analytic discourse is just like any other, and that the procedure outlined is representative of ordinary discourse. In fact, this is not really so. 'The patient must be left to do the talking', Freud says, 'and must be free to choose at what point he shall begin'. Implicit here are several forms of non-reciprocity characteristic of the analytic situation. To say that the patient *must be left* to do the talking, and *must be* free implies that the obligation to see that this is so devolves[2] upon someone other than the analysand[3]--the analyst, obviously, as the only other participant in the discourse. So what looks ostensibly like a statement that the power to determine the course of the conversation is in the patient's hands, that therefore the patient holds the power, actually entails the opposite: the analyst has the power to determine how the discourse shall proceed, and exercises this power by *allowing* it to proceed at the patient's whim. Moreover, although the analyst thus controls the discourse, he does not directly control choice of topic. He governs the inception and termination of the discourse, but not the subject matter. Thus we are dealing with a conversational situation replete with paradox. The one who appears to hold the power does not hold it. In normal discourse, as we have seen, power is normally shared among the participants, along with turn-taking and floor-holding. There are some common discourse types in which one participant holds the power. But normally, the wielder of power holds the floor at the same time--since his power comes about by virtue of the addressee's recognition of his greater authority--and determines the topics of discourse and, usually, initiates and terminates the discourse. The most typical example is the classroom lecture where, of course, interruption by other participants is frequently tolerated or even encouraged--but under the explicit control of the principal speaker. I can think of only one other type of discourse where power and floor-holding are divided among participants, and that is in the well-known tradition of the oral examination. It is at least in part because of this anomaly, I suspect, that well-prepared students often dread orals far more than any other academic ritual: they are uncomfortable with the contradictions of the situation. It is true, however, of orals that the holders of power determine the topics of discussion--so at least the distribution of authority is clearer than in the analytic setting.

What is principally of interest to us in this abrogation of the normal relationship between participants in a discourse is why they put up with it, or to put it another way, what each expects to get out of this anomalous discourse. For I think we can accept it as an underlying social principle that no reasonable human being will engage voluntarily in any social act unless he sees it as immediately or ultimately beneficial to him. Hence the need for a principle of benefit to participants: it provides a rationale for the continuation of the discourse. This benefit, as pointed out earlier, is effected via the Rules of Clarity, which enable the addressee to receive needed information, and the Rules of Rapport, which enable participants to feel comfortable and friendly in the discourse. The sharing of the power between the participants can also be thought of as a necessary entailment of the Rules of Rapport, in particular Deference and Camaraderie. Then a system in which all of these assumptions are invalidated would appear to deny as well the Principle of Benefit. Is it indeed true that no one is perceived as benefitting, and that the nonexistence of PB itself is one of the anomalies of psychoanalytic discourse? Or must we reinterpret PB according to context, and assume that, though the Principle remains in effect, in psychoanalytic discourse we must look in other than the usual places for the 'benefit'? The latter assumption, I think, is to be preferred, since with the former we would be left without any means of understanding why the participants participate; psychoanalytic discourse would be perhaps the only action voluntarily performed by people without benefit to the actors. The question of what the benefit is will be examined later, after other relevant issues have been explored.

Another instance of Rapport violation through non-reciprocity is found in the same paragraph, where the analyst tells the analysand, 'Before I can say anything to you, I must know a great deal about you'. Most ordinary conversation is equally revealing--or unrevealing--for both participants. In normal discourse it would be considered very odd for only one participant to talk about himself, and the other to comment on that, odd if the only thing one participant expected to hear were the personal revelations of the other. This would entail the violation of Rapport by both participants. The one making revelations would feel discomfort because he alone was violating Distance. The receiver of the confidences would likewise feel uncomfortable because he was abrogating Camaraderie. In situations where casual acquaintances unburden themselves to us when we do not wish to reciprocate, we feel caught in a social bind. But in the analytic setting this regularly occurs; indeed, in the guise of the 'rule of abstinence', the 'analytic mirror', and 'analytic anonymity', the analyst is expressly enjoined from any self-revelation at all--even that which would not be potentially embarrassing in a casual encounter. On the other hand, the analysand, under the terms of the Basic Rule, is expected to be much more confiding than is typical even of the most intimate social relationship. Here again, we may wonder why the participants prolong their encounter, since normally participants in such a one-sided discourse perceive themselves as deriving so little benefit that at least one attempts to disengage himself from the encounter, or at least change the subject, as soon as feasible.

Freud proceeds from here to discuss other differences between psychoanalytic and ordinary discourse. In the first paragraph, we noted, the analyst bore the heavier burden of learning a new mode of communication, which presumably came more naturally to the analysand. In the second paragraph, we view the situation from another point of view: the obligation resting on the analysand is at least as great. He must learn to ignore the rules he has implicitly worked under all his life. The Basic Rule is therefore less a liberating than a confining assumption for both participants. We notice at the outset that Freud's statement includes a paraphrase of the Principles of Communicative Competence. These principles, he says, are adhered to 'rightly': in ordinary discourse, there is a rationale behing them, however restrictive they may be. In fact, here is our second paradox: previously, an apparent invitation to the analysand to freedom from ordinary constraints was seen, viewed more closely, as highly constraining. Here, adherence to the communicative principles of ordinary discourse --presumably confining--appears as the desideratum, and the constraint lies in the injunction not to observe it. 'You will be tempted to say to yourself that this or that is irrelevant here ... You must never give in to these criticisms, but must say it in spite of them'. It should be noted too that, while the *must*--or the obligation--in the first paragraph is directed toward the analyst, in the second the injunction is phrased so that the *must* represents the obligation of the analysand. Another interpretation of the difference between the two statements may be that Freud is implicitly suggesting that the first set of injunctions is harder on the analysand than on the analyst, so that the latter must keep the former in line; but that this is not true of the second, so that the analysand can be left more or less to his own devices. The analyst is thus seen as the more responsible member of the pair, the one who is more apt to be rational; he will do what is difficult for him without prodding, but may need to prod the other participant into doing likewise. (More is said about the relative rationality assumed of the participants later in this paper, in the discussion of interpretability.)

It is not overly surprising, therefore, that only the obligation seen as devolving upon the analysand is codified as a Rule, the other being more in the form of advice or suggestion. For both participants, success in the discourse depends upon becoming explicitly aware of and therefore able to reject (in this context) a set of implicit rules governing ordinary conversation. This is reminiscent of the more general aim of psychoanalysis: by making the unconscious conscious, to gain the ability to overcome the unconscious, replacing it with conscious and rational behavior. Similarly, through making ordinarily implicit knowledge explicit (as Freud does in the instructions he gives here), one becomes able to suspend one's ordinary unthinking adherence to those principles, with sufficient justification.[4] The instructions to the analysand enjoin him to overlook both Clarity and Rapport--the latter, to be sure, being mentioned only more or less in passing in the last sentence: one must be honest even if it hurts one of the participants. This injunction is in direct violation of the overriding principle I mentioned earlier, that if in normal discourse there arises the possibility of a conflict between Clarity and Rapport, Rapport supersedes Clarity. This principle arose as a corollary of PB, it will be recalled. Here, Rapport is distinctly secondary; and again, PB must be viewed in some special way in the analytic setting, if we want to claim it is in effect at all.

Freud writes in this passage as though adherence by the analysand to the Basic Rule necessarily entailed that his contributions would be in violation of the Rules of Communicative Competence, or even as if while ordinary discourse functions under the Rules of Communicative Competence, analytic discourse functions under the Basic Rule: one chooses one or the other. I think it is not quite as clear-cut as that. We notice specifically in this passage injunctions to disregard Relevance, Quantity, and Manner ('... that this or that is irrelevant here, or is quite unimportant, or nonsensical, so that there is no need to say it'). While Freud does not speak about it here, it is an assumption of psychoanalytic theory that ordinary notions of truth--i.e. adherence to the maxim of Quality--must be suspended in the analytic setting: when the analysand's psychic truth conflicts with truth provable in reality, the former, for the purposes of the analysis and until the analysand discovers otherwise himself, is taken as the *real* truth,[5] just as the apparent real world irrelevance or triviality or meaninglessness of his contribution is ipso facto regarded within the analysis as relevant, material, and meaningful.

It is easier to understand the distinction as consisting of a difference in the participants' sense of the existence of a need for reconciling the underlying aim of the discourse with its superficial form.

In ordinary discourse, a violation of Clarity of Rapport is purely and simply deviant, because there is no use to which it may be put: as a contribution serves a conversational purpose by being of benefit by being in compliance, so it follows that a deviant contribution serves no purpose because it is of no benefit. But since the very deviance of a contribution in analysis is usable as grist for the analytic mill, it is beneficial according to the broader concept of benefit employed here. As we shall see at greater length further on in this paper, the benefit of analytic discourse lies outside of the immediate context of the conversation; the conversation is but a means to an end, where most ordinary conversations produce benefit in and of themselves. Hence we require it of ordinary discourse that the speaker's underlying intention in communicating match the explicit utterance as perceived by the addressee, since there is no possibility of justifying a contribution on grounds extrinsic to the discourse itself. But where a mismatch of this sort can be used toward an extrinsic goal, it is tolerated by the mutual consent of the participants.

Thus, the purposes of the analytic setting justify a different view of the abrogation of Clarity and Rapport--they are tolerated when they occur, but these violations are not assumed to be necessary in the analytic setting--when they occur, they are marked. An irrelevant contribution is neither overlooked nor regarded as directly relevant as it stands. In this sense, the Principle of Clarity, at least, is not really abrogated in the analytic setting; violations are still violations. The analysand is 'allowed' his violations. He is not--as he would be in ordinary discourse--made to feel uncomfortable purely by virtue of the fact that he has violated the rules. He is permitted a discrepancy between underlying aim and superficial form; it is still assumed that unless somehow prevented or distracted, a speaker would wish and intend to present his thoughts in conformity with Clarity and Rapport. Deviation, then, is assumed to reflect a special situation in the analysand's unconscious mind; otherwise there would be no conflict between Clarity and the Basic Rule, between speaking most intelligibly and saying what occurred to his conscious mind to say.

The implicit idea in this passage, then, is this: when the Rules of Communicative Competence are abrogated in accordance with the Basic Rule, this is a special situation and requires examination. In general, even though the Basic Rule countenances abrogation of the Principles, they will not be abrogated. As long as the analysand adheres to the Principles of Communicative Competence, there is nothing to interpret. The communication is within the realm of the normal. The distinctive feature of the analytic setting is that he is given an extra option--not really optional, of course--that of following trains of thought that do not directly benefit either participant. When taking this option precludes following the Principles, the analyst acts: he interprets. Freud does not say this in his instructions: the purpose for following the Basic Rule is not stated, only the cryptic remark, 'Later on, you will find out and learn to understand the reason for this injunction'. (That is, once interpretations are made, the analysand will see the necessity of his following the Basic Rule.)

Since the analysand's contribution does not, in any normal understanding of the term, benefit himself or the analyst, we may ask how and why both participate in the discourse. I said earlier that either we had to take a new view of our whole social organization and motivation for engaging in social activities, or redefine the notion of 'benefit' in this special context. First, we must recognize here as elsewhere the mutuality of the agreement to suspend the normal rules. Both participants agree, more or less implicitly, that they will not expect to gain from this discourse what they ordinarily gain. In this regard, we might say, production of 'free associations' differs from that of the psychotic's 'loose associations'. In both, the addressee does not see where the conversation is tending or how it relates to his interests, and in that sense both should be equally frustrating to him; but the former is made tolerable by the fact that he has entered into a voluntary agreement with the speaker to engage in this sort of discourse; it is voluntary and intentional on both their parts. Being party to a stream of loose associations is painful at least in part because one feels that one is being imposed upon; one has not asked for it, much less consented to it.

But certainly, even (or, we might say, especially) at its best, an analytic discourse is fraught with difficulties for the participants. The analyst himself will feel confused, not knowing how to tie it all together, which is, after all, his job; the analysand feels discomfort at saying things that are potentially embarrassing, and even in speaking in a mode unsuited to adult discourse, in not making sense. But another implicit reason why Freud explains so painstakingly to the analysand both the Basic Rule and the analysand's role in the analysis is precisely in order to enlist his cooperation in overlooking the normal expectation, thereby indicating that the benefit to be derived from the interaction is to be sought from another direction. The analysand indeed is to derive benefit from the discourse--but the discourse here is the means, not the end in itself. The benefit derived is not the usual one implied by adherence to Clarity and Rapport--increased knowledge (information) on the one hand, and a sense of acceptance (rapport) on the other; but it is curious that these are implied in Freud's statement of what a healthy person should be able to do, what abilities should be gained from analysis: love and work. So it is not that the benefits to the analysand are markedly different from those accruing to a participant in an ordinary discourse; they are just realized differently, and indirectly.

But both participants must gain from a conversation in order for it to continue. What does the analyst get? Increased knowledge, we might say, more insight into the human condition, satisfaction of his curiosity; and the sense of having helped, being useful: complementary to what the analysand derives as his benefits, and again closely related to what one expects to get from an ordinary interaction. These are, of course, less crucial benefits than the analysand derives, and as a result there must be some sort of equalization: on these grounds, one can justify theoretically the analyst's fee.

The other issue I have promised to examine concerns the notion of interpretation. The analyst, in making an interpretation of something the analysand has said, is in effect telling him why he said it, what it meant that he chose to utter it, utter it in a particular form; and what the content of the utterance signifies. This is, of course, the very heart of analytic procedure, and it is a bit curious that Freud, in what is otherwise a very lucid and detailed set of instructions, makes no mention of this aspect of the analyst's role, no more than a veiled hint that some such procedure may exist--a hint that we may understand in our reading of the passage, but which would have been cryptic to a wholly naive analysand (supposing this creature, like the naive speaker of a language, actually ever exists). We may further conclude that Freud felt, overtly or covertly, that he had to wait to make this part of the procedure obvious until he had the analysand's trust. Indeed, he says so later in the paper already cited, that interpretations are not to be made until such a bond has been established.

> The next question with which we are faced raises a matter of principle. It is this: When are we to begin making our communications to the patient? When is the moment for disclosing to him the hidden meaning of the ideas that occur to him, and for initiating him into the postulates and technical procedures of analysis?
>
> The answer to this can only be: Not until an effective transference has been established in the patient, a proper *rapport* with him (Freud 1958 (1913):139).

On the face of it, this reluctance to proceed at once with interpretation is a bit puzzling. Why must one wait till rapport is established? Ought not the analysand to welcome interpretations--as a light in the darkness, a show of interest in his situation, whatever? And in that case, the sooner, the better to establish this rapport? I think that in order to understand this seeming contradiction, we must examine more closely the concept of 'interpretation', asking under what conditions one person may interpret the words or actions of another.

To interpret is to make the unintelligible intelligible. One interprets for someone who cannot himself make his communication understandable. Thus one interprets for someone who cannot speak the language, one interprets a text written in a difficult and mysterious language by people with alien cultural assumptions. One can interpret a small child's utterances, or a poem. Each is cryptic in its own way, one because the child has not yet entirely learned how to communicate; the other, through a culturally sanctioned style of condensed and symbolic expression. Similarly, one interprets a dream, which, since it is a product of the unconscious mind, is assumed to be in a language that is not our normal rational mode of expression. On the other hand, to say that one must interpret a prose work such as an appliance's instruction manual is to make a critical comment about the style in which it is written. Interpretation in these cases mediates between what is unintelligible and irrational, and what is understandable and clear. As noted, we tolerate or even prefer unclear communication under some conditions. But in ordinary discourse, to be told that one is unintelligible, not making sense, or being irrational is almost certainly received as an insult of a particularly humiliating kind. If one violates Clarity to this extent, one is assumed to be doing so unintentionally (as is almost invariably the case), and therefore to be acting pathologically. (One must distinguish, as speakers can and do, between violations of Clarity done for purposes of Rapport, in which case the addressee both understands and appreciates the need for unclearness, and is able to discern the underlying intention; and unclarity for no reason that is apparent to the addressee, and therefore beyond his understanding.)

Thus, to say that one's productions require interpretation is to say that one has abrogated the Principle of Rationality. The addressee can no longer make sense of the speaker's productions through his use of projection and identification--they are beyond him. He thus, by interpreting, acknowledges that he feels the speaker and himself not to be part of the same group --there is no identity, no rapport, between them; the speaker is not one of 'us'. This is, of course, hurtful to a participant in normal discourse even more than the fact that interpretation implies that he is not in control of his mental processes. But certainly, given the fact that interpretation entails these assumptions on the part of the interpreter, it is evident that interpretation could disrupt the therapeutic dialog--unless there were sufficient love and trust already established (via the transference) that the analysand's positive feelings outweighed the negative. Trust and rapport are also strengthened by the participants' mutual agreement that the analysand will not insist on his rationality. Since both participants know that the analysand has voluntarily chosen this role, the fact that the analyst is interpreting his contributions does not rankle as it would otherwise.

Since the analyst interprets both Clarity and Rapport violations, he also must determine which he is dealing with, since the nature of his interpretation will differ in each case. A Clarity violation will lead to an interpretation of the content of the analysand's associations, most typically--the analyst will point out that there is something in the material itself that is creating unconscious conflict. A Rapport violation tends to be interpreted as a transference reaction: it indicates that the analysand is feeling some sort of conflict concerning the relationship between himself and the analyst. Of course, the analyst must decide, in each case, which it is; this is sometimes obvious and sometimes not. A violation may also be overdetermined: may involve a conflict of both kinds. Consider, for instance, a contribution of silence. The assumption is that something is always occurring in one's mind; if one cannot think what to say, one is failing to communicate fully and is thereby being irrational, and the silence itself is therefore interpretable. Depending on context, the analyst may choose to interpret silence either as a Clarity violation, against Quantity; a Rapport violation, against Camaraderie; or no violation at all, the analysand's taking time to reflect on something. In ordinary discourse, we make some of the same assumptions: a silence on the part of a participant may be viewed as 'cryptic' (Quantity) or 'brusque' (Camaraderie), as well as 'thoughtful'.[6] (Cf. Fliess 1949 for discussion of silence, and Loewenstein 1951, 1956, and 1957 for discussion of interpretation.)

In the course of this paper, I have looked at analytic discourse from the point of view of the analysand's contributions.

It is equally possible, and equally useful, to look at the analyst's (typically sparser) contributions as deviant from normal communicative acts. To do so at length would unnecessarily prolong this paper, but a few short remarks will suffice. The analyst's contributions--that is, his interpretations--themselves violate the Rules of Communicative Competence in comparable ways. His contributions are not seen, typically, as violating Clarity; even when he is silent, when he does not divulge requested information, or counters the analysand's question with a question, it is probably correct to consider it a violation of Rapport--specifically, Camaraderie. For he does not, typically, give evasive or unclear or irrelevant answers--which would violate Clarity, of course; but typically he responds by questioning the motivation behind the question: 'I wonder why you ask that?' And this is, of course, a reminder that the analysand's contribution must be regarded as irrational, as requiring interpretation. If in ordinary conversation we question the motives behind someone's utterance, it is potentially insulting--unless the participants are sufficiently intimate with each other that they have mutually agreed to suspend the normal requirements of Rapport--rather analogously to the analytic framework, though for different reasons.

This paper has presented arguments for the following hypotheses: (1) that an adequate theory of communicative competence will cover both normal and extraordinary forms of discourse; (2) that psychoanalytic discourse is learnable precisely because it assumes the normal Rules of Communicative Competence; (3) that differences between normal and psychoanalytic conversation occur by mutual consent of the participants, and therefore are tolerable; (4) that the Basic Rule of analysis and the ordinary Rules of Communicative Competence are not mutually incompatible, but violation of the latter in the analytic setting provides the basis for making interpretations.

NOTES

This research has been partially supported by Grant #1 R01 MH 26845-01 from the National Institute of Mental Health.

1. Looking ahead to the psychoanalytic discussion that occupies the bulk of this paper, it is useful to note here that the Principle of Rationality implies the adaptive use of two of the mechanisms of defense of psychoanalytic theory, 'identification' and 'projection'. Each participant in an ordinary discourse is assumed, throughout the discourse, to be unconsciously asking and answering two questions, serving to orient him to the contributions of the other: (1) If I were saying that, what would I intend by it? (identification). (2) How would he interpret my utterance, if I said it in a particular way? (projection).

The Principle of Rationality, then, is one example of the adaptive use of defensive processes, a concept that has been acknowledged by psychoanalytic theory from the inception of the study of the defenses (A. Freud 1936), discussed in some detail by Hartmann (1958), with perhaps the most relevant discussion by Schafer (1968).

2. I have discussed in my (1972) paper on 'The pragmatics of modality' the semantic-pragmatic ambiguity of *must*: that is, that in many sentences containing *must*, it is only by examining the context of the utterance (within or external to the discourse) that one can determine who is under the obligation. The point is germane to Freud's discussion, in that it suggests why the determination of the responsibility for following the rules of analytic discourse is not made explicit here.

3. In contrast to Freud's usage in the cited passage, as well as what is probably the prevailing practice in psychoanalytic writing, I have chosen to call the principals in the psychoanalytic relationship 'analyst' and 'analysand', rather than 'doctor' and 'patient' or any other variation. My reason is that I would like to use terms that suggest the special nature of the conversational relationship; 'doctor' and 'patient' are too general. I think that the use of 'doctor' and 'patient' also implies an activity on the part of one, based on the 'doctor's' normal role, and consequently a passivity on the other's part, that is contrary to the purpose of my discussion; and finally, since I am only tangentially concerned here with psychoanalysis as a therapeutic system, the invocation of the medical model in this discussion seems misleading and inappropriate.

4. Here we see perhaps the earliest example of consciousness-raising by linguistic education. One learns--this passage implies-- to do something unintuitive first by putting it into practice in one's verbal communication, which of all human behavior is perhaps most easily accessible to conscious awareness. Then, having learned these new strategies, one can put them to use elsewhere. These are the same tactics employed in feminist consciousness-raising and assertiveness training, where one first makes explicit--and learns the pitfalls of--familiar verbal devices; then learns new forms of speech to substitute for these; and finally, new forms of nonverbal behavior analogous to those new linguistic patterns.

5. For discussion cf. Sharpe (1950). The best known example of the distinction between real-world truth and psychic truth is one that caused Freud himself no little distress. His early patients invariably gave a history involving seduction in early childhood, by the father or a nursemaid. Freud assumed that these reports were true and developed a theory of the etiology of neurosis based on childhood seduction. It later turned out that most of these reports were untrue; the seductions were the figments of the patients' imaginations. Freud therefore was forced to abandon his theory, leaving the question of the etiology of neurosis not satisfactorily answered to

this day. But the important point is that the patients' symptoms in adult life came into existence as a result of the fantasied seductions; the 'untrue' belief was, for them, psychically 'true'. Since false recollection may cause indisputably real symptoms, in one sense such a recollection is 'truer' for one who holds it than the real-world corroborable 'truth' would be.

6. It should be noted that other than verbal actions are interpretable: for instance, striking deviations from the analysand's normal mode of entrance into the room, style of dress, posture, or gait; similarly, verbal contributions not in keeping with the analysand's expected style. We may reconcile these additions with our notion of interpretability by irrationality as follows: The analysand's 'normal' mode is coherent and consistent as a part of his personality, and as such is a form of communication. Just as a speech contribution must follow the Principles of communicative competence, so must one's whole mode of presentation of self. One's personal style is expected to be genuine (quality), effective (quantity), consistent (relevance), and purposeful (manner). A deviation from any of these is interpretable; an abrupt change is thus interpretable, at the least, as a relevance violation.

REFERENCES

Fliess, R. 1949. Silence and verbalization: A supplement to the theory of the analytic rule. International Journal of Psycho-Analysis 30.21-30.

Freud, A. 1936. The ego and the mechanisms of defense. London: Hogarth Press.

Freud, S. 1913. On beginning the treatment: Further recommendations on the technique of psycho-analysis. Standard edition, 12:121-144. London: Hogarth Press, 1958.

Hartmann, H. 1958. Ego psychology and the problem of adaptation. New York: International Universities Press.

Lakoff, R. 1972. The pragmatics of modality. In: Papers from the Eighth Regional Meeting of the Chicago Linguistic Society. Chicago: Chicago Linguistic Society.

Lakoff, R. 1973. The logic of politeness: Or minding your p's and q's. In: Papers from the Ninth Regional Meeting of the Chicago Linguistic Society. Chicago: Chicago Linguistic Society.

Lakoff, R. 1977. What you can do with words: Politeness, pragmatics and performatives. In: Proceedings of the Texas Conference on Performatives, Presuppositions, and Implicatures. Edited by Andy Rogers, Bob Wall, and John P. Murphy. Arlington, Va.: Center for Applied Linguistics.

Lakoff, R. (in preparation) Aspects of communicative competence.

Loewenstein, R. M. 1951. The problem of interpretation. Psychoanalytic Quarterly 20.1-14.

Loewenstein, R. M. 1956. Some remarks on the role of speech in psycho-analytic technique. International Journal of Psycho-Analysis 37.460-468.
Loewenstein, R. M. 1957. Some thoughts on interpretation in the theory and practice of psychoanalysis. The Psychoanalytic Study of the Child 12.127-150.
Schafer, R. 1968. Mechanisms of defense. International Journal of Psycho-Analysis 49.49-62.
Sharpe, E. F. 1950. Collected papers on psycho-analysis. London: Hogarth Press.

III. Language Attitudes

SOCIOLINGUISTIC CORRELATES OF SPEECH STYLE IN QUEBEC[1]

ALISON d'ANGLEJAN AND G. RICHARD TUCKER

McGill University

In this study we have examined the state of the French language in Quebec from a sociolinguistic perspective. This research which represents a new dimension in Canadian studies will interest scholars, educators, and administrators for both practical and theoretical reasons. The divergence of Quebec French from standard European French together with the recent attempts of the provincial government to influence the evolution of the language have permitted us to examine one small aspect of people's awareness of the role of language in their lives and their reactions to the attempts at language planning of a modern government in a developed country.

French is today the mother tongue of more than five million Canadians, 75% of whom live in the Province of Quebec. Although enclaves of French-speaking Canadians occur throughout the country, English is rapidly replacing French as the language of the French Canadian ethnic group in all areas other than Quebec, a trend also noted in the French-speaking areas in the northern part of the United States.

In Quebec, the high proportion of French Canadians plus the strong retention of French in the province (only 1.6% of Quebec's French ethnic population reported English as their mother tongue in 1961) has served to maintain the position of French as one of Canada's two official languages and to provide an important shield against linguistic and cultural assimilation (Lieberson 1970).

Although the British North America Act of 1867 recognized French and English as the two official languages of Canada, there is abundant evidence (Porter 1958, Royal Commission on Bilingualism and Biculturalism 1965) that the French language occupied a minor position in Canada and that even in Quebec, French Canadians were underrepresented in the higher echelons of business and industry where English became firmly entrenched as the working language. The eruption of terrorist activities in the early 1960's brought to light both the feelings of resentment held by many French Canadians with respect to their inferior status and the separatist aspirations of certain segments of their society. The following ten years which have been marked by sporadic outbursts of terrorism and the birth of an official Quebec separatist party have seen a parallel acceleration in language policy developments at both the federal and provincial levels.

In their historical survey of the development of language policy in Quebec, Pinault and Ladouceur (1971) pointed out that more has been done in the past ten years to guarantee the maintenance and development of French as the de jure and de facto working language of the province than during the preceding 190 years. For example, it is now mandatory for all English-speaking children to acquire a working knowledge of French within their school curriculum; a working knowledge of French has replaced Canadian citizenship as a requirement for certain professional licenses; and direct pressure has been exerted on large businesses and industries to collaborate with the government to make French the working language of employees at all levels.

In view of the significant role which French has played in preserving the people of Quebec and their culture from assimilation, and the relationship between language and nationalistic movements throughout the world, it is not surprising to find that language matters occupy a position of priority on the Quebec political and educational scene.

The French spoken in Quebec today by all but a small academic and professional elite differs at all levels of linguistic analysis from the accepted prestige form of the language spoken in France. Spilka (1970) attributed the high status of this standard model which has evolved from the Ile-de-France dialect to three main factors: (1) early and successful efforts at language standardization on the part of the State (the Académie Française entrusted with the defense and preservation of the French language was founded in 1635, and published its first dictionary in 1644; (2) the considerable prestige enjoyed by France and by French culture throughout the world; and (3) the absence of any serious political and economic challenge to France's superior position by other French-speaking nations. French colonies and former colonies have always remained subordinate to the mother country; in Canada, particularly, the French-speaking community has been ascribed an inferior status.

Denis (1949) described the evolution of the French language in Canada following the British conquest and the departure of the French-speaking elite. Cut off from contact with other French language centers, Canadian French quickly became archaic and offered little resistance to the influence of English. By the end of the 19th century, the contamination of French by borrowings from English reached such proportions that public campaigns were organized to awaken French Canadians to the fact that their language was in danger. These campaigns and corrective movements were ineffective in the face of the growing influence of the English language press and eventually of radio and television. These events led Valin (1970) to remark that if Quebec French was left to evolve naturally it could become unintelligible to speakers of standard French.

In 1961 the Quebec government established an Office de la langue française (OLF). This agency was assigned the task of revitalizing French in Quebec by bringing it closer to standard French and by upgrading the language of the underprivileged classes. The OLF regularly disseminates normative bulletins to educational institutions, businesses, and mass media which draw attention to the specific differences distinguishing Quebec French from standard French and provide appropriate standard French vocabulary lists to replace certain canadianisms and anglicisms now in common use.

In its first official publication, Cahier No. 1, the OLF stated that if the French language in Quebec is to survive the pressures of an English-speaking North American milieu, it must adhere to the same norms which prevail in other large francophone countries. No variation in morphology or syntax can be tolerated; phonetic and lexical variation should be reduced to an absolute minimum. It is interesting to note that this document does not deal with language variation in the objective terms of modern linguistics but is highly subjective and punctuated with value judgments of the following nature:

> Nous devons nous efforcer de produire les trentesix phonèmes (du français) avec la plus grande pureté possible. Mais nos prononciations vicieuses, notre relâchement articulatoire . . . nous écartent trop de la bonne voie à suivre dans ce domaine. Trop nombreux sont les sons que nous réalisons de façon défectueuse . . . Ce sont autant d'exemples de prononciation qui exigent un travail de redressement articulatoire . . . Quand à notre relâchement articulatoire dans le discours, il est absolument inacceptable (Cahier No. 1, p. 8, 1965).

Attitudes such as these are not new, and the tone is strongly reminiscent of that which has characterized pronouncements of the

Académie Française and an extensive list of French grammarians dating back to the sixteenth century.

According to Harmer (1954), the French at all levels of society display an intense interest in their own language and show remarkably little tolerance or sympathy toward either regional or social class deviation from the prestige form. It is understandable, therefore, that French Canadians who are now attempting to establish and strengthen cultural ties with France as a bulwark against the pressures of North America may feel sensitive and somewhat insecure with respect to their 'nonstandard' dialect. Miner (1939) remarked that the rural French Canadian is usually apologetic about his speech. Corrective measures have succeeded in making him lose pride in his language and he has no real basis for judging which of the words he uses are standard French and which are not.

The results of a number of empirical studies conducted in several countries support these generalizations. They suggest that regional dialect variables may come to elicit socially conditioned value judgments which in turn affect the attitudes of listeners toward speakers from various backgrounds. A speaker may be judged favorably or unfavorably by the prestige of the dialect that he speaks. Markel, Eisler, and Reese (1967) demonstrated that in the United States regional dialect is a significant factor in judging personality from speech style. Giles (1970) reported similar findings in England, while Tucker (1968) reported that speakers of American English were viewed more favorably than speakers of Filipino English or of Tagalog by listeners in the Philippines. The findings most relevant to this study were those reported by Lambert (1967). French and English Canadian university students were asked to rate the personality characteristics of ten speakers--five English and five French. In reality, five bilingual speakers were used with each speaker appearing in two guises. English students evaluated the English-speaking guises more favorably on most traits, while French students not only evaluated English guises more favorably than French guises, but also evaluated the French guises significantly less favorably than the English students did.

Labov's (1966) extensive study of the social stratification of speech in New York City drew attention to the importance of the relationship between speech and social class. Speakers from different social levels are characterized by distinctive phonological, syntactic, and lexical features which are easily identified by linguistically naive judges and which may be used by these judges as a basis for evaluating the speakers. Ellis (1967) showed that naive judges speaking one regional dialect of American English can accurately identify the social status of persons speaking different dialects.

An additional aspect of the relationship between language and social class was brought to light in Labov's (1967) study of social mobility which indicated that upwardly mobile people tend to adopt the linguistic style of the socioeconomic group just above their own. Brown (1969) reported similar findings in a French Canadian study. The speech styles of different socioeconomic levels can be accurately discerned by listeners, mainly on the basis of a gross upper class-lower class dichotomy. French Canadians tend to model their speech on those with whom they identify, i.e. those who are upwardly mobile adopt upper-class speech features.

Some of the possible psychological implications of speech style were discussed by Halliday (1968) who pointed out that the socioregional pattern of dialect distribution gives rise to socially conditioned moral and aesthetic value judgments. He warned that when attitudes of inferiority come to be shared by those who themselves speak the nonstandard or stigmatized dialect, and no other, they become harmful.

> A speaker who is made ashamed of his own language habits suffers a basic injury as a human being; to make anyone, especially a child feel so ashamed is as indefensible as to make him feel ashamed of the colour of his skin (Halliday 1968:165).

One might speculate that particular attention should be paid to these possible psychological implications in Quebec where French Canadians have been exposed to continual negative value judgments about the quality of their speech. To date, however, researchers have concentrated on the identification and description of the speech style of French Canadians from different geographic and social strata (e.g. Charbonneau 1955, Ellis 1965, Gendron 1966) while very few studies have examined sociolinguistic correlates of the linguistic variables. The one preliminary investigation in this area conducted by Chiasson-Lavoie and Laberge (1971) did find evidence of linguistic insecurity among lower-class French Canadians in Montreal.

The scarcity of data concerning possible correlates of speech style in French Canada together with the salience of language as a political and educational issue in the province motivated the present investigation. As a result of a pilot study which we conducted in Montreal in 1970 with 75 French Canadian junior-college students and teachers, the following areas were chosen for investigation:

(1) The awareness in people of regional and social dialect variation.
(2) The importance of language in general as a factor in social and academic success.
(3) The attitudes of people toward their own speech style and that of speakers from other social classes and regions.

(4) The willingness of people to accept standard European French as the prestige model.
(5) The reactions of people toward the systematic attempts by the government to standardize their language.

The present study was designed to investigate these questions, in a preliminary way, with groups of subjects from different occupations and different geographic locations throughout the province of Quebec.

Method

Subjects. All subjects (Ss) for this investigation were French Canadians who had been born and brought up in Quebec. Since many of the OLF materials are directed to schools, and since the educational system is traditionally one of the main vehicles by which language policy decisions are implemented, groups of teachers and students at the high-school level were selected as subjects. Students were from working class and lower-middle class backgrounds. In addition, groups of factory workers were included to study the reactions of Ss who might be less language conscious than the others. To obtain a relatively representative distribution of Ss and to be able to look at the possible effects of regional variation on language attitudes, Ss were selected from three geographical locations in Quebec: (1) Montreal, a large cosmopolitan, multilingual city; (2) Alma, a rural, predominantly French-speaking community; and (3) Quebec, a small monolingual city, and the Provincial capital. The sample is described in Table 1.

TABLE 1. Distribution of sample.

Location	Occupation	Male	Female	Total	Avg. age	Avg. no. yrs. experience
Montreal	Students	11	16	27	16.33	..
	Teachers	17	10	27	..	6.48
	Workers	13	14	27	24.58	..
Alma	Students	10	17	27	17.35	..
	Teachers	16	11	27	..	7.30
	Workers	12	15	27	30.81	..
Quebec	Students	11	16	27	16.93	..
	Teachers	20	7	27	..	7.15
	Workers	10	17	27	23.63	..
	Total	120	123	243		

Materials. Two complementary measures were used to assess the language attitudes of the Ss. In view of the low degree of constancy between attitude measures and actual behavior reported in studies reviewed by Agheyisi and Fishman (1970), we hoped that comparisons of the data resulting from two contrasting measures might help to validate the findings.

The first measure was a questionnaire comprising forty multiple choice and semantic differential type items. The appropriateness of each question as well as the format was determined in a pilot study. The questions focused on Ss' awareness of speech style differences, the importance they attributed to language, their awareness of government language policy, etc.

As a complementary measure, Ss were asked to evaluate the speech styles of twelve speakers and to indicate their probable occupational status. Samples were recorded from four lower-class and four upper-class French Canadians and from four Europeans. All were male, native speakers of French selected on the basis of their occupational status and country of origin. The lower-class speakers were a janitor, a maintenance man, a parking attendant, and a carpenter. They ranged in age from 40 to 50 years. All were native Montrealers. Upper-class speakers were a psychiatrist, an architect, and two university professors, all from Montreal, ranging in age from 30 to 45 years. European speakers were three French university students and a business man, ranging in age from 23 to 35. The voices were arranged in random order for the stimulus tape.

We decided for this portion of the study to obtain a sample of free speech rather than a sample of reading which allows variation in phonology but controls the use of syntax and lexical items. Giles (1970) draws an important distinction between the perception of accent as opposed to dialect. Dialect implies variation from the standard code at most levels of linguistic analysis, whereas 'accent' merely implies a manner of pronunciation with grammatical, syntactical, morphological, and lexical levels being regarded as more or less commensurate with the standard. Since this study is concerned with dialect variation and not reactions to accent only, a sample of free speech seemed the most appropriate stimulus. Furthermore, Agheyisi and Fishman (1970) suggest that in the typical 'matched-guise' experiment when judges evaluate speakers on the basis of a sample of reading, they may well be reacting to things such as the congruity, or lack of it, between the speaker, the topic, and the particular language variety. They feel that this congruity, or incongruity, should be studied rather than obscured.

The speakers used in this study were interviewed separately and informally on a specific topic, a record-breaking blizzard which occurred in Montreal during the first week of March 1971. This topic permitted them considerable freedom of expression. A 30 to 40 second sample of uninterrupted speech was selected from the output of each speaker. The final tape consisted of thirteen voices: four exemplars from each of the three categories and one additional French Canadian voice at the beginning of the tape which served as a 'practice' voice to acquaint Ss with the type of judgments they were to make for the following twelve voices.

The Ss were asked to make a series of rapid, subjective value judgments about each speaker: How intelligent does he sound? How likeable; educated; ambitious; tough; etc. ? Is his speech style an asset to him or a liability? What type of job would he probably hold? The Ss were encouraged to make their ratings using seven-point semantic differential-type scales quickly and intuitively.

An additional content-free tape recording was prepared in which the same speakers counted from one to twenty. Ellis (1967) found that a 20 second sample of counting was a sufficiently powerful stimulus to enable Ss to make accurate social class predictions. For this phase of the task, Ss were asked to indicate the probability that each speaker belonged to an upper or a lower occupational status group.

Testing procedure. Students in the three settings were group-tested in their respective classrooms. Teachers and workers were tested either individually or in small groups. The testing was carried out by two male French Canadian university students. All Ss first completed the objective questionnaire, then listened and evaluated one by one the thirteen voices on the free speech tape followed by the thirteen samples of content-controlled speech.

Method of data analysis. A variety of formal and informal data analyses were used in the present study. For the questionnaire, the frequencies of response by each of the nine groups of Ss were tabulated and converted to percentages for the multiple choice questions. The data for the questions answered with semantic differential rating scales were analyzed using separate two-way analyses of variance. The independent variables were geographic location (Montreal, Alma, and Quebec) and occupation (student, teacher, and worker).

For the voice data, separate three-way analyses of variance, with repeated measures, were used for each rating scale. Ratings for the four exemplars of each voice category were first averaged to obtain a single score for each speech style. The independent variables were geographic location (Montreal, Alma, and Quebec), occupation (student, teacher, and worker), and speech style (standard European French, upper-class French Canadian, and lower-class French Canadian).

Results and discussion

The data from the objective questionnaire and from the voice evaluations will be presented separately. Items from different parts of the questionnaire have been grouped according to topical area to facilitate discussion, and we have tried to draw attention to certain of the more general and consistent themes which occur throughout the data. We did not pay particular attention to significant main effects for location or to interactions involving location since the biographical information from our Ss revealed that many of them did not originally come from the locations in which they were interviewed.

Awareness of social class stratification. The responses to the first four questions indicated that a majority of the Ss from the three occupations in each geographical setting are conscious of speech variation. Underlying this consensus were minor variations in the patterns of responses. For example, the teachers in each setting showed relatively more awareness of variation (95% answered positively) than did the students (85%) or the workers (75%) when asked if they noticed that certain people in their community speak a style of French different from their own.

Furthermore, when Ss were asked to classify various occupational groups according to speech style, very clear patterns emerged. All Ss tended to cluster lawyers with university professors and radio announcers; and bus drivers with mailmen and janitors in a separate group. However, some of them assigned the occupation of bank clerk to one category; and some, to the other. This is not surprising since this latter occupation represents a point midway between high occupational status and low status according to Blishen (1958).

The Ss tended to classify their own speech style differentially according to their occupation. The following summary indicates the most frequently occurring groupings of Ss' own speech style by occupation and region:

Montreal	Students: bus driver or bank clerk
	Teachers: lawyer
	Workers: bus driver
Alma	Students: bank clerk
	Teachers: bank clerk
	Workers: bus driver
Quebec	Students: bank clerk
	Teachers: lawyer
	Workers: bank clerk

Apart from Montreal and Quebec teachers who viewed their own speech style as similar to that of lawyers, the highest category on the Blishen scale, most respondents grouped their speech with that of lower occupational status groups. This probably represents an accurate judgment since the students and workers came from lower-middle class and working class families. These data provide evidence that Ss do perceive clearly distinguishable differences in the speech of lower- and upper-class groups. The implications of these differences will be discussed after the voice data have been presented.

When asked to give the names of public figures whose speech style they particularly like or dislike, Ss in all groups mentioned prominent political figures (e.g. Robert Bourassa, Réal Caouette, René Lévèsque, Pierre Trudeau) who have appeared frequently on television at election time and whose speech style is familiar to most French Canadians. All groups showed a preference for the educated French Canadian speech model. Two political figures, Réal Caouette and Camil Samson, speakers of the low prestige nonstandard 'joual' form of Quebec French appeared consistently in the 'dislike' category. Pierre Trudeau who speaks a European style standard French was mentioned frequently in both the 'like' and 'dislike' categories. While these responses show interesting patterns and appear to complement the data from the two previous questions, it should be remembered that they may well be the reflection of individual political biases.

Awareness of regional variation. The responses to another series of questions indicated that a majority of Ss have encountered speakers from other dialect regions in Quebec, and are conscious of this type of variation in speech style. Table 2 provides a breakdown of the responses to three of these questions in percentages. Members of all groups report having experienced difficulty in understanding speakers from other regions (question B) with the highest figure reported by the Montreal sample (64%). This is understandable since Montrealers would more likely be travelling to areas of the province where speech deviates from the metropolitan norm than the Ss from Quebec and Alma who would perhaps be visiting Montreal, and who may have had prior exposure to the Montreal variety of French on radio or TV.

Responses indicated that Ss have little difficulty in making themselves understood when visiting other parts of the province (question C). Relative to other groups, workers from Alma reported slightly more difficulty in making themselves understood which suggests that the Lac St. Jean dialect differs noticeably from that of Montreal or Quebec.

Furthermore, all teachers and most students in the three areas indicated that they have encountered French-speaking Europeans

TABLE 2. Percentage of affirmative responses.

Questions:			A	B	C
Montreal	Students		93	64	26
	Teachers		89	80	28
	Workers		78	48	13
		$\bar{X}$ =	87	64	22
Alma	Students		81	42	8
	Teachers		100	52	11
	Workers		89	31	30
		$\bar{X}$ =	90	42	16
Quebec	Students		85	40	17
	Teachers		100	40	8
	Workers		81	38	22
		$\bar{X}$ =	89	39	16

A = Avez-vous eu l'occasion de visiter d'autres régions du Québec?
B = Si oui, avez-vous eu du mal à comprendre le français qu'on parle dans certaines de ces régions?
C = Avez-vous eu du mal à vous faire comprendre dans certaines de ces régions?

(see Table 3). A surprising finding is that nearly 50% of Montreal workers claimed that they had not met any Europeans (question D). This seems unlikely since the probability of encountering Europeans is greater in Montreal than in either Alma or Quebec. These Ss have probably met Europeans but may have remained unaware of this fact. All groups have experienced difficulty in understanding Europeans (question E), with the highest figure (44%) reported by students in Alma. Furthermore, all groups reported some degree of difficulty in making themselves understood by Europeans (question F), with Alma students again reporting the highest percentage (57%).

Attitudes toward speech style. Eight questions probed Ss' opinions about the existence of a recognized prestige form of French in Quebec, what this form might be and whether they are satisfied with their own speech style.

All groups report being moderately, but not entirely, satisfied with their own speech style ($\bar{X}$ = 3.76 on a 7-point scale). There were no significant occupation or location differences among the groups. The fact that Ss were not more satisfied with their speech style may

TABLE 3. Percentage of affirmative responses.

Questions:			D	E	F
Montreal	Students		89	28	42
	Teachers		100	23	19
	Workers		52	40	29
		$\overline{X}$ =	80	30	30
Alma	Students		93	44	57
	Teachers		100	37	30
	Workers		85	28	28
		$\overline{X}$ =	93	36	38
Quebec	Students		89	19	27
	Teachers		100	17	20
	Workers		59	30	38
		$\overline{X}$ =	83	22	28

D = Avez-vous eu l'occasion de rencontrer des européens de langue française (français, belges, suisses, etc.)?
E = Si oui, avez-vous eu du mal à comprendre le français parlé par ces personnes?
F = Avez-vous eu du mal à vous faire comprendre par ces personnes?

reflect accurately the feelings of people from these social strata. It may, on the other hand, be a consequence of the various speech improvement movements which have tended to make French Canadians self-conscious about their speech style.

The responses of all groups indicate that Ss listen to Radio-Canada with Ss from Alma listening relatively more frequently than groups in the other areas (Alma $\overline{X} = 1.78$, Quebec $\overline{X} = 2.26$, Montreal $\overline{X} = 2.46$; $F = 4.80$, $df = 2/234$, $p < .01$). This probably reflects the fact that there are no private radio or TV stations broadcasting in Alma, whereas many do exist in Montreal and Quebec.

The French spoken on Radio-Canada, a variety close to standard European French, represents the best form of Quebec French ($\overline{X} = 2.53$) for Ss from all areas. Among those who reported that they do not agree that Radio-Canada represents the prestige model, there is no consensus concerning an alternative although Ss in Montreal frequently proposed private radio and TV stations whose announcers incidentally tend to speak Quebec style French.

The responses of Ss show that they feel their speech has been only moderately influenced by Radio-Canada (Students $\overline{X} = 4.78$, Workers

$\overline{X}$ = 4.44, Teachers $\overline{X}$ = 3.65; F = 6.69, df = 2/234, $p < .01$). No particular significance is attached to this difference which may reflect a reluctance on the part of students to admit to being influenced by 'the establishment'.

When asked to indicate how their own speech style differs from the best form of French in Quebec, all groups rated vocabulary and pronunciation as the most important sources of difference. Grammar was rated least different by all groups. This finding is consistent with data reported by Chiasson-Lavoie and Laberge (1971) that Ss in Montreal were less conscious of grammatical variables than phonological ones. However, it is also likely that teachers, at least, might feel that their grammar coincides with the standard form, while workers might be unaware of their deviation in this area. A summary of the responses to this question appears in Table 4.

TABLE 4. Responses expressed in percentages.

Q: De quelle façon votre langage diffère-t-il de la meilleure forme de français au Québec?						
R:		N	P	G	V	I
Montreal						
Students		15	30	22	74	15
Teachers		19	52	4	37	44
Workers		0	58	0	35	31
	$\overline{X}$ =	11	47	9	49	30
Alma						
Students		0	48	19	81	41
Teachers		15	44	7	52	33
Workers		15	26	11	52	33
	$\overline{X}$ =	10	39	12	62	36
Quebec						
Students		7	48	11	52	22
Teachers		15	37	11	59	41
Workers		15	33	11	52	26
	$\overline{X}$ =	12	39	11	54	30

N = None; P = Pronunciation; G = Grammar; V = Vocabulary; I = Intonation

The Ss refused to accept the cliches that the French of Quebec is not so nice as European French ($\overline{X}$ = 4.77) and that Parisian French is the best French ($\overline{X}$ = 5.21). However, they did not respond at the extreme negative end of the scale which suggests that their disagreement with the statements is not absolute. This was one of the few places on either the objective or subjective questionnaires where Quebec French was not viewed less favorably than standard French and suggests that contrasting types of measures may probe different levels of the Ss' awareness.

There was a significant interaction in response to the statement that Quebec French is not so nice as European French between occupational group and location ($F = 3.83$, $df = 4/234$, $p < .01$) with students in Montreal showing the greatest disagreement with the cliche and students in Quebec the least.

The statement that people make fun of someone who speaks too well was questioned by all groups ($\overline{X} = 3.85$). There was, however, a significant difference among the means for the three locations (Montreal $\overline{X} = 4.14$, Alma $\overline{X} = 4.16$, Quebec $\overline{X} = 3.26$; $F = 4.76$, $df = 2/234$, $p < .01$) with Quebec Ss indicating a neutral position in contrast to the greater disagreement expressed by both the Montreal and Alma groups.

The Ss expressed only slight agreement with the statement that one is judged more by his way of speaking than by his intelligence although there was a significant difference among the responses by the three occupational groups (Students $\overline{X} = 3.17$, Teachers $\overline{X} = 3.43$, Workers $\overline{X} = 2.37$; $F = 7.90$, $df = 2/234$, $p < .01$). Note that the workers judged speech to be relatively more important than intelligence; a trend which was reversed on some other questions.

Finally, Ss reported that they consider speech style to be only moderately related to academic success. The difference among the mean scores for the occupational groups was significant (Students $\overline{X} = 2.80$, Teachers $\overline{X} = 3.64$, Workers $\overline{X} = 3.27$; $F = 3.59$, $df = 2/234$, $p < .05$) with students tending to express the greatest agreement that an educated person speaks better than an uneducated one.

Importance attributed to speech style. Ss clearly rated language as secondary in importance to both personality and intelligence as a factor which affects scholastic or university success, success in obtaining a good job, and success in making friends on a series of four questions. A summary of the rankings by group is presented in Table 5. This general pattern of findings, despite their previously expressed awareness of the direct relationship between speech style and occupational status, was not at all surprising since language must certainly be a less 'visible' factor than either intelligence or personality; and in fact we would not expect our linguistically naive Ss to show a conscious awareness of the subtle nature of the relationship between language and intelligence or language and social class.

TABLE 5. Summary classification of dress (D), intelligence (I), language (L), personality (P), and social class (S) by rank order of importance.

	Rank	Montreal S	T	W	Alma S	T	W	Quebec S	T	W
Success at school	1	I	I	I	I	I	I	I	I	I
	2	P	P	L	P	P	P	P	P	P
	3	L	L	P	L	L	L	L	L	L
	4	S	S	S	S	S	S	S	S	S
	5	D	D	D	D	D	D	D	D	D
Success at university	1	I	I	I	I	I	I	I	I	I
	2	P	P	L	P	P	P	P	P	P
	3	L	L	P	L	L	L	L	L	L
	4	S	S	S	S	S	S	S	S	S
	5	D	D	D	D	D	D	D	D	D
Success in finding a good job	1	P	P	P	P	P	P	P	P	P
	2	I	L	L	I	L	I	I	L	I
	3	L	I	I	L	I	L	L	I	L
	4	D	D	D	D	D	D	D	S	D
	5	S	S	S	S	S	S	S	D	S
Success in making friends	1	P	P	P	P	P	P	P	P	P
	2	L	I	I	I	I	L	I	I	I
	3	I	L	L	L	L	I	L	L	L
	4	S	D	D	S	S	S	S	S	S
	5	D	S	S	D	D	D	D	D	D

S = Students; T = Teachers; W = Workers

The evolution of language and language policy. Objective inferences about language change may be made by comparing the phonology, syntax or lexicon, for example, of the French spoken today in Montreal with that spoken two hundred years ago. A series of very systematic statements could be made to describe the nature of that change or even the change during the past fifty years. From a sociolinguistic perspective, however, it may be more interesting to examine people's awareness of language as a static or dynamic entity and their reactions to attempts to influence language change.

In response to the question whether language stays the same or changes, 80% of the respondents agreed that it changes. However, a disproportionately high number of workers in Montreal (33%) reported that it remains the same. This finding supports our earlier speculation that workers as a group may be less language conscious than our other Ss.

Respondents from all groups provided diverse and often extremely perceptive suggestions about the forces that might cause language to change. Almost all Ss cited the effect of radio and TV which suggests that their responses to the earlier question concerning Radio-Canada's influence on their speech may have been an understatement. Some of the other factors listed by Ss were improved educational opportunities, the effects of immigration, an awareness of poor speech habits, changes in generation and cultural isolation.

When the focus was shifted from language in general to Quebec French in particular, approximately 80% of the Ss again indicated an awareness that the French language in Quebec is evolving. Once more, workers differed from students and teachers with 29% of Montreal workers and 28% of the Quebec workers reporting that they do not think that the French language is evolving.

Having established that most Ss view language as dynamic, we next probed to determine whether they believed that it was possible and desirable to influence this natural process. Although the Ss in general believed that it is possible to influence the natural development of language ($\overline{X} = 2.37$), there was a significant interaction between occupation and location ($F = 3.18$, $df = 4/234$, $p < .05$). The Quebec teachers were relatively less sure ($\overline{X} = 3.22$) than the others that language evolution could be externally influenced, while the Quebec workers were relatively more sure ($\overline{X} = 1.85$).

The Ss expressed a slightly more conservative view when asked whether they felt that it was desirable to influence the natural evolution of language ($\overline{X} = 2.90$). There was, however, a significant main effect for location ($F = 5.11$, $df = 2/234$; $p < .01$) with Montreal students being relatively more conservative ($\overline{X} = 3.41$) than those from Quebec ($\overline{X} = 2.72$) or Alma ($\overline{X} = 2.58$). Once again there was a significant interaction between occupation and location ($F = 3.72$, $df = 4/234$, $p < .01$). The Montreal students in particular felt that it is inappropriate to interfere with the natural development of language. This is consistent with their responses to the earlier question where they reported that their speech was relatively uninfluenced by Radio-Canada. Again, these data may reflect anti-establishment feelings.

Finally, there was consensus ($\overline{X} = 1.85$) that the French spoken in Quebec does need improvement, although there was a significant location effect ($F = 3.17$, $df = 2/234$, $p < .05$) and a significant interaction between location and occupation ($F = 4.08$, $df = 4/234$, $p < .01$). As Figure 1 indicates, the Montreal students are relatively less adamant in their belief that the language needs improvement ($\overline{X} = 2.81$) than Ss from the other eight groups.

FIGURE 1. Interaction between occupation and location in response to whether Quebec French needs improvement.

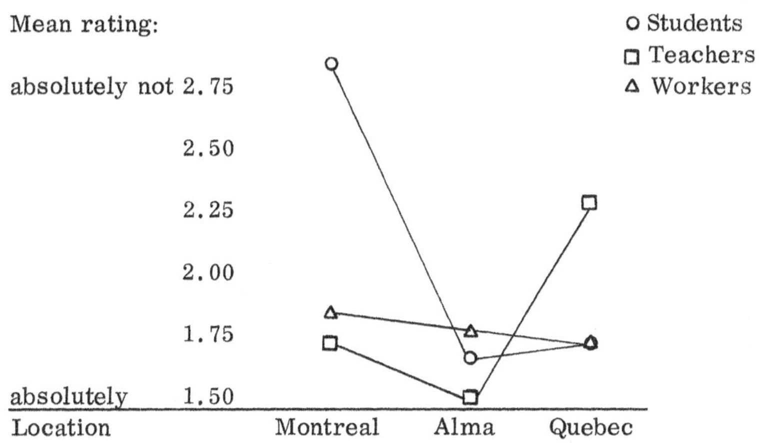

As a follow-up to the previous question, all Ss chose vocabulary and pronunciation most frequently (see Table 6) when asked to indicate what they considered to be the weaknesses, if any, of Quebec French. Grammar was in third place, followed by intonation. The workers in all locations chose pronunciation more frequently than vocabulary. These findings again coincide with those of Chiasson-Lavoie and Laberge (1971), and indicate that people are less conscious of deviant grammatical features in their speech. They are probably quite unaware of the intrusion of certain English syntactic structures in their French (e.g. Je n'ai jamais vu des choses qui vaillent la peine de se battre pour). Their reported high level of awareness of phonology as a weakness was complemented by the voice data where Ss made accurate social class distinctions after listening to a sample of speakers counting aloud.

TABLE 6. Perceived weaknesses in Quebec French by rank order of importance.

	Montreal			Alma			Quebec		
	S	T	W	S	T	W	S	T	W
Pronunciation	2	2	1	1	1	1	2	1	1
Vocabulary	1	1	2	2	2	2	1	2	2
Grammar	3	3	3	3	3	3	3	3	3
Intonation	4	4	4	4	4	4	4	4	4

S = Students; T = Teachers; W = Workers

The responses of the Ss to this series of questions revealed that they are aware of language variation, that they believe that languages are dynamic entities which evolve naturally; but that it may be possible to overtly influence the natural course of the evolution of a language. Furthermore, the Ss felt that the French spoken in Quebec was in need of improvement. In view of the fact that the government established the OLF in 1961 to promote and maintain the French language in Quebec, we next decided to probe Ss' awareness of this organization and their views about who, in general, should assume responsibility for language planning in Quebec.

A very clear pattern emerged when Ss indicated that European linguists and universities were not appropriate organizations for effecting language policy.

This reaction interested us since we had included the category 'European linguist' in the questionnaire when our attention was drawn to headlines in the Montreal press stating that the government had hired a team of European linguists to teach French Canadians correct language usage.

Students and teachers most frequently cited parents, teachers, and then the government in that order as the group to effect language policy while the workers most frequently selected teachers followed by the government. This latter finding suggests that the workers may feel themselves relatively incapable of helping their own children and implies an awareness on their part that their own parents were unable to help them. The rankings by each group are reported in Table 7.

TABLE 7. 'Qui devrait s'occuper d'améliorer our de préserver la langue française au Québec?'

The choices of each group expressed in rank order:	Students	Teachers	Workers
Government	3	3	2
Teachers	2	2	1
Parents	1	1	3
European linguists	5	5	5
University	4	4	4

Four questions probe directly the Ss' awareness of the activities of the OLF. Our pilot study conducted in Montreal revealed that students and teachers at the junior college level were generally aware of the OLF's existence, although they were occasionally unsure about the nature of its mandate which some thought to be the promotion of unilingualism. The data from the present study show that only 56% of the teachers, 32% of the students, and 26% of the workers had heard of the OLF. The low percentage for the workers suggests to us that the question may have been incorrectly phrased for this group. We should probably have questioned their exposure to the OLF's publicity to make French the working language of industry. Indeed, factory workers whom we tested referred to this campaign and occasionally thought our investigation was a part of it.

In general, those Ss who indicated awareness of the OLF also understood and supported its objectives and found them realistic. There was less tendency than in our pilot study to cite the promotion of unilingualism as an OLF goal.

Finally three questions were designed to probe Ss' feelings of insecurity or defensiveness with respect to their language. A majority of Ss (87%) reported that they generally accept correction and try to adjust their speech habits when errors are pointed out to them by a Quebecer; however, only 50% will accept corrections from a European. Since many workers previously reported that they had not met Europeans, this potentially interesting difference must be interpreted with caution.

The Ss' responses indicate a desire for 'correct' speech, (e.g Qu'est ce qui a le plus d'importance pour vous: que votre prononciation soit 'correcte' ou que votre prononciation garde son caractere Quebecois). Correctness over ethnicity in grammar was favored by 75% of all Ss, while a slightly lower percentage (70%) preferred correctness over ethnicity in vocabulary. In contrast, only 60% of the Ss indicated a preference for 'correct' pronunciation over 'Quebec' pronunciation. These data again lend credence to the belief that French Canadians are clearly aware of the phonological differences between their language and standard French, but relatively unaware of the extent to which their syntax diverges from standard patterns. In this respect, the normative bulletins of the OLF may be serving a particularly valuable function.

In the preceding section, Ss were asked to consider specific topics and express objective opinions. The data which we are about to present represent an attempt to probe, in a more subtle manner, their subjective reactions to variations in speech style and to substantiate, if possible, some of the previous findings.

Voice data. The Ss listened to speech samples collected from upper- (UFC) and lower-class (LFC) French Canadian speakers and from standard European French (SEF) speakers. They listened first to samples of spontaneous conversation, then to the same speakers counting aloud from one to twenty. After listening to each sample, Ss were asked to evaluate the speaker using selected semantic differential adjective scales and to answer a series of questions about the person's speech style.

On the basis of previous research (e.g. Labov 1966, Lambert 1967), we predicted that significant interactions would occur between the occupational group of our Ss and the speech styles of the stimulus voices which they judged. Furthermore, we predicted that there would be significant main effects for speech style.

The first noteworthy finding is the fact that Ss differentially assigned occupations to the speakers on the basis of their speech style ($F = 245.99$, $df = 2/234$, $p < .01$). All Ss tended to rate SEF speakers higher on the occupational scale ($\bar{X} = 2.18$) than they rated the UFC ($\bar{X} = 3.30$) or the LFC speakers ($\bar{X} = 3.50$). They appeared to differentiate more clearly between European and Canadian speakers, in general, than they did between the UFC and LFC speakers. This pattern recurs with other measures. In addition, there was a significant group effect ($F = 4.17$, $df = 2/234$, $p < .05$) with the workers, in general, tending to rate all speakers lower on the occupational scale ($\bar{X} = 3.09$) than did the students ($\bar{X} = 2.96$) or the teachers ($\bar{X} = 2.94$).

A methodological problem may account for the fact that the distinctions between the UFC and the LFC speakers were not more pronounced. The differences might have been greater had the Ss been asked to make a dichotomous choice between clearly upper-class and clearly lower-class occupations (cf. Brown 1969). Furthermore, our attempt for purposes of this analysis to adapt Blishen's (1958) social class categories to a 7-point scale, including intermediary and perhaps ambiguous categories such as bank clerk and radio announcer, may have precluded our obtaining more clearly defined differences.

When making judgments after listening to the counting samples, the Ss again reacted differentially and appropriately. A significant main effect for speech style ($F = 579.03$, $df = 2/234$, $p < .01$) was obtained when the Ss were asked whether the speaker was likely to be a mailman, bus driver, or janitor. The SEF speakers were perceived as least likely to hold this type of occupation ($\bar{X} = 5.57$), with the UFC next ($\bar{X} = 3.36$), and the LFC perceived as most likely ($\bar{X} = 2.39$). Furthermore, there was a significant interaction between occupation and speech style ($F = 15.06$, $df = 4/234$, $p < .01$) which is shown in Figure 2.

A complementary set of findings emerged when the Ss were asked whether these same speakers were likely to be lawyers, professors, or dentists. Again, there was a significant main effect for speech style ($F = 632.47$, $df = 2/234$, $p < .01$) with the SEF speakers being perceived as most likely to have these occupations ($\bar{X} = 2.46$), followed by the UFC ($\bar{X} = 4.60$), and the LFC ($\bar{X} = 5.71$) speakers. There was also a significant interaction between occupation and speech style ($F = 10.08$, $df = 4/234$, $p < .01$) which is shown in

FIGURE 2. Significant interaction between occupation and speech style in Ss' ability to discriminate lower-class speakers.

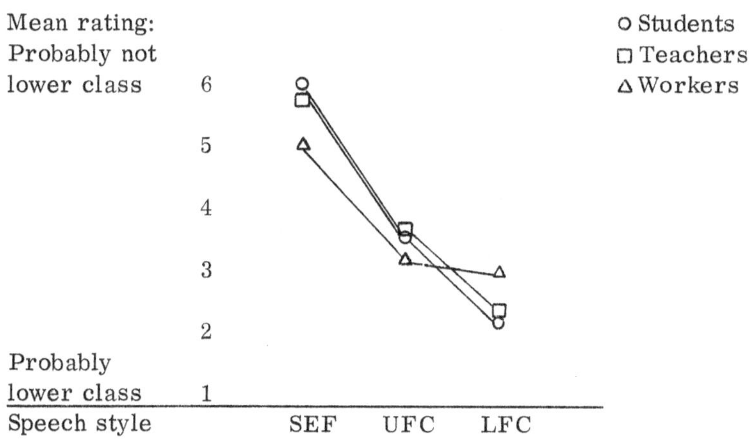

FIGURE 3. Significant interaction between occupation and speech style in Ss' ability to discriminate upper-class speakers.

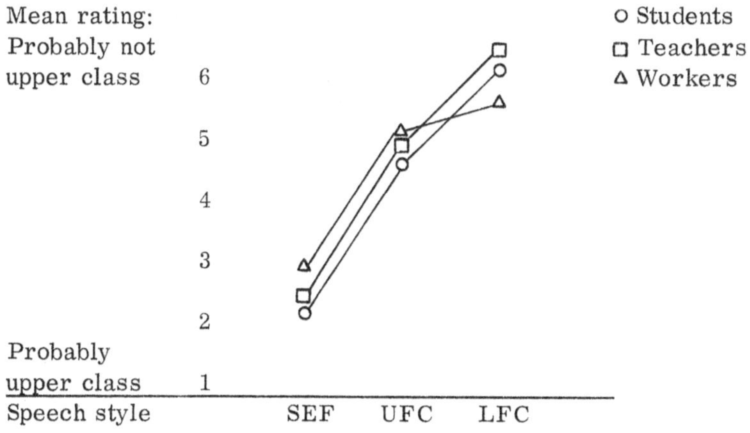

Figure 3. The patterns for these two significant interactions are remarkably similar. All Ss clearly discriminated between speakers on the basis of speech style although the workers appear to distinguish European from Canadian speakers while the students and teachers make finer discriminations among all three categories of speakers.

The Ss' reactions to the spontaneous speech samples revealed the existence of a powerful main effect attributable to speech style for all five adjective rating scales. The SEF speakers were consistently rated more intelligent, better educated, more likeable, more ambitious, and less tough than either the UFC or the LFC speakers. We had expected this pattern for the traits intelligent, educated, ambitious and tough; but we predicted that Ss would rate Canadian style speakers, particularly the UFC, as more likeable than the SEF speakers. This pattern, however, did not emerge. Quite to the contrary the Ss reacted more favorably to the European style of speech than to their own, a finding which complements the feelings of linguistic insecurity reported earlier. The mean ratings for each of the five adjective traits are as follows.

Trait	F ratio (2, 234 df)	$\overline{X}$ SEF	$\overline{X}$ UFC	$\overline{X}$ LFC
Intelligent	517.64	2.31	3.05	4.30
Educated	7999.99	2.02	3.13	4.95
Ambitious	276.07	3.09	3.68	4.77
Likeable	125.97	2.55	2.76	3.58
Tough	74.58	5.94	5.64	5.15

The next four questions probed the Ss general reactions to the speakers in a manner suggested by Labov (1966, 1967). Once again, we had predicted either significant main effects for speech style or significant occupation-speech style interactions. The Ss generally agreed that the speech style of the SEF speakers was most advantageous ($\overline{X} = 1.90$) followed by that of the UFC ($\overline{X} = 2.84$), and finally the LFC ($\overline{X} = 4.89$). The difference among these means was significant ($F = 816.55$, $df = 2/234$, $p < .01$).

In addition, there was a significant occupation-speech style interaction ($F = 3.60$, $df = 4/234$, $p < .01$) with the workers reacting slightly more favorably toward the LFC style, relative to the students and the workers, than they did toward the SEF or the UFC speakers. Moreover, when asked whether they would consider it personally advantageous to speak like any of the voice samples to which they had listened, the Ss again showed a unanimous preference for the SEF speakers ($F = 718.86$, $df = 2/234$, $p < .01$). The SEF speakers were rated most favorably ($\overline{X} = 2.36$), followed by the UFC ($\overline{X} = 3.30$), and then the LFC ($\overline{X} = 5.57$) speakers. Once again, there was a significant occupation-speech style interaction ($F = 5.52$, $df = 4/234$, $p < .01$). This interaction, shown in Figure 4 indicates that

FIGURE 4. Significant interaction between occupation and speech style in response to question: Trouvez-vous que ce serait un avantage pour vous de parler comme lui?

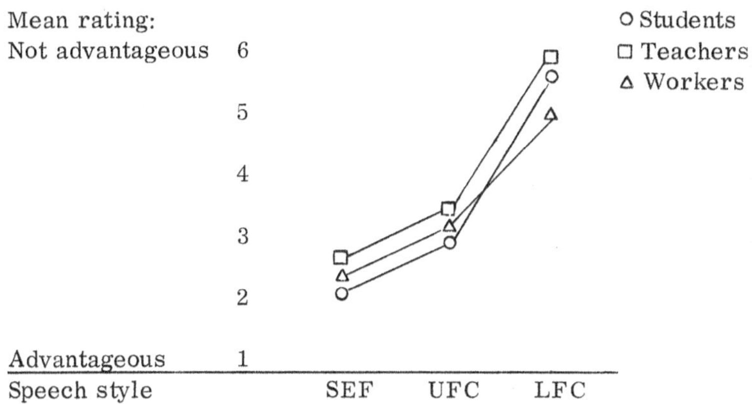

the workers perceived the LFC model to be relatively more favorable than did the teachers or students. This finding, together with the similar pattern observed previously suggests that although the workers view the SEF style of speech as an advantageous model, they feel that it could be relatively inappropriate in their own occupations. This finding certainly warrants further investigation.

Responses to the question 'Could this person be a friend of yours?' showed a significant main effect for speech style ($F = 160.11$, $df = 2/234$, $p < .01$) again pointing up the favorable reaction by all speakers to the SEF ($\bar{X} = 2.78$) and UFC ($\bar{X} = 2.74$) models in contrast to the LFC model ($\bar{X} = 4.00$). On this item, the judges made a clear distinction between educated and noneducated speech, but did not react differentially to the SEF and UFC models. The fact that the students rated the SEF voices less favorably than did either the teachers or workers, provides a hint that while they admire standard European French they might not completely accept it or identify with it.

Throughout this research, we have watched for evidence of linguistic insecurity and defensiveness in our Ss while hoping at the same time to discover whether Quebec style French could emerge as a symbol of national identity. We believe that we have uncovered a general malaise with respect to language which might well typify Ss such as ours who come from predominantly lower-class backgrounds. It may, however, also derive from the awareness, motivated by past and present speech improvement movements, that they speak a low prestige form of the language.

Accompanying this dissatisfaction with the way that they speak, we found a desire for correctness, for norms and for specific information regarding appropriate language usage. As Miner (1939) pointed out, French Canadians have been told for generations that they speak badly and have become apologetic about their speech. But previous speech improvement movements have failed to provide them with any practical means for effecting change. In this respect, we feel that the OLF may well come to play a valuable role in Quebec society although the present lack of objectivity and tendency toward negative value judgments which characterize some of its publications may not be conducive to building a positive self-image in the French Canadian people.

Among the Ss whom we studied, Quebec style speech does not yet appear to serve as a symbol of national identity differentiating French Canadians from other North Americans and also from European speakers of French. We speculated that they might reject SEF as a form of 'cultural imperialism' and show preference for the upper-class French Canadian model. They did not, and the consistent pattern of downgrading both UFC and LFC speech in favor of an SEF style reported by Lambert (1967) and by Brown (1969) again emerged.

While similar tendencies to downgrade their own group have been symptomatic of many minority groups in the United States, we have been unable to find indications of a trend toward an improved self-image comparable to that which has accompanied nationalistic movements among Black and Chicano groups. There are many incidental indications in contemporary Quebec which suggest that French Canadians do indeed have pride in their own language and culture as an entity distinct from that of France. Since the British conquest, they have clung to their language without the benefit of support from France; and a literary tradition distinctly different from that of France has grown up, with some writers choosing 'joual' as the most appropriate medium for expressing the realities of Quebec life (cf. Chantefort 1970). It seems surprising, therefore, that our Ss should indicate so great a willingness to abandon their own traditions and accept those of another cultural group.

A replication of this research, in perhaps five years, when people have had a greater exposure to SEF norms, would be interesting as a test of Labov's hypothesis that subjective evaluation often precedes changes in speech itself (1966). We accept the fact that the findings of this study may not be generalizable to other segments of French Canadian society. Furthermore, we must consider the possibility that our method and techniques did not allow us to assess validly the attitudes of our subjects. People are naturally sensitive about their language; French Canadians at present even more so than others. With these thoughts in mind, we hope to extend the study to other socioeconomic groups and to systematically vary both stimulus and response parameters.

Summary

The picture which emerges clearly from these data suggests an awareness of language variation on the part of French Canadian students, teachers, and workers from three disparate regions of Quebec. Furthermore, these Ss appear aware that there exists some undefined relationship between language and educational, occupational, and social mobility. They view language as a dynamic entity which can nevertheless be influenced by external forces.

The Ss perceive weaknesses in Quebec style French, particularly with respect to its phonology and lexicon; and they regard standard European French as the prestige form of the language. This dissatisfaction with the way that they speak appears to be accompanied by a desire for correctness, for norms, and for specific information regarding appropriate language usage to be supplied, ideally, by Canadians.

The results of this study suggest several important new research directions, and in addition provide baseline data against which to measure the effects of future changes in language policy.

NOTE

[1]We would like to thank Jack F. Griner, Jr., Director of Manufacturing, Frito-Lay Canada Ltd., for allowing us to interview workers in factories under his jurisdiction, and Roger Maréschal of Laval University who provided assistance in locating teachers and students for the study. We are grateful to Fernando Bravo-Ferrer and Réjean Racicot for their sensitivity and diligence in conducting the testing, and to Fred Silny who was responsible for the statistical analysis of the data. This research was supported in part, by grants from the Canada Council and the Defense Research Board to W. E. Lambert and G. R. Tucker.

REFERENCES

Agheyisi, R. and J. A. Fishman. 1970. Language attitude studies: a brief survey of methodological approaches. Anthropological Linguistics. 12.137-57.

Blishen, B. R. 1958. The construction and use of an occupational class scale. Canadian Journal of Economics and Political Science. 24.453-58.

Brown, B. L. 1969. The social psychology of variations in French Canadian speech styles. Unpublished doctoral dissertation, McGill University.

Cahiers de l'Office de la langue français, No. I. 1965. Norme de français écrit et parlé au Québec. Québec, Ministère des Affaires culturelles au Québec.

Chantefort, P. 1970. Diglossie au Québec: limites et tendances actuelles. Centre International de Recherches sur le Bilinguisme, Université Laval.

Charbonneau, R. 1955. Recherche d'une norme phonétique dans la région de Montréal. In: Etudes sur le parler français au Canada. Québec.

Chiasson-Lavoie, Michèle and Suzanne Laberge. 1971. Attitudes face au français parlé à Montréal et degré de conscience de variables linguistiques. Unpublished research paper, McGill University.

Denis, R. 1949. Les vingt siècles du français. Montréal, Fides. 359-77.

Ellis, D. S. 1967. Speech and social status in America. Social Forces. 45.431-37.

Ellis, P. M. 1965. Les phonèmes du français Maillardvillois. Canadian Journal of Linguistics. 13.94-98.

Gendron, J. D. 1966. Tendances phonétiques du français parlé au Canada. Paris, C. Klincksieck.

Giles, H. 1970. Evaluative reactions to accents. Educational Review. 22.211-27.

Halliday, M.A.K. 1968. The users and use of language. In: Readings in the sociology of language. Ed. by J. A. Fishman. The Hague, Mouton. 139-69.

Harmer, L. C. 1954. The French language today, its characteristics and tendencies. London, Hutchinson.

Labov, W. 1966. The social stratification of English in New York City. Washington, D.C., Center for Applied Linguistics.

_____. 1967. The effect of social mobility on linguistic behavior. In: Explorations in sociolinguistics. Ed. by S. Lieberson. The Hague, Mouton. 58-75.

Lambert, W. E. 1967. A social psychology of bilingualism. Journal of Social Issues. 23.91-109.

Lieberson, S. 1970. Language and ethnic relations in Canada. New York, Wiley.

Markel, N. N., R. M. Eisler, and H. W. Reese. 1967. Judging personality from dialect. Journal of Verbal Learning and Verbal Behavior. 6.33-35.

Miner, H. 1939. St. Denis, a French-Canadian parish. Chicago, University of Chicago Press.

Pinault, L. and L. Ladouceur. 1971. National language policies. Unpublished undergraduate research paper, McGill University.
Porter, J. 1958. Higher public servants in the bureaucratic elite in Canada. Canadian Journal of Economics and Political Science. 24.483-501.
Royal Commission on Bilingualism and Biculturalism. 1965. (Preliminary report). Ottawa, Queen's Printer.
Spilka, I. V. 1970. For a study of diglossia in French Canada. Unpublished mimeo, Université de Montréal.
Tucker, G. R. 1968. Judging personality from language use: a Filipino example. Philippine Sociological Review. 16.30-39.
Valin, R. 1970. Quel français devons-nous enseigner? In: Cahiers de l'Office de la langue française, No. 7. Québec, Gouvernement du Québec.

SOME RESEARCH NOTES ON DIALECT ATTITUDES AND STEREOTYPES

FREDERICK WILLIAMS

The University of Texas

The point has already been made by a number of researchers (e.g. Labov 1966, Shuy 1969, Williams 1970a) that linguistic attitudes are the other side of the social dialect coin. That is to say, if we have language features that are known to be correlated with the social stratification of speakers, then it seems plausible--and research has borne out--that such features may serve as cues in the listener's estimate of a speaker's social status. To date most studies in this area have placed the emphasis upon linguistic variables, or the features which are socially stratified, and how these variables may serve in attitudinal evaluations by listeners. In contrast, the aim of the present study is to examine some aspects of the attitudinal processes presumed to operate when persons make such judgments. Specific attention is given to the concept of social dialect stereotypes. My thesis is that, to varying degrees, persons have a stereotyped set of attitudes about social dialects and their speakers and these attitudes play a role in how a person perceives the cues in another person's speech. This paper (1) reviews a method for determining and measuring attitudes that some populations of teachers have reflected in their evaluations of children's speech, (2) summarizes how these measurements have been used to define operationally dialect stereotypes, and finally, (3) presents speculations on how the dialect stereotypes appear to enter into the processes of speech evaluations.

Attitude measurement. The chief measurement technique in the present series of studies is known as 'semantic differential' scaling. Typically a semantic differential scale involves the evaluation of a concept or stimulus by rating it on scales comprised of adjectival opposites. Thus, for example, a person might rate a speech sample in terms of the following scale:

fast ___:___:___:___:___:___:___ slow

If the respondent thought that the speaker sounded either extremely fast or slow, he would place a check mark in one of the extreme cells of the scale. He could indicate a lesser degree of extremity by marking in either of the second most extreme positions; the adjective quite is often used to identify these two cells. If the respondent evaluated the speaker as either somewhat fast or somewhat slow, he would mark either of the cells adjacent to the center of the scale. Finally if the intended rating is neutral or no judgment, the center cell is checked (sometimes persons are allowed to indicate no judgment simply by not marking the scale).

By having sets of such scales, it is possible to have a respondent rate multiple attitudes toward a stimulus; for example:

Speaker A:

fast ___:___:___:___:___:___:___ slow
unclear ___:___:___:___:___:___:___ clear
fluent ___:___:___:___:___:___:___ not fluent

Numbers can be assigned to the cells of the scales so that it is possible to convert check-mark responses into quantitative data and hence to calculate descriptive or inferential statistics. If, for example, we mark these scales with the digits '1' through '7', associating the '1' with the more favorable adjective in each of the above pairs, we might calculate that a group of people rating Speaker A and Speaker B show the following contrasts in their average evaluations:

	Speaker A	Speaker B
fast--slow:	3.6	4.1
clear--unclear:	2.9	2.8
fluent--not fluent	1.8	2.3

Beyond using averages to describe these evaluations, we could see, for example, whether the differences between the mean ratings for Speakers A and B on each scale were greater than would be expected by chance alone. In other words we would have a statistical basis for seeing whether there are statistically significant differences in the way Speakers A and B are evaluated by a given group of people.

It is possible to derive semantic scales empirically from a respondent population, and this was done at several points in the studies (Williams 1970b; Williams, Whitehead, and Miller 1971a, 1972) reflected in this paper. Briefly, the technique was to present small groups of respondents with audiotape or videotape speech samples, then to get persons to comment freely upon their impressions about the samples. In these studies the respondents were teachers or student teachers and the language samples from school children. The teachers were asked to describe their opinions of how well the child did in school, what his educational background seemed like, and what his speech and language seemed like. From these discussions, it was possible to identify adjectives that teachers typically used in talking about the children as well as the particular referends to which these adjectives were applied. Some sample scales developed in this way, although in a format slightly modified from that just presented, include:

The child seems:
hesitant ___:___:___:___:___:___:___ enthusiastic
The child sounds:
tense ___:___:___:___:___:___:___ relaxed
The child's family is probably:
low social status ___:___:___:___:___:___:___ high social status

At the first stages in the development of such scales, some fifty to sixty scales are usually prepared. Then by a program of pilot testing and various statistical methods used in scale development, it is possible to reduce the number of scales to those clusters of scales which seem to account for the most amount of differentiation among stimuli. Or, to put it more practically, scale development has allowed the identification of those clusters of scales that teachers seem to use the most in differentiating among different samples of children's speech.

In studies involving small groups of black and white teachers in Chicago (Williams 1970b), black and white teachers in Memphis (Williams and Shamo 1972), and black, white, and Mexican-American teachers in central Texas (Williams et al. 1971a, 1972; Williams, Whitehead, and Traupmann 1971) it has been found that two major clusters of scales account for the most amount of differentiation of children's speech samples. One of these clusters of scales has been made up of such adjective pairs as 'unsure--confident', 'active--passive', 'reticent--eager', and 'hesitant--enthusiastic'. Throughout the aforementioned studies clusters of this type have been interpreted as indexing an overall evaluation of a child's 'confidence-eagerness'. In other words, these scales taken together measure a global attitude by which the teachers differentiate children's speech. The subjective interpretation has been that evaluations on this dimension generally reflect the degree to which the child speaks continuously and fluently, carries the 'conversational ball' and reflects enthusiasm. Some objective evidence on this interpretation is that as the frequency of hesitation phenomena increases in speech samples, it can be mathematically demonstrated that the ratings of 'confidence-eagerness' tend to become more negative.

A second major cluster of scales found in the above studies was made up of such adjective pairs as 'standard American--marked ethnic style', 'White-like--non-white-like', 'low social status--high social status', and 'disadvantaged--advantaged'. This cluster in all of the preceding studies has been labeled as a broad evaluative dimension of 'ethnicity-nonstandardness'. Presumably evaluations on this dimension reflect the degree to which a child's speech characteristics are associated with low prestige markers, particular social status, or a particular ethnic group. It was found that to the degree that speech samples contained selected nonstandardizations (e.g., d for th substitutions, pronominal apposition, etc.), the more that the same samples were rated as sounding ethnic-nonstandard.

In a practical sense, the development of the above scales has provided a measurement technique for eliciting and eventually quantifying attitudinal evaluations of children's speech. In a more theoretical sense, it has indicated that among groups of teachers there seems to be a global two-dimensional framework for evaluation. In many of the reports mentioned above, it has been speculated that these two evaluative dimensions may be a reflection of at least two major dimensions of variations found in social dialect studies. There is the differentiation of the child's grammar (i.e. his linguistic system as manifested in performance), and this may be reflected in ratings of ethnicity-nonstandardness. There are variations in the fluency of performance using a particular grammar and this may be reflected mainly in the gross evaluations of 'confidence-eagerness'.

The two-dimensional model of 'ethnicity-nonstandardness' and 'confidence-eagerness' lends itself well for use in plotting graphic summaries of differentiations that respondents may make among different children. Figure 1 presents a two-dimensional plot where the mean ratings of children on 'ethnicity-nonstandardness' and 'confidence-eagerness' scales have been calculated, and where averages have been plotted in a two-dimensional space. The ratings in this figure are from a pilot phase of the Chicago research and involved teachers' evaluations of middle and low status white and black

FIGURE 1. Example of the two-dimensional plot of mean ratings.

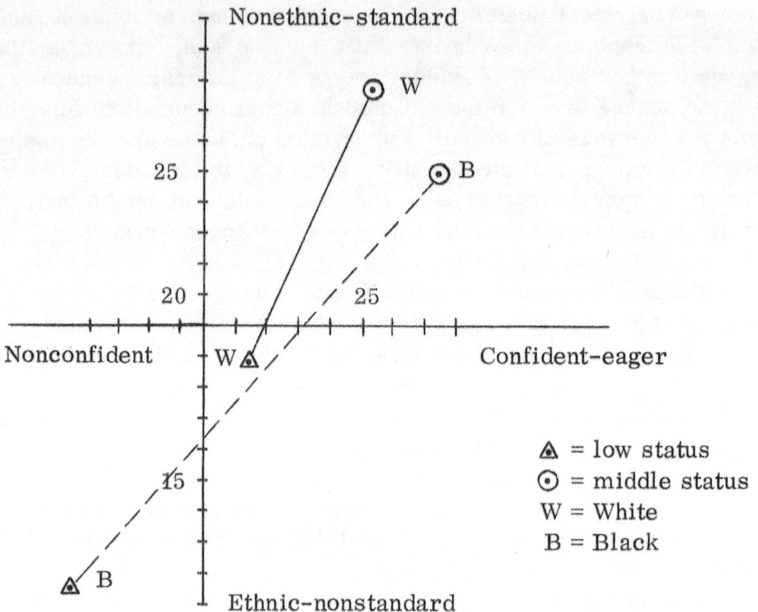

children. Each child had a set of ratings averaged across the respondents and the scales for each of the 'confidence-eagerness' and 'ethnicity-nonstandardness' dimensions. A point is then located on the diagram for the average ratings on these two dimensions for each of the stimuli. For example, the average ratings of middle class white children here were 27.5 on 'ethnicity-nonstandardness' and 25.2 in 'confidence-eagerness'. The intersection of those two coordinates in the two factor diagram defines the location of the plot for that stimulus. Note in Figure 1 how such plots provide for the simultaneous summary of the average ratings for the different stimuli on the two dimensions. Speaking more theoretically, we can say that the two-dimensional diagram is a model of the parameters of language or speech evaluation, at least in terms of the teacher populations studied.

The identification of stereotypes. The idea of measuring persons' stereotypes of particular dialects or speakers was arrived at in a somewhat backward way. A review of the literature of language evaluation studies (e.g. Shuy 1969) indicated that although some studies used very brief samples of speech (e.g. 3 to 10 seconds), it was often remarked that reliable ratings could be obtained with these samples.

In some unreported pilot studies by the present researcher, it was found that respondents would willingly fill in the rating scales not only for very short samples of speech but would also fill them in when simply told of a particular type of child who was to speak and where no tape was presented as a stimulus. This prompted the assumption that respondents were prone to employ an anticipation of attitudes (psychological set) toward a particular type of child and that these attitudes, if not prompted by a description of some type, would be elicited by the first relevant cues heard (or seen) in stimulus presentation. Such attitudes were assumed to reflect a 'stereotype'. The question, then, was what relation these stereotype attitudes had with ratings of speech samples. The next study focused upon this question.

Brief descriptions (Williams et al. 1971a) of low and middle status black, white, and Mexican-American children were presented to respondents as stimuli; and white student teachers were asked to evaluate children whom they associated with these descriptions on scales relative to the two-factor model described earlier. A sample of one such description, this referring to a low status Mexican-American child, is as follows:

> He is a Mexican-American boy who comes from a family of 10. His father is a gas station attendant. He lives in a lower class neighborhood.

In a preliminary evaluation session, respondents rated children associated with six such descriptions, representing low and middle status children from black, white, and Mexican-American groups in the central Texas area. Approximately one week after providing these ratings the group viewed and rated videotapes of children selected (by performance criteria) to represent the same six subgroups. Then at a period from three to five days after rating the videotapes, the respondents again evaluated stereotyped descriptions. This provided stereotyped descriptions rated at two different times and thus susceptible to comparison for consistency. The evaluations were a further basis for comparing the ratings of stereotype descriptions with ratings of samples of children's speech for representing the same categories. Figure 2 summarizes the results of the analysis of these data in terms of the two-factor model.

Note, first, in Figure 2 that for all three of the ethnic groups the stereotype evaluations obtained at two different times (m_1, m_2) were very consistent with one another. Note next that the stereotypes of the middle status children were always in the upper right-hand quandrant (indicating relatively high ratings on 'confidence-eagerness' and low ratings on 'ethnicity-nonstandardness') as against the lower status stereotypes appearing in the lower left quadrant, which reflected

FIGURE 2. Comparisons of stereotype and videotape ratings.

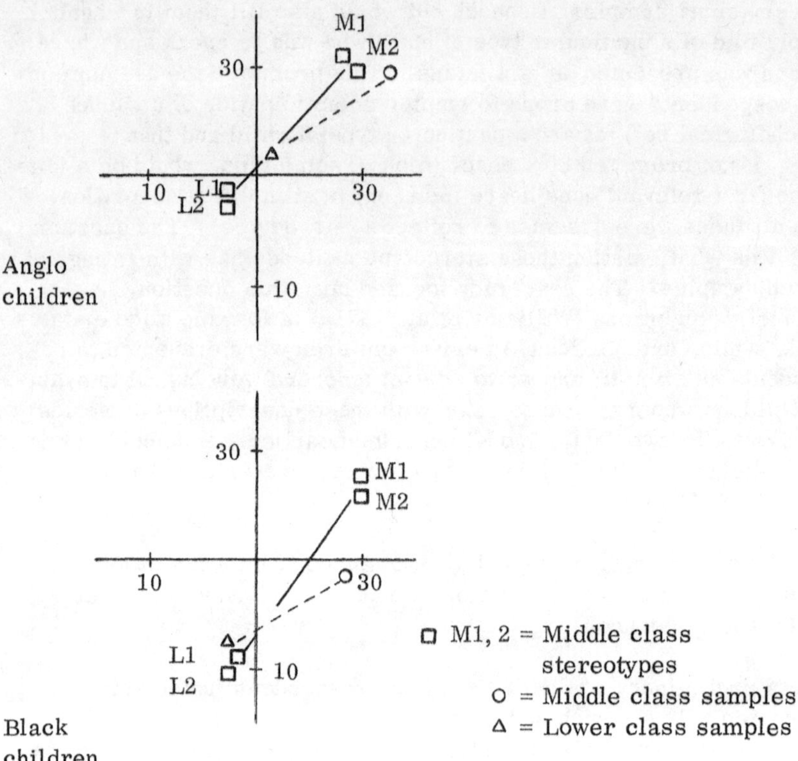

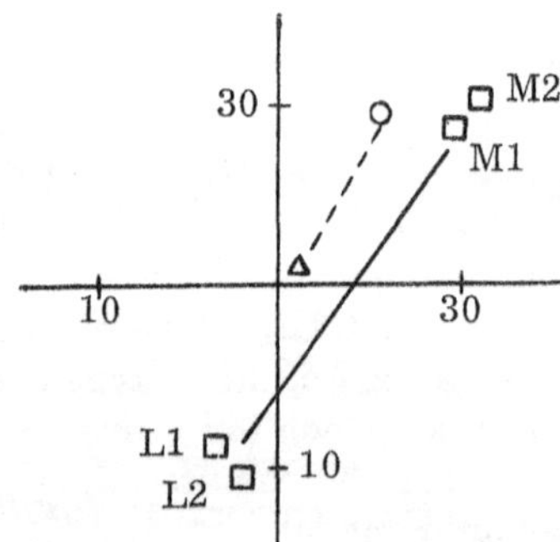

Mexican American
children

the opposite of the above ratings. Finally, it can be noted that for the most part, ratings of videotapes of the middle status and lower status children in each of the three ethnic groups tended in the direction of the stereotype ratings. There were exceptions to this; but such exceptions were usually only on one of the two dimensions. For example, on the ratings of the middle status black children, although the middle class videotape was rated as more 'ethnic-nonstandard' than was the stereotype, it was approximately the same as the stereotype in terms of confidence-eagerness.

The generalizations from this study were: (1) that one could readily obtain anticipated or stereotyped attitudes associated with a particular type of child, (2) that these would be consistent, (3) that they could be interpreted on the two-factor model, and (4) that they would show an interpretable relation with ratings of videotape samples.

A major problem in the study just described was that the verbal descriptions of the children used to elicit the stereotypes reflected directly on some of the scales relative to the two-factor model. In other words, the descriptions may have been sufficiently explicit so as to be more directly reflected in some of the scale ratings than they were a stimulus cue to have the individual respondent reflect his stereotype. Accordingly, in a further study (Williams, Whitehead, and Miller 1971a, 1972) it was found that ratings could be obtained simply by presenting a teacher with an ethnic label of a child and asking her to rate her experiences with, and anticipations of, children of that type. This time, the stimuli used to elicit stereotype ratings said nothing about status nor did they incorporate any adjectives which might directly influence the ratings. Figure 3 represents the stereotype evaluations of the labels 'anglo',[1] 'black', and 'Mexican-American' children as obtained from 125 white and 75 black teachers sampled from schools in central Texas.

At first it may be noted that these stereotypes are in somewhat different positions from those shown in Figure 2. This is anticipated because these stereotypes were not differentiated in their description by child status. Also some differences might be expected because these data came from groups of teachers practicing in the field, whereas the earlier data came from student teachers. In interpreting Figure 3, it can be noted that there is a general differentiation of the stereotypes of the three ethnic groups in the two-factor model, with the white children being located in the upper right quadrant, Mexican-Americans in the lower left, and black children tending toward the lower right. There is a greater differentiation between the white and black children's stereotypes in terms of 'ethnicity-nonstandardness' than in terms of 'confidence-eagerness'. The Mexican-American children's stereotypes were rated the least 'confident-eager' of all three groups, roughly similar to black children in terms of

FIGURE 3. Stereotype attitudes associated with 'anglo', 'black', and 'Mexican-American' children.

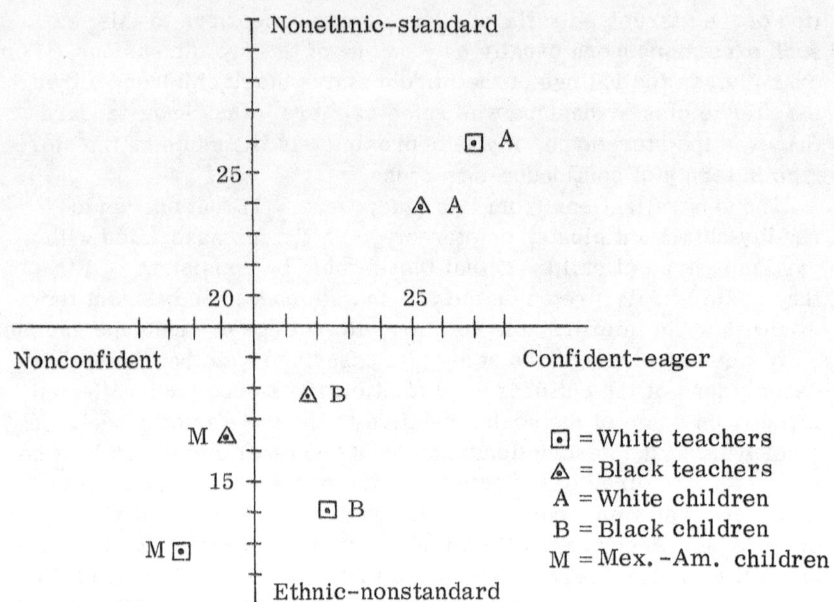

'ethnicity-nonstandardness' and markedly more 'ethnic-nonstandard' and less 'confident-eager' than the white children's stereotypes. It was evident, too, in this summary of stereotype ratings that the black and white teachers differed in their stereotypes. Black teachers tended to rate black children as less 'ethnic-nonstandard' than they were rated by white teachers. At the same time the black teachers rated white children as slightly more 'ethnic-nonstandard' and less 'confident-eager' than did white teachers. White teachers rated Mexican-American children as more 'ethnic-nonstandard' and slightly less 'confident-eager' than did black teachers.

By comparing the stereotype ratings with the ratings that the same groups of teachers gave of videotape samples of the speech of children from lower and middle status ethnic groups, it is possible to see how the stereotype related to different videotape ratings. Figure 4 is a summary of the low and middle status ratings of white children's videotapes by black and white teachers from central Texas schools. Note first that the videotape ratings all appear in the same quadrant as the stereotype ratings. More important is that the stereotype ratings have a tendency to stand between the middle and low status videotape ratings. For example, the geometric mean between the middle and the low status videotape ratings of anglo children by black teachers would almost perfectly define the location of the stereotype rating. The stereotype rating of white children by white teachers stands roughly between the two videotape ratings in terms of 'ethnicity-nonstandardness', but here the stereotype is rated as more 'confident-eager' than either of the videotapes.

The average ratings of the lower and middle status videotapes of black children are summarized in Figure 5. Here for both the ratings by black teachers and by white teachers the stereotyped rating falls almost at the mid point between the middle status and low status videotapes. In brief, the middle status tapes are rated more in the direction of 'nonethnic-sounding' and more 'confident-eager', as against the lower status tapes being rated the reverse of these from the stereotype. In this case, even more so than in the ratings of the white children, the videotapes of the different status groups tend to be differentiated away from the stereotype along a general diagonal direction that marks the patterns of differentiation in the model.

FIGURE 4. Ratings of white children's videotapes compared with stereotypes.

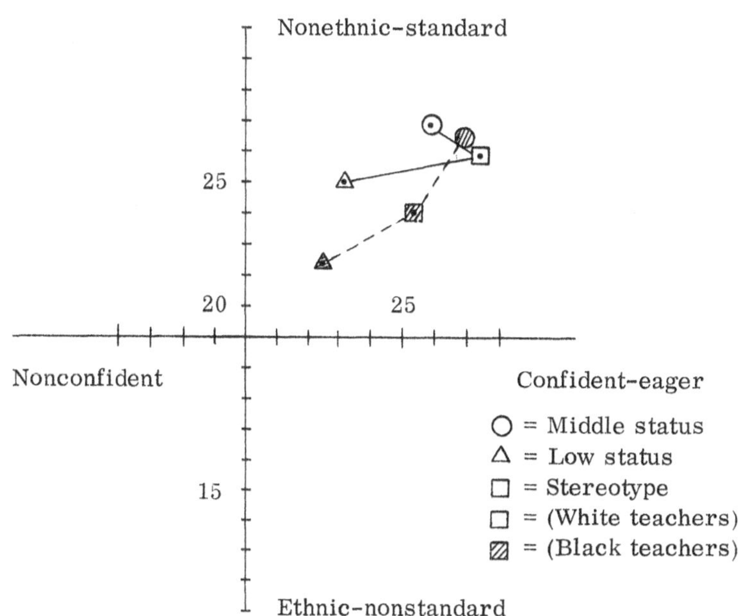

FIGURE 5. Ratings of black children's videotapes compared with stereotypes.

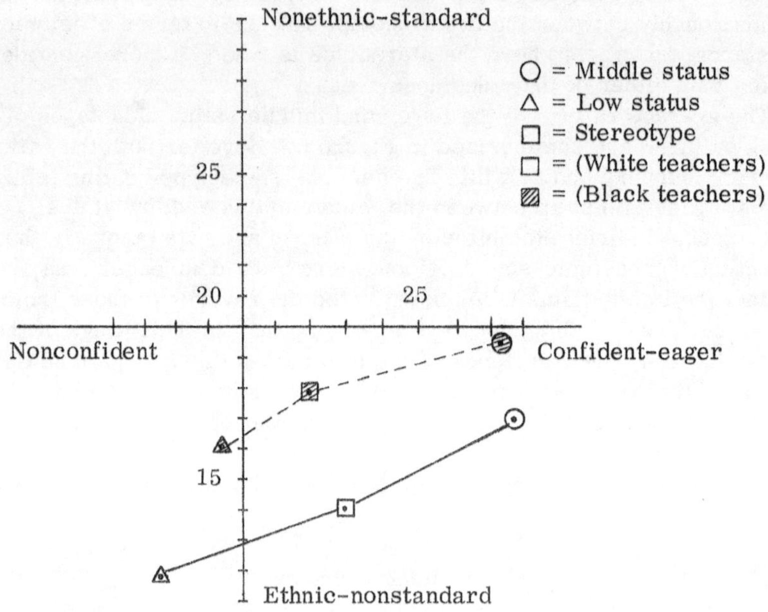

The videotape ratings of middle and lower status Mexican-American children and the stereotypes are summarized in Figure 6. Here there is no evidence of the stereotype standing between the middle status and lower status ratings of the children. In both cases of ratings by white teachers and black teachers the stereotypes are rated as less 'confident-eager' and more 'ethnic-nonstandard' than either of the tapes from the status groups. On the other hand, it can be noted that the middle and lower status tapes are differentiated from one another along the diagonal of the model. That is, the middle status tapes are rated as more 'confident-eager' and less 'ethnic-nonstandard' than the lower status opposites.

Some generalizations and speculations. In the stereotyping studies just described, it is evident that the stereotype judgments appear related to the judgments of speech samples. Although videotapes tend to show ratings that are biased in the same diagonal distribution as the stereotypes and even biased to the stereotypes themselves, the videotape ratings do not simply represent a person's report of the stereotype. Put another way, if a person's ratings of his speech stimuli were simply his stereotype or even extremely biased by his

FIGURE 6. Ratings of Mexican-American children's videotapes compared with stereotypes.

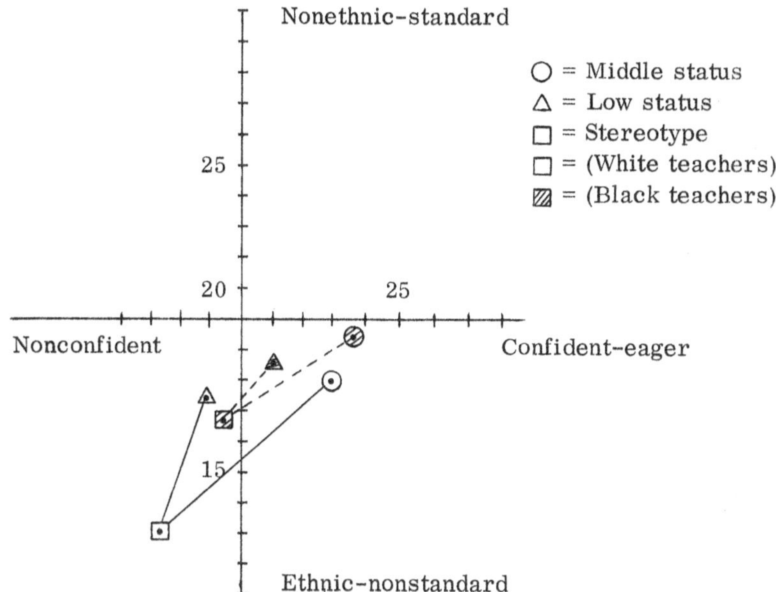

stereotype, we would expect to find the distribution of the videotape ratings on the two-factor model very close to those of the stereotype ratings. We find instead that the videotape ratings tend to be differentiated in a diagonal direction about the stereotypes. This is shown most clearly in the study just described, where the stereotype stimulus was simply a label of a child from a particular ethnic group, and the videotapes were chosen to represent status differentiations. Such status differentiations, with the exception of the Mexican-American children,[2] could almost be used to define or to predict the position of the stereotype. Or, by the same token, the stereotype could define, more or less, an anchor point about which videotapes are evaluated by the respondent.

In most of the considerations of the two-factor model prior to the stereotype research, it was assumed that persons provided attitudinal evaluations of children's audiotapes or videotapes by differentiating them relative to the neutral points on the model (or '20' in the preceding figures). That is, a child would be differentiated on 'ethnicity-nonstandardness' to the degree that the respondent would mark in cells away from the center (neutral) position on scales indexing that dimension, and would mark similarly for scales on 'confidence-eagerness'. The studies just discussed suggest that respondents may not differentiate the individual audiotape or videotape stimuli about the neutral point of the two-factor model, but instead may differentiate stimuli about a stereotype which is, more or less, an anchor point.

Of course, the present results do not unequivocally demonstrate that the stereotype is an anchor point; but they do offer quite suggestive evidence of it. The process of evaluation may be one where the stimulus may offer minimal cues which elicit a stereotype, then the stimulus is to various degrees differentiated by the respondent about the stereotype. This reasoning leads to a variety of implications. For one thing, it suggests that the teacher respondents do not evaluate children from different ethnic groups in a common way. Although it seems evident that the same two global dimensions of evaluation are used for the three ethnic groups of children, each child had a different 'starting point', so to speak, in how he was evaluated within the relative space of the two evaluative dimensions. Thus, for example, if a person's stereotype for black children tended to be biased in association with ethnic and nonstandard qualities and if the stereotype of the white child tended to be biased more toward the opposite extreme, it might be the case that the black child would have to sound more standard than the white child in order to obtain the same absolute rating. An alternative is that the respondent would have to free his or her ratings as much as possible from the stereotype bias that seems evident in the present studies.

Data from one further study (Williams, Whitehead, and Miller 1971b) show some evidence of how this bias may effect ratings. Figure 7 presents a plot of the average stereotype ratings by (white) student teachers of black, Mexican-American, and white children. It also presents the average ratings of three videotape presentations but where each had the same standard English audio track. The videotapes were side views of children whom could be seen speaking but whose utterances could not be lip read. Audio tracks of the standard English passage were dubbed onto the videotapes of the children from the three ethnic groups.[3] Note in Figure 7 that the same speech sample (the audio track) was rated quite differently depending upon which 'ethnic guise' it was presented with. Thus the black child with a standard English sound track was rated as more 'ethnic-nonstandard' than was the anglo child. The Mexican-American child is rated as markedly less 'confident-eager'. Of particular note, however, is that the biases in rating the standard English passage when paired with the two minority group children appear to be in the direction of the stereotype ratings of those two minority group children. The implication is that the visual image of the children on the tape served as an immediate cue of a type of child. This elicited a

FIGURE 7. Ratings of the same standard English audio samples with anglo, black, and Mexican-American video images.

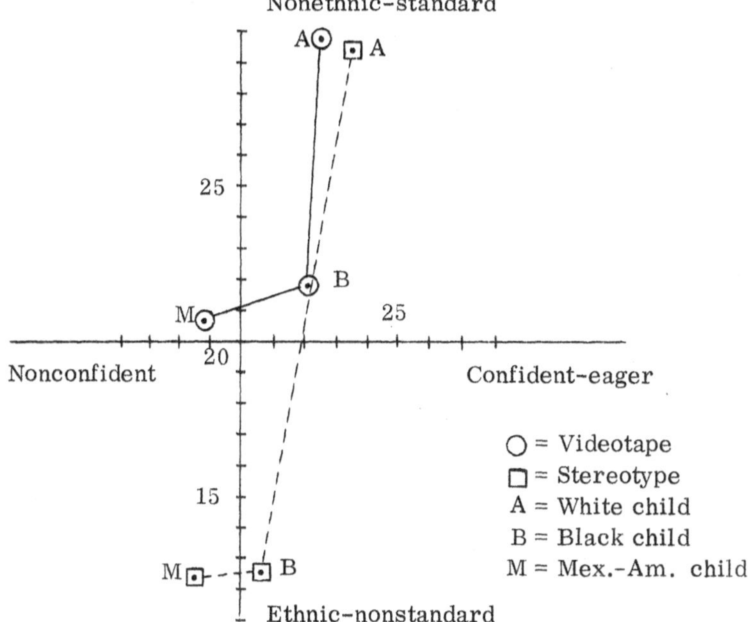

stereotype, and the presentation was judged relative to that stereotype. It is thought that this type of comparison represents the beginning of ways to test the degree to which ratings may be affected by manipulating the respondent's stereotypes. It is important to note, however, that this study only involved a relatively small group of student teachers and a limited number of stimuli. More important, some of the scales used in this research may apply equally well to the visual image as well as the audio track. Thus we can not assume that the respondent evaluates what is said as exactly distinct from what is seen. A further selection of scales that are more modality specific should aid in solving this problem in future studies.

At the outset of this paper it was said that my thesis was that persons have stereotyped sets of attitudes about dialects of speakers and that these attitudes play a role in how a person perceives another person's speech characteristics. Now stated more substantively, my thesis is that persons tend to employ stereotyped sets of attitudes as anchor points for their evaluation of whatever is presented to them as a sample of a person's speech. The description of this phenomenon in the present research is, of course, limited to the teacher and student populations which were sampled. My thesis is also limited at this point to the two-factor model of 'ethnicity-nonstandardness' and 'confidence-eagerness' which has been found in various groups of teachers. So, too, are the speech samples limited, mostly to standard English-speaking situations that could be classified as formal or semiformal. The extent to which this thesis of stereotyped attitudes affecting dialect perception would extend to other populations of evaluators, speakers, or speech situations, remains for further research. Fortunately, we appear to have the tools for that research.

NOTES

[1] The term for whites in central Texas.

[2] The exception of the Mexican-American children to this pattern between stereotypes and videotapes suggests some speculations. One is that the researchers' selection of the Mexican-American children for the videotapes was biased away from the stereotype--that is, they were more 'confident-eager' and nonethnic sounding than most respondents' stereotypes. Another speculation is that the stereotype of the Mexican-American child may be tied to the hesitancy of many of them to use English in formal situations and thus to say very little in teacher-pupil interactions; all of which might represent extremes in reticence and ethnic qualities to a white or black teacher.

[3] There were actually two standard English audio tracks used for each videotape; their average ratings are shown here. This was for research design requirements.

REFERENCES

Labov, W. 1966. The social stratification of English in New York City. Washington, D.C., Center for Applied Linguistics.

Shuy, R. 1969. Subjective judgments in sociolinguistic analysis. In: Linguistics and the teaching of standard English to speakers of other languages or dialects. Ed. by J. E. Alatis. Washington, D.C., Georgetown University.

Williams, F. 1970a. Language, attitude and social change. In: Language and poverty: perspectives on a theme. Ed. by F. Williams. Chicago, Markham.

_____. 1970b. Psychological correlates of speech characteristics: on sounding 'disadvantaged'. Journal of Speech and Hearing Research. 13.472-88.

_____, J. L. Whitehead, and L. M. Miller. 1971a. Attitudinal correlates of children's speech characteristics. USOE Research Report Project No. 0-0336.

Williams, F., J. L. Whitehead, and L. M. Miller. 1971b. Ethnic stereotyping and judgments of children's speech. Speech Monographs. 38.166-70.

_____, J. L. Whitehead, and J. Traupmann. 1971. Teachers' evaluations of children's speech. Speech Teacher. 20.247-54.

_____, J. L. Whitehead, and L. M. Miller. 1972. Relations between language attitudes and teacher expectancy. American Educational Research Journal.

_____ and W. A. Shamo. 1972. Regional variations in teachers' attitudes toward children's language. Central States Speech Journal.

ATTITUDES TOWARD SPANISH AND QUECHUA IN BILINGUAL PERU[1]

WOLFGANG WÖLCK

State University of New York at Buffalo

1.0. The language situation. Peru is, like all the other countries in South and Central America, a multilingual nation. As in the other cases, its multilingualism is primarily the result of contact between native American (Indian) languages and a colonial (European) language, and, to a lesser extent, between different indigenous languages. The Peruvian situation is unique in that this country contains within its national boundaries the main portion of the largest surviving native language group in the Americas. Quechua, as this language of the pre-colonial Inca empire is now commonly called, is still spoken by approximately seven million people in the Andean republics, with the bulk of its speakers in the southern and central Peruvian Andes mountains. According to the Peruvian national census of 1961, 40% of its total population of close to twelve million people speak Quechua as their first language. Of the other indigenous languages, only Aymara, the closest relative to Quechua, occupies by itself a clearly recognized slot, although with little more than 200,000 speakers it tends to be quantitatively overshadowed by Quechua. The multitude of languages spoken on the eastern slopes of the Andes and in the jungle area along the tributaries of the Amazon account for less than 100,000 people by the most generous assessment, the largest single component being the Campa, members of the Arawak family.[2] Among the Campa and Aymara, we find the largest number of bilinguals in indigenous languages, with Quechua as their second language. Moreover, trilingualism is quite frequent among these people through the addition of Spanish, the country's national language, to their reperotire. By far the most frequent point of contact, however, is clearly that between Spanish and Quechua: 20% of the total population above five years of age is said to be bilingual in Quechua and Spanish. This leaves about half the Quechua-speaking population monolingual and outside the socio-political life of that sector of Peru which would like to be considered representative of the role of this country in today's world.

The proportions become more extreme when we look at the Andean departments of Peru. There, as, e.g. in the Department of Ayacucho, Quechua is the mother tongue of 95%, Spanish of only 5%, of the population. Here, then, the proportion of bilinguals is somewhat higher than the national average, with a disproportion of two to one of men against women. The number of bilinguals is a little larger than, or equal to, the number of literates--with the same disproportion between males and females. In urban areas the percentages of bilinguals and literates are three times higher than in rural areas, where the proportion of literate males versus females often drops to three to one.

1.2. The Peruvian survey ('El Proyecto BQC'). Bilingualism--literacy--education--integration--is considered to be the safest route that promises to lead these 'marginated'[3] very sizable populations into bearable standards of living and that might even make them contribute to the country's GNP. Although Quechua had never been fully recognized or officialized on equal grounds with Spanish, it had always played some, however minor, role on the Peruvian educational scene. Recent governments and ministers of education have become increasingly more favorable toward 'bilingual education', i.e. using the native language of the Indian population as at least a means, if not a subject, of instruction to smooth the road toward literacy and further education. One such program started in 1964 under the auspices of the Plan for Linguistic Development of the Peruvian National University of San Marcos.[4] The results, though respectable, have been somewhat more modest than expected. In an effort to get to the roots of the problem, I was invited in early 1969 to begin a sociolinguistic survey of Quechua-Spanish bilingualism in Peru. The methodology of this project has been described in detail elsewhere.[5] As of this date, we have completed about 200 full-scale interviews in three locations, one a remote village in the Department of Ayacucho, another a district in the departmental capital of Ayacucho, and the most recent in the 'barriadas' of Lima, where we interviewed inmigrants from the first two locations. Most of the interviews were tape recorded and then transferred, i.e. abstrated, onto language background questionnaires. The responses are currently being tabulated and evaluated.

2.0. The attitude test. During the initial phase of the Project which began in the summer of 1969, while we were still largely involved in preparatory work for the general plan of the survey, we decided to devise a brief pretest or pilot study of language attitudes to be administered in our first two work sites. Besides developing and testing the instrument as such, one small immediate objective was the investigation of the validity of the two most current popular attitudes towards the language problem, which we shall call the 'hispanicist' and 'indigenist' attitudes, respectively. Extreme followers of the first position favor the speediest hispanicization of the non-Spanish speaking population over the retention of their own language, while the proponents of the latter doctrine tend to deny the usefulness or necessity of a knowledge of Spanish in their effort to preserve the native language and culture.[6]

The format we chose was that of a scaled instrument based on controlled language stimuli.[7] While we were quite aware of the separate tasks of preparing the stimuli and developing the rating scales, the importance of defining and selecting the evaluative terms for use in the instrument as a distinct job has become increasingly obvious since we began this study.[8]

2.1. The selection of the stimulus. To simulate as closely as possible the characteristics of conversational speech, we decided to use samples of connected free speech rather than isolated utterances as in the case of the Larsens' project. Carolyn and Vernon Larsen, of Social Science Research Associates in Chicago, were kind enough to let me see the materials they used in their study of reactions to black and white speech in Chicago.[9] Their study and its methodology clearly inspired this one. However, if isolated words are chosen as samples or stimuli, it is obviously only a very small subset of the phonological representations which can be at variance and will, therefore, be able to influence the judgment of the hearer. Yet it is most reasonable to assume that all levels of linguistic expression will be utilized by a hearer as diagnostic of the speaker's status, notably morphosyntactic features, lexical selection, ease of expression, articulatory distinctness, speed of delivery, and so on. The hearer should have access to all these potential variables when asked to judge another person's speech. Using connected speech, on the other hand, presents many problems that would not arise with isolated word stimuli. Some of the extra-linguistic variables in the message that might influence a rater's judgment are very difficult to control. The individual voice timbre can clearly not be neutralized. Others--

like contextual indicators of the speaker's status--can and must be eliminated from the passages used. Another important decision concerns the 'content' of the passages used for testing. Certain topics which might evoke different emotional reactions among different respondents and, therefore, influence their rating have to be avoided.

In addition, then, to insisting on as free as possible and continuous speech for our stimulus, we set up the following criteria for the choice of test passages. Some would apply to all stimuli used in attitude testing. Some, like the last, are specific to situations where cultural differences parallel linguistic ones.

(1) They should all have approximately the same content.

(2) The topic should be one of current validity, familiar to all speakers of the samples, and--possibly--the jury, to ensure ease and fluency in discussing it.

(3) The topic should have minimal emotional appeal. For example, choosing the description of a football (i.e. soccer) match in Latin America, even though it would satisfy criteria (1) and (2), might distract the rater from an evaluation of the speech sample to critical appraisal of the speaker's accuracy in reporting or interpreting the game. (Countries have been known to go to war over such matters.)

(4) The topic should be indigenous to both language communities, the Spanish and the Quechua-speaking group, and should be describable by a maximally independent vocabulary in both languages.

The topic which we eventually chose was bullfighting. Though it did not fulfill each separate criterion ideally, it combined a high degree of satisfaction over all of them.

Each speaker was asked to relate the events of a country bullfight which, by the way, is quite different from a Spanish-style bullfight as practiced in the Lima bullring. Country bullfights are an integral part of the independence-day celebration and are a free-for-all, fun-for-all event where anyone who has drunk himself into sufficient courage will confront the bull. Style and technique matter little, quite unlike the famous Spanish 'corrida'.

The bilingual test speakers were asked to describe the event in both Spanish and Quechua. We added a neutral specimen consisting of counting from 1 to 10, or 11 to 20, recorded for each speaker. Due to the rater fixed sequence of the events in the ceremony, it could be expected that the accounts would vary little in their content and its order. The recordings indeed showed many parallelisms, even though the informants had not received any special instructions beyond some general suggestions as to what we wanted them to talk about.

Besides the bullfighting stories, we recorded from each informant an account of a different event well-known in the area, a so-called 'pachamanca', which is a kind of picnic or cook-out with many libations, enjoyed among friends and family on special occasions. In terms of comparability or likeness of content, however, the 'corrida' was a much better topic.

The original recorded samples were left largely unedited. The only information that was cut out or masked over with played-in background noise concerned instances of possible explicit or implicit indicators of status. We also reduced extra-long pauses, although this may be objected to on the grounds that ease of expression is a possible index of status. All test samples were kept to approximately two and one-half minutes in length. If this required cuts, they were made at the beginning and/or the end of the original recording, where they coincided with paragraph or context boundaries. Within the sample no cuts were made unless it was to eliminate extralinguistic personal identifiers.

2.2. The informants. The speakers who produced the stimuli for the tests described here were chosen from two social and two linguistic groups. We used two Quechua-Spanish bilinguals of different social status, one of whom might be called a member of the middle class. He has a college education and comes from a moderately wealthy family. His parents are also bilingual. The other works as a driver and did not finish secondary school. His parents, who farm a small lot outside the departmental capital, know hardly any Spanish. He would be a member of the lower or lower middle class. The third speaker in this group was monolingual in Spanish and had spent only a few years in the area, working in the town's only large hotel as an accountant. He would also qualify for middle class membership. These three speakers were all males in their mid-twenties; two were interviewed by the same bilingual member of our team in Quechua, while I did the interviewing in Spanish. By situational criteria, the styles of the connected speech samples could be labeled informal, though not quite colloquial, rather like Joos's consultative style.[10] In age, average voice pitch, and volume, the speakers were very similar.

The total 'independent' controlled 'variables'--at least the ones we thought we controlled--in our stimuli were, then:

(1) the social class of the speaker,
(2) the language capacity of the speaker, i.e. whether he was monolingual or bilingual,
(3) the language used in the stimulus,
(4) the topic discussed in the stimulus passage.

2.3. The arrangement of the passages for testing. Up till now, we have worked with three different combinations of test passages. All our test tapes contain a total of six samples, each about two and one-half minutes long.

On the first test tape we had only two speakers, the higher- and the lower-class bilingual. We used passages in Spanish and Quechua from both, dealing with two different topics. In detail: In the first sample, the middle-class speaker talks about a picnic in Spanish; in the second, the lower-class speaker relates part of a bullfight in Quechua; in the third, the higher-class speaker does the same; in the fourth, the lower-class speaker describes the bullfight in Spanish; the fifth has the higher-class speaker depicting a bullfight in Spanish; the sixth and last is another two and one-half minute portion taken from the lower-class speaker's account of the bullfight in Quechua. It is distinct from the earlier, second passage on the tape, though only minimally, as the same speaker is talking about the same topic in the same language.

2.3.1. Variation of topic and consistency check. The rationale behind the topic variation was to see whether and how it would affect the response. The results, after tabulation and evaluation of the responses, showed that it did not.

Samples 2 and 6 were kept minimally distinct in content to avoid possible recognition of the speaker's identity by the audience. The purpose of introducing two near-identical samples was to test the jury's consistency in rating. This turned out to be an unnecessary precaution. No juror seemed to be aware that any one speaker was being used more than once. Even those who seemed to have noticed that some speaker had appeared more than once could not be specific about their hunches. On the basis of these results, we changed the arrangement on our second test tape and substituted an identical replay of the second sample--the lower-class speaker's bullfight story in Quechua--for the last sample as a better instrument for a consistency or reliability measure. In our latest re-arrangement of the test tape, we also discarded passage one, the only one left with a topic other than bullfighting, and put a recording of the middle-class monolingual's Spanish account of the bullfight in its place. On this test tape, then, the topic was invariant, and we had samples from three speakers--one from the middle-class monolingual in Spanish, and one each in Spanish and in Quechua from both the middle-class and the lower-class bilingual, with a repetition of the lower-class Quechua sample.

2.4. The rating scales. In devising a rating scale, we adopted the semantic differential technique as originally developed by Osgood and associates for cognitive studies,[11] together with an occupational suitability scale.

2.4.1. Semantic differential. In trying to establish the validity of a certain pair of polar terms for diagnostic purposes, we relied mostly on common, locally frequent concepts of evaluation and designation. Through observation and testing of associations, we first singled out a large number of apparently useful epithets. Reasons for later elimination of some were mostly of two kinds: One was that a common evaluative term turned out to vary too much in associations or that it had regionally distinct connotations, as was the case with the well-known Latin(-American) simpâtico, which to our surprise seems to refer exclusively to external attractiveness in the Peruvian Andes. Another reason was the impossibility of finding a parametrical antonym for a good term to make up a useful pair, as in the case of forastero for a non-local person or indio, where no good contrast exists. Negating the positive is no really good solution, although we sometimes used this way out, as in 'responsable--irresponsable', which is still better than 'amable--no-amable', while negation of adjectives and nouns in Spanish in this manner might even be rejected for reasons of grammaticality. We eventually decided upon the fifteen pairs of adjectives and nouns that can be found in the Appendix. An English translation of the terms is provided there.

The terms used in the scales were not chosen, or classified, by any other criteria like 'power versus solidarity',[12] 'cognitive versus affective', or any other such classificatory or general semantic notions.

Most of the concepts and attributes on the list will be reasonably clear. The English glosses, though they do not evoke associations completely identical to the Spanish, may help a little. One pair, though, definitely needs further comment. This is the distinction cholo--decente. Although its popular connotation is clearly negative, the anthropologist's neutral scientific use of the term cholo might help illustrate its meaning. The social anthropologist distinguishes between Indians, Cholos, and Mestizos by cultural integration and nativistic loyalty (Linton's term).[13] Thus cholo refers to a person who has left the Indian culture and has not yet been integrated into the Western, Spanish-speaking Mestizo culture. Popular usage collapses Indian and Cholo under the latter term, abstracting only the negative features in its employment. The term is emotionally loaded. Cholo, no estas en la sierra is the worst rapping a Limeño will give to another who steps out of line, as, for example, disturbing traffic through bad driving, or the like. Decentre, on the other hand, is the opposite of cholo in social status connotation. It implies being educated, respected, having adequate knowledge of Spanish.

The introduction of language competence scales (pairs B and K) was intended to serve as a preliminary subjective assessment of degrees of bilingualism.

2.4.2. The occupational suitability scale. Again, all the occupations selected for inclusion are well known to the juries which judged our samples. In deciding about distinctiveness, consistency of rating and ranking, we first presented a random list of over twenty occupations for hierarchical ranking to a large number of subjects (see Appendix). We selected those with a sufficiently small range of fluctuation. Certain seemingly clear cases turned out to be very ambiguous, as, for instance, hacendado, which to the rural poor would only mean a big landowner, while higher-class members would understand it as meaning any farmer, big or small. Chacarero, on the other hand--which, incidentally, is a Quechua loanword--refers usually to a small subsistence farmer.

A curious marginal result of this ranking poll was that female rankers would put jobs that are more indicative of material wealth first, before those involving intellectual prestige or academic training; the males would rank the other way around.

The hierarchical ascending scale of twelve occupations (see Appendix) was what we ended up with for the time being. It should be read top to bottom in left to right column sequence.

2.5.1. Administration of the test. The testing pad consisted of six identical rating sheets, one for each of the six test stimuli on the tape; an instruction sheet on top as introduction; and a personal data sheet at the end. Plus and minus sides of the pairs were randomly scrambled to avoid the possible suggestion of directionality to the respondent (see Appendix). We chose a six-interval scale, forcing the respondents to make a choice or leave a line blank. Odd-number interval scales leave the option of undecidedness, which may be different from the rater's decision not to respond to a certain pair at all. During the administration of the test, each stimulus was played to the responding audience or jury only once, sufficient time allowed for checking on the rating sheet, and then on to the next stimulus.

2.5.2. The respondents. Our raters, or jurors, were final-grade primary school boys, high school students, university students, and a small group of teachers--all male, with the exception of a few women teachers.

2.5.3. Tabulation of responses. The very first step in processing consisted of transferring the ratings of each stimulus separately onto a table with the pairs and occupations listed horizontally, the respondents vertically, and ratings being indicated by the number checked on each scale, i.e. a value between 0 and 5.

The next job was calculating the consistency of ratings for each respondent by comparing his responses to the two identical stimuli, number 2 and number 6. For our present purposes, we considered anyone with a higher average than 1.0 difference between the responses to the two identical passages as potentially unreliable for the other ratings. From the tables of individual ratings per stimulus, averages can be computed for any defined set of respondents. Such an average rating of a certain stimulus can then be plotted for each pair on an evaluation sheet where all contrasts are listed in the same direction, i.e. negatives on the left, positives on the right. The Appendix includes such 'profiles', shown as contrasting pairs on two scoring sheets.

3.0. Some test results. Before going into more detail, we would like to mention a general result which emerged immediately after the first tabulations, even though it may not be theoretically surprising. The terms on our scales fell neatly into two groups by differential reactions to the two sets. One set included the terms with some sort of institutional reference, like 'low-class--high class', 'educated--uneducated', 'urban--rural', while pairs with more emotive or associative value like 'ugly--pretty', 'weak--strong', 'kind--unkind', made up the other set. This post factum reinstatement of Osgood's classification (cognitive-affective) may be of some importance.

3.1. Language and social status. The profiles in the Appendix are plotted from the reactions to two Spanish stimuli by a class of male university students in their early twenties. The double line there shows their rating of the lower-class speaker's Spanish; the single line is for the middle-class speaker. The result that is typical of all the audiences we have worked with is that the higher-class speaker is given a clearly superior rating in the majority of cases, notably in those with a clear referent, like 'campo--ciudad' (rural--urban), 'empleado--jefe' (worker--boss), low-class--high-class, educated--uneducated, or on the occupational scale. The tendency for the lower-class speaker to come out relatively better on the affective judgment is already evident here, in the ranking of his Spanish performance. It comes out clearly in such pairs as 'amable--no amable', 'responsable--irresponsable'.

3.2. Quechua versus Spanish. Probably the most interesting result is the affective loyalty to Quechua which becomes evident when we compare the profiles of the responses to the same speaker's performances in Quechua and in Spanish (see Appendix). In this case the double line denotes Spanish, the single one Quechua. His Spanish always receives a higher ranking on the referential scale, i.e. higher-class, urban, more educated, than his Quechua. The rating by the affective criteria, however, shows a clear preference for Quechua. When speaking Quechua, he is rated stronger, more sincere, less arrogant, more ambitious, smarter, than when he speaks Spanish.

The results of the test indicate that, by identifiable social status criteria, Quechua is stigmatized but that there is, nevertheless, a great deal of native loyalty shown to the language, borne out on the affective scales.

3.3. Language competence. Another important bit of evidence, borne out by the reaction of all respondents alike, concerns the concept of linguistic competence measured by the pairs referring to knowledge of Quechua and Spanish, respectively (pairs B and K). First--and this might have been predicted--the lower-class speaker's Spanish was rated as inferior to the higher-class informant's, but--and this is curious--his Quechua was also rated poorer than the higher-status speaker's. The seemingly strange request for the knowledge of Quechua to be rated even if Spanish was spoken, and vice versa, gave most interesting though perhaps not entirely surprising results: When the lower-class speaker was using Spanish, he received an equal or higher ranking on knowledge of Quechua than when he spoke Quechua. His Quechua, on the other hand, was rated only minimally lower than his Spanish on the 'knowledge-of-Spanish' criterion. The higher-class speaker, conversely, received a low rating on Quechua when he spoke Spanish, and a similarly low rating on Spanish when he spoke Quechua.

When speaking Spanish, Speaker 1 (Spanish-Quechua bilingual) and Speaker 3 (Spanish monolingual) received equally low ratings on the knowledge-of-Quechua scale, Speaker 2 (low-class bilingual) a much higher rating than either 1 or 3. The lower-class bilingual's Quechua seems to have little societal value in the response of hearers. While it makes his Spanish worse, it does not help his Quechua performance any. That is, at least, the superficial impression. The linguist, however, will see in these results an interesting indication of grammatical integration: The grammar of the lower-class bilingual is obviously simpler in terms of identifying and collapsing more rules of the two systems into one, besides substituting more lexical items in both directions (or only in one), while the better educated bilingual has a much less fused grammar. The established concept and interpretation of 'interference'[14] does not seem to fit this bilingual situation, but may have to be complemented and, in this instance, replaced by the process which, for the time being, we have called 'fusion'.[15]

3.4. Differences between groups of raters.

3.4.1. Degree of bilingualism. The stablest bilinguals showed the least difference between ratings of Spanish and Quechua stimuli on the 'referential' scales. There appears to be an inverse proportion between the degree of bilingualism and the status differentiation between the two languages. Language dominance, whether Quechua or Spanish happens to be the dominant language, seems to have little effect on this principle. If plotted in a diagram, the curve showing the proportion between the degree of bilingualism and the evaluative status distinction between the two languages would approach the following form:

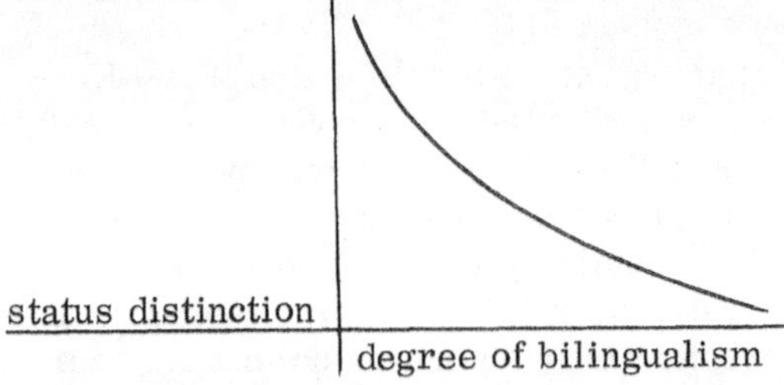

On the 'affective' scale, there is a gradual decrease in the amount of positive evaluation of Quechua the more heavily Spanish-dominant the bilinguals are:

(1) The Quechua-dominant bilinguals rate Quechua as less lazy or more industrious, smarter, stronger, more honest, less arrogant, more pleasant or kinder, nicer ('amable'), i.e. more positively on practically all the affective scales.
(2) The stable or matched bilinguals ('ambilinguals') show distinct positive evaluation for Quechua only on the strength, amiability, and smartness scales.
(3) The Spanish-dominant group shows a differential rating that is positive for Quechua only on the strength and attractiveness ('bonito') scales. On most of the other affective markers the two languages come very close; on the 'lazy-ambitious' scale there is even a change-over in favor of Spanish. Quechua seems to be rated here only as an aboriginal culture with its rather stereotyped epithets of being 'earthy' and 'quaint'.

3.4.2. Quechua speakers versus non-Quechua speakers. In only one jury, the one composed of university students, were we able to separate the Quechua speakers' from the non-Quechua speakers' reactions. In general, the results of this comparison conformed pretty much to the tendencies already observed as accompanying an increase in the dominance of the Spanish language, of which Spanish monolingualism may here be considered the end point.

One prominent difference, however, exists in the accuracy of the evaluation of linguistic competence of the bilingual speakers. The Quechua-Spanish bilinguals among our respondents showed a high and accurate degree of sensitivity to bilingual interference with regard to both languages, the monolinguals much less so.[16] The bilinguals were also much more sensitive to class dialects or styles within Quechua. They ranked the higher-class speaker clearly into the 'decente' range, even when he spoke Quechua, while for the monolinguals he was simply a 'cholo'.

To the bilinguals, the higher-class speaker is suspect, even when he speaks Quechua. He is less amiable ('amable') than the lower-class speaker, whereas the monolinguals rate the opposite way; the same is true for the arrogance scale.

NOTES

[1]An earlier report on this study was delivered at the 1970 meeting of the International Linguistics Association. The research reported in this paper was supported by a Latin American Studies grant from the Ford Foundation, an Indiana University Summer Faculty Fellowship, and by funds from the 'Plan de Fomento Lingüístico' of the Universidad Nacional Mayor de San Marcos in Lima, Peru. I am grateful to the current director of the Plan de Fomento Lingüístico, Dr. Inés Pozzi-Escot, and to its former director, Dr. Alberto Escobar, for their cooperation and encouragement. Any credit for this work I have to share with my Peruvian and North American research associates.

[2]These and later figures are based on the reports of the Sexto Censo Nacional de Población de 1961, Lima: Instituto Nacional de Planificación, Dirección Nacional de Estadística y Censos, 1965-1970; in particular on the following volumes: III: Idioma, alfabetismo, asistencia escolar, nivel de educación. Centros poblados I: Amazonas, Ancash, Apurimac, Arequipa, Ayacucho, and on the special volume for the Department of Ayacucho (in preparation; the tables were made available to us). Figures for 'jungle' languages are from C. F. and F. M. Voegelin: Languages of the World: Native America, Anthropological Linguistics, vol. 6, no. 6 (1964) and vol. 7, no. 7 (1965) and from information received from the staff of the Summer Institute of Linguistics in Peru. For location and classification see also

Čestmír Loukotka, Classification of South American indian languages, Los Angeles, University of California, 1968.

[3]A gloss attempting to capture the flavor of the official Peruvian euphemism commonly applied to these people, 'marginado', pushed to the margin, i.e. left out.

[4]Descriptions of this program are Inés Pozzi-Escot: La Educación rural en el Peru: El problema de los quechua-hablantes, Actas del Primer Seminario de Investigación y Ensenanza de la Lingüística, Concepción 1971:99-104, and her paper, La situacion lingüística en el Peru y su repercusión en la enseñanza del castellano, read at the First International Workshop in Andean Linguistics in Buffalo, New York, August 1971. Another program of bilingual education is being undertaken by members of the Summer Institute of Linguistics. Cf. Donald Burns, Bilingual education in the Andes of Peru. In: Language problems of developing nations. Ed. by J. A. Fishman, C. A. Ferguson, and J. Das Gupta. New York, John Wiley, 1968:403-13, and his Cinco anos de educacion bilingue en los Andes del Perú, report presented to the First International Workshop in Andean Linguistics, Buffalo 1971.

[5]See W. Wölck, El Proyecto BQC: Metodología de una encuesta sociolingüística sobre el bilingüismo Quechua-Castellano. In: Lingüística e indigenismo moderno de América. Ed. by G. J. Parker, A. G. Lozano, and R. Ravines. Estudios presentados al XXXIX Congreso Internacional de Americanistas, Lima (in press); and Teoría y práctica de la encuesta sociolingüística, in Proceedings of the 6th Symposium of the Interamerican Program for Linguistics and Language Teaching, San Juan (Puerto Rico) 1971.

[6]Cf. the debates in the proceedings of the Mesa redonda sobre el monolinguismo Quechua y Aymara y la educación en el Perú. Documentos Regionales de la Etnohistoria Andina 2. Lima, Casa de la Cultura, 1966.

[7]For a critical summary and bibliography of some of the practices in attitude testing, see Rebecca Agheyisi and Joshua A. Fishman: Language attitude studies: a brief survey of methodological approaches, Anthropological Linguistics. 12(5).137-57 (1970).

[8]See W. Wölck, Language as a basis for social attitudes, paper presented during the Sociolinguistics Forum of the 1971 Linguistic Institute.

[9]Vernon S. and Carolyn H. Larsen, Reactions to pronunciations, part of: Language barriers to communication. Chicago Sociolinguistics Project. (mimeographed) (1967).

[10]Cf. Martin Joos, The isolation of styles. In: Monograph Series on Languages and Linguistics No. 12 (10th Annual Round Table). Washington, D.C., Georgetown University Press, 1959, pp. 107ff.,

and The five clocks, Bloomington, Indiana, Research Center for Anthropology, Folklore, and Linguistics, Publication 22, 1962.

[11]Charles E. Osgood, G. J. Suci, and P. H. Tannenbaum, The measurement of meaning. Urbana, University of Illinois Press, 1957.

[12]As used by Joan Rubin, Bilingual use in Paraguay. In: Readings in the sociology of language. Ed. by J. A. Fishman. The Hague, Mouton, 1968:512ff.

[13]Ralph Linton, Nativistic movements, American Anthropologist. 45.230-40 (1943).

[14]As defined in Uriel Weinreich, Languages in contact. The Hague, Mouton, 3rd pr. 1964.

[15]In W. Wölck, Interference or fusion? A new look at the bilingual's grammar. To be presented at the 11th International Linguistics Congress.

[16]This parallels and again confirms Labov's observation of the high sensitivity on the part of the users of certain stigmatized forms to the occurrence of such forms in others, bearing out their 'linguistic insecurity'. Cf. William Labov, The social stratification of English in New York City. Washington, D. C., Center for Applied Linguistics, 1966, chaps, XI and XII.

APPENDIX

I. Scoring pad

Desearíamos saber lo que Usted piensa acerca del habla (conversación) o de las personal que hablan, luego de escucharlas a través de cintas grabadas. No interesa la historia, sólo el habla y la persona que habla.

Instruciones. A. Damos una lista de pares de palabras contrarias con seis espacios entre ellas. Usted puede marcar su opinión con un aspa (X) en el espacio que mejor corresponda a la realidad.

Suponiendo que el par de palabras sea 'agradable--desagradable' luego de escuchar la cinta grabada si le parece: Muy agradable puede marcar así:

Agradable _X:___:___:___:___:___ Desagradable

Si le parece más o menos agradable puede marcar así:

Agradable ___:_X:___:___:___:___ Desagradable

Si le pareco poco agradable puede marcar así:

Agradable ___:___:_X_:___:___:___ Desagradable

Si le parece muy desagradable puede marcar así:
Agradable ___:___:___:___:___:_X_ Desagradable
Si le parece más o menos desagradable puede marcar así:
Agradable ___:___:___:___:_X_:___ Desagradable
Si le parec poco desagradable puede marcar así:
Agradable ___:___:___:_X_:___:___ Desagradable

Advertencias.
(1) Sólo debe haber un aspa entre dos pares de palabras.
(2) Sólo una vez se va a escuchar la cinta grabada.
(3) Hay una hoja para cada ejemplo de habla en la cinta grabada.

Les agradecemos su atención y colaboración y les pedimos que en la última hoja dé su nombre y otros datos que necesitamos.

Ejemplo número ___*

A.

feo ___:___:___:___:___:___ bonito
sabe quechua ___:___:___:___:___:___ no sabe quechua
empleado ___:___:___:___:___:___ jefe
fuerte ___:___:___:___:___:___ débil
ciudad ___:___:___:___:___:___ campo
mentriroso ___:___:___:___:___:___ sincero
clase alta ___:___:___:___:___:___ clase baja
amable ___:___:___:___:___:___ no amable
humilde ___:___:___:___:___:___ prepotente
sabe castellano ___:___:___:___:___:___ no sabe castellano
ambicioso ___:___:___:___:___:___ flojo
cholo ___:___:___:___:___:___ decente
sabido ___:___:___:___:___:___ tonto
irresponsable ___:___:___:___:___:___ responsable
ignorante ___:___:___:___:___:___ educado

B. Ocupación

_____ peón _____ empleado
_____ obrero _____ negociante
_____ chacarero _____ maestro
_____ artesano _____ sanitario
_____ chofer _____ abogado
_____ albañil _____ médico

*Identico para ejemplos nos. 2-6.

____________________	____________________	____________________
Nombre	Apellido Paterno	Apellido Materno

Edad________________ Sexo___________

Centro de enseñanza____
Año______________________ Grado de Instrucción__________________
Profesor____
Dirección____
Lugar de Nacimiento____
¿Sabe Ud. Quechua? Sí_____ No _____
Ocupación del padre____
Viajes realizados (A dónde? ¿Por cuánto tiempo?)___________________
____
Fecha__________________

II. Ranking list of occupations

1. médico	2. aboqado	3. maestro
4. fabricante	5. empleado	6. sanitario
7. chofer	8. albañil	9. hacendado
10. artesano	11. obrero	12. negociante
13. mozo	14. peón	15. chacarero

III. Attitude profiles (Univ. Nac. San Cristobal de Huamarga, Ayacucho, Jury)

Language: Spanish
Speaker I: Middle class; Speaker II: Lower middle class

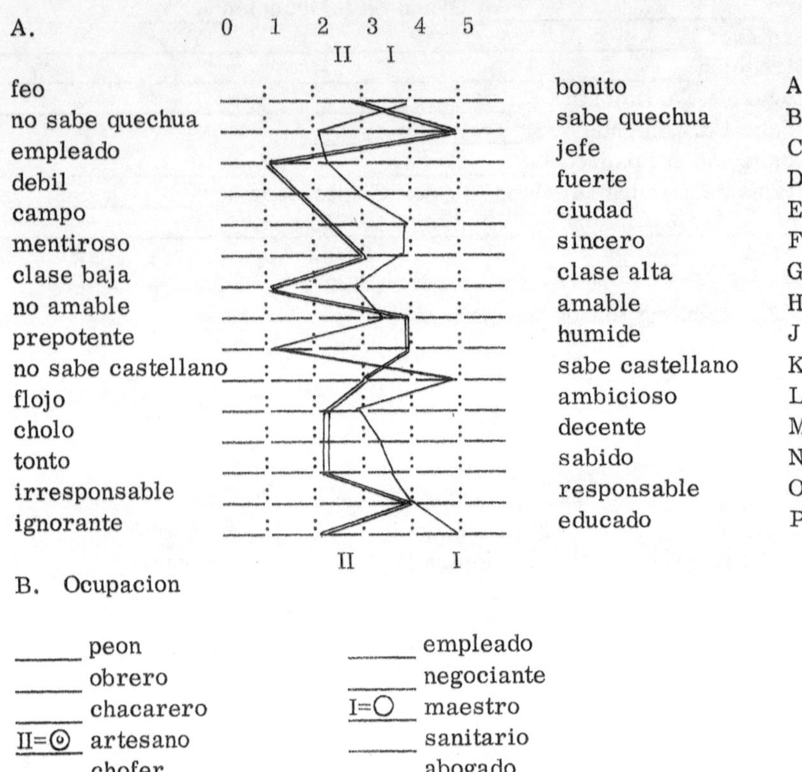

B. Ocupacion

____	peon	____	empleado
____	obrero	____	negociante
____	chacarero	I=○	maestro
II=⊙	artesano	____	sanitario
____	chofer	____	abogado
____	albañil	____	medico

Jury: Univ. students (UNSCH)

Stimuli: Quechua (—) and Spanish (=) by lower middle class speaker

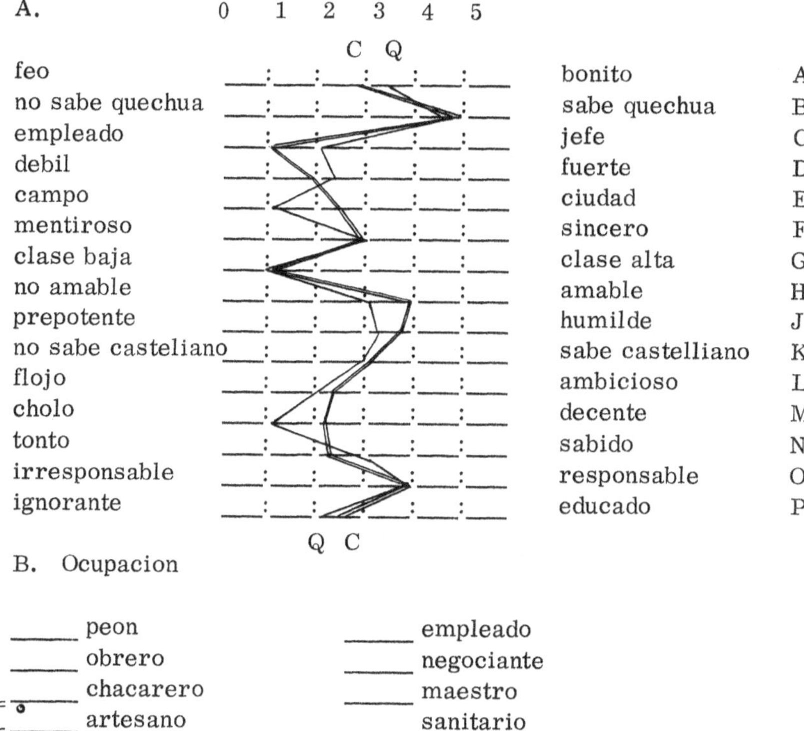

B. Ocupacion

_____ peon	_____ empleado
_____ obrero	_____ negociante
_____ chacarero	_____ maestro
Q= ◦ C= _____ artesano	_____ sanitario
⊙ _____ chofer	_____ abogado
_____ albañil	_____ medico

A.

ugly	pretty	A
does not know Quechua	knows Quechua	B
employee	boss	C
weak	strong	D
country	city	E
dishonest	honest	F
lower class	higher class	G
unpleasant	pleasant	H
arrogant	unassuming	J
does not know Spanish	knows Spanish	K
lazy	ambitious	L
'cholo'	'decent folk'	M
dumb	smart	N
irresponsible	responsible	O
uneducated	educated	P

B.

peon	employee
workman	merchant
peasant	health officer
artesan	teacher
driver	lawyer
brick mason	doctor

TEACHERS' ATTITUDES TOWARD BLACK AND NONSTANDARD ENGLISH AS MEASURED BY THE LANGUAGE ATTITUDE SCALE[1]

ORLANDO L. TAYLOR

Federal City College and Center for Applied Linguistics

Introduction. Teachers' handling of classroom language problems, especially those occurring in classrooms with large numbers of 'nonstandard' speakers, is probably influenced greatly by their attitudes toward a number of topics, including language and cultural differences. Because of this, the claim could be made that language interaction between teachers and students in schools with substantial black and other minority group children would be better understood by comparing teachers' actions with their professed attitudes toward nonstandard language generally, and Black English in particular. Despite admitted problems in obtaining the 'true' feelings of people on any subject, it is possible that language attitude data can assist in determining some of the underlying bases of classroom language problems related to language differences.

One approach used by the author to assess teachers' attitudes on language differences has involved the development and administration of a Language Attitude Scale (LAS). The scale was designed to solicit data on what teachers think about nonstandard and Black English, and how (or if) this dialect should be used in the classroom.

Description of LAS. LAS is a Lickert-type scaling instrument. As such, it involves self-evaluation of opinions, in five gradations, on a set of language statements.[2]

There are two forms of LAS. Each form contains twenty-five items distributed as follows across four content categories:

	# Pro Black English items	# Con Black English items
(1) The structure and inherent usefulness of nonstandard and Black English dialects	4	4
(2) Consequences of using and accepting nonstandard and Black English in the educational setting	4	4
(3) Philosophies concerning the use and acceptance of nonstandard and Black English dialects	4	4
(4) Cognitive and intellectual abilities of speakers or speakers of nonstandard and Black English	—	1
Total	12	13

The items on each of the forms were selected from an initial pool of 117 items as a function of their ability to discriminate teachers with positive Black English attitudes from those with negative Black English attitudes. Judgments of item sensitivity were made following administration of the 117 items to a group of 186 teachers from throughout the United States on the basis of response patterns on each item of the most Pro Black English teachers (top 25%) versus those of the most Con Black English teachers (bottom 25%). Score differences between these two extreme groups were analyzed by means of the t-test. All of the items selected for the two forms of LAS elicited statistically significant response differences at or beyond the .05 confidence level and, indeed, were among those items which elicited the highest t-scores for all of the items within a given content and Pro Black English/Con Black English category. Also, t-values for items were closely matched across forms of LAS. The twenty-five items selected for each form of LAS, together with their t-values, are presented as a function of the four content categories in Tables 1 and 2.[3]

For statistical purposes, an arbitrary scoring system was adopted for coding subjects' responses to LAS items. The system assigned numerical values to responses as follows:

(a) 1 point for strong disagreement with a positive statement;
(b) 2 points for mild disagreement with a positive statement;
(c) 5 points for strong agreement with a positive statement;
(d) 4 points for mild agreement with a positive statement;
(e) 1 point for strong agreement with a negative statement;
(f) 2 points for mild agreement with a negative statement;
(g) 5 points for strong disagreement with a negative statement;
(h) 4 points for mild disagreement with a negative statement; and
(i) 3 points for any no opinion response.

Administration of LAS to a nationwide group of teachers. Numerous assertions have been made about teachers' attitudes toward language behavior and variety, especially as related to Black English. To date, no controlled study has been reported which discusses, in-depth, teachers' attitudes on the various questions which might be related to the topic of nonstandard and Black English. Further, teachers' attitudes on these subjects have not been presented as a function of such variables as race, sex, age, geography, teaching experience, grade taught, etc. LAS was administered to a large cross section of teachers to obtain data of these types.

Methodology

Subjects. A total of 422 teachers were selected for the survey in the following manner. First, one rural and one large urban school system were randomly picked from each of nine Federal Census districts--New England, Middle Atlantic, South Atlantic, East North Central, East South Central, West North Central, West South Central, Mountain, and Pacific.[4] Second, at least twenty teachers (ten males and ten females) were selected in each of the settings in such a way that the racial and cultural compositions of the communities were reflected.

Materials. Form 1 of the Language Attitude Scale was administered to all teachers in the presentation order indicated in Table 3.

Scoring. Ss' responses to each LAS item were scored as described above.

TABLE 1. Items for Form 1 of LAS and their t-values as a function of content and Pro/Con Black English categories.

Content and Pro/Con Black English categories	t-values	Statements
1+	11.4320	Black English sounds as good as Standard English
	7.6299	Black English is cool.
1-	10.8797	Black English is an inferior language system.
	8.1893	Black English is too imprecise to be an effective means of communication.
2+	10.7057	The encouragement of Black English would be beneficial to our national interests.
	10.8535	Societal acceptance of Black English is important for development of self-esteem among black people.
	12.1888	When teachers reject the native language of a student, they do him great harm.
	13.3329	If use of Black English were encouraged, speakers of Black English would be more motivated to achieve academically.
2-	9.4058	It would be detrimental to our country's social welfare if use of Black English became socially acceptable.
	9.2400	The continued use of a nonstandard dialect of English accomplishes nothing worthwhile for an individual.
	10.0289	Allowing and accepting the use of nonstandard English in the classroom will retard the academic progress of of the class.
	8.6754	A decline in the use of nonstandard English dialects would have a positive influence on social unity.

TABLE 1. Continued.

Content and Pro/Con Black English categories	t-values	Statements
3+	10.7609	There is much danger involved in accepting Black English.
	13.3749	Widespread acceptance of Black English is imperative.
	10.0014	A child should not be corrected by teachers for speaking his native non-standard dialect.
	9.4497	We should encourage the continued use of nonstandard English dialects.
3-	10.5426	It is ridiculous to encourage children to speak Black English.
	11.3447	One of the goals of the American school system should be the standardization of the English language.
	9.7386	Teachers have a duty to insure that students do not speak nonstandard dialects of English in the classroom.
	14.6180	Black English should be discouraged.
4-	7.9709	A black child's use of Black English thwarts his ability to learn.

TABLE 2. Items for Form 2 of LAS and their t-values as a function of content and Pro/Con Black English categories.

Content and Pro/Con Black English categories	t-values	Statements
1+	9.8320	Black English is a clear, thoughtful, and expressive language.
	8.8513	Nonstandard English is as effective for communication as is Standard English.
1-	10.3585	Black English is a poorly structured system of language.
	8.5710	Complex concepts cannot be expressed easily through nonstandard dialects like Black English.
2+	10.7042	Black English should be encouraged because it is an important part of black cultural identity.
	11.1051	Acceptance of Black English by teachers is vitally necessary for the welfare of the country.
	12.0885	To reject Black English is to reject an important aspect of the self-identity of black people.
	13.0718	Attempts to eliminate Black English in schools results in a situation which can be psychologically damaging to black children.
2-	9.9305	Continued usage of nonstandard dialects of English would accomplish nothing worthwhile for society.
	9.0287	Allowing Black English to be spoken in schools will undermine the schools' reputation.
	12.8343	The scholastic level of a school will fall if teachers allow Black English to be spoken.
	6.0698	The elimination of nonstandard dialects of English is necessary for social stability.

TABLE 2. Continued.

Content and Pro/Con Black English categories	t-values	Statements
3+	10.6665	In a predominantly black school, Black English as well as Standard English should be taught.
	13.5259	Nonstandard English should be accepted socially.
	10.5426	Teachers should allow black students to use Black English in the classroom.
	8.9206	Teachers should avoid criticism of nonstandard dialects of English.
3-	10.5593	The sooner we eliminate Black English, the better.
	11.0097	The sooner we eliminate nonstandard dialects of English, the better.
	10.4839	The possible benefits to be gained from approval of Black English do not alter the fact that such approval would be basically wrong.
	13.9351	A teacher should correct a student's use of Nonstandard English.
4-	7.9740	Children who speak only Black English lack certain basic concepts such as plurality and negation.

TABLE 3. Randomized presentation order for LAS, Form 1.

Content and Pro/Con Black English categories	Number	Statements
2-	1	The scholastic level of a school will fall if teachers allow Black English to be spoken.
1-	2	Black English is a misuse of Standard English.
2+	3	Attempts to eliminate Black English in school result in a situation which can be psychologically damaging to black children.
2-	4	Continued usage of a nonstandard dialect of English would accomplish nothing worthwhile for society.
1-	5	Black English sounds as good as Standard English.
3+	6	Teachers should allow black students to use Black English in the classroom.
3-	7	Black English should be discouraged.
2+	8	Black English must be accepted if pride is to develop among black people.
1-	9	Black English is an inferior language system.
1+	10	Black English is cool.
2-	11	Black English should be considered a bad influence on American culture and civilization.
1-	12	Black English sounds sloppy.
2+	13	If use of Black English were encouraged, speakers of Black English would be more motivated to achieve academically.
1+	14	Black English is a clear, thoughtful, and expressive language.
1-	15	Black English has a faulty grammar system.
2+	16	When teachers reject the native language of a student, they do him great harm.

TABLE 3. Continued.

Content and Pro/Con Black English categories	Number	Statements
3-	17	A teacher should correct a student's use of Nonstandard English.
3+	18	In a predominantly black school, Black English as well as Standard English should be taught.
3+	19	Widespread acceptance of Black English is imperative.
3-	20	The sooner we eliminate nonstandard dialects of English, the better.
2-	21	Acceptance of nonstandard dialects of English by teachers will lead to a lowering of standards in schools.
3+	22	Nonstandard English should be accepted socially.
1+	23	Nonstandard English is as effective for communication as is Standard English.
3-	24	One of the goals of the American school system should be the standardization of the English language.
4-	25	One successful method for improving the learning capacity of speakers of Black English would be to replace their dialect with Standard English.

Data analysis. Teachers' responses were analyzed as a function of the following variables:

(1) geographical location of teaching assignment
(2) sex
(3) race
(4) field(s) of college degree(s)
(5) number of years of teaching experience
(6) grade assignment
(7) racial composition of school
(8) parents' education

Teachers' responses were submitted to a cross-tabulation computer program which allowed the viewing of each variable as a function of any other variable or group of variables. Means were then computed for each content category and the above variables to reveal the relative frequency-of-occurrence of responses in each of the five response categories.

The distribution of means across the five response categories was analyzed for each content category as a function of the sub-variables of the above variables by means of the Kolmogorov-Smirnov Test one sample. Following this operation, the Kolmogorov-Smirnov Test (two sample) was used to compare the distribution of scores across response categories for selected sub-variables of variables.

Results

Results obtained from the nationwide teacher survey are presented in Tables 4 and 5. The data are summarized as a function of each Content Category. The summaries for each category include statements on (1) the overall response pattern, (2) statistically significant main effects, and (3) statistically significant differences between selected sub-variables of main effects.

Content Category 1: Structure of Nonstandard and Black English. As shown in Table 4, there was a relatively equal distribution of teachers in the five response categories. In general, the pattern showed that 40% of the teachers responded in the two positive response categories; 40% responded in the negative response categories; and 20% revealed a neutral attitude.

Table 4 also shows that teachers in the South Atlantic rural area had significantly more negative than positive attitudes to statements in Category 1. Pacific Urban teachers, on the other hand, had significantly more positive than negative attitudes to statements in this category. None of the other geographical sub-variables was significant.

In terms of the race of teachers, black teachers revealed significantly more positive than negative attitudes toward statements in Category 1. Similarly, teachers from schools which were predominantly black had significantly more positive than negative responses. However, teachers from predominantly white schools indicated significantly more negative than positive attitudes.

Responses as a function of field of degree, years of teaching, grade taught, sex of teacher, and parents' education showed essentially flat curves with very similar proportions of Ss responding in each of the five response categories. Thus, none of the sub-variables in these areas produced significant differences in response patterns.

TABLE 4. Mean percentage of teachers responding to statements in four Content Categories as a function of biographical variables and response categories; and results of Kolmogorov-Smirnov one-sample test.

Key: N = Number of observations per variable.
* = Distribution of scores significantly different from chance.

Response categories:
Con BE = Con Black English
M Con BE = Mildly Con Black English
M Pro BE = Mildly Pro Black English
Pro BE = Pro Black English

Geography:
SA-U = South Atlantic--Urban
MA-U = Middle Atlantic--Urban
ENC-U = East North Central--Urban
ESC-U = East South Central--Urban
WNC-R = West North Central--Rural
SA-R = South Atlantic--Rural
ENC-R = East North Central--Rural
P-U = Pacific--Urban
NE-R = North East--Rural

Content Category 1: Structure and inherent usefulness of Nonstandard English Dialects

		Response categories:					Kolmogorov-Smirnov One-sample test	
Variables	N	Con BE	M Con BE	Neither	M Pro BE	Pro BE	D	p
Overall		20.7	18.3	20.5	17.9	22.3	.02	NS
Geography								
SA-U	46	18.5	18.6	22.0	17.2	23.7	.037	NS
MA-U	36	13.4	23.7	21.8	18.0	23.2	.066	NS
ENC-U	84	24.9	20.6	22.3	18.4	13.9	.078	NS
ESC-U	30	24.8	17.9	20.0	16.9	20.5	.048	NS
WNC-R	21	9.2	26.8	28.0	20.8	13.4	.049	NS
*SA-R	37	53.7	11.6	16.5	11.5	6.7	.108	.05
ENC-R	13	34.9	29.0	10.7	15.6	9.8	.337	NS
*P-U	150	12.9	15.4	19.8	19.7	32.3	.149	.05
NE-R	6	4.2	14.6	18.8	22.9	39.6	.122	NS
Sex								
Male	80	20.3	24.6	17.4	18.0	19.7	.224	NS
Female	342	20.9	16.8	21.3	18.0	23.0	.049	NS

TABLE 4. Continued.

Variables	N	Con BE	M Con BE	Neither	M Pro BE	Pro BE	Kolmogorov-Smirnov one-sample test D	p
Race								
*Black	111	18.0	14.9	21.7	16.5	28.9	.129	.05
White	281	21.1	20.5	20.2	18.5	19.7	.018	NS
Oriental	17	23.0	10.3	20.0	18.6	28.1	.081	NS
Field								
Education	238	20.1	18.9	21.8	17.6	21.0	.024	NS
Arts-Science	35	19.0	18.5	24.6	15.5	22.4	.025	NS
Law	2	6.3	37.5	12.5	12.5	30.7	.137	NS
Business	9	33.4	19.4	8.7	16.8	18.2	.134	NS
Years teaching								
Under 1	32	14.2	15.8	22.5	20.6	26.9	.109	NS
1-2	51	14.6	18.6	18.8	18.5	29.6	.095	NS
3-5	68	15.3	14.5	23.2	18.8	28.2	.102	NS
6-10	76	25.0	19.4	18.9	16.3	20.4	.050	NS
10 years	176	25.3	19.9	20.5	17.2	17.2	.053	NS
Grade taught								
1st	178	11.3	20.5	19.4	17.7	28.6	.111	NS
2nd	40	23.0	15.2	20.6	18.3	23.0	.030	NS
3rd	38	18.9	22.3	23.1	18.5	17.2	.043	NS
4th	33	24.7	11.5	22.2	16.9	25.4	.047	NS
5th	39	15.8	22.6	18.8	20.7	22.2	.042	NS
6th	34	20.9	19.8	19.8	19.1	20.8	.009	NS
7th	5	10.0	21.9	23.8	26.3	18.1	.010	NS
8th	8	43.8	9.4	21.9	6.3	18.8	.238	NS
9th	6	59.2	19.6	15.0	0	6.3	.039	NS
10th	15	27.7	19.1	15.5	19.6	18.1	.077	NS
11th	19	37.5	20.2	16.9	16.1	9.3	.177	NS
12th	20	38.8	17.5	12.5	17.5	13.8	.188	NS
Gen. Elem.	23	13.4	19.9	26.1	19.9	20.0	.067	NS
Gen. High Sch.	1	0	0	62.5	0	37.5	.400	NS
Speech	1	0	0	12.5	25.0	62.5	.400	NS
Reading	4	9.4	27.0	38.5	9.4	15.6	.149	NS
Racial composition of school								
*Predominantly black	179	17.6	14.5	20.0	17.3	30.6	.106	.05
*Predominantly white	143	29.4	22.3	19.8	17.7	10.9	.115	.05
Mixed	48	10.8	19.9	21.3	21.4	26.7	.107	NS

TABLE 4. Continued.

Variables	N	Response categories: Con BE	M Con BE	Neither	M Pro BE	Pro BE	Kolmogorov-Smirnov one-sample test D	p
Parents' education								
High school graduate	129	18.6	15.3	23.5	19.4	23.1	.61	NS
BA/BS	60	25.6	17.4	20.2	16.7	20.1	.051	NS
Graduate degree	39	13.3	16.7	24.4	15.6	30.0	.100	NS
Content Category 2: Consequences of using and accepting Nonstandard English dialects in the educational setting								
Overall		13.3	12.1	17.5	24.6	32.5	.172	NS
Geography								
SA-U	46	12.7	11.9	19.9	22.6	35.5	.55	NS
MA-U	36	8.7	15.4	17.9	20.6	37.3	.180	NS
ENC-U	84	15.6	16.2	17.3	28.0	21.8	.109	NS
ESC-U	30	14.8	11.9	18.2	29.3	25.8	.051	NS
*WNC-R	21	4.8	10.1	13.7	45.2	26.2	.314	.05
SA-R	37	40.1	14.4	21.9	9.9	13.7	.201	NS
ENC-R	13	14.4	23.9	19.2	25.9	16.2	.056	NS
*P-U	150	7.7	8.2	15.3	24.1	44.7	.241	.05
NE-R	6	6.3	4.2	16.7	18.8	54.2	.328	NS
Sex								
*Male	80	12.2	15.3	16.6	23.5	32.4	.159	.05
*Female	342	13.6	11.4	17.8	24.9	32.4	.172	.05
Race								
*Black	111	12.7	9.4	18.3	20.8	38.9	.204	.05
*White	281	12.6	13.7	17.4	26.3	30.0	.163	.05
Oriental	17	16.3	5.2	17.8	22.5	38.2	.207	NS
Field								
*Education	238	12.5	13.0	18.8	25.7	30.0	.157	.05
Arts-Science	35	10.4	12.2	21.9	21.5	34.1	.155	NS
Law	2	12.5	18.8	12.5	31.3	25.0	.162	NS
Business	9	32.0	19.4	11.1	13.9	23.6	.120	NS
Years teaching								
*Under 1	32	9.1	10.3	14.5	23.2	42.9	.261	.05
*1-2	51	9.1	12.3	13.8	23.5	42.4	.248	.05

TABLE 4. Continued.

Variables	N	Response categories: Con BE	M Con BE	Neither	M Pro BE	Pro BE	Kolmogorov-Smirnov one-sample test D	p
Years teaching								
*3-5	68	9.7	6.9	16.9	23.4	43.1	.267	.05
6-10	76	14.6	16.3	17.1	24.7	27.3	.120	NS
*10+ years	176	17.2	13.7	18.8	26.0	24.3	.112	.05
Grade taught								
*1st	178	9.9	10.1	16.5	27.9	33.6	.235	.05
2nd	40	14.7	13.3	13.7	32.9	26.5	.183	NS
3rd	38	7.9	16.8	17.6	26.9	30.8	.153	NS
4th	33	18.2	9.9	17.1	21.0	33.8	.148	NS
5th	39	7.8	14.0	19.9	25.6	34.7	.183	NS
6th	34	7.6	14.4	20.9	21.3	35.7	.171	NS
7th	5	10.0	5.0	10.0	25.0	50.0	.350	NS
8th	8	31.3	14.1	26.6	9.4	18.8	.012	NS
9th	6	40.4	19.2	21.3	8.8	10.4	.204	NS
10th	15	20.0	10.0	16.7	27.5	25.8	.133	NS
11th	19	35.5	10.5	12.5	19.7	21.7	.155	NS
12th	20	24.8	15.2	17.0	19.0	24.0	.04	NS
Gen. Elem.	23	11.2	14.4	21.7	22.2	30.5	.144	NS
Gen. High Sch.	1	12.5	0	25.0	0	62.5	.275	NS
Speech	1	12.5	0	12.5	25.0	50.0	.035	NS
Reading	4	6.3	15.6	15.6	46.9	15.6	.181	NS
Racial composition of school								
*Predominantly black	179	11.5	8.9	14.5	23.6	41.4	.251	.05
Predominantly white	143	18.3	16.0	18.7	28.9	18.1	.070	NS
Mixed	48	5.9	21.1	15.7	21.8	40.3	.141	NS
Parents' education								
*High school graduate	129	11.6	11.8	16.7	25.9	34.0	.191	.05
BA/BS	60	16.9	9.8	20.1	19.0	34.2	.142	NS
*Graduate degree	39	9.9	7.1	16.7	28.2	40.4	.236	.05

TABLE 4. Continued.

Variables	N	Response categories: Con BE	M Con BE	Neither	M Pro BE	Pro BE	Kolmogorov-Smirnov one-sample test D	p
Content Category 3: Philosophies concerning use and acceptance of Non-standard English dialects in educational and other social settings								
Overall		16.7	17.6	17.9	20.5	24.8	.078	NS
Geography								
SA-U	46	18.9	14.3	20.6	19.3	27.0	.063	NS
MA-U	36	13.3	20.8	16.3	26.5	23.1	.096	NS
ENC-U	84	13.1	22.8	20.5	27.5	14.1	.041	NS
ESC-U	30	22.9	20.3	18.4	20.9	17.4	.032	NS
*WNC-R	21	4.8	26.2	16.7	35.7	17.9	.123	.05
SA-R	37	50.7	16.0	13.8	10.8	18.7	.307	NS
ENC-R	13	15.4	31.7	19.2	26.0	7.7	.123	NS
*P-U	150	10.3	13.2	17.3	23.2	37.1	.198	.05
NE-R	6	6.3	2.1	10.4	20.8	60.4	.412	NS
Sex								
Male	80	13.3	18.6	17.2	24.5	24.1	.109	NS
*Female	342	17.0	17.4	18.1	22.5	24.9	.075	.05
Race								
Black	111	18.5	15.3	20.8	18.9	26.6	.054	NS
*White	281	15.0	19.1	17.4	24.5	23.9	.085	.05
Oriental	17	16.7	12.1	13.8	22.8	34.6	.174	NS
Field								
Education	238	15.5	18.5	20.0	24.4	21.6	.060	NS
Arts-Science	35	14.1	17.5	21.1	18.5	28.9	.088	NS
Law	2	6.3	31.3	6.3	43.8	12.5	.161	NS
Business	9	34.7	15.3	11.1	23.6	15.3	.141	NS
Years teaching								
Under 1	32	14.5	16.5	17.0	21.0	31.0	.121	NS
1-2	51	12.4	20.4	15.1	23.6	28.5	.121	NS
3-5	68	11.5	14.3	19.7	21.0	33.9	.155	NS
6-10	76	19.8	19.4	15.5	25.8	19.5	.053	NS
10+ years	176	20.4	18.2	18.7	23.2	19.6	.027	NS
Grade taught								
1st	178	12.8	17.8	18.0	24.4	27.1	.114	NS
2nd	40	17.0	20.2	11.5	25.4	26.0	.113	NS

TABLE 4. Continued.

Variables	N	Response categories: Con BE	M Con BE	Neither	M Pro BE	Pro BE	Kolmogorov-Smirnov one-sample test D	p
Grade taught								
3rd	38	10.2	20.4	21.3	30.9	17.2	.098	NS
4th	33	21.6	14.6	17.7	17.0	29.1	.091	NS
5th	39	8.8	19.9	19.1	27.8	24.4	.112	NS
6th	34	15.1	18.7	18.1	23.1	25.0	.062	NS
7th	5	20.0	20.0	17.5	17.5	25.0	.050	NS
8th	8	47.1	4.9	14.3	17.7	15.9	.271	NS
9th	6	43.3	24.6	15.4	7.0	9.6	.233	NS
10th	15	27.8	15.4	13.5	27.1	16.2	.078	NS
11th	19	35.2	19.9	12.7	17.4	14.8	.151	NS
12th	20	31.5	25.7	6.3	20.8	15.7	.172	NS
Gen. Elem.	23	10.4	18.0	23.6	23.5	24.5	.116	NS
Gen. High Sch.	1	0	0	87.5	12.5	0	.400	NS
Speech	1	12.5	0	12.5	37.5	37.5	.350	NS
Reading	4	0	24.0	26.0	25.0	25.0	.200	NS
Racial composition of school								
*Predominantly black	179	14.4	14.6	17.2	21.7	32.1	.110	.05
Predominantly white	143	20.1	23.5	18.3	25.7	12.3	.076	NS
Mixed	48	11.7	14.2	16.1	23.4	34.6	.180	NS
Parents' education								
High School graduate	129	14.2	15.6	19.0	24.3	27.1	.112	NS
BA/BS	60	21.6	14.5	18.6	19.0	26.3	.053	NS
Graduate degree	39	9.5	16.1	15.5	23.5	35.4	.199	NS
Content Category 4: Cognitive and intellectual abilities of speakers of Black English								
Overall		13.0	17.3	17.8	21.8	30.2	.121	NS
Geography								
SA-U	46	6.7	22.2	20.0	15.6	35.6	.157	NS
MA-U	36	5.6	36.1	16.7	11.1	30.6	.145	NS

TABLE 4. Continued.

Variables	N	Response categories: Con BE	M Con BE	Neither	M Pro BE	Pro BE	Kolmogorov-Smirnov one-sample test D	p
Geography								
ENC-U	84	12.4	22.2	24.7	23.5	17.9	.076	NS
ESC-U	30	26.7	20.0	13.3	26.7	13.3	.062	NS
*WNC-R	21	0	19.0	0	42.9	38.1	.409	.05
*SA-R	37	41.7	25.0	13.9	11.1	8.3	.266	.05
ENC-R	13	15.4	7.7	15.4	61.5	0	.216	NS
*P-U	150	9.4	7.4	18.8	20.3	43.6	.244	.05
*NE-R	6	0	0	0	16.7	83.3	.600	.05
Sex								
*Male	80	12.7	19.0	7.6	27.8	32.9	.213	.05
*Female	342	13.0	16.9	20.1	20.4	29.6	.102	.05
Race								
*Black	111	9.2	15.6	25.7	14.7	34.9	.154	.05
*White	281	13.3	17.3	15.1	25.2	29.1	.144	.05
Oriental	17	17.6	11.8	11.8	23.5	35.3	.165	NS
Field								
*Education	238	13.2	18.0	20.5	20.9	27.4	.089	.05
Arts-Science	35	14.3	20.0	20.0	17.2	28.6	.058	NS
Law	2	0	50.0	0	0	50.0	.300	NS
Business	9	22.2	33.3	22.2	11.1	11.1	.177	NS
Years teaching								
Under 1	32	9.4	12.5	15.6	21.9	40.6	.226	NS
*1-2	51	3.9	19.6	13.7	23.5	39.2	.240	.05
*3-5	68	7.5	13.4	17.9	26.9	34.3	.213	.05
6-10	76	11.9	21.1	19.7	22.4	25.0	.081	NS
10+ years	176	20.2	18.5	17.4	19.7	24.3	.044	NS
Grade taught								
*1st	178	9.1	19.5	11.9	20.8	37.8	.197	.05
2nd	40	17.5	15.0	12.5	27.5	27.5	.150	NS
3rd	38	10.8	10.8	21.6	27.0	29.7	.184	NS
4th	33	12.1	9.1	36.4	18.2	24.2	.189	NS
*5th	39	5.1	18.0	15.4	20.5	41.0	.220	.05
6th	34	12.1	12.1	18.2	27.3	30.3	.180	NS
7th	5	0	20.0	20.0	0	60.0	.400	NS
8th	8	50.0	0	25.0	12.5	12.5	.150	NS
9th	6	40.0	40.0	20.0	0	0	.400	NS

TABLE 4. Continued.

Variables	N	Response categories: Con BE	M Con BE	Neither	M Pro BE	Pro BE	Kolmogorov-Smirnov one-sample test D	p
Grade taught								
10th	15	20.0	26.7	6.7	26.7	20.0	.064	NS
11th	19	47.4	10.5	5.3	21.1	15.8	.274	NS
12th	20	20.0	30.0	10.0	25.0	15.0	.100	NS
Gen. Elem.	23	4.6	27.3	22.7	13.6	31.8	.120	NS
Gen. High Sch.	1	0	0	0	0	100.0	.800	NS
Speech	1	0	100.0	0	0	0	.600	NS
Reading	4	0	25.0	25.0	50.0	0	.200	NS
Racial composition of school								
*Predominantly black	179	13.0	10.7	15.8	17.1	42.4	.126	.05
Predominantly white	143	16.8	23.8	16.1	28.7	14.7	.050	NS
*Mixed	48	4.4	15.2	19.6	21.7	39.1	.204	.05
Parents' education								
*High school graduate	129	13.4	14.2	17.3	22.8	32.3	.160	.05
BA/BS	60	15.5	13.8	20.7	22.4	27.6	.107	NS
Graduate degree	39	5.1	23.1	10.3	23.1	38.5	.217	NS

TABLE 5. Comparisons (Kolmogorov-Smirnov Test) of results between sub-variables for national teacher LAS.

Variables compared	Statement category: 1		2		3		4	
	D	p	D	p	D	p	D	p
Sex								
M-F	.072	NS	.025	NS	.034	NS	.112	NS
Race								
B-W	.087	NS	.088	NS	.035	NS	.059	NS
W-Or.	.084	NS	.082	NS	.092	NS	.072	NS
B-Or.	.050	NS	.036	NS	.12	NS	.092	NS
Field								
Ed-A&S	.015	NS	.04	NS	.072	NS	.031	NS
Ed-Bus	.138	NS	.259	NS	.192	NS	.251	NS
Years teaching								
Less 1--3-5	.012	NS	.028	NS	.052	NS	.063	NS
3-5--10+	.178	.05	.181	.05	.14	NS	.179	.05
Less 1--10+	.163	NS	.176	NS	.118	NS	.164	NS
Race of school								
B-W	.198	.05	.181	.05	.197	.05	.147	NS
W-Mix	.210	.05	.124	NS	.222	.05	.208	NS
B-Mix	.068	NS	.078	NS	.031	NS	.086	NS
Parents' education								
HS-BA	.91	NS	.067	NS	.074	NS	.064	NS
BA-MA	.130	NS	.131	NS	.136	NS	.117	NS
HS-MA	.068	NS	.064	NS	.075	NS	.083	NS
Grade								
1-3	.136	NS	.102	NS	.082	NS	.088	NS
1-5	.090	NS	.052	NS	.040	NS	.055	NS
1-8	.290	NS	.260	NS	.245	NS	.383	.05
3-5	.071	NS	.029	NS	.072	NS	.122	NS
3-8	.403	NS	.297	NS	.369	NS	.584	.05
3-11	.186	NS	.276	NS	.250	NS	.366	NS
5-8	.280	NS	.303	NS	.383	NS	.620	.05
5-11	.217	NS	.277	NS	.264	NS	.453	.05
8-11	.093	NS	.135	NS	.119	NS	.300	NS

TABLE 5. Continued.

Variables compared	Statement category: 1		2		3		4	
	D	p	D	p	D	p	D	p
Geography								
SA[U]-MA[U]	.025	NS	.045	NS	.056	NS	.128	NS
SA[U]-ENC[U]	.083	NS	.100	NS	.109	NS	.183	NS
SA[U]-ESC[U]	.041	NS	.071	NS	.100	NS	.224	NS
MA[U]-ENC[U]	.089	NS	.145	NS	.060	NS	.124	NS
MA[U]-ESC[U]	.063	NS	.061	NS	.112	NS	.111	NS
ENC[U]-ESC[U]	.046	NS	.051	NS	.098	NS	.163	NS
SA[U]-P[U]	.116	NS	.118	NS	.129	NS	.132	NS
MA[U]-P[U]	.110	NS	.108	NS	.129	NS	.248	.05
MA[U]-NE[R]	.213	NS	.211	NS	.349	NS	.59	.05
ENC[U]-ENC[R]	.184	NS	.208	NS	.122	NS	.208	NS

Key:
- M = Male
- F = Female
- B = Black
- W = White
- Or = Oriental
- Ed = Education
- A&S = Arts & Science
- Bus = Business
- [U] = Urban
- [R] = Rural

In comparing selected sub-variables on Content Category 1, it is interesting to note that even though black teachers indicated more positive attitudes than white teachers, there was no statistically significant difference between the two groups. Similarly, there were no statistically significant differences between teachers who were of different sexes, who taught different grades, or who were from different geographical areas (even though the Pacific area produced the most favorable attitudes).

It should be noted, however, that the relatively younger teachers with three to five years experience had significantly more positive attitudes than older teachers with more than ten years experience. However, very inexperienced teachers with less than one year of experience fell in between both groups and had more neutral responses. Teachers in schools which were predominantly black had significantly more positive attitudes than teachers in schools with predominantly white student populations. Similarly, teachers in schools which had mixed student populations had significantly more positive attitudes than teachers from predominantly white schools.

Content Category 2: Consequences of using and accepting Nonstandard English. Table 4 shows that the response pattern across the five response categories for Content Category 2 reveals that teachers have more positive than negative attitudes in this area. In general, 57% of the teachers responded in the two positive categories; 25% responded in the negative categories; and 17% revealed neutral feelings.

In terms of geography, Table 4 shows that teachers in the West North Central Rural and the Pacific Urban areas had significantly more positive than negative responses in Category 2. Also, both male and female teachers indicated significantly more positive than negative attitudes in this category, as did both black and white teachers. The results for the 'field of degree' variable indicated that teachers with Education School backgrounds were the only ones to produce a statistically significant trend toward positive attitudes. It should be noted, however, that teachers with Arts and Sciences backgrounds had approximately the same distribution of attitudes as Education teachers, but significance was not realized because of the relatively small N.

In the variable category 'years teaching', all groups except the 6-10 years experience group showed significantly more positive than negative attitudes. Of all the grades sampled, only first grade teachers produced significantly more positive than negative responses. (The very large N for the first grade category probably contributed to the finding.) Similarly, only those teachers from predominantly black schools were significantly more positive than negative in their attitudes, although teachers in schools with other racial characteristics produced non-significant trends in the same direction. Finally, teachers whose parents were high school or graduate degree holders had significantly more positive than negative attitudes on Content Category 2 statements. Teachers with parents with B. A. degrees showed a similar trend, but the N was too small to reach significance.

Comparisons of selected sub-variables reveal an interesting difference between teachers with 3-5 years experience and those with 10 or more years experience. Teachers in the former group produced significantly more positive attitudes than those in the latter group, whose attitudes were approximately evenly distributed across the five response categories. Also, a comparison of attitudes of teachers from predominantly black and predominantly white schools produced a statistically significant difference, with teachers from black schools revealing significantly more positive attitudes than those from predominantly white schools, who show a more even distribution of attitudes. None of the remaining comparisons of sub-variables was significant.

Content Category 3: Philosophies concerning use and acceptance of Nonstandard English. Table 4 reveals that teachers' attitudes were slightly more positive than they were negative. The magnitude of this trend, however, was not as great as Category 2. In general, 45% of the teachers responded in the two positive categories; 33% in the two negative categories; and 18% were neutral.

On the geographical variable, Table 4 shows that teachers in the West North Central Rural and the Pacific Urban areas showed significantly more positive than negative responses. Teachers in none of the remaining geographical areas produced a significant trend. Also, female teachers indicated significantly more positive attitudes than males. Males demonstrated a similar pattern, but their N was too small for significance to be reached. In terms of race, black, white, and Oriental teachers all displayed a trend of producing more positive than negative responses to the statements in this category. However, only the result for white teachers was significant because of their relatively large N.

Teachers in predominantly black schools also produced a significant trend toward positive responses. Teachers in predominantly white schools demonstrated a more negative trend, though it was not as significant. There were no significant effects obtained whatsoever on the variables of: field of study, years teaching, or grade taught.

In comparing selected sub-variables (Table 5), significance was achieved only for comparisons within the variable of racial composition of schools. Teachers from predominantly black schools professed significantly more positive attitudes toward statements from Category 3 than teachers from predominantly white schools. Similarly, teachers from mixed schools professed significantly more positive attitudes than teachers from predominantly white schools. None of the remaining comparisons was significant.

Category 4: Cognitive and intellectual abilities of speakers of Black English. Teachers demonstrated a slight trend toward positive attitudes to the one statement from Category 4 (Table 4). Fifty-two percent of their responses fell in the two positive response categories; 31% fell in the two negative categories; and 18% were neutral. Within the geographical variable, Table 4 shows that teachers in the West North Central Rural, Pacific Urban, and New England Rural areas all produced significantly more positive than negative attitudes. However, South Atlantic Rural teachers demonstrated significantly more negative than positive attitudes in this category.

Both black and white teachers, as well as male and female teachers, indicated significantly more positive than negative attitudes to the statement in this response category. Also, teachers with Education School backgrounds produced significantly more positive than negative responses. Teachers with backgrounds in other university divisions produced a similar trend, but significance was not achieved because of relatively small cell sizes.

On the experience variable, Table 4 shows that those with one to two years and three to five years of experience produced significantly more positive than negative attitudes in this Content Category. Teachers with under one year of experience and over ten years of experience showed no significant trends away from a normal distribution.

Further, teachers in grades one and five both showed significantly more positive than negative attitudes toward the statement in Category 4. No further significant trends were obtained in this variable. Also, teachers from predominantly black and mixed schools both showed significantly more positive than negative attitudes to the statement, while teachers from predominantly white schools showed a non-significant trend toward more negative attitudes. Finally, teachers whose parents held high school degrees showed significantly more positive attitudes. Teachers with parents from other education categories produced a similar trend, but the N was too small to achieve significance. Comparisons between selected sub-variables (see Table 4) show that teachers with three to five years of teaching experience showed significantly more positive attitudes to the statement in this category than teachers with ten or more years of experience. Similarly, teachers in the Pacific Urban area showed significantly more positive attitudes than those from the Middle Atlantic Urban area, even though teachers in the latter area had a slightly positive trend. Finally, several interesting results were achieved from comparisons of teachers at different grades. First, third, and fifth grade teachers produced significantly more positive responses than eighth grade teachers. (It should be noted, however, that grade eight had a small N.) Also, fifth grade teachers produced significantly more positive attitudes than eleventh grade teachers. None of the remaining sub-variable comparisons achieved significance.

Discussion

The most obvious finding of this survey is that teachers' attitudes relating to various topics of Nonstandard and Black English vary from topic to topic. Thus, teachers do not appear to have a single, generic attitude toward dialects, but, rather, differing attitudes depending upon the particular aspect of dialect being discussed.

Similarly, there appears to be great attitudinal variation within topic categories of Nonstandard and Black English as a function of several biographical variables. For this reason, results of such surveys should be discussed in terms of these variables, as well as the topics, if a valid picture is to be drawn.

If one were forced to make a statement about an overall trend, the best that could be said is that excluding topics dealing with the structure of Nonstandard and Black dialects, the majority of teachers throughout the country tend to reveal positive to neutral opinions. In the category pertaining to attitudes about structure, they are about evenly distributed. This finding is extremely interesting in that, contrary to popular opinion, a substantial number of American teachers are favorably disposed toward language variation, at least as measured by the present instrument. If this picture is correct, then it is obvious that school officials and language specialists have a lot of positive potential to capitalize upon to change school practices vis-a-vis dialects. In other words, enough positive attitudes seem to already be present, even though specific educational procedures and materials may be unavailable. Obviously, of course, there is a substantial core of negative attitudes which must be dealt with.

Across all four Content Categories, there were some trends related to biographical variables that are rather persuasive. Among the most important of these is the finding that teachers with three to five years of teaching experience had significantly more positive attitudes toward dialect than teachers just beginning their careers or those with ten or more years of experience. The implication of this result is that teachers who are relatively new to the teaching profession are less entrenched in their attitudes than teachers who have been teaching for long periods of time. If this finding is valid, it means that teachers with three to five years of experience are a good population for trying out new classroom procedures and methodologies. One might gather that in addition to the non-entrenchment factor, teachers in the three to five years experience category responded as they did not only because they are younger, but because they have probably been more exposed to recent thinking about language and cultural variety. If this assumption is true, then the very youngest teachers should have shown a much stronger positive trend than they did. Perhaps their relatively conservative trend was unrelated to their age or absence of new information, but, instead more related to uncertainty associated with entering the teaching profession and insecurity in trying radically different approaches.

Another overall trend is that teachers from predominantly black schools are more positive in their attitudes than teachers from predominantly white schools. It should be noted, however, that if the school population is predominantly black there is a strong chance that there are more black teachers, which may account for the trend. (It should be recalled that slightly fewer black teachers responded negatively than white teachers in all Content Categories, although significance was not achieved.) If true, however, the black teachers' non-negativeness was certainly not great enough to account for the observed trends. Also, teachers from mixed schools (which generally had white teachers) tended to be more positive than teachers in schools with a predominantly white population. The implications of the findings are clear. Teachers in schools where there were only white children, as opposed to schools where there were representative amounts of children of other races, tend to have the most negative attitudes concerning nonstandard dialects. Of course, one does not know whether these teachers went to mixed schools because they had 'liberal' attitudes on the topics or whether their attitudes developed as a result of working with children who speak nonstandard dialects on a daily basis. Both possibilities seem feasible, though other research done by this author suggests the latter as being more likely.

Implications of the present findings to the topic of bussing to achieve racial balance in schools are interesting, but frightening. The data suggest that the bussing of black children into predominantly white schools is likely to cause them to come into direct contact with teachers who are most likely to have negative attitudes toward their dialect and its use in the schools. However, given experiences with these new children, their attitudes might change to conform with those which seem to prevail for teachers in mixed schools. If true, the bussing may be more useful for the educational enrichment of the teacher than for the pupils. In any case, the whole topic needs to be reevaluated in the context of apparent attitudes on the subject.

It is interesting to note that there are no differences in attitudes between the male and female teachers on any of the response categories. Similarly, teachers did not differ significantly as a function of race, although always more black teachers were slightly more positive. This latter point is especially interesting in that it does not support numerous loosely made claims that middle class black teachers are more likely to engage in self-hate to the point that they reject their children more than white teachers. On the other hand, it is significant to note that black teachers are not as supportive of black children as some might expect, or as younger black students are, who are overwhelmingly pro-Black English. Perhaps this trend is related to age and the changing attitudes of blacks toward themselves, especially among the young. At this point, however, black teachers appear to be teachers first!

Results for geographical area comparisons are somewhat surprising on two counts. There appear to be at least two hypotheses which could be advanced to predict geographical differences in dialect attitudes. One argument would be that Southern teachers would be more positive toward black dialect than Northern teachers because there is relatively less divergence between black-white speech in the South than in the North. The other argument would posit that Northern teachers would be more positive than Southern teachers to black dialects because of different racial views, i.e. Southern teachers might be presumed to have more negative attitudes toward blacks and, therefore, more negative attitudes toward black speech. Neither of the opposing hypotheses was born out by the data.[5] Indeed there appears to be little difference between professed attitudes of Northern and Southern teachers on the topic, a fact which should lead us to talk less about regional attitudes than of national teacher trends. The only exception to this generalization would be in the Pacific Urban group which seem quite different from the other teachers, probably because they were selected from a highly cosmopolitan, 'liberal', and third-world setting in the Bay area of Northern California.

As stated, the Content Categories appear to be independent. However, attitudinal differences reflected in the categories are of importance. It has been noted, for instance, that the most negative attitudes were expressed toward the category dealing with the structure of nonstandard and black dialects while the most positive attitudes were expressed in the area of the consequences of using dialects in the schools. Thus, it appears that linguistic structure is the topic that teachers find most objectionable about nonstandard dialects. Language structure, after all, is what teachers are formally taught in schools and college, whereas positions in the other three categories are more judgmental, subjective, and less substantiated by data. In a sense, this finding is hopeful, in that the part of dialect that is most objectionable is the part that is taught to teachers, and hence, the most likely to be affected through education.

Although teachers' attitudes on structure are not positive, they are willing to profess positive attitudes toward use of different dialects in school settings. It would appear that the teachers may not like a Nonstandard dialect, but are willing to attempt to use it in hopes of finding a useful teaching tool. However, teachers' actual philosophies (or attitudes on various philosophies) are not as positive as their attitudes on consequences. For example, teachers are more likely to agree more strongly with items such as, 'When teachers reject the native language of a student, they do him great harm' than they do with items like 'Teachers should allow black students to use Black English in the classroom'. Nevertheless, most teachers are apparently open and willing to try new approaches to teaching.

There was only one item in the category concerning cognitive abilities of speakers of nonstandard dialects, thus it must be discussed with great caution. However tentative, there are some fascinating implications of the results of this survey for current tests and measures used to evaluate students' intelligence. In general, teachers seem willing to indirectly question the validity of using language foreign to the students for evaluating his IQ. In other words, given that teachers seem to recognize that language is not a valid indication of intelligence, they have implicitly called into question the validity of standardized tests which utilize Standard English as indicators of the intelligence of nonstandard speakers. Of course, most teachers do not recognize the contradiction implied by their separate views on language as unrelated to intelligence on the one hand and the primacy of Standard English on the other. Effective training should make this point clear.

NOTES

[1]The research reported in this paper was conducted as a part of a larger project conducted at the Center for Applied Linguistics and sponsored by the Ford Foundation. The author acknowledges the contributions of David Swinney, presently at the University of Texas, and Alfred Hayes, presently at Federal City College (D. C.), for their contributions to the research reported herein.

[2]Since the time of the original development of this scale, several sociolinguists have proposed more sophisticated types of approaches for assessing language attitudes, e.g. commitment type scales.

[3]A randomized presentation order for the twenty-five items in each form, as well as administration instructions, are available from the author of this paper.

[4]A map of the U. S. Census districts may be obtained from the U. S. Census Bureau.

[5]It should be noted that the geographical hypothesis may be incapable of being tested by the present data because a substantial core of Southern data was collected from a city which was geographically Southern, but socially and politically Northern. Also, the geographical data may be distorted by the fact that the racial composition of teachers' classes was not utilized in the statistical analyses. In most cities, black teachers usually taught black students. However, Southern white teachers usually taught white students and Northern white teachers typically taught students of all racial backgrounds. Because of the pattern of 'de facto' segregation in teacher assignments, there is no way to determine, for instance, whether the Southern data were more 'liberal' because of the preponderance of black teachers with black students and white teachers with white students.